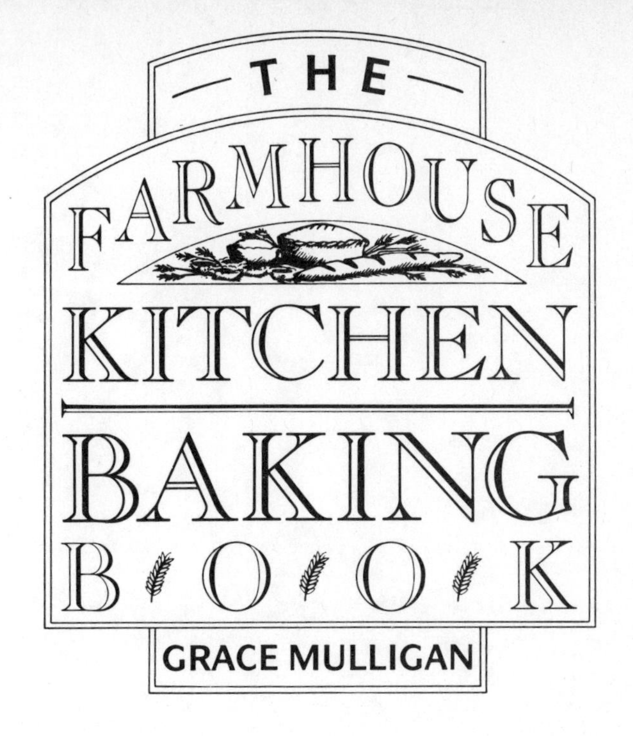
THE
FARMHOUSE
KITCHEN
BAKING
BOOK
GRACE MULLIGAN

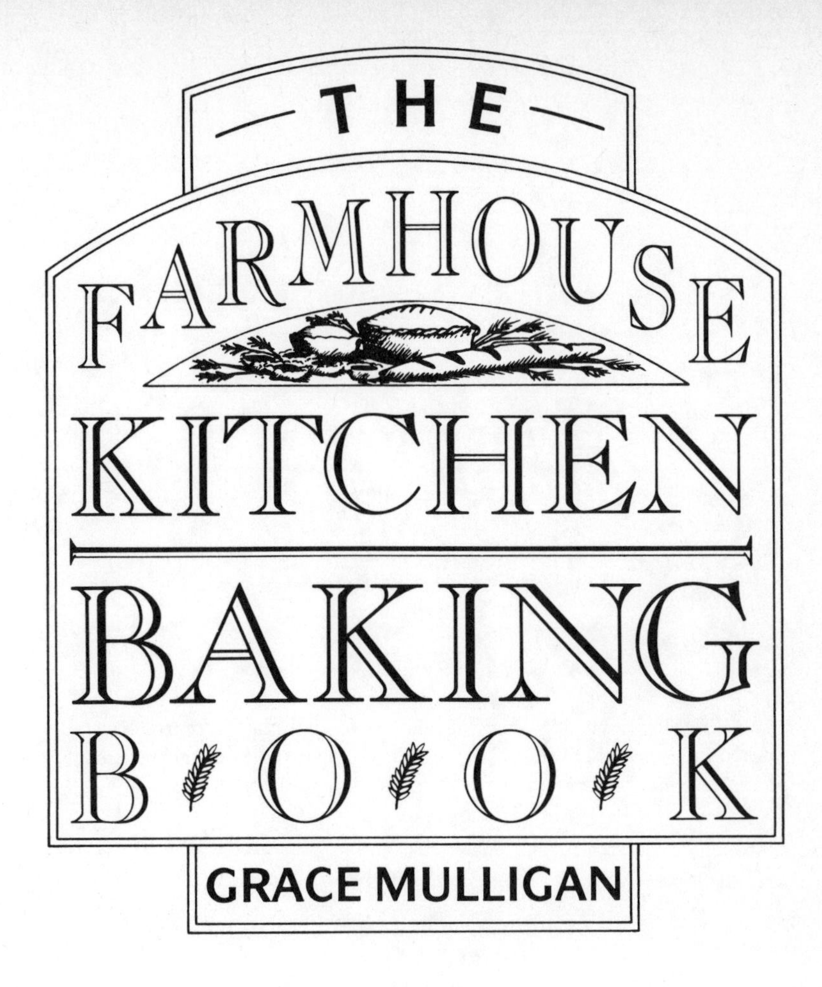
THE
FARMHOUSE
KITCHEN
BAKING
BOOK
GRACE MULLIGAN

YORKSHIRE
TELEVISION

DIAMOND
BOOKS

This edition published 1995 by
Diamond Books
77–85 Fulham Palace Road
Hammersmith, London W6 8JB
Reprinted 1995

First published 1988 in association with
Yorkshire Television Enterprises Ltd by
William Collins Sons & Co.

ISBN 0 261 66685 1

Typeset in Great Britain by Rowland Phototypesetting Ltd,
Bury St Edmunds, Suffolk
Printed in Finland by WSOY

Diagrams: Lorna Turpin
Front cover: *The White Tablecloth* by John Shirley-Fox,
courtesy of the Bridgeman Art Library
Photograph of author: Brian Cleasby

CONTENTS

INTRODUCTION

ALTHOUGH I enjoy all kinds of cooking, baking still comes very high on my list of favourite things. From the letters I get from viewers of my television series, Farmhouse Kitchen, I know that baking is not a dying art but more of a freshly discovered pleasure. They also tell me how much they appreciate the extra hints and tips I give as I go through a recipe and I have included these tips and suggestions all through this book – I do dislike a 'bald' recipe which only lists ingredients and gives the barest instructions.

The sheer magic of baking has never dimmed for me. It is always fascinating to put a raw mixture into a hot oven, watch it through a glass door and bring out the finished result all golden and fragile. Although I would not be without my freezer, the very best way to enjoy your baking is when it is at its freshest – still warm and fragrant from the oven. No apple tart emerging from its expensive colour co-ordinated designer carton can compare with that.

I was born and brought up in Dundee in the old county of Angus. Scottish bakeries are famous for their range of tea breads, and we lived opposite the bakery for a group of shops called Wallaces Land O'Cakes. Their doors were often open and we children could watch the men at work amongst the flour. It wasn't unusual to see ten to fifteen varieties of scones and buns in their shops, quite apart from all the cakes and tarts. I remember particularly the bran farls and treacle scones, which we ate with butter from the local dairy. I loved going to that shop. It was bright and clean, the walls were covered with pale green tiles, some with pictures of hens and cows. The girl skilfully used wooden butter pats, or 'hands', as they were called, to scoop off a lump of butter from the huge barrel-shaped hunk of butter which sat on a marble slab. I can still hear the slapping noises she made while shaping the butter into a neat oblong. If there was time she would use a carved wooden stamp to pattern the butter. I always preferred the cow to the buttercup!

From the same baker we bought marvellous light cream cookies as a special treat on Saturdays. Other times it would be warm and juicy rhubarb tarts made with hot water pastry. A sign would go up, 'New season's rhubarb tarts' and I always think of that when I cut the early rhubarb grown in our garden. I use a lot of fruit in my baking and with four children to cook for I've had plenty of opportunity to experiment. I know they always loved to come home to the fragrant smell of baking.

Knowing the keen interest we have all developed in reading the small print on the labels of packets and bottles and our desire to eat pure and natural ingredients, I think one of the best ways of ensuring this is to make your own bread and to bake at home as much as possible. It is, of course, very much

cheaper, too. One of the things I often do in a television programme is to buy something like a quiche and then make a home-made version, costing out all the ingredients used. Almost always you can make two items at home for the price of one of the shop-bought variety – and it's better.

I cannot remember baking when I was very young but I do remember some rock cakes which lived up to their name. It was many years later that I discovered that if a recipe has few ingredients it usually means that there is a fair bit of skill needed to put them together. I do hope you will try your skills out on my recipes, and that you will get that sense of real pleasure when you can say – I made it myself.

WEIGHTS AND MEASURES

CONVERSION CHART

Metric grammes (g)	Imperial ounces (oz)
7	¼
15	½
25	1
50	2
75	3
125	4
150	5
175	6
200	7
225	8 (½ pound)
250	9
275	10
300	11
325	12
350	13
400	14
425	15
450	16 (1 pound)

Metric grammes (g)	Imperial pounds (lb)
675	1½
900	2
kilogrammes (kg)	
1.1	2½
1.3	3

Metric millilitres (ml)	Imperial fluid ounces (fl oz)
150	5 (¼ pint)
300	10 (½ pint)
450	15 (¾ pint)
600	20 (1 pint)

Follow *either* the metric or the imperial measures – never mix the two.

SPOON MEASURES

All spoon measures used in this book are level unless otherwise stated.

OVEN TEMPERATURE CHART

Description	Gas	Fahrenheit °F	Centigrade °C
Very low	¼	225	110
Low	½	250	120
Slow	1	275	140
Cool	2	300	150
Moderate	3	325	160
	4	350	180
Moderately hot	5	375	190
Fairly hot	6	400	200
Hot	7	425	220
	8	450	230
Very hot	9	475	250

The oven temperatures used throughout this book are for a conventional oven. For fan-assisted ovens, refer to the manufacturer's handbook as temperatures and cooking times are generally reduced.

INGREDIENTS
AND
EQUIPMENT

INGREDIENTS

FATS

BUTTER

Both salted and unsalted butter have much the best flavour for baking. While good quality butter is harder to cream, I do not care for some of the very cheap butters which have such a high salt content. They are often very sloppy when soft. Although good quality margarine can nearly always be substituted for butter, it is sometimes very important to use butter for its flavour, e.g. in shortbread.

MARGARINE

Block margarine

The harder margarines which do not liquefy readily at room temperature are ideal for cake making by the rubbing-in method and for pastry making.

Tub margarine

The softer-textured tub margarines, which liquefy very readily, are ideal for the creaming method and also for the all-in-one method of cake making. They are incorporated very swiftly and easily.

Polyunsaturated margarines, e.g. sunflower margarine

These are satisfactory in all baking but take care to avoid the ones at the very cheap end of the market which are very waterlogged.

LOW-FAT SPREADS

Some of these work well in baking but it is better to check what is written on the wrapping. That should tell you whether or not the spread is suitable for baking.

SOLID VEGETABLE OIL

This is oil in block form. I tend to use this in pastry making instead of lard, using half solid oil and half block margarine.

LIQUID OILS

Liquid oils, e.g. corn oil or sunflower oil, can be used successfully in cake and pastry making, if it is important for you to cut down on saturated fats for liver or gall bladder diseases, or for weight loss. When making cakes and scones with oil an extra raising agent is needed as well. You may substitute 2 tablespoons oil for each 25 g/1 oz butter or margarine and add also 1 teaspoon baking powder to each 125 g/4 oz self-raising flour.

LARD, DRIPPING AND SUET

These were commonly used for baking but less so now. Suet can be used to make sweet or savoury pastries (*see pages 28 and 29*), or use it, tied in muslin, to grease frying pans or girdles (*see below*). Lard is used in the popular Lardy Cake (*see page 107*).

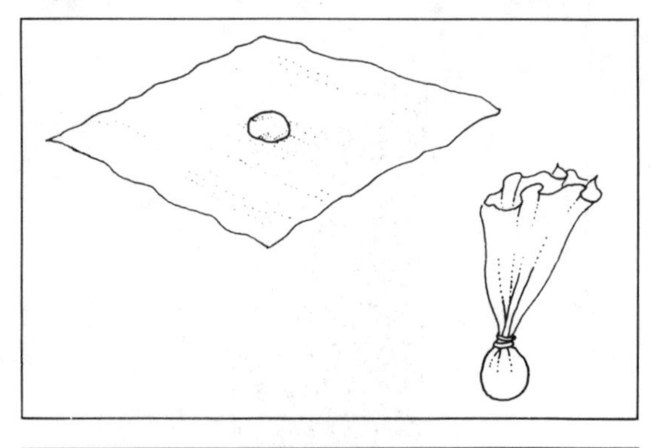

FLOURS

There are many different kinds of flour on the market today. It is important therefore to choose the correct flour for the type of baking you are doing. Flours vary in composition and are defined according to their rate of extraction – i.e. the percentage of the whole cleaned wheatgrain that is present in the flour – and the type of wheat from which they are milled.

Wholemeal or wholewheat flours

These flours contain 100% of the wheatgrain with nothing added or taken away. They produce a heavier texture when baked than other flours.

Wheatmeal or brown flours

These usually contain 85%–90% of the whole wheatgrain, and most of the bran and wheatgerm. Brown bread is therefore a lighter texture than wholemeal bread.

White flours

These usually contain 72%–74% of the whole wheatgrain, although lower extraction flours can be produced. All the bran and wheatgerm is removed so white bread has a good volume and texture. During milling some nutrients are lost, and our law requires that iron and the B vitamins thiamine and nicotinic acid must be added to white flour to compensate for this loss. (Calcium is also added to all flours except wholemeal.) Since white flour is fortified in this way there is little significant difference between the nutritional value of white, brown and wholemeal bread and flour except in their fibre or roughage content. However, as fibre is essential in the diet, choosing wholemeal or brown bread and flour is an excellent way of incorporating it in your daily diet.

TYPES OF FLOUR

Plain white flour

Very versatile and is used in cake making, puddings, sponges, shortcrust pastry and for thickening purposes in sauces, soups etc.

Plain wheatmeal or brown flour

Used for exactly the same things as plain white. However, baked goods made with wheatmeal or brown flour will have a limited rise and closer texture.

Plain and strong flour – wholemeal, wholewheat and white

These flours are the best to use for good bread because of their high gluten content. Strong flour is also used for choux pastry and Yorkshire puddings.

Self-raising white flour

In practice this means that 450 g/1 lb of self-raising white flour is equivalent to 450 g/1 lb plain white flour with 4 × 5 ml/4 teaspoons of baking powder added. (Some cooks prefer to vary the quantity of the raising agent and it would, therefore, be better to use plain flour and add the raising agent separately.) Use for cakes, puddings, sponges etc.

Self-raising wheatmeal flour

This flour is widely available and is much finer than it used to be and is therefore suitable for all types of baking.

Self-raising wholemeal or wholewheat flour

These are high-fibre flours with strong flavour, but they rise less than white self-raising flour and give a closer texture. Good in cakes and fruit loaves.

Special sponge flour, self-raising

This white soft flour is particularly good for sponges as it produces a larger cake and an even, fine rise.

Cornflour

Cornflour is smoother and lighter than ordinary flour. It is sometimes added to plain flour when making shortbread, biscuits and cakes. I have always believed that fairy cakes are so-called because cornflour is used in the recipe.

SPECIALITY FLOURS

Other flours and meals are available. Some are milled from cereals such as rye, buckwheat, barley and oats and add their own flavours to baking. These flours tend to be expensive and because of their low gluten content or, as in the case of barley and oat flour, no gluten at all, they are usually mixed with other flours to make unusual breads. Some flours, Granary for example, contain a mixture of various cereals like malted wheat and rye.

SIFTING FLOUR

By passing flour through a sieve – either a wire or plastic one – you are adding air. This gives a lighter texture to the finished cake or pastry. Sometimes also, flour which has been standing for a long time in a damp cupboard becomes compacted and lumpy. I automatically sift all my flour even if the packet cover tells me it is super sifted. It is beneficial to sift even wholemeal flour for the same reasons. Bran will be retained in the sieve and should be returned to the mixing bowl.

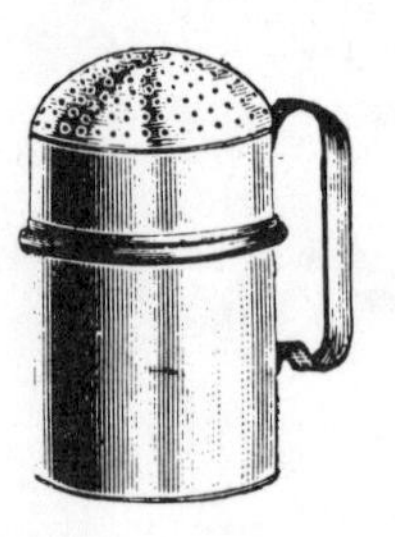

Super-sifted flour

This is available in both plain and self-raising and is specially prepared. The grinding and sifting techniques used produce flour with a free-running quality which in turn reduces the tendency for the mixture to become lumpy and stick together when liquid is added. The flour is therefore easier to use.

STORING FLOURS

The best way to store flour is to keep it in its bag in as cool a place as possible. If the kitchen tends to get damp and steamy put the bag into a tin with a lid or in a storage jar with a lid.

If you store flour loose do not add new flour to old.

Plain white flour keeps best of all for 4–6 months. Self-raising white flour keeps for 2–3 months. Wholemeal and brown flours should be used within 2 months.

Bare measure

By this phrase I mean that the weight of whatever is being measured should just touch the relevant mark on the weighing machine and no more, e.g. 50 g/2 oz (bare measure) plain flour means just fractionally under the 50 g/2 oz measure and no more.

RAISING AGENTS

Raising agents give lightness to baking and there are several types. Air sifted into flour and beaten in during the mixing process is also a raising agent.

BAKING POWDER

Probably the most widely known raising agent, this is a blend of bicarbonate of soda and cream of tartar or other acid. Baking powder is sold in cartons and tins. I like to sift it into my mixture along with the flour in the following proportions:

For each 225 g/8 oz plain flour:
1 teaspoon for rich cakes*
2 teaspoons for medium rich cakes
4 teaspoons for scones and sweet loaves

* *Rich cakes have half to equal quantities of fat to flour and to sugar, e.g. sandwich cakes, all-in-one cakes, Madeira and Christmas cakes. Baking powder is also used for some scones and small cakes.*

BICARBONATE OF SODA

Sometimes used alone, as in gingerbread, or with an acid such as cream of tartar, sour milk, vinegar etc., as in scones. Used alone, it has an effect on the colour and texture, darkening and softening the cake. It is therefore good for cakes which have less than equal quantities of fat to flour and sugar.

Bicarbonate of soda with cream of tartar

Many cooks favour the old way of adding bicarbonate of soda and cream of tartar separately to a mixture, e.g. in soda bread.

EGGS

When beaten in very carefully to a cake, eggs trap air bubbles which in turn cause the cake to rise and become light.

YEAST

Yeast is another widely known raising agent and is available fresh, dried and freeze dried, or the 'instant' types now available. Full information on yeast is on page 168.

SWEETENING AGENTS

SUGARS

White and brown sugars are nutritionally similar. The choice therefore between white and brown sugar for baking depends entirely on what you are making. Brown sugars have a distinctive taste and this can be used to advantage, e.g. in rich fruit cakes, fruit loaves and also in fudge-flavoured icing and fillings. (*See also page 251.*)

White granulated sugar

This is widely used for baking when the melting method is used, e.g. simple fruit cakes, gingerbreads etc. The crystals, which are more coarse than caster sugar, are dissolved before the cake is mixed. A spotty surface on a light cake often indicates that granulated sugar was used instead of caster sugar.

White caster sugar

This is the sugar most often used in home baking. It is free flowing and has fine crystals which dissolve easily. It is used for sponges and light cakes.

Icing sugar

This is made by grinding sugar crystals to a fine powder. It dissolves rapidly and is easily made into icings and fillings for decorating cakes and sponges. Icing sugar is also used when a very fine texture is required, e.g. in some biscuits and in sweetening uncooked cheesecakes. It is also used in a decorative way by dredging it lightly over baked and cooled sponges and fairy cakes.

Brown sugars

These range in colour from golden beige to dark brown. The molasses present in them provide the colour and distinctive taste. Like demerara sugar, they are often used in coffee but occasionally their flavours can be used to advantage in baking, e.g. Christmas cakes and ginger cakes or parkins.

Demerara sugar

This sugar is also flavoured with molasses. It has larger crystals than any of the other sugars and is occasionally used decoratively on top of a cake, e.g. sprinkled over the raw fruit loaf before it goes into the oven.

Brown fine grain sugar

This sugar has come onto the market fairly recently. It is free flowing and while not as fine as caster sugar it can be used instead of the white sugar with good results. I like it very much in meringues (*see page 135*).

Light soft brown sugar/ Dark soft brown sugar

Both these sugars are used extensively in baking when a full flavour is required or for icings and fillings, the dark having a slightly stronger flavour than the light. The texture is slightly damp and care must be taken to store them carefully in a dry place as they harden easily. When used in icings and fillings, the finished texture is very slightly grainy. I particularly like the taste of soft brown sugar with dates, e.g. Fudge and Date Sponge (*see page 219*).

Vanilla sugar

See page 17.

GOLDEN SYRUP

One of the ingredients often used to sweeten cakes made by the melting method and also the flapjack type of tray bake. Its thick and sticky texture make it difficult to measure. One method is to weigh the pan to be used and, while it is still on the scales, pour the syrup into it. To soften the texture and make it easy to measure out just one spoonful, set the opened tin or jar in a pan of gently simmering water. Golden syrup is sometimes referred to as light treacle.

TREACLE (BLACK/DARK)

Black treacle with its dominating flavour is used to sweeten gingerbreads and parkins. It is also sticky like golden syrup and can be measured in the same way as described above. Confusion often arises because in the north of England the word treacle means golden syrup. Where I come from treacle is always the black variety and treacle tart is invariably made with golden syrup.

HONEY

Runny or clear honey is the kind used in baking. Its stickiness is dealt with in exactly the same way as for golden syrup and treacle. Icings, butter cream and whipped double cream may all be enhanced with flavoured honey, e.g. orange blossom honey.

Note

All cakes and buns made with syrup, treacle and honey tend to brown easily. It is therefore important to follow the recipe carefully and allow the baked article to be in the oven only as long as is necessary.

EGGS

Fresh eggs are available from size 1 (the largest) to size 7 (the smallest). I like large eggs for baking but a good medium egg would be size 4.

Approximate sizes used in the recipes in this book:
large egg = size 1 or 2
medium egg = size 4 or 5
small egg = size 6 or 7

STORING EGGS

Eggs should be stored at room temperature and not in the fridge and they should keep in good condition for up to 10 days. Try to use your eggs in rotation, that is, do not mix freshly bought ones with the ones you have had for a week. Buy them from a shop with a good turnover – buy little and often would be a good motto.

One exception to the rule that fresh eggs are always best is when making anything which requires the eggs or egg whites to be whipped until fluffy. Eggs which are one week old are better, for example, in meringues and fatless sponges and they give more volume.

BEATING EGG WHITES

Must be done in a gleaming clean bowl. The least trace of oil or fat will prevent the egg white from fluffing up. Bowls made from glass, porcelain, stainless steel are fine. Plastic is not so good. In the old days and still in many restaurants today a copper bowl was used because the chemical reaction between the metal and the egg white produces a much bigger volume of foam. However, the egg whites must not be left standing in the copper bowl or they start to discolour. Some chefs still insist that there is nothing to beat hand mixing in a copper bowl for egg whites!!

STORING EGG WHITES

Storing and using egg whites can sometimes be a problem when the yolks have been used for something else. They stay fresh in the fridge for 4–5 days if they are tightly covered. They also freeze for up to 2 months.

Use spare egg whites to make meringues. To make whipped cream go further – just whip the cream then whip the egg white until stiff and fold the two together. Use immediately to serve with fruit or with a dessert.

STORING EGG YOLKS

If the yolk is not broken, pour some cold water over it to keep it moist and it will keep for up to 2 days in the fridge.

Use spare egg yolks to mix pastry, to thicken a sauce, make mayonnaise or just add one yolk to one large whole egg and use as two eggs.

Storing egg yolks in the freezer is not as successful as storing egg whites. They dry out easily unless they are in a plastic box with a very tight lid. Break the yolks up well and use within 2 weeks.

DRIED FRUIT

APRICOTS

I usually buy the soft, ready-to-eat variety because of the difficulty of drying thoroughly dried apricots which have been soaked overnight.

CURRANTS

Some currants are very seedy, especially the larger ones, and I prefer to use very small currants. Vostizza currants come in two sizes, small and pinhead, and the name refers to the plant itself. I buy mine loose from a fruiterer who bags up his own, or from a wholefood shop which sells them from the box they came in.

DATES

Packet dates are a good store cupboard fruit and are available already stoned in small oblong cellophane-covered blocks. Cut them finely to add to scones, tea breads etc., but beware of the odd stone left in a fruit by mistake. When you are buying them, watch out for dates which have gone very hard.

RAISINS

The two sorts of raisins most commonly available are the small 'black' raisins and the larger sticky ones of a lighter colour. The true muscatel flavour is more prominent in the larger raisins. I tend to use these more at Christmas in mincemeat and Christmas puddings. The smaller darker ones are good in fruit cakes and tea breads.

SULTANAS

These are another variety of dried seedless grape. They are a golden brown colour and very sweet. I have the impression that bakers in Scotland use sultanas more often, and I tend to use them along with raisins and currants in fruit loaves and cakes.

Preparation of fruit

I have always washed and dried fruit before using it. This includes currants, sultanas and raisins, and by far the most in need of washing are currants. Once you have seen the grit and colour of the water after washing them you will always do it in future. I am convinced a fruit cake is much better and more moist if this is done. A master baker, who now teaches, once wrote to me after a television programme to emphasize his agreement. He felt that fruit cakes with burnt fruit on the outside were due solely to the fact that the fruit was not washed and rehydrated in the first place.

To wash fruit – pour boiling water over it, leave until cool then squeeze out the water and spread the fruit to dry on a paper towel or a tin.

Large raisins and sultanas are much better chopped small so that all the fruit in a heavy fruit cake is about the same size. This gives the finished cake a perfect even texture.

PEEL

Orange, lemon and citron peel can be bought ready chopped and mixed. However, I prefer to buy the whole pieces of candied peel and prepare it myself. I am convinced the texture is softer and has a much nicer flavour. To prepare these pieces, wash off all the caked sugar, dry the peel and use your scissors to chop it into small pieces about the size of currants.

FLAVOURINGS

ALCOHOL

Used with great care, alcohol can enhance lots of savoury and sweet baking. Spirits and flavoured liqueurs come in miniature bottles, and wine can also now be bought in cans and bottles small enough to be economical. Fruit juices like apple or orange make a good substitute if you prefer not to use alcohol.

ESSENCES

Essences are often used in baking to give a delicate flavour to the food. It is worthwhile buying real essences rather than the artificial ones even though they cost twice as much. They should always be used sparingly as they are very concentrated. The two most popular are:

Almond

A very useful flavouring, not at all harsh; used in biscuits and sponges.

Vanilla

Real vanilla has a lovely round flavour which once tasted you will always remember.

FRESH FRUIT RINDS

Fresh fruit rinds are particularly useful for both flavouring and decoration. I store the empty shells from lemons and oranges, which have been used for juice only, in the freezer. It is then easy to grate the frozen shells for, say, just a couple of teaspoons of lemon rind. Another way is to finely grate the peel from fresh fruit and leave it on a plate or on kitchen paper to dry over a couple of days. Store the grated and dried peel in a jar in the fridge. (*See also page 253.*)

ORANGE FLOWER WATER AND ROSE WATER

Both delicate flavourings enjoying a slight revival. Use with restraint to flavour cream and icing to enhance a cake or dessert.

HERBS

Both fresh and dried herbs are useful in sweet and savoury baking. My own herb garden is right at my back door and contains eleven different herbs, including fennel, lovage, chervil and three kinds of thyme.

When using fresh herbs prepare them carefully. Wash or wipe the leaves and chop them small. I use my scissors rather than a knife. Be particularly careful, especially in the autumn, to remove the brittle stems of things like thyme and sage.

Dried herbs are handy if you have no means of growing your own. I cannot grow basil in the north so I use dried basil in winter and buy a pot of fresh basil for my windowsill in summer. Check before using a dried herb that it is not at the 'old hay' stage. Something which has been sitting in a jar for years will do nothing for your baking. Remember also that dried herbs are much more potent than fresh ones – you should cut the quantity by half when using them as opposed to fresh herbs.

NUTS

Nuts such as walnuts can add a strong flavour to many cakes or loaves, while almonds impart a more delicate taste. They can be used whole, chopped or ground. (*See also page 252.*)

SEEDS

Sesame and sunflower seeds are just two of the many seeds which will add flavour and texture to breads and other baking. Sometimes they are used as toppings (*see page 173*), e.g. on a bread plait before the plait goes in the oven. In other recipes they are baked into the dough, e.g. a fruit loaf or tray bake, to give extra flavour. Often the recipe suggests that the seeds be lightly toasted before using. This intensifies their flavour but do be careful – they burn easily. (*See also page 252.*)

SPICES

Spices, I am glad to say, are increasingly much more cherished than they used to be, and turn up in all sorts of savoury as well as sweet dishes. Indian and Chinese spices are almost as well known as our own traditional ones.

Try to buy all spices in minute quantities so that they do not sit on your shelf for ever. They are also better stored out of the sunlight.

VANILLA SUGAR

Often used in fatless sponges, custards and creams etc. A dried vanilla pod is immersed in a jar of caster sugar where its flavour permeates the sugar and is extremely pleasant. The black shrivelled pod lasts for a very long time.

FOOD COLOURINGS

Available in a wide range of colours, these should be used very carefully as they are extremely concentrated and once added to the mixture the colour cannot be taken away.

I always think of my daughter, Grainne, whenever I mention them. She made gooseberry fool for her 'O' level cookery exam and was trying to pour one or two drops of green food colouring into her gooseberries, when she dropped the whole bottle in. A speedy mopping up operation saved the day but she finished up with only two servings instead of four.

They are, however, useful for a variety of things including colouring icings and fillings.

GELATINE

Gelatine is sold in powder form in packs of five sachets. It is used in baking to help set fruit in pies or, more often, on top of cheesecakes. Each sachet will set 600 ml/1 pint liquid to a jelly. Always add gelatine to the liquid, not the other way round. It will quickly dissolve when sprinkled onto very hot liquid in a cup. If, after stirring, it does not dissolve then the cup can be set in a pan of simmering water until it does. Do not let the gelatine mixture boil.

KEEPING QUALITY

All baking is at its best when freshly made. The only exception is the gingerbread/parkin type of mixture which, when freshly baked, is fairly firm. Two or three days in a closed tin and the texture softens or gives.

When a cake is described as rich this means the proportion of fat is high. It has nothing to do with the amount of fruit in the cake. A rich cake will keep in good condition longer than a plainer cake.

Pastry tarts or pies are certainly much better when freshly cooked and the crispness of the pastry is still there. Left for one or two days, the filling begins to soften the pastry. They can be reheated but the pastry will not recover entirely.

Home-made biscuits do not have the ability to stay as crisp as shop-bought biscuits will over many weeks. They must be stored in an airtight tin. If they become soft they can easily be crisped up again in a hot oven.

USEFUL EQUIPMENT

BAKING TINS

It pays to buy good quality tins and to look after them. Nonstick tins are a great advantage but need to be protected from scratching, and certainly you should not cut up anything while still in a tin.

There is a huge variety of sizes on the market so the word approximately should go before each size I quote, e.g. in my own collection I have Swiss roll tins in four different sizes.

BASIC SET OF TINS FOR A HOME BAKER

1 × 20-cm/8-inch round cake tin, about 9 cm/3 inches deep

1 × 18-cm/7-inch square cake tin, about 9 cm/3 inches deep

2 × 18-cm/7-inch round but straight-sided sandwich tins, about 4 cm/1½ inches deep

Small Swiss roll-type tin

Large Swiss roll-type tin

Tray of bun tins, the dozen size is best

Wire cooling tray

If you are a breadmaker, add to your list

2 × 900-g/2-lb loaf tins

2 × 450-g/1-lb loaf tins

OTHER USEFUL TINS

Brioche tins
Brioche tins are traditionally shaped like scalloped bun tins. Their fluted and flared sides not only pattern the rich yeast dough but allow it to spread out amply as it proves. They come in either small individual or larger sizes. They can be used for pastry cases as well as jellied moulds etc.

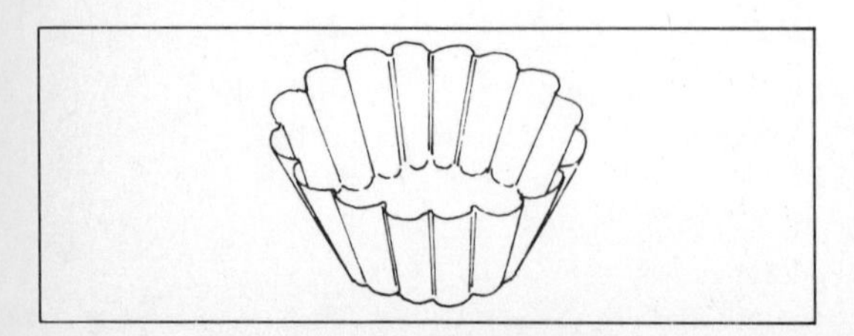

Bun tins
Deeper than patty tins, these are used for little cakes, tartlets or pies. They are usually bought set in a sheet of six or twelve. These tins can also be used with paper cases into which you spoon the cake mixture. The bun tins support the cakes while they bake.

Dariole mould tins
These little flowerpot-shaped tins are the ones I use for English madeleines. They are also sometimes called castle pudding tins. Grease them well and lay a tiny circle of greaseproof paper in the bottom to ensure they turn out really well.

Flan rings
These are just narrow metal frames, round or oblong, which are greased and set on a baking tray then lined with pastry and filled. When the tart is cooked it is easy to lift the metal ring away and slide the tart onto a serving plate. You can also buy rings fitted with an inner scalloped ring to give a decorative edge to the pastry.

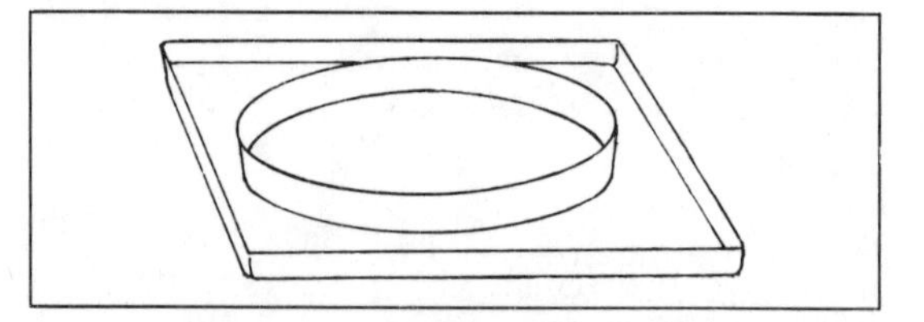

Loose-bottomed tins or flan tins
These come in all sizes from shallow quiche tins to very large springform cake tins. They are particularly useful if you are serving something hot like a quiche, the pastry shape of which, with its filling, is much more fragile when hot. With a loose-bottomed tin, you can stand it on a bowl of a smaller diameter. The frame drops down, leaving you with the quiche base to support the pastry but the sides free for slicing.

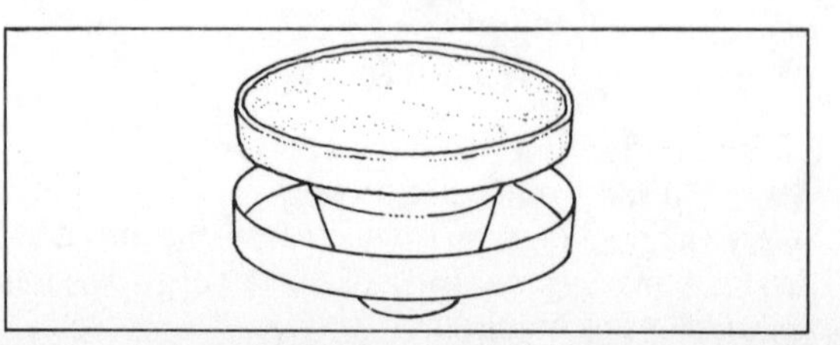

Patty tins
These shallow little tins are for making tartlets in the traditional English shape. If they are loose, they are placed on baking trays, but they can also be bought in a sheet of six or nine.

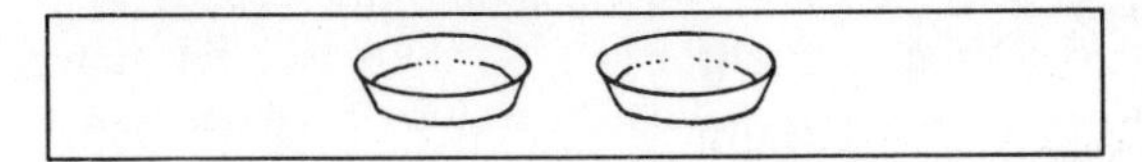

Pizza tins
Pizza tins are very flat with hardly any turn up at the edges, which makes serving the pizza really easy. They come in two or three sizes, often with a nonstick surface. Do not cut the pizza on a nonstick tin as this will damage the surface. Slide it off onto a hot serving plate and then cut into slices.

Sponge flan tins
It is unfortunate that this tin is also called a flan tin because it is just a sponge cake tin with a raised middle section. When the sponge is turned out, it has a dip in the middle to hold a filling such as fruit or jelly.

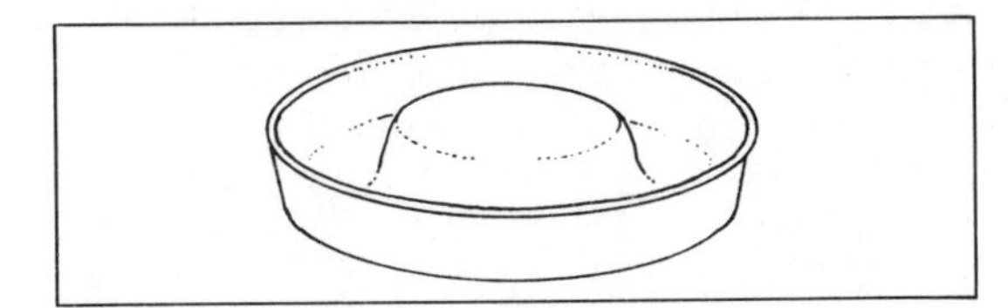

GENERAL EQUIPMENT

Baking beans
Instead of using dried, and sometimes old, beans and peas to hold down the greaseproof paper when you are baking a pastry shell, you can now get ceramic or metal 'beans' which are easy to deal with and washable.

Baking trays or sheets
Buy heavy quality ones, flat and smooth. Necessary to conduct heat underneath pies, quiches, scones and biscuits.

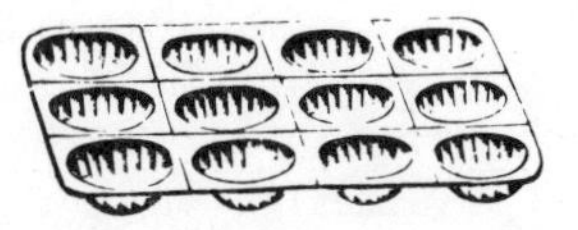

Flour dredger
To sprinkle a fine dusting of flour over a rolling surface. If the holes are small enough, this can also dredge icing sugar over cooked sweet pies, tarts and the tops of sponges.

Food processor or liquidizer
For shredding, slicing and grating. A processor reduces fat and flour, ready for mixing into pastry, in seconds.

Kitchen scissors

Knives
A sharp knife for chopping, cutting and shaping, plus a flat-bladed knife for mixing.

Measuring jugs
Glass or plastic jugs with imperial and metric volumes marked on the side. It is handy to have two.

Metal grater
For obtaining zest from orange and lemon rinds. Use the large holes for cheese or breadcrumbs.

Mixing bowls
I hesitate to suggest sizes since they will depend on amount of baking done and the family to be catered for. However, a medium and large size is useful, as well as a small heatproof bowl.

Pastry brush
For applying egg wash, glazes etc.

Pastry and chopping boards
I use an old wooden board. These are very expensive now and so are the newish 'soft' plastic boards which are excellent. The hard plastic boards are easy to clean but slippery to use.

Pastry cutters
Plain or fluted metal for scones, biscuits and pastry cases.

Piping equipment
If you are very keen on decorative work, e.g. icings, piped biscuits or piped fancy decorations, it is handy to have a complete piping set. (*See page 243.*)

Plastic sieve
Used for flour and icing sugar.

Rolling pin
Can be glass, wood or ceramic. Glass rolling pins are often hollow and can be filled with ice-cold water to keep pastry cool. I prefer my wooden pin.

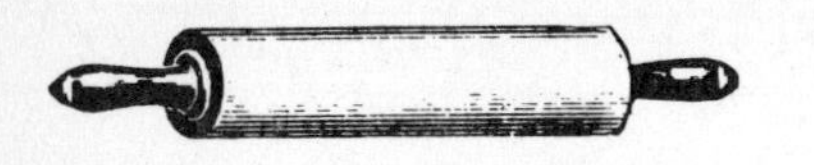

Spatulas
Flat rubber or plastic heads used for mixing and scraping clean a bowl of dough or soft mixtures. Much more efficient than a spoon.

Spoons
Wooden ones for stirring and mixing. Long-handled perforated draining spoon for cooked fruit etc. A set of measuring spoons to give accurate measurements is also very useful.

Weighing machine
A pair of balance scales with both metric and imperial weights or a set of kitchen scales.

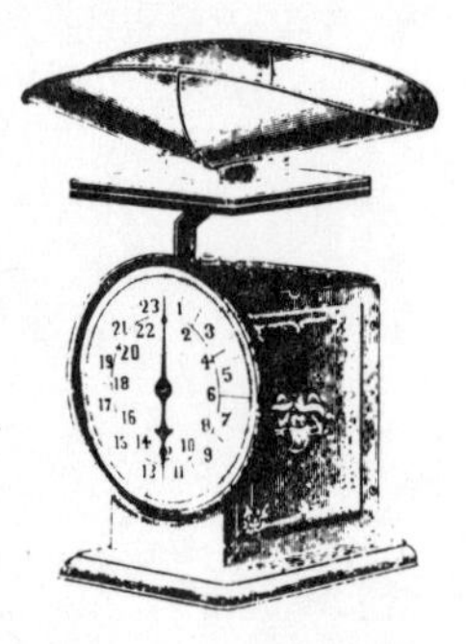

Whisks or beaters
Wire, balloon or loop-headed, hand rotary, electric hand-held, electric mixer with beater, whisk and dough hook, small 'stick' electric mixer – all the above can be used for whipping eggs, batters, creaming fat and sugar etc.

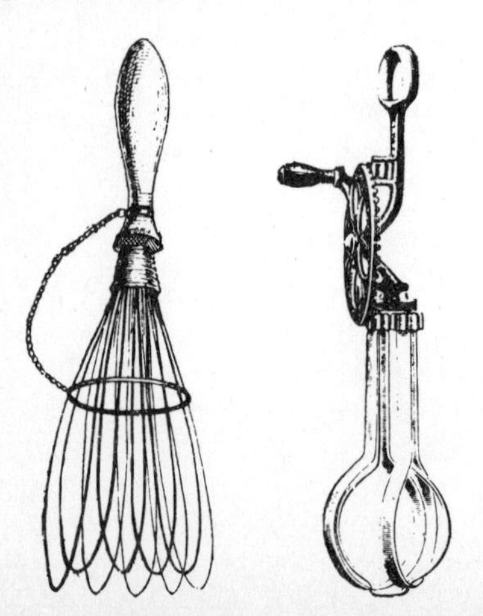

PREPARATION OF TINS

Greaseproof paper and nonstick paper

Greaseproof paper is most often used for lining cake tins and is available in rolls or in flat packs. It is also possible to buy papers to fully line round and oblong tins. These have crinkly sides which expand to fit the tin. Commercial bakers use them. For lining the bases of round tins, circles of paper are available to save you the trouble of making your own.

Nonstick paper is silicone treated, and is very helpful when making biscuits or anything with a high sugar content like macaroons or meringues. You can buy it in rolls or flat packs. With care it can be used two or three times – just wipe the paper carefully when warm and allow it to dry.

GREASING AND LINING BAKING TINS

Despite the fact that I use some nonstick tins, I have to admit that I always grease them as well. Use a small knob of margarine or lard and, using a piece of kitchen roll, smear this evenly over the inside of the tin. My own way of doing this is to keep a small jar of solid vegetable oil in the fridge. I melt it by standing the uncovered jar in a pan of simmering water (or give the jar 1 minute on high power in a microwave oven) and then use a brush to paint a thin film over the tins. I then add a circle of greaseproof paper for sandwich cakes. For richer cakes, the tins should be greased and fully lined (*see page 21*). Cakes requiring long cooking (over 1 hour) benefit not just from lined tins but also from a thick collar of brown paper placed round the outside of the tin and a thick wad under the tin as well. This helps prevent scorching.

LINING TINS

Round tin

It is important to allow about 5 cm/2 inches of paper to extend above the rim of the tin. Using the tin as a template, cut two circles of greaseproof paper to fit the bottom of the tin. Cut a strip of paper slightly longer than the circumference of the tin and deep enough to allow for the extra 5 cm/2 inches plus another 2.5 cm/1 inch. Now fold back the strip about 2.5 cm/1 inch along the long edge.

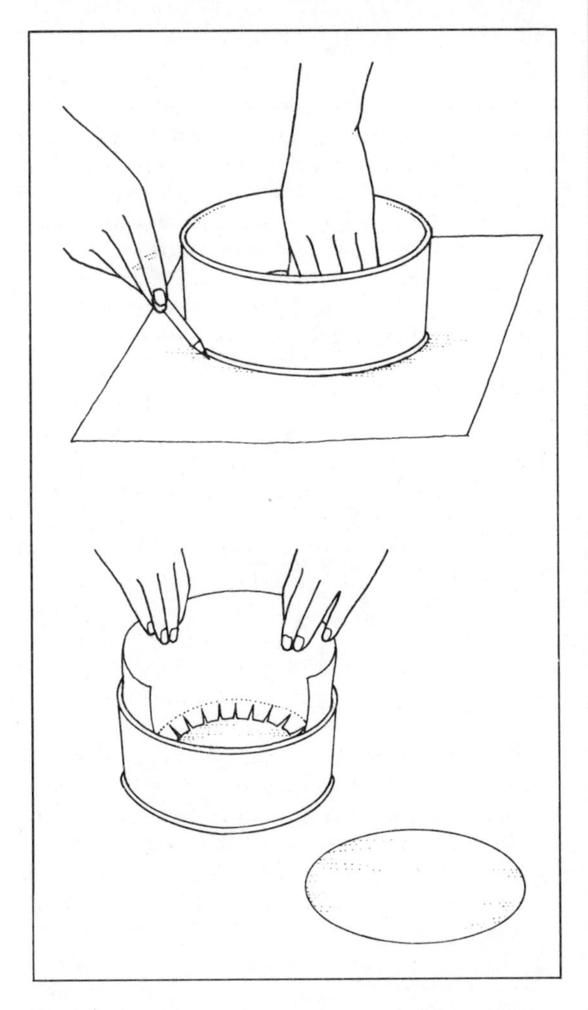

Open up this fold and snip it at intervals with scissors, cutting at a slight angle up to the fold. Grease the tin and lay in one of the paper circles. Press it down. Press the long strip of paper round the sides. The snipped edge will overlap itself to give a good fit round the base of the tin. Grease the paper circle in the bottom of the tin again and press in the second circle of paper. You will find this holds the side papers in position.

Square tin

This is rather easier to line. One way is to cut two long strips of greaseproof paper measuring the width of the side. Grease the tin, then lay the paper in across one way. Grease the inside bottom layer of paper then lay in the other strip in the opposite direction.

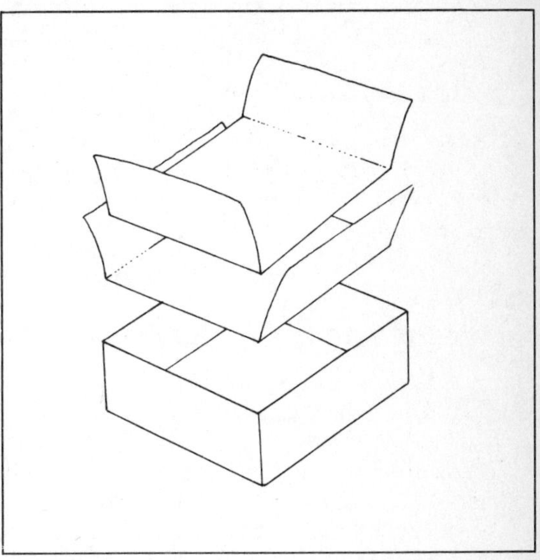

Alternative method for square tin

Cut a piece of greaseproof paper by measuring the length and width of the tin and adding twice its depth. Lay the tin on the middle of the paper. Then make four straight cuts from the edge of the paper up to the corners of the tin. Grease the tin and fit the paper inside, folding and overlapping at the corners.

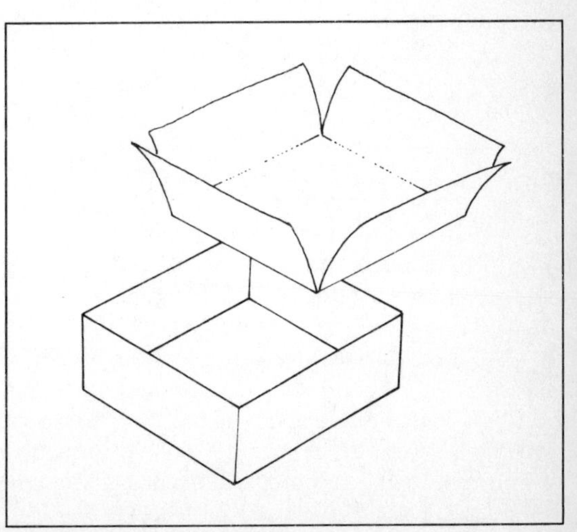

Oblong tin

A long tin or loaf tin may be lined with a continuous strip of paper running down one long side, across the bottom and up the other long side. The short ends can easily be released by sliding a knife down between the loaf and the tin. Grease the tin first and then lay in the greaseproof paper.

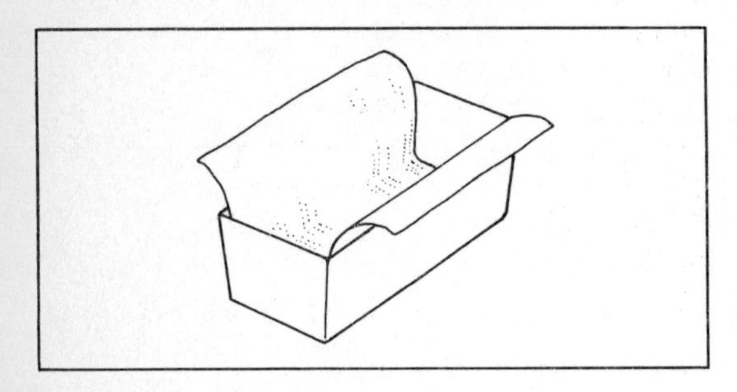

Greasing and lining flat tins

I find it easier to lightly grease a flat tin (like a Swiss roll tin) and lay the greaseproof paper on top. The grease holds it in position. This is important in a fan oven when the paper can get blown up at the corners. Place the empty tin on a sheet of paper 5 cm/2 inches larger than the tin and draw round the tin. Brush the inside of the tin with oil. Make a cut from each corner of the paper to each corner of the marked line. Place the paper into position in the tin, smoothing it across the base of the tin and overlapping the cut edges to give sharp corners.

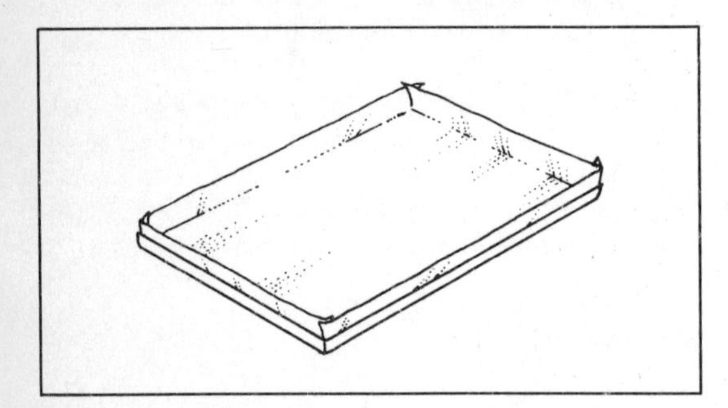

CLEANING TINS

All tins and baking trays must be washed carefully after use. I keep a toothbrush for getting into the corners, especially in square or oblong tins. If you can get them into the oven after washing to dry off in the residual heat of the oven, so much the better.

If you are a breadmaker you probably won't use your bread tins for anything else. A wipe with a damp cloth will be all they will need and the older they get the better they will be.

USING THE OVEN

OVEN TEMPERATURES

Conventional ovens

I always say a recipe is just a guide. This is especially true of oven temperatures. No two ovens are alike and I am reluctant to lay down rules for where to put what. You will know your oven better than anybody else but, generally speaking, the top third of the oven is the hottest. In both gas and electric ovens use the top third for all pastries and bread. I put sponges and sandwich cakes just above the middle, and things which cook slowly, like large cakes and gingerbreads, need to go in so that the top of the cake is level with the middle of the oven.

Try to avoid opening the oven door before at least half the cooking time has elapsed as this might cause the cake to sink. Remember also to preheat your oven about 15 minutes before you need to use it so that it has time to reach the temperature mentioned in the recipe.

Fan ovens

No preheating is needed for either gas or electric fan ovens, and cooking times and temperatures should be reduced in accordance with the oven handbook.

As hot air is circulating evenly within the oven, the food can be placed on any shelf and several things baked at the same time without the need to rotate their positions.

BAKING AND COOLING

Since oven temperatures vary so much, deciding whether or not something is cooked is often a matter of judgement. In baking you can nearly always see what is happening. Try not to open the oven until at least halfway through the recommended cooking time.

The degree of brownness is a good indicator and, for cakes, and cake-type loaves, a careful feel with the fingers will indicate if there is still a wobble under the surface. The old test of a metal skewer, when inserted into the food, coming out clean if something is fully baked and sticky if not, is not always very reliable, especially if the skewer happens to pierce something moist like fruit. A better indication of doneness is, I think, the slight shrinking from the sides of the tin.

The cooling process should not be hurried. Try to avoid handling a red-hot cake as it will be very fragile. It is much better to leave things in or on the tins or trays until they firm up and cool down a little. I always run a knife between the tin and cake or loaf, give a gentle knock two or three times with the tin on its side like a wheel, and then drop the cake or loaf out onto my open hand.

Place the food to be cooled on an open-mesh wire tray to allow the air to circulate freely around it and the heat to be dissipated.

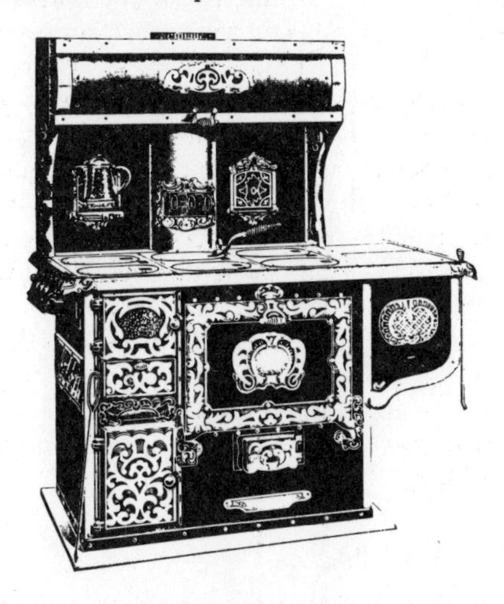

USING A MICROWAVE OVEN

Generally speaking, anything which can be cooked by boiling, steaming or poaching will do well in a microwave oven. However, baking needs dry heat and in my opinion is not something which a microwave oven does well, although the newer machines which combine microwave power and conventional heat are much more successful than microwaves alone.

Melted cake mixtures cook fairly well in a microwave, as do gingerbreads made in small quantities. If you are very pressed for time, a sponge cake which will be eaten at one sitting can be put together easily and cooked in the microwave. I prefer to make this sort of cake in a ring mould as I am certain it cooks more evenly.

I do, however, use my microwave in many other ways to assist my baking. It is ideal for:

- softening butter or margarine
- warming flour prior to bread making
- melting chocolate, syrup and honey
- browning flaked almonds and coconut
- rising dough prior to bread making
- warming lemons before squeezing
- dissolving gelatine
- drying herbs

USING THE FREEZER

Freezing cakes, buns and scones etc. is a good way to keep your baking in good condition longer. In fact, now that there are only two of us at home, I tend to freeze my cakes in slices and remove only what I need. I do not like cooked tarts and pastries with wet fillings from the freezer. I much prefer to freeze them uncooked or, better still, to freeze the pastry only in its raw state for open tarts. Fruit and meat fillings can be cooked and frozen in small quantities ready to fill a tart or a pie.

I have given freezing suggestions with most recipes, but here are a few more tips.

Do read the instructions for using your freezer.

Freeze food when it is very fresh.

Freeze food in quantities most likely to be used.

Pack food carefully using packaging made especially for freezer use – polythene freezer bags, heavy duty foil, plastic-lidded boxes and trays.

Exclude as much air as possible when wrapping food to be frozen.

Label each package well with details of contents, number of servings and the date.

Note recommended storage time and use, if possible, within that time. Food kept over the storage time is still quite safe to eat but it will begin to lose flavour and texture.

To freeze small items like cakes or buns, it is more satisfactory to open-freeze them first then pack into lidded plastic boxes to preserve their shape. This way they will not stick together. Open-freezing means laying the items uncovered on a tray in the freezer until they are frozen solid then packing them in boxes.

Raw bread dough freezes well, as do cooked loaves (*see page 171*).

Pastry freezes well either raw or cooked. The raw pastry may be frozen at the rubbed in stage (*see page 26*), in a ball or shaped into tartlets or flans. Pack and freeze in rigid plastic boxes.

SWEET AND SAVOURY PASTRIES, PIES AND TARTS

Pastry in all its varied guises is not difficult to make, but the old story about needing cool hands is true. Very hot hands create a lot of problems when making pastry, and while frequently resting the dough in the fridge does help, food processor pastry would be the best answer if you have hot hands.

Raw pastry freezes well as do baked pastry shells. I am not quite so keen on freezing tarts and flans which have a wet filling touching the pastry. I much prefer to freeze the tart or flan case raw.

Another shortcut is to freeze pastry crumbs. Make a large batch of flour and fat at the rubbed-in stage and then freeze it. Because it is crumbly, it defrosts quickly and in fact the pastry benefits if the crumbs are still well chilled when it is rolled out.

INGREDIENTS

It is nothing short of amazing the way in which three ingredients, flour, fat and water, can be manipulated to produce all the many types of pastries we use in baking.

FLOUR

Traditionally, plain white flour is used for making most pastries. Pass the flour through a sieve to incorporate as much air as possible.

Some people prefer self-raising flour. This gives a different texture – more crumbly than crisp – and I like it best when making simple jam and lemon curd tarts.

Wholemeal flour makes a strongly flavoured pastry particularly suited to savoury dishes. It is difficult to handle in an ordinary shortcrust recipe but try it with half plain wholemeal flour and half self-raising white flour for a good result. Use the special wholemeal flour recipe (*see page 30*) if you are using all wholemeal flour. You will find it pliable and easy to use.

Use strong flour (bread flour) for choux pastry, hot water crust and flaky pastry.

Notes on all the various flours available are on page 10.

FATS

Full information on fats is on page 10.

Lard

Lard is still a great favourite with many people who bake meat pies and savoury tarts. It gives a soft short pastry. A firm-textured lard is easier to rub in than some of the newer soft-textured ones.

Margarine

As with lard, the same rule applies – the firm-textured block margarine is better than the soft variety.

Butter

Pastry made with all butter has a lovely flavour and a very crisp texture. However, it is not easy to handle. It is usually used in rich sweet shortcrust pastry especially for the French type of small fruit tart (*see page 51*).

Half lard and half margarine

The combination of half lard and half margarine is an old one for making pastry. In the end it is probably a matter of personal taste. Butter makes a lovely crisp pastry but its flavour often permeates the dish; also it is expensive and rather more difficult to rub in. Lard, on the other hand, makes a very crumbly pastry – almost too short – but the flavour goes really well with savoury dishes like a bacon and egg pie. I do not like block margarine on its own nor would I use a soft margarine. By using the mixture of half lard and half margarine I get a smooth pliable pastry which handles easily and does not crack.

Suet

Suet is only used for making suet pastry which is very soft and spongy. Because suet comes in a packet ready to be mixed, the rubbing-in stage is omitted and so there is a saving in time. However, to achieve a good flavour and texture, self-raising flour is used, with additional baking powder and a beaten egg added in the mixing. You can prepare your own suet by getting it from the butcher and grating it yourself. However, separating the skin from the suet before you start is a tedious job.

SUGAR

Sugar is not used very much in pastry making. The only pastry in this book in which there is sugar is the rich sweet shortcrust (*see page 28*). Caster sugar is best but I do know one or two people who prefer sifted icing sugar to get a very smooth-textured pastry. Do not use granulated sugar or the pastry will be speckled.

LIQUID

Apart from hot water crust pastry, all pastries need water as cold as possible. The quantity needed is very variable – different flours absorb different amounts of water. Always take care when adding water, too much will make the pastry hard and too little will make the dough difficult to roll because it is dry.

MAKING PASTRY

MIXING THE DOUGH

I like a narrow deep bowl if I am making pastry by hand, and I prefer to make up not more than 325 g/12 oz flour.

Take every opportunity to add air to the mixture – sift the flour into the bowl and rub in the fat with the fingertips, lifting the mixture as high as you safely can.

Mix the pastry with ice-cold water and add just enough to bring it together. I use a long-bladed knife, the old-fashioned kind with a white handle. Use the knife to mix and stir, pressing the mixture against the side of the bowl. Once the pastry is forming use your hand to knead the mixture in the bowl, turning it over and over until all the fat and flour is incorporated.

Set the pastry aside at this point in a cool place (not in the fridge) to rest before rolling out.

ALLOWING PASTRY TO REST

There is no doubt that allowing pastry to rest for 10–15 minutes after it has been mixed gives a better result. It stops shrinkage and the pastry is more crisp, so try to get into the habit of doing this. I usually rest pastry once after it is mixed and again after I have shaped it into whatever I am making.

Recipes often suggest chilling pastry – however, I really recommend that you do not put it in the fridge. I find it is often over-chilled and extremely hard to handle and I like to put mine somewhere colder than my kitchen.

ROLLING THE PASTRY

Make a space on a flat surface or use a laminated board or a wooden pastry board. Dust it lightly with flour and dust the rolling pin with flour. Knead the pastry slightly to achieve a smooth crack-free surface underneath then turn it over and start rolling.

Begin with both hands out flat, and with a gentle flow of short light movements ease the pastry to the shape and size you want. When shaping the pastry, always move the pastry round and do not try to use the rolling pin in any direction other than away from you and in a straight line.

To lift pastry into a tin, e.g. a flan case, use the rolling pin – drape the pastry over it and lay the outer edge of the pastry on the edge of the tin, then unroll the pastry so that it flops into the tin. Ease

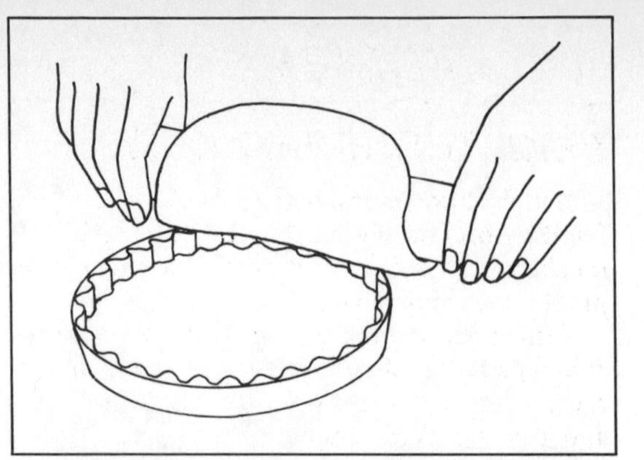

the base of the pastry circle down into the tin and press the pastry gently to the sides, paying particular attention to the angle at the base. Trim away any excess pastry on the top edge and prick all over the base to let any air escape which is trapped. The holes seal up perfectly when the heat reaches the pastry so do not worry about fillings leaking. They are much more likely to leak if the pastry is unevenly rolled and one bit is thinner than another.

TO BAKE A FLAN CASE OR PASTRY SHELL BLIND

The word 'blind' means that the pastry is cooked or partially cooked before the filling is added. To prevent the pastry bubbling up while cooking, dried peas or beans are used to fill the pastry shell. Ceramic and metal beans are also now available.

When baking a deep flan with 5-cm/2-inch sides, line the base of the raw pastry case with a large circle of greaseproof paper. Cover this paper with dried peas or beans and pile them up the sides to support the pastry until it is cooked. Remove the beans and paper 10 minutes before the end of cooking time to enable the pastry to crisp up.

Flan cases with just 2.5-cm/1-inch sides do not need the 'dried bean' treatment to hold up the sides. Just keep an eye on the pastry while it is baking. If the base bubbles up or the sides slide down just push them back into position with a fork.

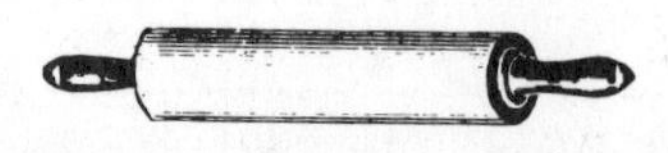

EQUIPMENT

BAKING TINS AND TRAYS

Although I have several fluted porcelain flan dishes I still go back to my reliable tin ones. Metal is a much better conductor of heat than either heat-proof glass or porcelain.

Remember to oil or grease your tins well. I use an old pastry brush to make sure of getting into all the corners. After use wash the tins in hot water and pay particular attention to the joins where crumbs may stick. Dry the tins in the residual heat of your oven.

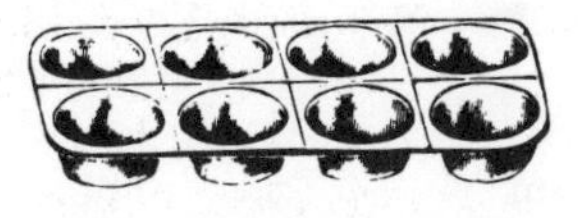

DEEP PIES, FLANS AND QUICHES

Old-fashioned deep fruit pies and meat pies are usually baked in stoneware or enamelware pie dishes with a generous rim. There is only one layer of thickish pastry and that is on top where it seals in all the moisture and flavour and also remains crisp.

Flan tins come in two depths but usually with loose bottoms. The shallow flan tin, with about 2.5-cm/1-inch straight sides, is usually for tea-time tarts like Bakewell and Almond. The deeper flan tin with sides about 5 cm/2 inches deep, usually sloping outwards, is more often used for savoury flans like Bacon and Egg. There are also metal flan rings which you sit directly onto a baking tray.

All these tins come in a huge variety of sizes. Here is a guide to the amount of pastry needed for different sizes. Don't forget that e.g. 225 g/8 oz shortcrust pastry means the amount of flour used to make the pastry would be 225 g/8 oz plain flour. On the other hand, if you buy frozen pastry 225 g/8 oz would refer to the total weight, i.e. flour, fat and water together.

For flans or flan rings

15 cm/6 inch	–	125–150 g/4–5 oz flour
20 cm/8 inch	–	175–200 g/6–7 oz flour
25 cm/10 inch	–	225–250 g/8–9 oz flour

OTHER USEFUL EQUIPMENT

Bowls
I like narrow deep bowls to mix pastry in rather than wide flat ones. The bowls I have are plastic with a lip at one side like a handle.

Dredger
This is handy for sprinkling dry flour over your working surface or rolling pin.

Knife
I use a long-bladed old-fashioned knife with a white handle to bring the pastry together.

Palette knife
A long flexible palette knife is handy when rolling out a large piece of pastry. You can slide it under to release the pastry should it be sticking to the board.

Pastry funnel
To support pastry over fillings in pies.

Plastic bag
Slip any raw pastry which you are not working with into the bag to keep it from drying out.

Rolling pins
I prefer a wooden rolling pin. Mine is very short because it originally had handles which I removed.

Spatula
A rubber spatula is always handy for scraping mixture down the sides of the bowl.

Working surface
A wooden pastry board is very nice to work on especially if you are cutting out small pastries such as tartlets. However, it has to be really large. The plastic working surface of modern kitchen units is also perfectly suitable for most rolling out.

SHORTCRUST PASTRY

225 g/8 oz plain white flour
1 pinch salt
50 g/2 oz block margarine, at room temperature, cut into small pieces
50 g/2 oz firm lard, at room temperature, cut into small pieces
Very cold water

1. Sift the flour and salt into a mixing bowl.
2. Rub the fats into the flour. Use your fingertips and lift the mixture up and down to incorporate more air. (This stage can be done in a food processor, then return the mixture to the bowl.)
3. When the mixture starts to resemble damp breadcrumbs, use a jug to sprinkle about 4 tablespoons cold water over the surface of the crumbs.
4. Using a long, round-bladed knife, start mixing and cutting and pressing the mixture against the side of the bowl. If the mixture still looks crumbly, add a very little more water. Use your hand to knead the mixture round and round the bowl until it leaves the sides more or less cleanly.
5. When you have a smooth ball of pastry, wrap it in foil or a polythene bag and rest the dough in the fridge for 20 minutes before using.

RICH SWEET SHORTCRUST PASTRY

This is a lovely pastry for rich dessert flans and tartlets. The egg helps to give it an excellent texture which is firmer than ordinary shortcrust.

225 g/8 oz plain white flour
1 pinch salt
150 g/5 oz butter, softened
25 g/1 oz caster sugar
1 teaspoon lemon juice
1 medium egg yolk
2–3 tablespoons cold water

1. Sift the flour and salt into a mixing bowl.
2. Rub in the butter as lightly as possible. (This stage can be done in a food processor. Return the mixture to the bowl if you have used a processor.) Stir in the sugar.
3. Mix together the lemon juice, egg yolk and 2 tablespoons of water. Using a round-ended knife, stir this into the flour and start to bring it together by pressing the mixture against the side of the bowl. If the mixture still looks crumbly, add more water. Use your hand to knead to a smooth firm dough.
4. Wrap the dough in foil or a polythene bag and rest it in the fridge for 10–15 minutes before using.

SHORTCRUST PASTRY IN A FOOD PROCESSOR

325 g/12 oz plain white flour
1 pinch salt
175 g/6 oz mixed block margarine and firm lard straight from the fridge, cut into small pieces
3 tablespoons water

1. Place the flour, salt and fats into the bowl and, using the steel blade, process on a medium speed for a few seconds until the mixture resembles breadcrumbs.
2. With the machine running on a low speed, add the water through the feed tube and process for a few seconds until one or two balls of pastry are formed. Stop the machine. Remove the pastry from the bowl and combine together by hand to avoid over-processing.
3. The dough will be warm so wrap it in foil and rest it in the fridge for 10–15 minutes before using.

ALMOND SUET PASTRY

Makes a very well-flavoured firm pastry. Useful with wet, juicy fruit fillings.

175 g/6 oz self-raising white flour
125 g/4 oz prepared packet suet
50 g/2 oz ground almonds
25 g/1 oz caster sugar
2–3 drops almond essence
1 medium egg, beaten
Cold water

1. Sift the flour into a mixing bowl and stir in the suet, ground almonds and sugar.
2. Add the almond essence, the egg and enough cold water to make a firm dough – 1 tablespoon should be enough.
3. Use your hand to knead the dough in the bowl until smooth.
4. Wrap the dough in foil or a polythene bag and rest it in a cool place for 10–15 minutes before using.

TO MAKE A PASTRY SHELL OR FLAN CASE, 20 CM/8 INCHES ACROSS

Many recipes call for a cooked pastry shell to which a filling is then added. Make the shell according to the instructions below and then bake blind *(see page 26)*.

Use either a 20-cm/8-inch loose-bottomed flan tin, 5 cm/2 inches or 2.5 cm/1 inch deep, or a flan ring placed directly onto a greased baking tray.

Remember to rest the pastry for 10–15 minutes before rolling out, and again after the pastry has been fitted into the tin. This helps to prevent shrinkage and ensure the pastry shell has a good shape. If you like fairly thin pastry, you may have a little left over after rolling out.

1 quantity shortcrust pastry *(see page 27)*

1. Grease the flan tin, or flan ring and baking tray.
2. On a lightly floured board, roll out the pastry to a circle – 5 cm/2 inches wider than the diameter of the 2.5-cm/1-inch deep tin, or 10 cm/4 inches wider than the 5-cm/2-inch deep tin.
3. Lift the pastry on your rolling pin *(see page 26)* and ease it into the tin or ring. Smooth the pastry from the centre outwards, pressing it well into the angle at the bottom. Ease the pastry up the sides of the tin, avoid making folds, and trim off any surplus with a sharp knife.
4. Using a fork, prick the base of the pastry all over and set aside in a cool place for 10–15 minutes. The pastry is now ready to fill and bake, or to be baked blind *(see page 26)*.
5. Bake in a hot oven, Gas 7, 425°F, 220°C, for 10–12 minutes. Remove the dried peas or beans and paper and bake for a further 7–8 minutes until the pastry is crisp and brown. Allow to cool.

Store in an airtight tin until needed. Can be frozen but may need to be crisped up in a hot oven for 10 minutes before using.

SUET PASTRY

A useful everyday pastry with a firm texture.

225 g/8 oz self-raising white flour
1 teaspoon baking powder
125 g/4 oz prepared packet suet
1 medium egg
1 tablespoon cold water

1. Sift the flour and baking powder into a mixing bowl and stir in the suet.
2. Mix the egg with the water and, using a round-ended knife, stir the egg and water into the flour to make a firm dough.
3. Cover the dough with foil or polythene and rest it in the fridge for 10–15 minutes before using.

WHOLEMEAL PASTRY

This pastry can also be made in a food processor following the instructions on page 28 for making shortcrust pastry in a food processor.

225 g/8 oz plain wholemeal flour
75 g/3 oz mixed solid vegetable fat and butter, cut into pieces
1 teaspoon sugar
1 pinch salt
1 fat pinch baking powder
125 ml/4 fl oz water
1 teaspoon vegetable oil

1. Sift the flour into a mixing bowl, adding any residue of bran left in the sieve.
2. Rub the fats into the flour and add the sugar, salt and baking powder.
3. Add the water and vegetable oil and mix to a fairly wet dough.
4. Set the dough aside for a few minutes to absorb all the water, then turn out on a lightly floured board and knead with your hand until the dough is smooth. The dough is now ready to use.

CHEESE PASTRY

225 g/8 oz plain white or wholewheat flour
1 pinch salt
½ teaspoon mustard powder
1 pinch cayenne pepper
75 g/3 oz mixed block margarine and lard, cut into small pieces
75 g/3 oz finely grated strongly flavoured cheese (e.g. Cheddar and Parmesan mixed)
1 medium egg yolk
2 tablespoons cold water

1. Sift the flour, salt, mustard and cayenne pepper into a mixing bowl, adding any residue of bran left in the sieve if using wholewheat flour, and rub in the mixed fats. (Or mix in a food processor.)
2. (Return the mixture to a bowl if you have used a processor.) Stir in the cheese.
3. Mix the egg yolk with the water and pour into the bowl. Using a round-ended knife, start to bring all the ingredients together. If the mixture still looks crumbly add extra water. Use your hand to knead to a smooth, firm dough.
4. Wrap the dough in foil or a polythene bag and rest it in the fridge for 10–15 minutes before using.

HOT WATER CRUST PASTRY

Apart from its use in pork and game pies, this pastry has all but disappeared in most places. However, it is still used in Scotland for little meat pies, and a type of individual fruit tart you only find in bakers' shops there. I think it is particularly useful for fruit tartlets because it does not absorb liquid in the way that shortcrust does. Its texture is more brittle than crumbly. To make it, lard and water are boiled together and poured straight into the flour. The pastry has to be used warm or it starts to crack. I found it easy to warm up again in my microwave cooker the last time I used it on television to make pork pies.

275 g/10 oz strong white flour
½ teaspoon salt
125 ml/4 fl oz water
125 g/4 oz lard

1. Sift the flour and salt into a large mixing bowl.
2. Put the water and lard into a small pan and bring to the boil.
3. When the lard has melted, immediately pour the liquid into the flour.
4. Using a spoon or knife, mix thoroughly until the mixture is cool enough to knead with your hand then knead to a smooth, firm dough.
5. Allow to cool a little before using.

PIE PASTRY

This is another pastry suitable for pork and game pies. It is not necessary to use boiling water as the egg makes the pastry soft and elastic.

275 g/10 oz plain white flour
1 teaspoon salt
140 g/4½ oz lard, cut into small pieces
1 medium egg, beaten
6 tablespoons water

1. Sift the flour and salt into a mixing bowl and rub in the lard.
2. Mix the egg with the water and stir this into the mixture. Use your hand to knead in the bowl to a soft dough.
3. Set the dough aside in a cool place for at least 1 hour before using.

CHOUX PASTRY

The most delicate of all pastries – most often associated with éclairs and profiteroles, but good with savoury fillings, too.

60 g/2½ oz strong white flour
1 pinch salt
50 g/2 oz unsalted butter, cut into small pieces
125 ml/4 fl oz water
2 medium eggs, well beaten

1. Sift the flour and salt onto a piece of paper. (This makes it easy to add to the hot water and butter.)
2. Put the butter and water into a pan and bring to the boil.
3. Immediately the butter has melted, tip the flour and salt into the pan, using the paper as a funnel. Take the pan off the heat and beat the mixture vigorously with a wooden spoon until it leaves the sides of the pan.
4. Allow the mixture to cool slightly, then beat in the eggs, a little at a time. At this point the mixture should be slack enough to pipe easily but firm enough to retain its shape.
5. Allow the mixture to cool in the pan and then use immediately.

VARIATION

You can flavour the pastry by adding an extra pinch of salt and a pinch of cayenne pepper. Savoury choux pastry is very nice with a filling of cream cheese and chives. Make the choux buns quite tiny to offer with drinks before a meal.

NEW FLAKY PASTRY

I was very sceptical about making a flaky pastry this way but it really is excellent – providing you keep your hands out of it until the last minute.

175 g/6 oz block margarine
225 g/8 oz plain white flour
1 pinch salt
Ice-cold water

1. Put the margarine in the freezer for 25 minutes.
2. Sift the flour and salt into a large mixing bowl and, with a small bowl, take out enough flour to use for dipping.
3. Using a piece of foil, grip the frozen margarine and grate it, on the largest holes of a metal grater, into the mixing bowl. Try to cover the surface of the flour with the grated fat. As soon as the block becomes sticky, dip it into the small bowl of flour. When all the margarine has been grated, add the remaining flour in the small bowl to the mixture.
4. Using a knife, cut and mix into the flour and margarine mixture and add enough cold water to make a firm dough. At the last moment, when the mixture is crumbly, use your hand to knead it gently to a ball.
5. Wrap the dough in foil or a polythene bag and chill for 30 minutes before using.

TRADITIONAL FLAKY PASTRY

This takes a little time to make but it is rather less difficult than puff pastry. Although both can be bought frozen ready-made, the home-made variety is unrivalled for taste and texture. In hot weather, or if you have hot hands, the pastry may be chilled between rollings.

225 g/8 oz strong white flour
1 pinch salt
75 g/3 oz butter, cut into small pieces
150 ml/¼ pint cold water
Squeeze lemon juice
75 g/3 oz lard, cut into small pieces

1. Sift the flour and salt into a mixing bowl and rub in approximately half the butter.
2. Mix the water with the lemon juice, then add to the flour mixture. Using a knife first, and finishing with your hand, knead gently to make a soft but not sticky dough.
3. Turn out the dough on a lightly floured board and roll out to an oblong about 41 cm/16 inches long. Square the corners so that you have a neat shape, and mark the dough lightly into thirds horizontally.
4. Take about half the lard and, using a knife, put dabs all over the top two thirds of the dough, leaving a border around the edge. Fold the bottom third up over the centre section of dough and fold the top third down over this, keeping the corners as square as possible. Seal the edges by pressing with the rolling pin then give the pastry a half turn so that the fold is at the right side.
5. Roll out the pastry as before until it is about 41 cm/16 inches long, and repeat the process with the remaining butter.
6. Roll out the pastry again and repeat with the remaining lard. Roll and fold once more without the addition of any fat.
7. Wrap the dough in clingfilm or foil and chill in the fridge for 20–30 minutes. The dough is now ready for use.

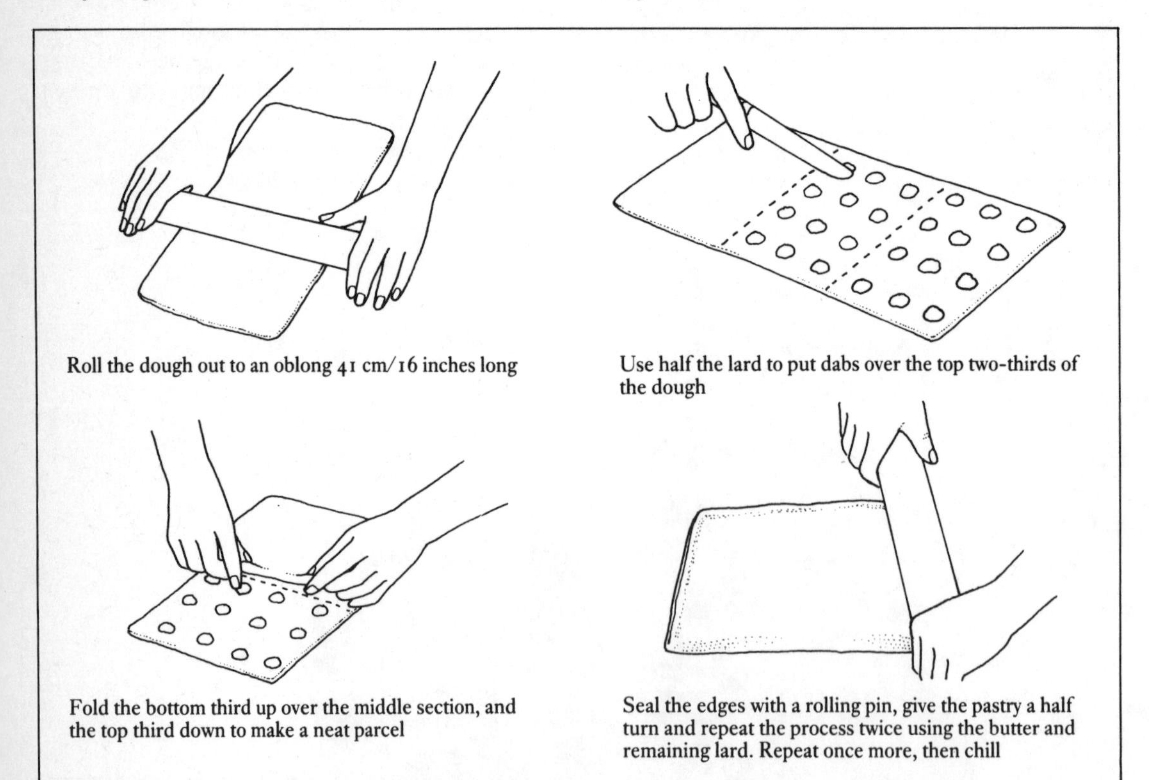

Roll the dough out to an oblong 41 cm/16 inches long

Use half the lard to put dabs over the top two-thirds of the dough

Fold the bottom third up over the middle section, and the top third down to make a neat parcel

Seal the edges with a rolling pin, give the pastry a half turn and repeat the process twice using the butter and remaining lard. Repeat once more, then chill

ROUGH PUFF PASTRY

This is an economical puff pastry.

225 g/8 oz strong white flour
1 pinch salt
75 g/3 oz good quality block margarine
75 g/3 oz firm lard
1 teaspoon lemon juice
About 150 ml/¼ pint iced water

1. Sift the flour and salt into a large mixing bowl.
2. Cut the fats into 1-cm/½-inch pieces and stir them into the flour.
3. Add the lemon juice and mix with enough water to give a firm dough. Do not try to break up the pieces of fat. Shape the dough into a long brick shape, cover and set it aside for 10 minutes in a cold place.
4. On a well floured board, lightly roll out the pastry until it is about 5 mm/¼ inch thick and make it about three times as long as it is wide. You will need to keep flouring your rolling pin. Fold the bottom third up and the top third down so that you have three layers. Using the rolling pin, press the edges firmly to seal in the air. Cover and chill again for 10 minutes.
5. Return the pastry to the board, giving it half a turn so that the sealed short ends are top and bottom. Repeat the rolling, folding, sealing and chilling three more times. Wrap the dough in clingfilm or foil and chill again for 30 minutes before using.

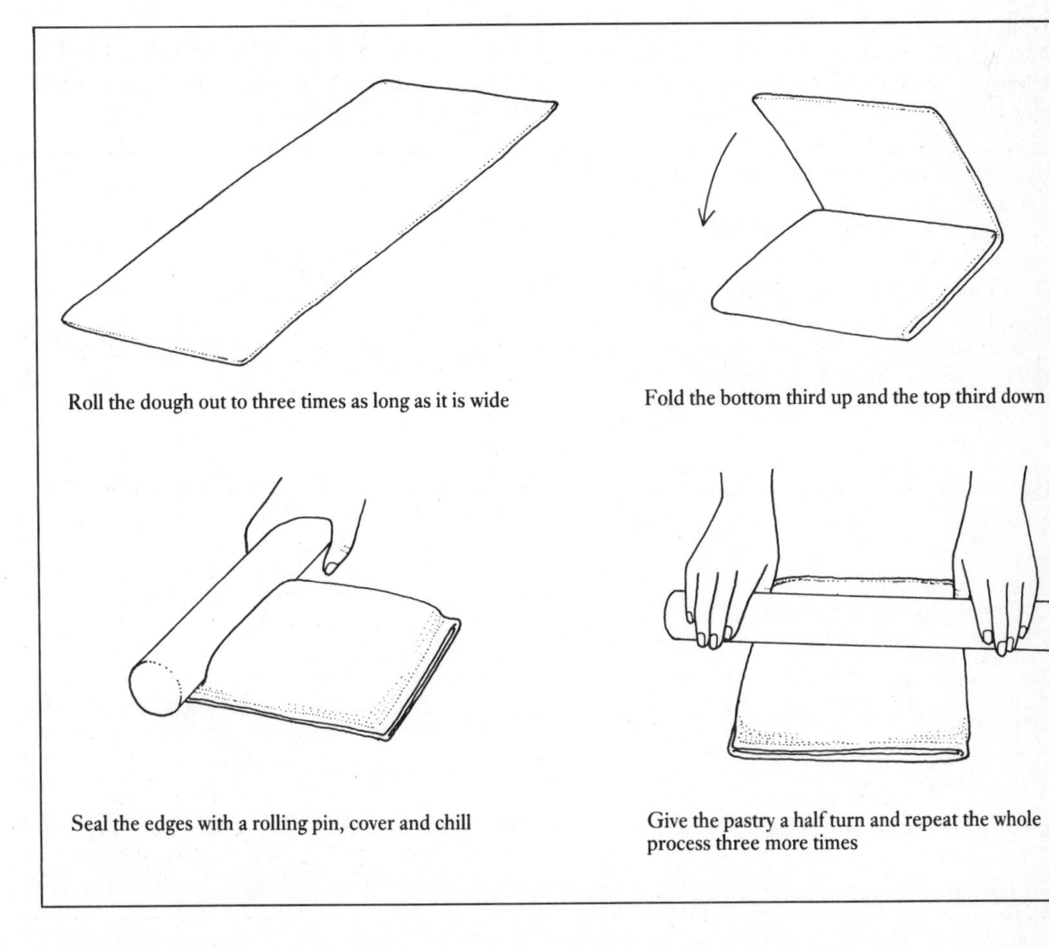

Roll the dough out to three times as long as it is wide

Fold the bottom third up and the top third down

Seal the edges with a rolling pin, cover and chill

Give the pastry a half turn and repeat the whole process three more times

STEAK AND KIDNEY PIE

This classic combination takes a lot of beating. Make plenty of rich gravy to serve separately.

Serves 6–8

2 tablespoons oil
900 g/2 lb steak and kidney, chopped
1 large onion, peeled and chopped
2 tablespoons plain wholemeal flour
600 ml/1 pint beef stock made with a stock cube
2 heaped teaspoons horseradish sauce
Salt and pepper
A dot of gravy browning
325 g/12 oz suet pastry *(see page 29)*
Milk or beaten egg to glaze

1. Heat the oil in a large, heavy-based pan.
2. Check that as much fat and skin as possible is removed from the meat, and that the core and skin are completely removed from the kidney. Brown the meats on all sides in the hot oil. You may have to do this in two batches. Remove the meats with a slotted spoon and set aside.
3. Add a little more oil to the pan if necessary, and brown the onion.
4. Return the meats to the pan and sprinkle over the flour. Stir well and add enough stock to barely cover the meat. Bring to the boil and remove any scum which rises to the surface. Stir in the horseradish sauce and reduce the heat to a steady simmer.
5. Cover the pan and cook, stirring occasionally, for about 1½–2 hours, or until the meat is tender. Stir carefully to avoid breaking up the chunks of meat. Check the seasoning, stir in the gravy browning and leave to go cold.
6. When ready to bake, preheat the oven to hot, Gas 7, 425°F, 220°C.
7. To assemble the pie, roll out the pastry on a floured board to about 1 cm/½ inch thick and about 2.5 cm/1 inch wider than the outer rim of a 1.5-litre/2½-pint pie dish.
8. Using a slotted spoon, transfer the cold steak and kidney to the pie dish. Add just enough gravy to keep the meat moist – about 2 tablespoons – and position a pie funnel in the middle of the dish. Reserve the remaining gravy.
9. Cut a 2.5-cm/1-inch strip from the outer edge of the pastry long enough to fit round the pie dish rim. Moisten the rim with water and press the pastry strip all round it. Moisten the upper surface of the strip, lift the pastry lid on a rolling pin and cover the pie. Press the edges firmly to get a good seal.
10. Make a small hole over the top of the pie funnel. Using a sharp knife and with the pie carefully lifted in your left hand and the handle of the knife angled under the dish, trim off the surplus pastry. Use the trimmings to cut out a few leaves, if wished.
11. Using a fork, make a decorative pattern all round the sealed edge, then brush over the top of the pastry with the milk or beaten egg. Decorate the top with the pastry leaves, if using, and brush them with milk or beaten egg.

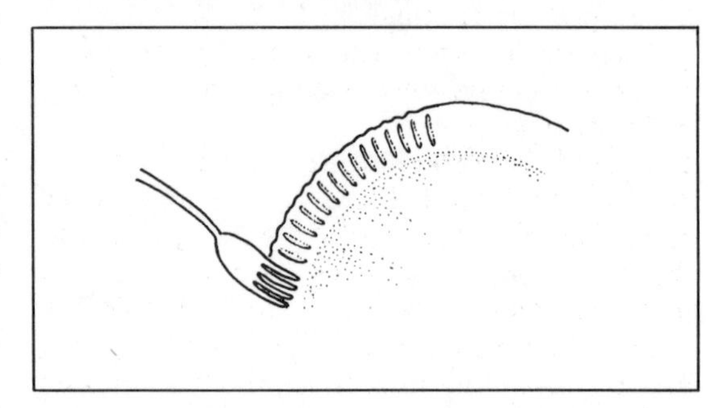

12. Place the pie dish on a baking tray and bake for about 30–40 minutes, or until the pastry is crisp and golden in colour.
13. Reheat the reserved gravy, adding extra stock if necessary to give a generous amount. Serve with the pie.

Store in the fridge for 2–3 days. Unlike other pastry dishes where the wet filling is in contact with the pastry, I think this pie freezes really well for up to 2 months.

CHEESE AND ONION PIE

This is the easiest pie to make that I know, but you must be very fond of onion and cheese together. Use wholemeal pastry for a change.

Will cut into 8 generous wedges

325 g/12 oz wholemeal pastry *(see page 30)*
2 large Spanish onions (about 450 g/1 lb), peeled and finely minced or chopped
225 g/8 oz strongly flavoured cheese (mature farmhouse Cheddar or Canadian Cheddar), grated
Pepper
25 g/1 oz butter, cut into small pieces
A little milk
25 g/1 oz sesame seeds

1. Grease a 23-cm/9-inch pie plate, or flan ring and baking tray. Preheat the oven to fairly hot, Gas 6, 400°F, 200°C.
2. Divide the pastry in two, roll out half and line the pie plate or flan ring.
3. Squeeze out as much moisture as possible from the onions and mix them with the cheese. Season well with pepper.
4. Spread the onion mixture over the pastry and dot the butter all over. Brush the edges with water.
5. Roll out the other half of the pastry and cover the pie, sealing the edges well. Trim off the surplus pastry and neaten the edge with fork marks all round. Make a small hole in the centre of the pie, brush all over with milk and sprinkle the sesame seeds on thickly.
6. Bake for about 30 minutes, or until the pastry is crisp and firm.

Best eaten on the day it is made, but will keep in the fridge for up to 2 days. Because the mixture in this pie is fairly dry it freezes well for up to 3 months.

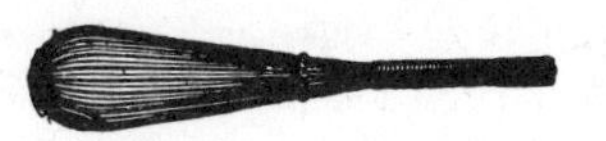

FIDGET PIE

There are examples of this pie from many parts of Britain but all contain apple, onion and bacon. It is a tasty combination, made the old way in a deep pie dish with one layer of pastry on top.

Serves 4–5

325 g/12 oz bacon pieces, or streaky bacon, chopped
225 g/8 oz onions, peeled and very finely sliced or minced
450 g/1 lb Bramley cooking apples, peeled, cored and sliced
2 teaspoons fresh sage leaves, chopped, or 1 teaspoon dried sage
Pepper
150 ml/¼ pint stock
175 g/6 oz shortcrust pastry *(see page 28)*
A little milk

1. Grease a 1.5-litre/2½-pint pie dish. Preheat the oven to moderate, Gas 4, 350°F, 180°C.
2. If you are using bacon pieces, trim off the skin then slice the bacon finely and chop into pieces.
3. Layer the onion, bacon, apple and sage into the dish, season well with pepper and pour in just enough stock to come halfway up the dish.
4. Roll out the pastry on a floured surface to about 2.5 cm/1 inch bigger than the pie dish. Gather up the pastry trimmings, reroll and cut a narrow strip to fit the rim of the dish. Brush the rim with a little water and press the narrow strip onto it. Moisten the pastry strip with water then cover the pie with the pastry, pressing down well to make a good seal. Trim off the surplus pastry and use this to cut out a few decorative leaves. Make a small hole in the centre of the pie. Brush the pastry with milk, decorate the surface with the pastry leaves and brush with milk again.
5. Place on a baking tray and bake for 1¾ hours.

Best eaten on the day it is made, but will store in the fridge for up to 3 days. Freezes well for 2 months.

RABBIT PIE

This is the old fashioned type of deep pie with only one top crust. I use suet pastry and a deep pie dish with a rim – 1.5-litre/2½-pint capacity.

Serves 6

1 × 1.3-kg/3-lb rabbit, jointed, or 1.1 kg/ 2½ lb frozen chopped rabbit meat, thawed
2 medium onions, peeled and chopped
1 bay leaf
225 g/8 oz streaky bacon pieces, de-rinded and chopped into cubes
1 litre/1½ pints vegetable stock made with a stock cube
Salt and pepper
125 g/4 oz pork sausagemeat
1 teaspoon plain flour
2 pinches dried sage
1 tablespoon oil
½ teaspoon dried sage
40 g/1½ oz plain white flour
4 tablespoons water
325 g/12 oz suet pastry *(see page 29)*
1 small egg, beaten

1. Wash the rabbit joints or pieces and put them into a large pan with the onions and bay leaf.
2. Add the bacon to the rabbit pieces and pour in the vegetable stock.
3. Bring to a boil and remove any scum which rises to the surface. Season with salt and pepper. Lower the heat and cook covered for about 1 hour or until the meat is tender.
4. Meanwhile, divide the pork sausagemeat into six balls. Season the teaspoon of flour with the 2 pinches dried sage and roll the balls in it.
5. Heat the oil in a frying pan and fry the balls fairly briskly until nicely browned. Set aside.
6. Using a slotted spoon, remove the rabbit, onion and bacon pieces and place in a 1.5-litre/2½-pint greased pie dish. Discard the bay leaf. Set aside as many bones as possible but try to keep the rabbit in pieces rather than shredded. Add the sausagemeat balls to the dish, sprinkle the ½ teaspoon dried sage over the top, and place a pie funnel in the middle of the dish.
7. Now, thicken the stock left in the pan. In a small bowl, mix the 40 g/1½ oz flour with the water. When it is smooth, pour it into the pan with the stock and cook gently, stirring all the time, until the liquid thickens. Pour enough of this stock over the rabbit to come halfway up the dish. Reserve the remaining stock to serve as gravy. Allow the contents of the pie dish to go cold before covering with pastry.
8. Preheat the oven to hot, Gas 7, 425°F, 220°C.
9. On a floured surface, roll out the pastry to an oval shape, about 2.5 cm/1 inch bigger than the size of the dish and about 1 cm/½ inch thick. Cut a narrow strip from the outer edge of the pastry long enough to fit round the pie dish rim. Moisten the rim with water and press the pastry strip all round it. Moisten the upper surface of the strip, lift the oval of pastry on your rolling pin and cover the pie. Press the edges firmly to get a good seal.
10. Make a small hole over the top of the pie funnel. Using a sharp knife and with the pie carefully lifted in your left hand and the handle of the knife angled under the dish, trim off the surplus pastry. Use the trimmings to cut out a few leaves or flowers.
11. Using a fork, make a decorative pattern all round the sealed edge, then brush over the top of the pastry with the beaten egg. Decorate the top with the leaves or flowers and brush them with egg as well.
12. Place the pie dish on a baking tray and bake for 30 minutes, or until the pastry is brown and crisp.

Best eaten freshly made. Store in a cold place for no more than 3 days before eating. This pie will freeze well cooked, or at stage 8 with the raw pastry.

CHICKEN AND LEEK PIE

To get really tender chicken it is best to gently poach it in a flavoured stock. However, this recipe is almost as successful with the cold remains of a roast chicken.

Serves 8

2 small chicken breasts – about 325 g/12 oz (or cold cooked chicken)
600 ml/1 pint water
1 small onion, peeled and sliced
Sprig of tarragon, or ¼ teaspoon dried tarragon
2 full rashers smoked bacon, de-rinded, grilled and chopped
40 g/1½ oz butter
675 g/1½ lb leeks, washed, topped and tailed and sliced in thin rings
Salt and pepper
225 g/8 oz new flaky pastry *(see page 31)*

FOR THE SAUCE

300 ml/½ pint chicken stock from poached chicken, or use a stock cube
25 g/1 oz plain white flour
25 g/1 oz butter
Sprig of tarragon, or ¼ teaspoon dried tarragon
Salt and pepper

1. First, cook the chicken. Slice each chicken breast horizontally in two. Put these into a pan with the water, onion and tarragon and bring to the boil. Remove any scum which rises to the surface and reduce the heat to a simmer. Cook, covered, for about 30 minutes, or until the chicken is tender. Allow to cool in the stock.
2. Drain and reserve the stock. Chop the chicken in cubes and put into a large bowl with the bacon.
3. Melt the 40 g/1½ oz butter in a pan. Add the leeks, cover and cook gently over a low heat until soft. Season with salt and pepper. Stir into the bowl with the chicken and bacon.
4. Make a thick white sauce. Put 300 ml/½ pint of the reserved chicken stock into a small pan with the flour, butter and tarragon. Whisk the mixture over a low heat until the flour is dispersed. Set aside the whisk and stir with a wooden spoon until you have a smooth, thick white sauce. Season well with salt and pepper and allow to cool.
5. Stir in enough of the sauce to hold together the leeks, chicken and bacon. You may not need it all.
6. Preheat the oven to hot, Gas 7, 425°F, 220°C.
7. Divide the flaky pastry in two and roll out one half to a circle about 23 cm/9 inches across. Use a plate or a pan lid to get a good shape. Put this circle directly onto a greased oven-proof plate, if you have one big enough, or onto a metal pie plate.
8. Gather up the pastry trimmings, reroll and cut a narrow strip of pastry about 1 cm/½ inch wide. Brush the outer edge of the pastry base with beaten egg and press the narrow strip onto it.
9. Spoon the chicken mixture onto the pastry and pile it up in the centre as high as you can. Moisten the pastry strip with a little water.
10. Roll out the other piece of pastry to a circle about 25 cm/10 inches across, and cover the pie. Trim off the surplus pastry and use this to cut out some leaves or flowers. Make a decorative finish to the pastry by knocking up the sealed edge with horizontal cuts to give a layered effect. Now press your thumb round the edge of the pie and, using the back of a knife, pull the pastry back in between each thumb print to give a scalloped effect.
11. Make a small hole in the centre of the pie and decorate the surface with the pastry leaves or flowers. Using a sharp knife, lightly score the pie with a sun-ray effect into eight sections. Brush the beaten egg all over the top of the pie.
12. Bake for 15 minutes then reduce the heat to fairly hot, Gas 6, 400°F, 200°C, and bake for a further 15 minutes.

Best eaten freshly made. Store in a fridge for up to 3 days, or freeze for up to 2 months.

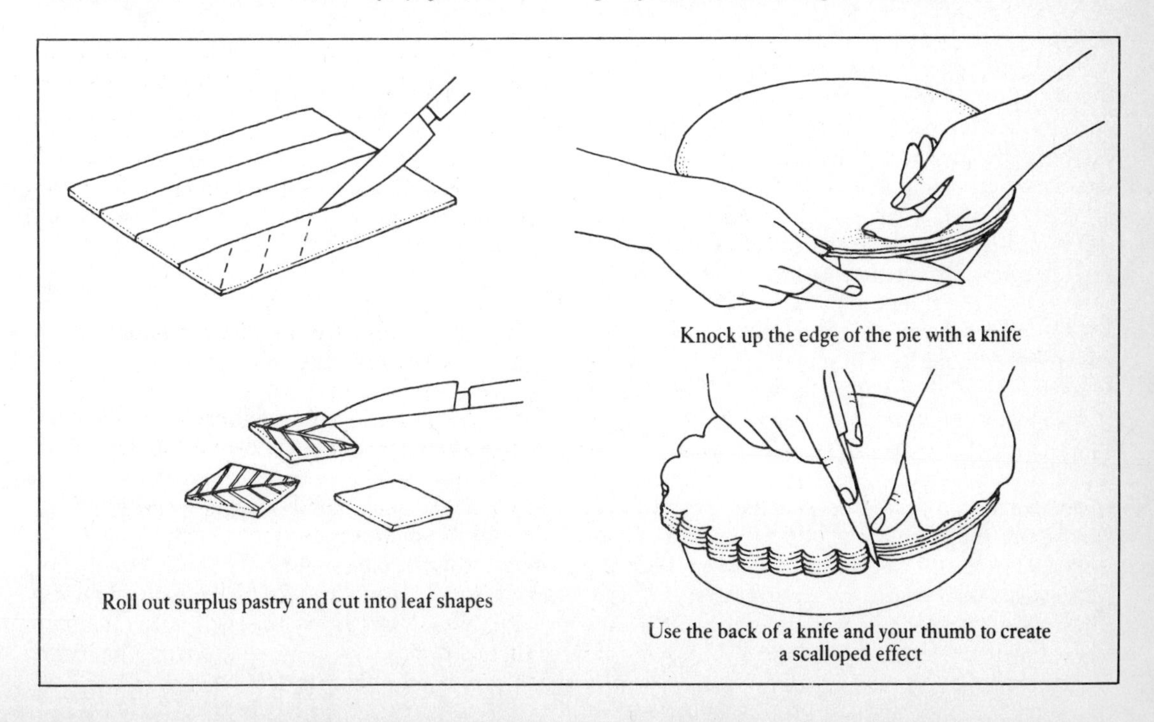

Knock up the edge of the pie with a knife

Roll out surplus pastry and cut into leaf shapes

Use the back of a knife and your thumb to create a scalloped effect

PORK PIE

Traditionally, the pork should be chopped into pieces no bigger than a raisin; I use scissors for this. Use a loose-bottomed pie tin. Start the day before.

Will cut into 8 small wedges

FOR THE SAVOURY JELLY

***Traditional method*:**

1 pig's trotter, split in two

1 bay leaf

6 peppercorns

600 ml/1 pint water

***Alternative method*:**

300 ml/½ pint cold meat stock (you can use a stock cube)

½ packet powdered gelatine (1 heaped teaspoon)

FOR THE PIE

275 g/10 oz hot water crust pastry *(see page 30)*, **or pie pastry** *(see page 30)*

450 g/1 lb pork cut from the shoulder, trimmed of fat and gristle and cut into very small pieces

¼ teaspoon white pepper

¼ teaspoon ground mace

2 pinches each salt, ground cinnamon, ground ginger

1 small egg, beaten

1. If making the savoury jelly by the traditional method, put the trotter, bay leaf and peppercorns into a roomy pan with the water. Bring to the boil and remove any scum which rises to the surface. Reduce to a steady simmer, cover and cook for about 2½ hours.
2. Stir hard to break up the trotter, then remove from the heat. Strain off the liquid and put aside to set. Discard the trotter, bay leaf and peppercorns.
3. The next day, remove any fat from the top of the jelly. (If the liquid has not set into a firm jelly, melt it down again, this time in an open pan, and simmer for a further 20–30 minutes. Allow to set again.)

   If making the savoury jelly by the alternative method, put the stock into a heatproof jug or bowl and sprinkle the powdered gelatine over the surface. Place the jug or bowl into a pan of hot water and simmer until the gelatine dissolves. Stir well, then leave overnight to set to a firm jelly.
4. Grease a loose-bottomed pie tin, 15 cm/6 inches across and 7.5 cm/3 inches deep. Use a brush to get into the bottom angle.
5. Make the hot water pastry or pie pastry according to the recipe and allow it to cool slightly.
6. Preheat the oven to fairly hot, Gas 6, 400°F, 200°C.
7. Place the pieces of pork in a mixing bowl. (If you prefer, you can mince the pork using the coarse blade in the mincer.) Stir in all the seasonings.
8. Take about two-thirds of the pastry and pat it into a flat round. Fold this in four and quickly ease it into the base of the tin. Unfold it and work the pastry up the sides to the top of the tin as evenly as possible. You may have to do a bit of patching up as this pastry is very floppy. Try to work it so that the angle at the bottom of the tin is well shaped.
9. Put the pork in the pastry case but do not pack it down. Take the remaining pastry and roll it to a circle. Brush the top edge of the pie in the tin with egg and press on the pie lid. Make a firm join all round and then, using a sharp knife, trim off the surplus pastry.
10. Make a small hole in the lid. An old custom was to insert a 'chimney' – made by rolling a small piece of card – to make sure the steam could escape. I like to make a pastry tassel – cut a strip of pastry 5 × 2.5 cm/2 × 1 inch, then cut very fine strips across the 2.5-cm/1-inch width, almost to the other side. Roll this up (*see diagram*) and ease it into the steam hole. Leaves and flowers can also be added and fixed with the beaten egg.

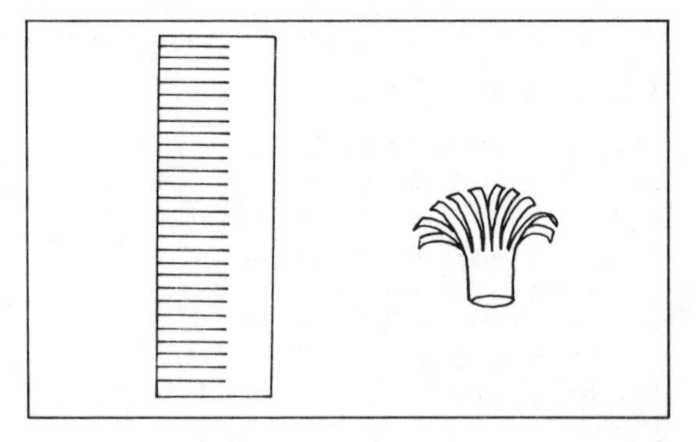

11. Before baking, brush the pie lid with two or three coats of beaten egg, allowing each coat to dry before adding the next. (If you like a very shiny gloss to the pie, you can take the cooked pie out of its tin and paint it all over with egg and return it to the oven on its baking tray. Do this several times if you wish.)
12. Put the pie on a baking tray and bake for 30 minutes, then reduce the heat to moderately hot, Gas 5, 375°F, 190°C, and bake for a further hour.
13. Remove from the oven and leave in the tin for about 15 minutes, then remove and cool on a wire tray.

14. Melt the savoury jelly in a small pan over gentle heat. Season with salt and pepper and allow it to cool for 15 minutes.
15. Gently ease the pastry tassel out of its hole and, using a small funnel, pour the cooling jelly into the still warm pie. Allow time for the jelly to settle and then pour in some more. The jelly should percolate in between the meat. The pie should hold about 150 ml/¼ pint melted jelly. When the pie is cold return the pastry tassel to its hole.

Best eaten on the day after it is made. Store in a cool place. If it is stored in a fridge, see that it is allowed to come back to room temperature before serving. I do not like the pie if it has been in the freezer.

VARIATION

This same mixture and quantity can be baked in an oblong tin measuring 19 cm/7½ inches long × 10 cm/3½ inches deep. Putting three very tiny hard-boiled eggs down the centre of the meat is a pleasant addition. The loaf shape is also easier to cut.

PICNIC PIE

A useful meaty pie for many different occasions.

Will cut into 8 small wedges

175 g/6 oz shortcrust pastry *(see page 28)*
225 g/8 oz pork sausagemeat
50 g/2 oz streaky bacon, finely chopped
1 small eating apple, peeled, cored and finely chopped or grated
2 teaspoons fresh chopped parsley
1 medium egg, beaten
Salt and pepper

1. Lightly grease a baking tray. Preheat the oven to moderately hot, Gas 5, 375°F, 190°C.
2. On a floured board, roll out half the pastry and line a 15-cm/6-inch flan ring set on the baking tray. Trim off the surplus pastry.
3. In a mixing bowl, mash together the sausage-meat, bacon, apple, parsley and half the egg. Season well with salt and pepper.
4. Pack this mixture into the pastry case and level it off.
5. Roll out the remaining pastry. Moisten the upper border of the pastry bottom and cover with the lid. Seal the edges together and trim off the surplus pastry. Make a small hole in the centre and brush the top with the remaining egg.
6. Bake for 30 minutes. Reduce the heat to moderate, Gas 4, 350°F, 180°C, and bake for a further 15 minutes. Cool on a wire tray.

Eat fresh if possible or store in the fridge for 2–3 days. This pie will freeze for up to 2 months, either cooked or raw.

SAVOURY BEEHIVES

I am always looking for interesting variations of favourite recipes. This is the cheeriest sausage roll variation I know. Children always smile when they get one!

Makes 8

225 g/8 oz shortcrust pastry *(see page 28)*
450 g/1 lb beef sausagemeat
2 teaspoons chopped parsley
2 pinches dried thyme
Pepper
1 small egg, beaten

1. Grease two baking trays. Preheat the oven to fairly hot, Gas 6, 400°F, 200°C.
2. On a floured board, roll out the pastry fairly thinly and cut out eight 5-cm/2-inch circles. Cut the remaining pastry into long strips about 5 mm/¼ inch wide. Gather up the trimmings, reroll and cut into more strips. Place the pastry rounds on the baking trays.
3. Mix the sausagemeat with the parsley, thyme and pepper. Divide it into eight pieces and shape each piece like a small pyramid. Wet your hand slightly to help put one pyramid on each pastry circle.
4. Starting at the base of each pyramid, coil a pastry strip round the sausagemeat, using water to help them stick, and slightly overlapping them as you go.
5. Brush the finished 'beehives' with the beaten egg and bake for 30 minutes until crisp and golden in colour. Cool on a wire tray.

Store in an airtight tin for up to 4 days. Will freeze for up to 2 months.

CORNISH PASTY

The position of the join on a Cornish pasty is not always on top – I understand it depends on where you live. In Cornwall the traditional filling also can vary from area to area. Anyway, this recipe is a good variation on a theme, and I'm putting the join on top!

Serves 1 hungry person or 2 fairly hungry ones.

125 g/4 oz shortcrust pastry, made with white or wholemeal flour *(see page 28)*
A little milk

FOR THE FILLING
125 g/4 oz skirt steak, braising steak or good quality stewing steak
1 small potato, peeled and very finely sliced
1 small onion, peeled and very finely sliced (*not* diced)
A small piece of swede or turnip, peeled and very finely sliced
Salt and pepper

1. Grease a baking tray. Preheat the oven to hot, Gas 7, 425°F, 220°C.
2. Cut away as much fat as possible from the meat, then slice the meat very finely and chop the slices into small pieces, but do not mince.
3. Mix the potato, onion and swede or turnip together in a large mixing bowl.
4. Roll out the pastry on a lightly floured board to a circle about 20 cm/8 inches across.
5. Place half the mixed vegetables down the centre of the pastry and season with salt and pepper. Cover the vegetables with the meat, season again and top with the remaining vegetables. Season again.
6. Moisten the outer edge of the pastry and bring both the edges up to meet in the middle over the top of the filling. Squeeze the edges together and crimp them with finger and thumb. The pasty should look like a fat purse.
7. Brush the pasty with milk and make a small slit at the top on each side of the sealed edge.
8. Bake on a greased baking tray for about 20 minutes, or until the pasty starts to look brown. Reduce the heat to moderately hot, Gas 5, 375°F, 190°C, and bake for a further 30 minutes.

Best eaten on the day it is made, or freeze for up to 2 months.

SAUSAGE ROLLS

Freshly made, this very British take-away snack has no rivals. Use good-quality, fresh sausagemeat and cook in a really hot oven for best results. Vary the thickness and size of the rolls according to taste.

Makes about 20 × 5-cm/2-inch long rolls – picnic size

225 g/8 oz new flaky pastry *(see page 31)*, **or shortcrust pastry** *(see page 28)*
450 g/1 lb good-quality, freshly made sausagemeat
75 g/3 oz onion, grated and drained
1 heaped teaspoon fresh sage leaves, finely chopped, or ½ teaspoon dried sage
Pepper
1 medium egg, beaten
A little flour

1. Preheat the oven to hot, Gas 7, 425°F, 220°C.
2. On a floured board, roll out the pastry as thinly as you can to an even rectangle. Trim and square the edges.
3. In a mixing bowl, thoroughly mix the sausagemeat with the onion and sage. Season with plenty of pepper. Divide this mixture into three portions.
4. Sprinkle flour over a board and, using the palm of your hand, roll out each piece of sausagemeat until you have a fairly even strip of rolled meat about the thickness of a fat cigar.
5. Lay this strip a little way in along the bottom edge of the pastry. Moisten the lower edge of the pastry and roll this edge over the meat to join the pastry at the other side. It should overlap by about 5 mm/¼ inch. Cut the long sausage roll from the main piece of pastry and press the pastry join. Turn the elongated sausage roll over so that the join is underneath and press gently to flatten. Cut the roll into 5-cm/2-inch lengths.
6. Brush the sausage rolls with beaten egg and, using a pair of scissors, nick three vents in the top of each. Repeat this process until all the meat is used up.
7. Set the sausage rolls on baking trays and bake for about 25 minutes, or until the pastry is brown and crisp. Cool on wire trays.

Best eaten hot and fresh but will keep for 3–4 days in a tin in the fridge, or freeze for up to 2 months.

SAUSAGE PLAIT

This is an economical dish using sausagemeat. Shop around for sausagemeat which is low in fat and, if possible, minced with a coarse blade, which gives the finished plait more texture.

Serves 4 generously

225 g/8 oz shortcrust pastry *(see page 28)*, **or flaky pastry** *(see page 32)*
1 small egg, beaten

FOR THE FILLING
225 g/8 oz pork sausagemeat
50 g/2 oz apple, peeled, cored and finely chopped
1 teaspoon dried sage, or 1 heaped teaspoon freshly chopped sage leaves
2 tablespoons cooked mixed vegetables, e.g. carrot, peas, green beans
Pepper

1. Grease a baking tray. Preheat the oven to hot, Gas 8, 450°F, 230°C.
2. Roll out the pastry on a floured board to an oblong about 25.5 × 20 cm/10 × 8 inches. Lightly score the pastry lengthways into three.
3. Form the sausagemeat and the apple into a neat roll measuring about 25.5 cm/10 inches long. Roll it in the chopped herbs and set aside for 20 minutes to firm up.
4. Lay the roll of sausagemeat on the centre section of the pastry and press it down lightly with your hand. Sprinkle the vegetables on top and season well with pepper.
5. Using half the egg, brush all the pastry edges. Fold the two short ends in over the sausagemeat and then slash the two outside pastry sections diagonally.
6. Plait the pastry strips from both sides over the middle section. Finally, brush the whole plait with beaten egg and set it on the baking tray.
7. Bake for 10 minutes, then reduce the heat to fairly hot, Gas 6, 400°F, 200°C, and bake for a further 30 minutes, or until the pastry is crisp and the sausagemeat cooked.

Best eaten freshly made. Store uncooked in a fridge for no more than 24 hours, or freeze, cooked or uncooked, for up to 2 months.

FILLING VARIATIONS

1 × 200-g/7-oz can of tuna, drained and chopped
4 tablespoons mixed cooked vegetables

Spoon the tuna onto the pastry and top with the vegetables. Continue as above.

225 g/8 oz cooked beef mince
2 tablespoons mixed cooked vegetables

Spoon the beef mince onto the pastry and top with the vegetables. Continue as above.

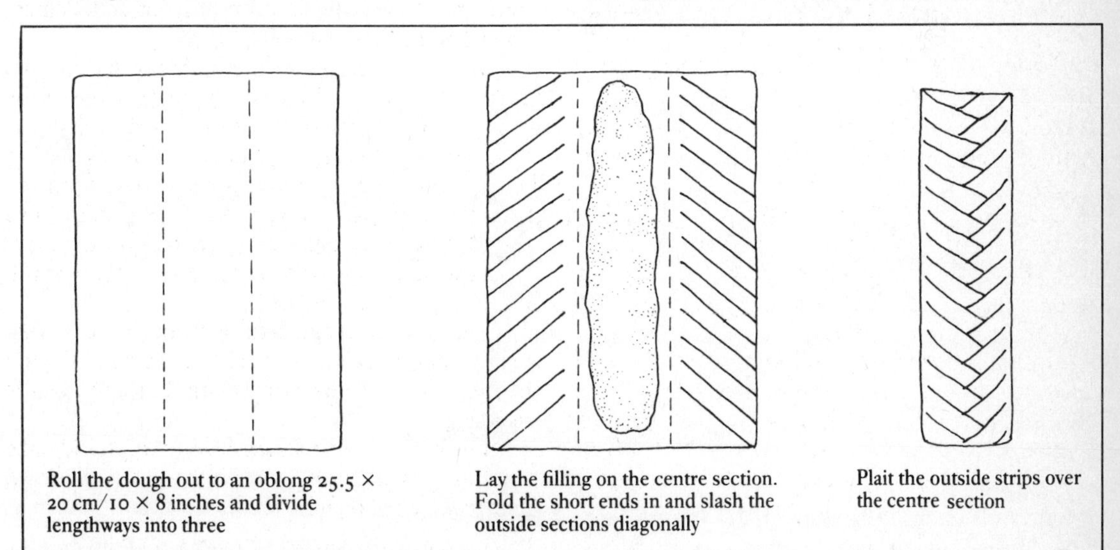

Roll the dough out to an oblong 25.5 × 20 cm/10 × 8 inches and divide lengthways into three

Lay the filling on the centre section. Fold the short ends in and slash the outside sections diagonally

Plait the outside strips over the centre section

VEGETABLE TARTLETS

This is a handy way of preparing vegetables in advance for a party. The fillings can be very varied but basically a purée of cooked vegetables is put into individual tartlet cases and topped with two or three lightly cooked, chunky, colourful vegetables. The tartlets can then be reheated at the last minute which ensures that the vegetables do not become dry. A food processor is a great help in preparing the vegetables.

Start the day before by soaking the haricot beans.

Makes 6

50 g/2 oz haricot beans, soaked overnight
125 g/4 oz wholemeal or white shortcrust pastry *(see page 28)*
25 g/1 oz butter
450 g/1 lb leeks, trimmed, washed and very finely chopped
Salt and pepper
2 medium-sized carrots, scraped, topped and tailed and cut into batons (small sticks)
2 thin, small courgettes, wiped, topped and tailed and sliced in thin circles

1. Soak the haricot beans overnight, drain and boil in fresh water until cooked but firm. Drain and set aside.
2. Grease six individual quiche tins which measure 7.5 cm/3 inches across and 1 cm/½ inch deep. Preheat the oven to moderately hot, Gas 5, 375°F, 190°C.
3. Roll out the pastry on a floured board and cut out rounds 10 cm/4 inches across. Gather up the trimmings, reroll and cut. Ease the pastry rounds into the quiche tins, press down firmly and trim off the surplus pastry. Place a circle of foil or grease-proof on the pastry and weigh this down with some baking or dried beans. (You can dispense with the dried bean treatment if you are able to watch the tartlets as they cook, and if any puff up press them down with a wooden spoon handle.)
4. Put the tartlets on a baking tray and bake for about 10–15 minutes until crisp and brown. Set aside until needed.
5. Melt the butter in a pan and stir in the leeks. Cook covered, shaking and stirring from time to time, for about 10 minutes. Season lightly and leave to cool.
6. Simmer the carrots and courgettes separately in water until barely cooked. Drain both and set aside until needed.
7. Just before you are ready to serve, and with the pastry cases still on the baking tray, spoon the cooked leeks to cover the base of each one. Top with the haricot beans, carrots and courgettes in a decorative pattern. Reheat in a moderate oven, Gas 4, 350°F, 180°C, for about 15 minutes.

VARIATIONS

BASE

Puréed peas: cook frozen peas in just a knob of butter

Broad beans: discard the skins of cooked beans and purée the insides

TOPPING VEGETABLES

Young swede, peas or broccoli stems: simmer in water or steam

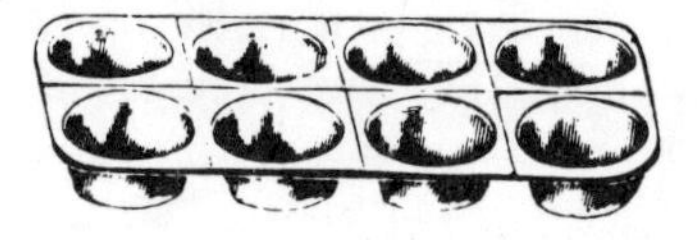

ZUCCHINI (COURGETTE) TART

This open tart or quiche is good enough to serve as a main course with a crisp green salad, especially if you give it its Italian name! Buy the courgettes when they are firm, shiny and dark green.

Will cut into 4 large or 8 smaller wedges

225 g/8 oz zucchini (courgettes), wiped, topped and tailed
25 g/1 oz butter
1 small onion, peeled and finely chopped
1 teaspoon chopped fresh tarragon, or ½ teaspoon dried tarragon
2 large eggs
150 ml/¼ pint each of single and double cream or 300 ml/½ pint milk
1 tablespoon grated Parmesan cheese
Salt and pepper
1 pre-baked 20-cm/8-inch shortcrust pastry shell *(see page 29)*

1. Chop the courgettes into cubes about the size of large raisins.
2. In a roomy pan, melt the butter, add the onion, tarragon and courgettes and cover. Shake over a low heat until barely cooked. Set aside to cool.
3. Preheat the oven to moderate, Gas 4, 350°F, 180°C.

4. In a mixing bowl, beat the eggs into the combined creams or milk, and stir in half the cheese. Using a slotted spoon, remove the cooled courgettes and onion from the pan and add to the cream mixture. Season to taste with salt and pepper.
5. Set the pastry shell either in its original baking tin or straight onto a baking tray. Mix the filling well and pour into the shell. Sprinkle the remaining cheese over the top.
6. Bake for about 30–40 minutes, or until set.

Best eaten on the day it is made.

VARIATIONS

Using 2 large eggs and 300 ml/½ pint milk, or cream, as a base. Use the same baking times:

SPINACH AND CHEESE TART

225 g/8 oz frozen cooked spinach (or 450 g/ 1 lb fresh cooked spinach, well drained)
125 g/4 oz cottage cheese
1 tablespoon grated strong cheese (Parmesan or Cheddar)

Mix the above ingredients in a food processor before adding the eggs and milk (or creams) and seasoning. Pour into the pastry base and bake as above.

EGG AND PRAWN TART

125 g/4 oz peeled prawns
1 large hard-boiled egg, peeled and chopped
2 teaspoons chopped parsley

Stir together with the eggs, milk (or creams) and seasoning and pour into the pastry base. Bake as above.

KIPPER TART

225 g/8 oz kippers, cooked, boned, skinned and flaked
1 teaspoon mustard powder
2 teaspoons chopped parsley

Stir together with the eggs, milk (or creams) and pour into the pastry case. Bake as above.

HAM AND EGG FLAN

This flan is made with cooked ham instead of bacon. To make sure that the base of the pastry is cooked, I like to heat an empty baking tray so that it is very hot when the raw pastry and raw filling are slid onto it. Try also to use a loose-bottomed flan tin. It is so much easier to stand the hot tin on a smaller round tin, allowing the outer frame to drop down. Your flan is then ready to serve.

Will cut into 12 small wedges

25 g/1 oz fat or solid vegetable oil
1 small onion, peeled and finely chopped
Salt and pepper
1 pre-baked 20-cm/8-inch shortcrust pastry shell *(see page 29)*
50 g/2 oz Cheddar cheese, grated
125 g/4 oz cold cooked ham
2 large eggs, beaten
300 ml/½ pint milk

1. Set the oven to fairly hot, Gas 6, 400°F, 200°C, and put a baking tray in to heat up.
2. Melt the fat or vegetable oil and fry the onion gently until soft. Season well, then set aside to cool.
3. Leave the pastry shell in the loose-bottomed flan tin in which it was cooked and spread the cooled onion into it. Put half the cheese on top of the onion, followed by the ham.
4. Whisk the eggs into the milk. Beat again and pour most of this mixture into the flan, holding back some of the custard until you get the flan tin in place on the hot baking tray in the oven. (It's a wobbly walk otherwise!) Add the remaining custard and sprinkle on the remaining cheese.
5. Bake for 20 minutes, then reduce the heat to moderate, Gas 4, 350°F, 180°C, and bake for a further 10 minutes.

Eat on the day the flan is assembled and baked.

SMOKY BACON FLAN

Eggs and bacon together are always marvellous but try this flan using smoked bacon. Do not throw the rind away – fry it very gently in a nonstick pan until it is really crisp. Drain on kitchen paper and crush into very small pieces. Sprinkle over food to give texture and flavour, e.g. over Cauliflower Cheese or anything which is of a soft texture.

Will cut into 8 small wedges

25 g/1 oz lard or solid vegetable oil
1 medium onion, peeled and finely chopped
1 pre-baked 20-cm/8-inch shortcrust pastry shell *(see page 29)*
4 full rashers of smoked bacon, de-rinded, lightly grilled and chopped
50 g/2 oz strong Cheddar cheese, grated
2 large eggs, beaten
300 ml/½ pint milk

1. Heat the lard or vegetable oil in a frying pan and soften the onion. Allow to cool.
2. Set the pastry shell either in its original tin or in a ring on a baking tray. Preheat the oven to moderate, Gas 4, 350°F, 180°C.
3. Spread the cooled onion on the pastry base, then cover with the bacon and half the cheese.
4. Beat the eggs into the milk and pour over the bacon and onion. (This is best done as near to the oven as possible to avoid spillage.) Sprinkle the remaining cheese on top.
5. Bake for about 30–40 minutes until the filling is set and golden in colour. Serve hot or cold.

Best eaten on the day it is made.

VOL-AU-VENTS

As their French name suggests, the pastry for these savouries must be light and flaky. I think they are very fiddly to do but everybody seems to like them.

Vol-au-vents may be round or oval. They can be served hot or cold with a variety of savoury or sweet fillings. Sweet vol-au-vents are simple to do. Fill them when cold with whipped sweetened cream, and a blob of good jam or a little fruit on top and serve cold.

For buffet meals, make tiny vol-au-vents, 4 cm/1½ inches across. Medium-sized ones should measure 7.5 cm/3 inches across, and a large vol-au-vent to serve 4 should be 20 cm/8 inches across.

One large vol-au-vent to serve 4

225 g/8 oz flaky pastry *(see page 32)*
1 small egg, beaten
Extra flour for rolling

1. Lightly flour a pastry board and roll out the pastry either in a round or an oval, approximately 2 cm/¾ inch thick and about 20 cm/8 inches across. Use a plate or a pan lid as a guide.
2. Lay the pastry on a damp baking tray. (Run cold water over the surface and do not dry.)
3. Using a sharp knife, cut another round or oval about 2 cm/¾ inch in from the edge of the pastry. However, do not cut right through the pastry but just about halfway through. This inner ring or oval marks out the lid of the vol-au-vent.
4. Brush the top of the vol-au-vent with the beaten egg. Set aside in a cold place to rest for 30 minutes, then brush again with beaten egg.
5. Bake above the middle of a hot oven, Gas 7, 425°F, 220°C, for about 10 minutes, or until well risen. Reduce the heat to fairly hot, Gas 6, 400°F, 200°C, and bake for a further 25–30 minutes.
6. Turn out onto a wire tray to cool. Lift off the pastry lid with care and press down the layers inside to make room for the filling. If the layers are still damp you can remove and discard one or two but take care to leave a firm base to take the filling *(see page 45)*.
7. Fill just before serving and reheat in a moderate oven, Gas 4, 350°F, 180°C, for 15–20 minutes.

SMALL VOL-AU-VENTS

This method is a little different from that for the large vol-au-vent.

Makes about 12 × 4 cm/1½ inches across, or 8 × 7.5 cm/3 inches across

225 g/8 oz flaky pastry *(see page 32)*
1 small egg, beaten
Extra flour for rolling

1. Preheat the oven to hot, Gas 7, 425°F, 220°C.
2. Roll out the pastry very thinly – about 5 mm/¼ inch thick.
3. Cut as many circles or ovals as you can and, using a smaller cutter, take out the centre portion from half of them. You now have a number of circles and the same number of rings.
4. Brush the beaten egg round the outer edge of each circle and place a ring on top. Brush the surface of the ring. Reroll the trimmings by piling them on top of each other and rolling again. The pastry will not be as good as the first batch so see that the family eat these!
5. Place the vol-au-vents on a baking tray and bake above the middle of the oven for about 8 minutes. Reduce the heat to fairly hot, Gas 6, 400°F, 200°C, and bake for a further 10 minutes.

Store the cooked but unfilled vol-au-vents in an airtight tin for up to 2 weeks, or freeze in the uncooked state for 2 months. Protect in the freezer by putting them into a rigid plastic box. I do not advise freezing filled vol-au-vents.

SAVOURY FILLINGS FOR VOL-AU-VENTS

To fill 10 small vol-au-vents

PRAWN AND EGG

FOR THE PRAWN STOCK
Prawn shells
Up to 300 ml/½ pint milk

FOR THE SAUCE
40 g/1½ oz butter
40 g/1½ oz plain white flour
Salt and pepper
175 g/6 oz prawns, chopped small and shells reserved for the stock
2 large hard-boiled eggs, chopped
1 dessertspoon chopped fresh parsley

1. First, make the prawn stock by simmering the prawn shells in a little water. Stir vigorously to extract as much flavour as possible. Strain and add milk to make up 300 ml/½ pint. (Or you can use all milk.) Allow to go cold.
2. To make a quick, all-in-one pan sauce, put the cold stock, butter and flour into a small pan. Whisk vigorously over a low heat to disperse the flour. Stirring continuously, bring the mixture to the boil and continue cooking until the sauce is thick and smooth – about 3–4 minutes. Remove the pan from the heat, allow to cool a little and season well with salt and pepper.
3. Stir in the prawns and the egg. Set aside until needed.
4. Lay the cooked vol-au-vents on a baking tray and fill with the prawn mixture. Reheat in a moderate oven, Gas 4, 350°F, 180°C, for about 15 minutes. Serve immediately.

MUSHROOM AND BACON

300 ml/½ pint cold chicken stock (you can use a stock cube)
40 g/1½ oz butter
40 g/1½ oz plain white flour
Salt and pepper
2 full rashers bacon, de-rinded, grilled and finely chopped
1 dessertspoon cooked peas
175 g/6 oz mushrooms, chopped, lightly cooked and drained

1. To make a quick all-in-one pan sauce, put the cold stock, butter and flour into a small pan. Whisk vigorously over a low heat to disperse the flour and, stirring continuously, bring the mixture to the boil. Continue cooking until the sauce is thick and smooth – about 3–4 minutes. Remove the pan from the heat, allow to cool a little and season well with salt and pepper.
2. Stir in the bacon, peas and mushrooms. Set aside until needed.
3. Lay the cooked vol-au-vents on a baking tray and fill with the mushroom mixture. Reheat in a moderate oven, Gas 4, 350°F, 180°C, for about 15 minutes. Serve immediately.

APPLE PIE

This is the traditional apple pie, cooked on a metal pie plate, with a crust above and below.

Serves 8

700 g/1½ lb Bramley cooking apples, peeled, cored and sliced
50 g/2 oz granulated sugar
225 g/8 oz shortcrust pastry *(see page 28)*
A little milk
Caster sugar for sprinkling

1. Put the apples, sugar and as little water as possible in a pan with a lid and shake over a low heat. Remove from the heat once the apples start to soften on the outside. Set aside to become cold.
2. Set the oven to fairly hot, Gas 6, 400°F, 200°C, and put a metal baking tray in to heat up. Grease a 24-cm/9½-inch metal pie plate.
3. On a lightly floured board, roll out half the pastry to a circle, lift the pastry on your rolling pin and press it gently onto the metal plate. Trim off the surplus pastry and reserve.
4. Using a slotted spoon, spread the half cooked, cold apples over the pastry bottom, leaving a good 2.5-cm/1-inch border. With a pastry brush, moisten the border with a little water.
5. Roll out the remaining pastry and cover the fruit. Press the edges together well and, using a knife, trim off the surplus pastry – hold the plate up in your left hand and angle the knife so that the handle is under the plate. This way the pastry will not shrink so easily.
6. 'Knock up' the edge of the pie and finish off with a scalloped design: press your thumb round the edge of the pie and, using the back of a knife, pull the pastry back in between each thumb print to give a scalloped effect (*see page 37*).
7. Roll out the pastry trimmings and cut into decorative leaves or flowers, then stick them on the pastry with a little milk. Brush over the entire surface of the pie with milk and sprinkle with caster sugar. Cut two or three slits in the pastry and put the pie on the hot baking tray.
8. Bake for about 30–35 minutes until crisp and brown.

Best eaten on the day it is made, or store in the fridge for 2–3 days. May go soggy on freezing.

VARIATIONS

Flavour the apples with 3–4 whole cloves or 1 teaspoon ground cinnamon.

BLACKBERRY AND APPLE PIE

Cook 75 g/3 oz blackberries with the apples.

PLUM PIE

Replace the apples with 700 g/1½ lb plums stewed with 50 g/2 oz sugar. Drain well.

RHUBARB PIE

Replace the apples with 1.1 kg/2½ lb rhubarb, stewed without sugar since it is very watery. Drain in a nylon sieve then add sugar to taste.

LEMON MERINGUE PIE

Good lemon flavouring does not come out of a packet or out of a plastic lemon. The rind of a real lemon imparts the true zinging flavour to any lemon dish. Grate the lemon rind on a metal grater and use a clean brush to get the rind out of the holes. If you use a lemon zester, take care to pare away only the yellow rind and not the white pith beneath. Chop the rind carefully.

Will cut into 12 pieces

40 g/1½ oz cornflour
Grated rind and juice of 2 large lemons (approximately 4 tablespoons juice)
125 g/4 oz caster sugar
15 g/½ oz butter
2 large egg yolks
1 pre-baked 20-cm/8-inch shortcrust pastry shell *(see page 29)*

FOR THE MERINGUE
2 large egg whites
125 g/4 oz caster sugar
½ teaspoon cornflour

1. In a 600-ml/1-pint measuring jug, blend the 40 g/1½ oz cornflour with the lemon juice. Add 125 g/4 oz sugar, the grated lemon rind and enough water to make up to 300 ml/½ pint.
2. Pour this liquid into a small pan and cook gently until thick.
3. Remove from the heat and beat in the butter and egg yolks.
4. Pour this mixture into the pastry shell and set aside for 30 minutes until cool and set.
5. To make the meringue topping, in a clean, grease-free bowl, whisk the egg whites until stiff. Whisk in 50 g/2 oz caster sugar until firm.
6. Sift the remaining sugar with the cornflour and, using a rubber spatula or a large metal spoon, fold gently into the meringue mixture.
7. Spread the meringue carefully over the surface of the filling. Take particular care to seal the edges so that no lemon filling is seen. Use the flat of a knife to pull out delicate spikes all over the meringue, and bake in a cool oven, Gas 2, 300°F, 150°C, for about 25–30 minutes.

Eat the tart on the same day it is assembled. The pastry base may be frozen either cooked or raw.

FILLING VARIATIONS

325 g/12 oz stewed apples, drained and flavoured with cinnamon

450 g/1 lb stewed rhubarb, drained and sweetened

325 g/12 oz stewed plums, drained, stoned and sweetened

MINCEMEAT

Good Christmas mince pies are made with home-made mincemeat. I like to use the Vostizza currants best to make mine, which I get from a wholefood shop. Start the day before.

Makes about 1.3 kg/3 lb

225 g/8 oz seedless raisins, washed and dried
125 g/4 oz sultanas, washed and dried
125 g/4 oz eating apples, peeled, cored and finely chopped
50 g/2 oz packet suet
225 g/8 oz currants, washed and dried
Grated rind and juice of 1 lemon
Grated rind and juice of 1 orange
125 g/4 oz dark soft brown sugar
1 tablespoon golden syrup
1 teaspoon mixed spice
1 teaspoon ground cinnamon
¼ teaspoon grated nutmeg
50 g/2 oz whole almonds, skinned and finely chopped
4 tablespoons brandy or whisky

1. Chop the raisins and sultanas in a food processor for a few seconds, or chop by hand.
2. Mix all the ingredients, except the brandy or whisky, together in a large mixing bowl and set aside overnight.
3. Next day, to prevent fermentation, put the bowl of mincemeat in a very low oven, Gas ¼, 225°F, 110°C, for 2½ hours. Stir well once or twice and leave to cool, then stir in the brandy or whisky.
4. Spoon into clean dry jars, cover and store in a cool place or in the fridge for up to 3 months.

MINCE PIES

I think these are best served warm.

Makes about 12

150 g/5 oz shortcrust pastry *(see page 28)*
325 g/12 oz home-made mincemeat *(see page 47)*
125 g/4 oz cream cheese
Icing sugar for dredging

1. Lightly grease twelve deep bun tins. Preheat the oven to moderate, Gas 4, 350°F, 180°C.
2. On a floured board, roll out the pastry thinly and cut an equal number of 7.5-cm/3-inch and 6-cm/2½-inch circles. Ease the larger circles into the bun tins.
3. Spoon a heaped teaspoon of mincemeat into each tart and top with a small teaspoon of cream cheese.
4. Moisten the edges of the remaining circles, cover each tart and seal well.
5. Bake for 25–30 minutes until golden in colour. Leave in the bun tins to cool down a little but remove before they are absolutely cold.
6. Dredge with icing sugar just before serving.

Mince pies store well in an airtight tin for up to 1 week. Best frozen unbaked, for up to 2 months.

DEEP CUSTARD TART

The traditional custard tart is not made in a flan ring but in a deeper tin with sloping sides and a narrow base.

Serves 4

175 g/6 oz shortcrust pastry *(see page 28)*
225 ml/8 fl oz milk (2 tablespoons less than 300 ml/½ pint) – use gold top milk if possible
25 g/1 oz vanilla sugar *(see page 17)*
2 large eggs
Freshly grated nutmeg

1. Set the oven to hot, Gas 7, 425°F, 220°C, and put a baking tray in to heat up.
2. Grease a round deep tin, 18 cm/7 inches across, sides 4–5 cm/1½–2 inches deep which narrow to a base of 7.5 cm/3 inches across.
3. Roll out the pastry on a floured surface to a circle about 25 cm/10 inches across. Lift the pastry on your rolling pin and ease it into the tin to line the base and sides. Work the pastry well into the base and trim the edges. Put the tin in the fridge until you are ready to fill it.
4. Warm the milk in a pan and add the sugar. Remove from the heat and stir until the sugar has fully dissolved. This step is important.
5. Beat the eggs lightly with a fork. Strain them through a nylon sieve into the milk mixture and gently beat again.
6. Take the pastry out of the fridge and place on the hot baking tray. Pour the custard into the pastry (do this near the oven) and grate nutmeg over the top.
7. Bake for 15 minutes. Reduce the heat to fairly hot, Gas 6, 400°F, 200°C, and bake for a further 25 minutes, or until the filling is set. Test this by giving the tin a shake and watching for a wobble which will indicate more baking time is needed.
8. Remove from the oven and leave the tart in the tin for 15–20 minutes to cool.
9. Use two plates to turn it out of the tin. This needs to be done swiftly. Put one plate over the top of the tart and turn the plate and the tart over. The tart will drop out onto the plate. Cover the bottom of the tart with another plate and immediately turn the two plates over. Another way you can try is to drop the tart upside-down on your open hand which is covered with a clean tea towel, immediately place a plate over the bottom and swiftly turn it over again. Good luck!

Eat on the day it is made. Not suitable for freezing.

CURD TART

Eat hot as a pudding or cut into small pieces for tea.

Will cut into 12 pieces

1 pre-baked 20-cm/8-inch shortcrust pastry shell *(see page 29)*
225 g/8 oz curd cheese, or home-made curd *(see below)*
25 g/1 oz butter, softened
1 tablespoon caster sugar
1 tablespoon golden syrup
1 large egg, beaten
40 g/1½ oz currants, washed and dried
1 tablespoon rum

1. Set the pastry shell either in its original baking tin or straight into a flan ring on a baking tray. Preheat the oven to moderate, Gas 4, 350°F, 180°C.
2. Break up the curd cheese in a mixing bowl so that it is fairly smooth.
3. Add all the remaining ingredients and mix well. Pour the curd mixture into the pastry shell.
4. Bake for about 30 minutes until set.

Like most filled pastry, this tart is best eaten the day it is made. I do not like it frozen. The pastry case, however, freezes well in its raw state.

HOME-MADE CURD

This easily made curd is beautifully moist and makes an excellent curd tart. Gold top milk will yield 350 g/13 oz curd, and silver top milk will yield 300 g/11 oz curd.

2 pints Channel Island milk – gold top or silver top
1 rounded teaspoon Epsom salts or 2 teaspoons liquid rennet or 2 rennet tablets*, crushed

* *Buy liquid rennet or rennet tablets at a chemist's shop. They can also be used for making junket.*

1. Pour the milk into a large pan, bring to boiling point and boil for 1 minute.
2. Remove from the heat and stir in either the Epsom salts, liquid rennet or crushed tablets. The curd should be visible straight away as you stir.
3. Allow to go cold, then strain through a nylon sieve. The liquid is excellent for making bread or scones. Store the curd no more than 2 days.

VARIATION

If you like a very firm curd, mix 1 heaped dessertspoon flour with a little cold milk and add it to the milk before it comes to the boil.

FRENCH TARTE AUX POMMES

This is really an almond tart with apples, and the almond filling is made just like a cake. Calvados is an apple liqueur.

Serves 8 for a hot pudding, or can be cut into 12 smaller pieces for tea

175 g/6 oz rich sweet shortcrust pastry *(see page 28)*
75 g/3 oz butter, softened
75 g/3 oz caster sugar
1 medium egg, beaten
75 g/3 oz ground almonds
2–3 drops almond essence
40 g/1½ oz plain white flour, sifted
1 tablespoon Calvados
Apricot jam, sieved and warmed
3 dessert apples, peeled, cored and halved
Icing sugar for dredging

1. Roll out the pastry on a floured board and line a 23-cm/9-inch flan ring set on a baking tray. Trim the edges and set aside in a cool place.
2. Preheat the oven to fairly hot, Gas 6, 400°F, 200°C.
3. In a mixing bowl, cream the butter and sugar until pale and fluffy. Beat in the egg, a little at a time. Fold in the ground almonds and almond essence, then the flour and Calvados.
4. Spread a very thin layer of apricot jam over the base of the raw pastry. Pour in the almond mixture.
5. Slice the apple halves and arrange on top of the almond mixture.
6. Bake for about 15 minutes to set the pastry, then reduce the heat to moderately hot, Gas 5, 375°F, 190°C, and bake for a further 10 minutes.
7. Remove the tart from the oven and dredge the surface with icing sugar. Return the tart to the oven for a further 10 minutes to glaze the apples.

Best eaten on the day it is made, but will keep in good condition in the fridge for 2–3 days. I do not advise freezing this tart.

TREACLE TART

This is rather a flat tart so use a pie plate rather than a flan tin. Serve hot as a pudding or cold for tea.

Will cut into 12 small pieces

175 g/6 oz wholemeal shortcrust pastry *(see page 30)*
4 tablespoons golden syrup
125 g/4 oz fresh wholemeal breadcrumbs
Grated rind and juice of ½ lemon

1. Grease a 20-cm/8-inch pie plate. Set the oven to moderately hot, Gas 5, 375°F, 190°C.
2. Roll out the pastry on a lightly floured board and cover the pie plate. Trim off the surplus pastry and set aside.
3. Warm the syrup in its jar by sitting it, without the lid, in a pan of hot water placed briefly in the oven. Measure it out into a mixing bowl and add the breadcrumbs, lemon rind and juice. Mix well and spread on the centre of the pastry.
4. Gather up the pastry trimmings, reroll to an oblong shape and cut out long narrow strips about 5 mm/¼ inch wide. Twist the strips slightly and lay them lattice fashion over the tart. Use a fork to neaten the outer edge by marking it all round.
5. Bake for about 30 minutes.

Best eaten on the day it is made or store in an airtight tin for 2 days. Do not freeze.

WALNUT TARTS

I never think these tarts look very attractive but they taste delicious.

Makes 12

225 g/8 oz wholemeal pastry *(see page 30)*
1 medium egg, beaten
125 g/4 oz light soft brown sugar
Grated rind of 1 lemon
2 teaspoons fresh lemon juice
4 tablespoons golden syrup, warmed
40 g/1½ oz butter, softened
125 g/4 oz walnut pieces, chopped

1. Grease twelve 7.5-cm/3-inch tartlet tins. Preheat the oven to moderate, Gas 4, 350°F, 180°C.
2. Roll out the pastry on a lightly floured surface until it is very thin and cut out rounds about 10 cm/4 inches across. Line the tins with the pastry rounds, and trim off the surplus pastry.
3. Make the filling by beating the egg, sugar, lemon rind and juice, and golden syrup very thoroughly. Beat in the butter and stir in the chopped walnuts. Divide the filling between the pastry cases.
4. Bake for 15–20 minutes. Cool and remove from the tins onto a wire tray.

Best eaten on the day they are made, or store in an airtight tin for up to 1 week. Freeze for up to 2 months.

YORKSHIRE CURD TARTS

This favourite northern recipe can be made with the now popular quark if curd cheese is difficult to get. If the quark is wet set it in a nylon sieve over a bowl and leave for 1½–2 hours until well drained. Cottage cheese is another substitute but needs to be beaten to smooth it down a little.

Makes about 20

175 g/6 oz shortcrust pastry *(see page 28)*
40 g/1½ oz butter
50 g/2 oz caster sugar
50 g/2 oz currants, washed and dried
225 g/8 oz curd cheese, beaten slightly, or quark
1 medium egg, beaten
1 pinch each ground nutmeg and cinnamon

1. Lightly grease about twenty patty tins. Preheat the oven to hot, Gas 7, 425°F, 220°C.
2. On a lightly floured board, roll out the pastry and cut out 7.5-cm/3-inch rounds. Reroll the trimmings and cut again to get about twenty rounds.
3. Ease the pastry rounds into the patty tins.
4. In a roomy pan, melt the butter and stir in all the remaining ingredients.
5. Spoon this mixture into the pastry cases – about two-thirds full is enough. Bake for 15–20 minutes. Allow to rest in the tins for 10 minutes, then turn out onto a wire tray to cool.

Best eaten warm and fresh. Store, after cooling, in an airtight tin for 2–3 days, or freeze for up to 1 month.

STRAWBERRY TARTS

Makes about 20 small tarts

225 g/8 oz rich sweet shortcrust pastry *(see page 28)*
3 tablespoons good strawberry jam, the strawberries chopped small
175 g/6 oz full fat cream cheese
2 teaspoons caster sugar
3 teaspoons milk
225 g/8 oz fresh strawberries, washed and dried
4 tablespoons redcurrant jelly

1. Grease twenty small patty tins. Preheat the oven to moderately hot, Gas 5, 375°F, 190°C.
2. On a floured board, roll out the pastry very thinly then use a 7.5-cm/3-inch cutter to cut pastry rounds. Gather up the trimmings, reroll and cut until you have about twenty circles.
3. Fill the tins with the pastry rounds, pricking the bottom of each one.
4. Bake for about 10 minutes, or until golden in colour. Remove the pastry cases and cool on wire trays.
5. Put a tiny spot of strawberry jam in the base of each tart.
6. Put the cream cheese and sugar into a mixing bowl and beat with enough of the milk to give a soft consistency. Put a good teaspoonful in each tart and smooth it down.
7. Slice each strawberry into three, cutting from the top to the bottom. Arrange the slices over the cream cheese and press down gently.
8. Melt the redcurrant jelly in a cup placed in a pan of simmering water. Paint this glaze carefully over the sliced fruit and leave to set.

Eat on the day they are made. The pastry tart cases can be frozen either cooked or raw for up to 2 months.

JAM OR LEMON TARTS

Everybody thinks that jam tarts are easy to make but, in fact, it is very easy for things to go wrong. Either they are overbaked and the jam or lemon curd is like toffee, or they are underbaked and the pastry is uncooked under the jam. The difficulty is that pastry needs a hot oven and since the jam and lemon curd are already cooked they burn easily.

One solution is to bake the tartlet cases blind, i.e. empty (*see page 26*), and fill them when cold with jam or curd which has been slightly warmed by standing the jar in a pan of hot water on the stove.

Alternatively, put just a small teaspoon of jam or curd in each tart, then, when the pastry is cooked and still hot, stir another teaspoon of cold jam into the hot jam in the tart. Home-made jam or lemon curd make the best tarts.

Makes about 24

225 g/8 oz shortcrust pastry, white or brown *(see page 28)*
225 g/8 oz raspberry, blackcurrant or strawberry jam
225 g/8 oz lemon curd

1. Grease twenty-four patty tins, each measuring about 6 cm/2½ inches across. Preheat the oven to moderately hot, Gas 5, 375°F, 190°C.
2. On a lightly floured board, roll out the pastry very thinly and stamp out rounds measuring 7.5 cm/3 inches. Gather up the trimmings, reroll and cut until you have about twenty-four rounds. Ease the pastry rounds into the tins.
3. Fill half the tarts with the jam and half with the lemon curd, or bake blind and fill (*see above*). Bake for about 15 minutes. Cool on a wire tray.

Eat fresh or store for 1–2 days only in an airtight tin. Freeze the unfilled tartlets, raw or baked, for up to 2 months for best results.

LEMON CURD TARTLETS

These are really individual lemon meringue tartlets. They are at their very best when made with home-made lemon curd.

Makes 14

175 g/6 oz plain white flour
1 pinch salt
40 g/1½ oz solid vegetable fat, cut into small pieces
40 g/1½ oz block margarine, cut into small pieces
1 medium egg yolk
Ice cold water to mix
175 g/6 oz good quality lemon curd
2 medium egg whites
1 pinch cream of tartar
125 g/4 oz caster sugar

1. Make the pastry cases first. Sift the flour into a bowl and rub in the fats and salt until the mixture resembles breadcrumbs. Stir in the egg yolk and enough ice cold water to make a firm dough. Wrap in a plastic bag and set aside for 20–30 minutes to rest.
2. Preheat the oven to fairly hot, Gas 6, 400°F, 200°C. Prepare fourteen deep patty tins by brushing them with oil or fat.
3. On a lightly floured board, roll out the pastry fairly thinly and, using a large fluted cutter about 7.5 cm/3 inches across, cut out pastry rounds. Gather up the trimmings, reroll and cut until you have fourteen rounds.
4. Ease the pastry rounds into the patty tins. Press down gently and prick the pastry all over with a fork. Bake blind (*see page 26*) for about 10–15 minutes. If you are going to be in the kitchen, you need not line each case with foil and weigh down with beans but keep an eye on the tartlets as they bake. If the pastry bubbles up in the middle pat it down again with the round end of a knife handle.
5. Allow the tartlets to cool in the tins for 10–15 minutes, then lift them carefully onto a wire tray.
6. To assemble the tartlets, half fill each one with lemon curd.
7. Put the egg whites and the cream of tartar into a clean grease-free bowl and, using an electric or rotary whisk, whisk until the egg whites are stiff.
8. Add the caster sugar, about 1 tablespoon at a time, and keep whisking until all the sugar is incorporated and you have a very thick meringue. Spoon into a piping bag fitted with a star nozzle and pipe a large whirl on each tartlet, pulling up a good peak.
9. Put the tartlets into a fairly hot oven, Gas 6, 400°F, 200°C, for no more than 3 minutes, to colour the meringue pale gold – it will be soft like marshmallow and not crisp. Do not leave any longer or the lemon curd will boil up. Allow to cool a little in the tins and then remove very carefully.

When cold, the empty tartlet cases can be stored in an airtight tin for about 1 week, or freeze for up to 3 months. Eat the filled tartlets on the day they are assembled. Not suitable for freezing.

PINEAPPLE TARTLETS

A rich tartlet with contrasting soft filling and crisp pastry case.

Makes 10

125 g/4 oz rich sweet shortcrust pastry *(see page 28)*
4–5 pineapple rings (canned in natural juice)
150 ml/5 fl oz double cream
125 g/4 oz icing sugar, sifted
2 teaspoons water
1 drop lemon food colouring

1. Well grease ten deep tartlet tins. Preheat the oven to moderately hot, Gas 5, 375°F, 190°C.
2. Roll out the pastry on a lightly floured surface as thinly as possible and, using a 7.5-cm/3-inch cutter, stamp out rounds. Reroll the trimmings and cut again until you have ten rounds.
3. Ease the pastry into the tins and bake blind (*see page 26*) for 10–15 minutes. Allow to cool.
4. Chop the pineapple into small pieces and dry on kitchen paper. Put the pineapple into the pastry cases.
5. Whip the cream very firmly, spoon over the pineapple pieces and level off each top. Set the tartlets in a cold place to allow the cream to firm up.
6. Mix the icing sugar and water with a drop of lemon colouring to make up a thickish icing. Dribble a spoonful of icing over each tartlet and allow to set.

Eat on the day they are made. The empty tartlet cases will store in an airtight tin for up to 7 days, or freeze for up to 2 months.

TRADITIONAL ECCLES CAKES

Makes 18

50 g/2 oz butter
225 g/8 oz currants, washed and dried
50 g/2 oz candied orange peel, washed and finely chopped
50 g/2 oz light soft brown sugar
1 teaspoon ground cinnamon
½ teaspoon freshly ground nutmeg
Grated rind of 1 medium orange
225 g/8 oz new flaky pastry *(see page 31)*
1 medium egg white
Caster sugar for sprinkling

1. Melt the butter in a small pan, add all the remaining ingredients, except the pastry, egg white and caster sugar, and remove from the heat. Stir well and set aside to go cold.
2. Grease two or three baking trays. Preheat the oven to hot, Gas 7, 425°F, 220°C.
3. Roll out the pastry on a lightly floured board to a thickness of about 3 mm/⅛ inch. Cut out circles about 7.5 cm/3½ inches across. Gather up the trimmings, pile them on top of each other, reroll and cut until you have about eighteen circles.
4. Place a teaspoon of the filling in the middle of each circle. Brush the inner edge of the circle with water and fold the pastry over the filling. Brush the joins with water and press the edges firmly. Turn the circle over so that the join is underneath. Reshape the circle and roll it gently with a rolling pin until you can see the currants shining through the thin pastry.
5. Brush the surface with egg white and sprinkle with caster sugar. Using a sharp knife, make three slits across the surface.
6. Lay the Eccles cakes on the baking trays, and bake for 15 minutes until the pastry is brown and crisp. Cool on a wire tray.

Store in an airtight tin for up to 1 week. They also freeze well at the raw pastry stage or the fully finished stage, cooked or uncooked, for up to 2 months.

MINT PASTY

This should be made when you have some fresh mint in the garden. Do not use dried mint.

Will cut into 12 squares

75 g/3 oz block margarine
225 g/8 oz plain white flour, sifted
1 pinch salt
1 medium egg yolk
3 tablespoons fresh mint, chopped
75 g/3 oz currants, washed and dried
50 g/2 oz butter, softened
50 g/2 oz caster sugar
1 medium egg white

1. Lightly grease a baking tray. Preheat the oven to hot, Gas 7, 425°F, 220°C.
2. In a mixing bowl, rub the margarine into the flour and salt. Mix with the egg yolk and just enough water to make a firm dough.
3. Divide the pastry into two. Roll out one portion to a square measuring 20 cm/8 inches. Trim the edges and lift the pastry onto the baking tray.
4. Prepare the mint leaves by cutting away any hard ribs from some of the larger leaves. Use scissors to finely chop the rest. Mix the currants, butter, sugar, and mint, reserving about 25 g/1 oz sugar.
5. Spread the mixture evenly over the pastry, leaving a narrow border clear. Moisten this border with water.
6. Roll out the other piece of pastry and cover the tart. Make fork marks all round the square and a small hole in the centre. Brush with the egg white and sprinkle the reserved 25 g/1 oz caster sugar over.
7. Bake for about 15 minutes, or until crisp and brown. Cool on a wire tray.

Store in an airtight tin for 3–4 days, or freeze for up to 2 months.

CHOCOLATE ÉCLAIRS

Choux pastry is nearly always associated with chocolate and coffee éclairs or profiteroles. It can also be very good used for savouries. Choux pastry is really not difficult to make.

Makes 14

60 g/2½ oz choux pastry *(see page 31)*

FOR THE ICING

50 g/2 oz plain chocolate, broken into small pieces
125 g/4 oz icing sugar, sifted
1 tablespoon boiling water
1 teaspoon vegetable oil

FOR THE FILLING

225 ml/8 fl oz double cream, whipped

1. Line two baking trays with nonstick paper. I find it easier to grease the tins lightly first so that the paper stays in place. Preheat the oven to hot, Gas 7, 425°F, 220°C.
2. Put the raw choux pastry into a piping bag fitted with a 1-cm/½-inch plain nozzle. Pipe éclairs about 6 cm/2½ inches long straight onto the trays.
3. Bake one tray at a time – they cook better without any further steam from another tray. Bake for 10 minutes, then reduce the heat to moderately hot, Gas 5, 375°F, 190°C, and bake for a further 20–30 minutes, or until the éclairs are crisp and golden in colour.
4. Remove from the oven and cut a little slit in each éclair to release the steam. Return to the oven for 5 minutes to dry out, remove then bake the second batch. Cool the éclairs on wire trays.
5. To make the chocolate icing, put the chocolate into a heatproof bowl set over a pan of simmering water and stir until melted. Add the icing sugar, water and oil and stir until smooth. A little more water may be needed. Remove from the heat but keep warm over hot water.
6. When the éclairs are cold, spoon the whipped cream into a piping bag fitted with a 5-mm/¼-inch plain nozzle. Slit each éclair down one side only and pull open. Pipe in a layer of cream and fold the lid over. Fill each éclair in the same way.
7. Dip the top of each éclair in the chocolate icing, allow to set and dry.

Once filled, eat on the same day. Store unfilled éclairs in an airtight tin, or freeze for up to 2 weeks. Open freeze first then lay the éclairs in a single row in a polythene box and cover.

VARIATION

COFFEE ÉCLAIRS

Make and fill as for Chocolate Éclairs but ice with the following coffee icing. In a small bowl, dissolve 2 teaspoons instant coffee in 1 tablespoon boiling water. Add 150 g/5 oz sifted icing sugar and stir well. Repeat the dipping process as above and allow to dry.

APPLE FLAN WITH MERINGUE

This used to be a great favourite with my children. Like the apple pie recipe on page 46, you can vary the fruit filling.

Serves 8

700 g/1½ lb Bramley cooking apples, peeled and cored
50 g/2 oz granulated sugar
1 pre-baked 20-cm/8-inch shallow shortcrust pastry shell *(see page 29)*
2 large egg whites
75 g/3 oz caster sugar

1. Slice the apples into fairly thick slices. Put them with the granulated sugar and a little water in a pan with a lid. Shake and stir over a low heat until the apples are just beginning to soften. Remove from the heat and set aside to become cold.
2. Preheat the oven to cool, Gas 2, 300°F, 150°C.
3. Set the cooked pastry flan on a metal baking tray. Drain the cold apples and put them in the bottom of the flan.
4. Using a hand or electric whisk, beat the egg whites until they are stiff and peak easily. Set aside the whisk and, using a metal spoon, quickly fold the caster sugar into the egg whites. Spoon this meringue mixture evenly over the apples, taking care to spread it all over especially round the pastry edge.
5. Bake for 30–40 minutes, or until the meringue is dry and brown on the outside and soft inside.

Best eaten the same day. The pastry case freezes well, either cooked or raw, for up to 3 months.

FRESH FRUIT FLAN AND CRÈME PÂTISSIÈRE

Fresh fruit and a crisp pastry are delicious but add to them a rich custard cream and the result is perfection.

Serves 4 generously, or 6

FOR THE CRÈME PÂTISSIÈRE
300 ml/½ pint rich milk (gold top is best)
1 vanilla pod
1 large egg plus the yolk of 1 egg
50 g/2 oz caster sugar
25 g/1 oz plain white flour, sifted

1 pre-baked 18-cm/7-inch rich sweet shortcrust pastry shell *(see page 29)*
Fresh fruit *(see below)*

1. Put the milk into a pan with the vanilla pod, bring just to the boil and remove from the heat. Leave to infuse for 30 minutes.
2. In a large bowl, beat the egg, the egg yolk and sugar until pale, then whisk in the flour. Mix until smooth.
3. Take the vanilla pod out of the milk and wash and dry it for future use.
4. Pour the milk into the egg mixture. Stir, then return the mixture to a clean saucepan and put over a gentle heat. Bring to the boil and stir continuously until the mixture thickens. Beat hard if any lumps form. Simmer for a further 2–3 minutes.
5. Leave to cool, and use on the day it is made or not later than the day after.
6. Just before serving, pour the crème into the pastry shell and arrange the fresh fruit on top.

Best eaten on the day it is made. The flan case freezes well, either cooked or raw.

SUGGESTED FRUITS

175 g/6 oz fresh strawberries, sliced in half

75 g/3 oz each of green and black grapes, each one cut in half and pips removed

225 g/8 oz fresh raspberries. (Dredge with caster or icing sugar just before serving.)

2 medium sized peaches. Peel the peaches by dropping them one at a time into boiling water and then into cold water. Peel the peaches, stone and slice them. Poach the peach slices very slightly in a light syrup made from 25 g/1 oz sugar dissolved in 300 ml/½ pint of water. Simmer until the sugar dissolves then lay the peaches in the simmering water for 8–9 minutes. Remove the slices with a slotted spoon, cool then lay them in the tart.

RICH TOFFEE AND NUT FLAN

This flan is very rich.

Will cut into 12 small wedges

125 g/4 oz seedless raisins
150 ml/¼ pint water
1 tablespoon cornflour
Grated rind and juice of 1 medium orange
50 g/2 oz dark soft brown sugar
Grated rind and juice of ½ lemon
50 g/2 oz pecan nuts (or walnuts), finely chopped
1 pre-baked 20-cm/8-inch shortcrust pastry shell *(see page 28)*

TO DECORATE
150 ml/¼ pint double cream
1 dessertspoon rum

1. Put the raisins into a pan with the water. Simmer for a few minutes or until the raisins are soft, then drain.
2. Mix the cornflour to a paste with 1 tablespoon each of orange and lemon juice and add the sugar.
3. Stir the cornflour mixture and lemon and orange rinds into the raisins and cook until thick – the consistency should be like jam. If the mixture is too thick, add more lemon juice. Allow to cool.
4. When the mixture is cold, add the chopped nuts and pour into the pastry shell.
5. Whip the cream until thick, add the rum and whip again. Put this cream into a piping bag with a 1-cm/½-inch star nozzle and pipe a lattice design across the surface of the flan.

Eat on the same day. Store the undecorated flan for 4–5 days in the fridge, or freeze for up to 2 months.

CUT-AND-COME-AGAIN CAKES AND SPONGES

I forget where I first heard the expression 'cut and come again' to describe a cake. I hesitate to say I invented it, but it does fit in with the old habit of having something in the tin for the unexpected visitor. In the days before domestic freezers, the cake or loaf would keep more moist in the tin than individual cakes or buns. Some cakes, gingerbreads and parkins, because of their low fat content, are quite hard when freshly baked. Two or three days in a closed tin and they soften.

Although the traditional shape for cakes is round, oblong and square cakes are very much easier to slice neatly. However, they are much more vulnerable at the corners during baking as the heat hits the corners from two directions and they can scorch easily. I was reminded of this recently when I baked a cake in a Christmas tree-shaped tin. It was a great success, but I had to protect all the sharp points on the tree with added corners of foil while it was in the oven.

Speaking of foil, I usually put a circle of foil in the bottom of each storage tin. Not only does it prevent any flavour from the tin going into the cake, but it is also useful for lifting the cake out. If the cake is very fragile, it is also helpful to put it on the lid and place the bottom part of the tin over it. Do, though, label it 'this way up' – I once had a beautifully decorated chocolate cake upended when my son thought my tin was upside down and straightened it for me!

THE BASIC METHODS

There are several different basic methods for cake and sponge making.

RUBBING-IN METHOD

The fat used is crumbled or rubbed into the flour. Try to use only the tips of your fingers and lift the mixture out of the bottom of the bowl as you do it. This allows more air in. Continue until the mixture resembles dried breadcrumbs. Or use the metal blades of a food processor, which does the job in seconds. The other dry ingredients are then added and, finally, the liquid is stirred in.

Because rubbed-in cakes have half or less than half fat to flour they should be eaten or frozen quickly. Cakes made by this method are called plain cakes and have an open texture.

SPONGES MADE BY THE WHISKING METHOD

The eggs and sugar are whisked at high speed until very thick and creamy and then sifted flour is folded in very lightly. Some sponges are made richer with the addition of melted butter. An electric mixing machine with a whisk attachment is very good for making whisked sponges, as is a hand-held electric mixer. A small rotary whisk is slowest of all but gives good volume eventually. I do not think the whisk attachment in a food processor is very efficient for this type of mixing.

Really light sponges, Swiss rolls and sponge drops are all made by this method, and it is this sponge which is used as a base for ice cream and fruit desserts.

MELTING METHOD

This is a very simple method. The fat and sugar are melted, allowed to go cold and then all the other ingredients are folded in.

Moist cakes such as gingerbreads and some fruit loaves are nearly always made this way.

CREAMING METHOD

In this method the fat and sugar are beaten together until they are pale and fluffy. The sugar is then beaten in, followed by the eggs and, finally, the flour is folded in.

Cakes made by this method have a high proportion of fat to flour and are called rich cakes. (The amount of fruit in a fruit cake has nothing to do with the cake being called rich.) Christmas cakes, Madeira cakes and some sandwich cakes are all made this way, and have a close texture.

ALL-IN-ONE METHOD

The availability of the soft margarines has made this method the easiest of all. The ingredients all go into the bowl together and are beaten by hand or machine for just 3–4 minutes, when the mixture should be smooth. The texture is more open than cakes made using the creaming method. The All-in-One Plain Sponge on page 73 is made by this method.

EGGLESS FRUIT AND NUT CAKE

This recipe was given to me by a friend who is allergic to eggs.

Makes 1 × 15-cm/6-inch square cake

50 g/2 oz raisins, washed, dried and chopped
50 g/2 oz currants, washed and dried
50 g/2 oz walnut pieces, chopped
225 g/8 oz plain white flour
1 teaspoon bicarbonate of soda
125 g/4 oz butter or block margarine, cut into small pieces
1 tablespoon black treacle, warmed
150 ml/¼ pint milk
75 g/3 oz caster sugar
2 tablespoons white vinegar

1. Lightly grease a 15-cm/6-inch square tin. Preheat the oven to moderate, Gas 3, 325°F, 160°C.
2. Put the raisins, currants and walnuts into a small mixing bowl and mix thoroughly.
3. Sift the flour and bicarbonate of soda into another bowl and rub in the butter or margarine until the mixture resembles coarse breadcrumbs.
4. Add the fruit and nuts, treacle, milk and sugar and, using a spatula, fold in so that there are no dry pockets of flour. Lastly, very lightly fold in the vinegar.
5. Pour this mixture into the tin and level it off.
6. Bake for about 1¼–1½ hours, or until the cake is shrinking from the sides of the tin. Allow to firm up in the tin for 10 minutes, then turn out, peel off the lining paper and cool on a wire tray.

When cold, wrap in greaseproof paper and store in an airtight tin for up to 10 days, or freeze for up to 2 months.

FRUIT AND NUT CAKE

This is a lovely fruit cake and easy to make. It really is much nicer with the walnuts which add a delicious extra texture. Try chopping the raisins and sultanas small to give a finer result. You can also substitute wholemeal flour and this will give you a slightly firmer cake.

Makes 1 × 20-cm/8-inch round cake, or 1 × 18-cm/7-inch square cake

175 g/6 oz butter or block margarine, softened
175 g/6 oz light soft brown sugar
200 g/7 oz plain white flour
1 teaspoon baking powder
125 g/4 oz tiny currants, washed and dried
125 g/4 oz sultanas, washed and dried
125 g/4 oz raisins, washed and dried
50 g/2 oz glacé cherries, washed, dried and chopped
40 g/1½ oz walnuts, chopped
3 large eggs, beaten

1. Grease and line the base and sides of either a 20-cm/8-inch round cake tin or an 18-cm/7-inch square cake tin. Preheat the oven to moderate, Gas 3, 325°F, 160°C.
2. In a large mixing bowl, cream the butter or margarine and sugar until pale and fluffy.
3. Sift the flour and baking powder into the mixture and add the dried fruit and walnuts. Stir in the beaten egg.
4. Spoon the mixture into the tin and smooth the surface.
5. Bake for about 1 hour 40 minutes, or until firm and golden in colour. Allow to firm up in the tin for a short time then turn out, peel off the lining paper and cool on a wire tray.

When cold, wrap in greaseproof paper and store in an airtight tin for up to 2 weeks, or freeze for up to 3 months.

HONEYED FRUIT CAKE

This fruit cake is made with oil instead of butter or margarine (*see page 10*).

Makes 1 × 18-cm/7-inch square cake, or 1 × 20-cm/8-inch round cake

225 g/8 oz plain wholemeal flour
1½ teaspoons bicarbonate of soda
1 teaspoon ground cinnamon
225 g/8 oz currants, washed and dried
125 g/4 oz raisins, washed and dried
2 large eggs, beaten
75 ml/3 fl oz vegetable oil
200 ml/7 fl oz milk
225 g/8 oz clear honey, slightly warmed

1. Grease and line the base and sides of either an 18-cm/7-inch square tin or a 20-cm/8-inch round tin. Preheat the oven to cool, Gas 2, 300°F, 150°C.
2. Sift the flour, bicarbonate of soda and cinnamon into a large mixing bowl, adding any residue of bran left in the sieve. Stir in the currants and raisins.
3. In another bowl, whisk the eggs, oil and milk. Pour this into the dry ingredients, add the honey and mix thoroughly. Spoon the mixture into the tin and level the surface.
4. Bake for about 1½ hours, or until the cake is risen, feels fairly firm to the touch and is starting to shrink from the sides of the tin. Allow to firm up in the tin for 10 minutes then turn out, peel off the lining paper and cool on a wire tray.

When cold, wrap in greaseproof paper and store in an airtight tin for up to 1 week, or freeze for up to 4 months.

WHOLEWHEAT FRUIT CAKE

A good, filling fruit cake which is ideal for packed lunches because it does not crumble. It's made by the melting method (*see page 57*) so is easy to put together.

Makes 1 × 20-cm/8-inch round cake, or 1 × 18-cm/7-inch square cake

175 g/6 oz currants, washed and dried
125 g/4 oz raisins, washed and dried
175 g/6 oz dark soft brown sugar
125 g/4 oz block margarine
50 g/2 oz mixed peel, finely chopped
1 teaspoon ground nutmeg
1 teaspoon bicarbonate of soda
225 ml/8 fl oz water
225 g/8 oz plain wholemeal flour
1 teaspoon baking powder
40 g/1½ oz glacé cherries, washed, dried and finely chopped
40 g/1½ oz walnuts, finely chopped
2 large eggs, beaten

1. Grease and line the base and sides of an 18-cm/7-inch square tin or a 20-cm/8-inch round tin. Preheat the oven to moderate, Gas 4, 350°F, 180°C.
2. Put the currants, raisins, sugar, margarine, peel, nutmeg, bicarbonate of soda and water into a roomy pan. Bring gently to the boil, then set aside to go cold. Stir well once or twice while cooling then turn the mixture into a large bowl.
3. Sift the flour and baking powder into the cooled mixture, adding any residue of bran left in the sieve, and fold in. Add the cherries, walnuts and eggs and mix thoroughly. Spoon the mixture into the tin and level the surface.
4. Bake for about 1¼ hours, or until the cake is risen, firm to the touch and just beginning to shrink from the sides of the tin. Allow to firm up in the tin for about 10 minutes, then turn out, peel off the lining paper and cool on a wire tray.

When cold, wrap in greaseproof paper and store in an airtight tin for up to 1 week, or freeze for up to 3 months.

DUNDEE CAKE

Coming from Dundee myself, this is one of my most used recipes. It is not difficult. Lightly fruited with sultanas and currants, it is traditionally topped with rings of almonds.

Makes 1 × 20-cm/8-inch round cake

175 g/6 oz tub margarine
125 g/4 oz light soft brown sugar
3–4 drops almond essence
200 g/7 oz plain white flour
1 teaspoon baking powder
175 g/6 oz sultanas, washed and dried
175 g/6 oz currants, washed and dried
50 g/2 oz red glacé cherries, washed, dried and finely chopped
25 g/1 oz ground almonds
3 large eggs, beaten
Whole or split almonds, blanched

1. Grease and line the base and sides of a 20-cm/8-inch round tin. Preheat the oven to moderate, Gas 3, 325°F, 160°C.
2. In a large mixing bowl, thoroughly cream the margarine, sugar and almond essence, ensuring there are no lumps in the sugar.
3. Sift the flour and baking powder into another bowl and stir in the fruit, cherries and ground almonds. Fold this into the creamed mixture together with the eggs and combine thoroughly but do not beat.
4. Spoon the mixture into the tin and carefully level the surface.
5. To blanch the almonds, pour boiling water on them and allow to stand for 2–3 minutes when the skins should slide off easily. If they don't, put them back in the water again. Arrange the blanched almonds in circles on top of the cake mixture.
6. Bake for about 1½ hours, or until the cake is firm and shrinking from the sides of the tin. Allow to firm up in the tin for 10 minutes then turn out, peel off the lining paper and cool on a wire tray.

When cold, wrap in greaseproof paper and store in an airtight tin for 2–3 weeks, or freeze for up to 3 months.

SULTANA CAKE

The corn oil replaces butter or margarine in this tasty cake (*see page 10*).

Makes 1 × 18-cm/7-inch square cake, or 1 × 20-cm/8-inch round cake

175 g/6 oz self-raising white flour
175 g/6 oz plain wholemeal flour
½ teaspoon bicarbonate of soda
1 pinch salt
Grated rind of 1 orange
125 g/4 oz sultanas, washed and dried
3 large eggs, beaten
200 ml/7 fl oz corn oil
4 tablespoons orange marmalade
150 g/5 oz light soft brown sugar
4 tablespoons milk

1. Grease and base line an 18-cm/7-inch square cake tin, or a 20-cm/8-inch round cake tin. Preheat the oven to moderate, Gas 3, 325°F, 160°C.
2. Sift both flours, the bicarbonate of soda and the salt into a large mixing bowl, adding any residue of bran left in the sieve. Stir in the orange rind and sultanas.
3. In another bowl, whisk together the eggs, oil, marmalade, sugar and milk. Stir in the dry ingredients until well blended.
4. Spoon into the tin and level the surface.
5. Bake for about 1 hour 35 minutes, or until the cake is risen, firm to the touch and beginning to shrink from the sides of the tin. Leave to firm up in the tin for 10 minutes, then turn out, peel off the lining paper and cool on a wire tray.

When cold, wrap in greaseproof paper and store in an airtight tin for 1 week, or freeze for up to 3 months.

ORANGE AND SULTANA CAKE

Another fruit cake made with oil (*see page 10*). The flavours go very well together.

Makes 1 × 20-cm/8-inch round cake

150 g/5 oz self-raising white flour
150 g/5 oz self-raising wholemeal flour
125 ml/4 fl oz vegetable oil
2 large eggs, beaten
2 tablespoons milk
1 tablespoon orange juice (concentrated orange juice, preferably)
150 g/5 oz light soft brown sugar
175 g/6 oz sultanas, washed and dried
Grated rind of ½ orange

1. Grease and base line a 20-cm/8-inch round cake tin. Preheat the oven to moderate, Gas 4, 350°F, 180°C.
2. Sift the white flour and wholemeal flour into a large mixing bowl, adding any residue of bran left in the sieve.
3. In another bowl, whisk together the oil, eggs, milk, orange juice and sugar. Make sure that the sugar has dissolved, then fold in the flour, sultanas and orange rind. Mix well, then spoon into the tin and level the surface.
4. Bake for about 1 hour, or until the cake feels firm to the touch and is beginning to shrink from the sides of the tin. Leave to firm up in the tin for 10 minutes, then turn out onto a wire tray, peel off the lining paper and allow to cool.

Store in an airtight tin for 5–6 days, or freeze for up to 3 months.

APPLE LATTICE CAKE

An unusual apple cake which not only tastes good but looks pretty, too. The mixture is almost like shortbread when it is first made, with a pleasant crispness. Make it in an ordinary cake tin if you don't have a loose-bottomed one.

Makes 1 × 20-cm/8-inch cake

200 g/7 oz self-raising white flour
1 pinch salt
1 teaspoon ground cloves
150 g/5 oz unsalted butter, softened
75 g/3 oz caster sugar
1 large egg, beaten
325 g/12 oz Bramley cooking apples, peeled and cored
1 tablespoon lemon juice
2 tablespoons apricot jam
50 g/2 oz demerara sugar
Icing sugar for dredging

1. Grease and base line a loose-bottomed 20-cm/8-inch cake tin, 4 cm/1½ inches deep. Preheat the oven to moderate, Gas 3, 325°F, 160°C.
2. Sift the flour and salt into a mixing bowl, and add the ground cloves.
3. In another bowl, cream the butter and sugar until pale and light. Beat in the egg, a little at a time. Fold in the flour. You should have quite a soft mixture.
4. Spoon about three-quarters of the mixture into the bottom of the tin, making a hollow in the centre of the mixture.
5. Slice the apples and sprinkle with the lemon juice to prevent them going brown. Lay the slices in overlapping rows in the middle of the cake mixture.
6. Soften the apricot jam a little, if necessary, and brush over the surface of the apples. Don't worry if this is a little difficult as the jam will melt. Sprinkle the demerara sugar over the jam.
7. Roll the remaining cake mixture into long strips about as thick as your little finger and lay them in rows across the apples – you will only be able to fit in about 5–6 strips. Neaten off the edges.
8. Bake for about 1¼ hours when the cake should be quite brown. Allow to firm up in the tin for about 10 minutes if you are using a loose-bottomed cake tin. If not, leave it in the tin until almost cold as it is rather fragile when hot. Dust thickly with icing sugar and peel off the lining paper before serving.

Best eaten fresh but will store in an airtight tin for up to 4 days, or freeze for up to 3 months.

DANISH APPLE CAKE

Why this type of cake is called Danish I do not know. It never looks very good because the apple juice usually dribbles down the side of the cake but its flavour is very good indeed. I think it is best made in a square tin as you can cut it up more easily.

Makes 1 × 20-cm/8-inch square cake

225 g/8 oz plain white flour
½ teaspoon baking powder
1 pinch salt
125 g/4 oz butter or margarine, softened
125 g/4 oz light soft brown sugar
1 large egg, beaten
400 g/14 oz cooking apples, peeled, cored and sliced
½ teaspoon ground cloves
1 tablespoon light soft brown sugar
Icing sugar for dredging

1. Grease and line the base and sides of a 20-cm/8-inch square tin. Preheat the oven to moderate, Gas 4, 350°F, 180°C.
2. Sift the flour, baking powder and salt into a large mixing bowl.
3. In a small pan, melt the butter or margarine and stir in the sugar. Pour this into a cold bowl to cool it down. Whisk the beaten egg into the mixture and, using a spatula or a large metal spoon, fold in the flour. Spoon about two-thirds of the mixture into the bottom of the tin, and level it off.
4. Lay the apple slices neatly in overlapping rows on top of the cake mixture and sprinkle the ground cloves and soft brown sugar over them. Spoon the remaining cake mixture on top of the apples, spreading it evenly.
5. Bake for about 45 minutes when the cake should be firm to the touch and beginning to shrink from the sides of the tin. Allow the cake to firm up in the tin for about 45 minutes because it will be fragile with the fruit in it. Use the lining paper to help lift it out of the tin and onto a wire tray to cool. Remove the lining paper and serve dredged with icing sugar.

Eat as soon as possible. This cake will freeze for up to 1 month if absolutely necessary.

VINEGAR CAKE

Vinegar cakes were popular during the war when eggs were scarce. One tablespoon of vinegar was said to equal one egg! Eat this thinly sliced and buttered.

Makes 1 × 18-cm/7-inch square cake

175 g/6 oz lard or margarine, cut into pieces
450 g/1 lb self-raising white flour, sifted
225 g/8 oz currants, washed and dried
50 g/2 oz sultanas, washed and dried
225 g/8 oz caster sugar
2 teaspoons mixed spice
1 pinch salt
4 tablespoons white vinegar
250 ml/8 fl oz milk

1. Grease and base line an 18-cm/7-inch square tin. Preheat the oven to moderate, Gas 3, 325°F, 160°C.
2. In a large mixing bowl, rub the lard or margarine into the flour until it resembles bread-crumbs.
3. Stir in the prepared fruit, sugar, spice and salt. Add the vinegar and enough of the milk to give a soft consistency.
4. Spoon the cake mixture into the tin and level the surface.
5. Bake for about 1½ hours, or until the cake is firm to the touch, risen and just beginning to shrink from the sides of the tin. Leave to cool in the tin for 10 minutes, then turn out, peel off the lining paper and cool completely on a wire tray.

Store in an airtight tin for 3–4 days, or freeze for up to 3 months.

BANANA CAKE

Some fruit shops which sell nuts often keep dried banana chips as well. I buy mine from a wholefood shop.

Makes 1 × 20-cm/8-inch round cake

125 g/4 oz self-raising white flour
1 teaspoon baking powder
125 g/4 oz butter, cut into pieces and softened
125 g/4 oz light soft brown sugar
2 medium eggs, beaten
1 teaspoon vanilla essence
3 tablespoons milk
1 large ripe banana, peeled and mashed to a pulp
75 g/3 oz banana chips, roughly broken

1. Grease and base line a 20-cm/8-inch cake tin. Preheat the oven to moderate, Gas 3, 325°F, 160°C.
2. Sift the flour and baking powder into a large mixing bowl, and add the butter, soft brown sugar, eggs, vanilla essence and milk. Beat well for 2 minutes or until very smooth. Fold in the mashed banana.
3. Spoon the mixture into the tin, level the surface and cover the top with the banana chips.
4. Bake for about 25–30 minutes, or until the cake is well browned and just beginning to shrink from the sides of the tin. Allow to firm up in the tin for a few minutes, then turn out onto a wire tray, peel off the lining paper and allow to cool.

Store in an airtight tin for 2–3 days, or freeze for up to 3 months.

CHERRY CAKE

Glacé cherries come in three colours: red, green and yellow. The most widely used, of course, are the red ones. Because of recent worries about food colourings, a 'natural' glacé cherry is now available without added colour. It is about the colour of a raisin.

Cherry cakes are notorious for the fruit sliding to the bottom. This is why I recommend you cut each cherry in two, wash off all the syrup in hot water, dry the cherries on paper towels and then chop ready for baking. The smaller you chop the cherries the less likely they are to slide to the bottom of the cake.

Makes 1 × 18-cm/7-inch square cake, or 1 × 20-cm/8-inch round cake

175 g/6 oz butter, softened
175 g/6 oz caster sugar
1–2 drops almond essence
3 large eggs, beaten
125 g/4 oz self-raising white flour
50 g/2 oz plain white flour
75 g/3 oz ground almonds
150 g/5 oz glacé cherries, cut in two, washed, dried and chopped

1. Grease and line the base and sides of an 18-cm/7-inch square tin, or a 20-cm/8-inch round tin. Preheat the oven to moderate, Gas 3, 325°F, 160°C.
2. In a warm mixing bowl, beat the butter and sugar to a pale cream, add the almond essence and beat again.
3. Gradually beat in the eggs a little at a time, adding just a little of the measured flour if the mixture looks like separating.
4. Sift the self-raising and plain flours into a mixing bowl, then stir in the ground almonds and the cherries.
5. Fold the dry ingredients into the butter and egg mixture and mix well. Spoon into the tin and level the surface.
6. Bake for about 1¼ hours, or until the cake is firm to the touch and beginning to shrink from the sides of the tin. Allow to firm up in the tin for 10 minutes, slide a knife blade carefully round the outside of the cake and turn it out onto a wire tray. Peel off the lining paper and allow to cool.

When cold, wrap in greaseproof paper and store in an airtight tin for up to 10 days, or freeze for up to 3 months.

CHERRY AND ALMOND CAKE

This cake is baked at a low temperature because anything made with ground almonds burns and browns very quickly. For this reason, too, the base and sides of the tin are lined. Washing the cherries of all syrup ensures they don't sink to the bottom of the cake in a thick layer.

Makes 1 × 20-cm/8-inch round cake, or 1 × 18-cm/7-inch square cake

225 g/8 oz butter, softened
225 g/8 oz caster sugar
3 large eggs, beaten
4–5 drops pure almond essence
75 g/3 oz glacé cherries (any colour), cut in two, washed, dried and chopped
225 g/8 oz plain white flour
1 heaped teaspoon baking powder
125 g/4 oz ground almonds
40 g/1½ oz nibbed almonds

1. Grease and line the base and sides of a 20-cm/8-inch round tin, or an 18-cm/7-inch square tin. Preheat the oven to cool, Gas 2, 300°F, 150°C.
2. In a large mixing bowl, cream the butter and sugar until pale and fluffy. Add the eggs a little at a time, beating well between each addition, then beat in the almond essence. Stir in the chopped cherries.
3. Sift together the flour and baking powder and fold this into the creamed mixture, along with the ground almonds. Spoon the mixture into the tin and level the surface. Sprinkle the nibbed almonds all over.
4. Bake for about 2 hours. Look at the cake after 1 hour and if it is getting rather brown on top, crumple a piece of greaseproof paper and put it over the cake, inside the paper lining. The cake will be ready when a skewer inserted in the middle of the cake comes out clean, and the cake is shrinking from the sides of the tin. Allow to firm up in the tin then turn out, peel off the lining paper and cool on a wire tray.

When cold, wrap in greaseproof paper and store in an airtight tin for up to 4–5 days, or freeze for up to 2 months.

HAZELNUT AND CHERRY CAKE

You can buy ground hazelnuts from most 'baking-aids' shelves in supermarkets or at your local wholefood shop. However, to get a really intense hazelnut flavour, it is better to grind your own (*see page 252*).

Makes 1 × 20-cm/8-inch square cake

200 g/7 oz self-raising white flour
75 g/3 oz glacé cherries (any colour), cut in four, washed and dried
1 teaspoon baking powder
1 pinch salt
175 g/6 oz tub margarine
3 large eggs, beaten
175 g/6 oz caster sugar
75 g/3 oz ground hazelnuts
Icing sugar for dredging

1. Grease and line the base and sides of a 20-cm/8-inch square tin. Preheat the oven to moderate, Gas 4, 350°F, 180°C.
2. Sprinkle 25 g/1 oz of the measured flour over the dried cherries and stir to coat them. (This will prevent them sinking to the bottom of the cake while cooking.)
3. Sift the remaining flour with the baking powder and salt into a large mixing bowl.
4. Add the margarine, eggs, sugar and ground hazelnuts, and beat together, using a wooden spoon or a rigid spatula, until the mixture is smooth. Fold in the coated cherries, ensuring they are well distributed. Spoon this mixture into the tin and level the surface.
5. Bake for about 1¼ hours, or until the cake has risen, feels firm to the touch and is just beginning to shrink from the sides of the tin. Allow to firm up in the tin for 10 minutes, then turn out onto a wire tray, peel off the lining paper and leave to become cold. When the cake is cold, dredge with icing sugar.

Store in an airtight tin for 4–5 days, or freeze for up to 3 months.

ALMOND AND APRICOT CAKE

Makes 1 × 20-cm/8-inch round cake

175 g/6 oz butter, softened
75 g/3 oz caster sugar
3 tablespoons clear honey
3 large eggs, beaten
200 g/7 oz self-raising white flour, sifted
25 g/1 oz ground almonds
75 g/3 oz apricots, ready-to-eat kind, finely chopped
2–3 drops almond essence
3–4 tablespoons milk
40 g/1½ oz nibbed almonds, toasted
175 g/6 oz icing sugar

1. Grease and line the base and sides of a 20-cm/8-inch round cake tin. Preheat the oven to moderate, Gas 4, 350°F, 180°C.
2. In a large mixing bowl, cream the butter and sugar until pale and fluffy, then beat in the honey.
3. Beat in the eggs a little at a time, adding some of the measured flour if the mixture looks like separating.
4. Fold the ground almonds into the flour together with the apricots, almond essence, egg and butter mixture and enough of the milk to make a fairly stiff mixture.
5. Spoon the mixture into the tin and level the top.
6. Bake for about 1 hour, or until the cake is firm to the touch and just beginning to shrink from the sides of the tin. Allow to firm up in the tin for 5 minutes then turn out onto a wire tray, peel off the lining paper and leave to become cold.
7. Meanwhile, toast the almonds. Place them on a metal tray and put under a hot grill to brown – watch carefully, they burn easily. Set them aside to cool.
8. Sift the icing sugar into a small mixing bowl and gradually add 2–3 teaspoons water to give a thick but spreadable icing. Spread evenly over the top of the cake and press the toasted almonds in while the icing is still soft.

Store the decorated cake for 2–3 days in an airtight tin, or freeze for up to 2 months.

WALNUT CAKE

Look for very pale walnuts and buy them from a shop which has a good turnover. They deteriorate much more quickly than other nuts. If you use them rarely, keep some in your freezer.

Makes 1 × 20-cm/8-inch round cake

175 g/6 oz tub margarine
175 g/6 oz caster sugar
3 large eggs, beaten
225 g/8 oz plain flour, white or wholemeal
1½ teaspoons baking powder
75 g/3 oz walnuts, chopped
2–3 tablespoons milk (3 tablespoons if you are using wholemeal flour)

FOR THE COFFEE ICING
40 g/1½ oz butter
1 tablespoon milk
1 teaspoon water
1 teaspoon coffee granules
225 g/8 oz icing sugar, sifted
Extra walnut pieces

1. Grease and base line a 20-cm/8-inch round tin. Preheat the oven to moderate, Gas 3, 325°F, 160°C.
2. In a large mixing bowl, cream the margarine and sugar until light and fluffy. Beat in the eggs a little at a time, adding just a spoonful of the measured flour if the mixture looks as if it will separate.
3. Sift the flour and baking powder into another bowl, and stir in the walnuts. Fold the dry ingredients into the egg mixture together with the milk. Mix well.
4. Spoon the mixture into the tin and level the surface.
5. Bake for about 1¼ hours, or until the cake is risen, firm to the touch and shrinking from the sides of the tin.
6. Leave in the tin to firm up for about 10 minutes, then turn out onto a wire tray, peel off the lining paper and leave to become cold.
7. To make the coffee icing, in a small pan, melt together the butter, milk, water and coffee granules. Allow to go cold.
8. Beat the icing sugar into the cooled liquid until you have a thick but spreadable icing. Spread the icing over the cold cake and decorate with a border of walnut pieces.

Store in an airtight tin for 5–6 days, or freeze for up to 3 months.

NUTTY RING CAKE

This is more like a ring of nuts stuck together with very little cake. Marvellous if you like nuts, but you'll need a sharp knife to slice it.

Use the soft, ready to eat dried figs.

Will cut into 20 slices

200 g/7 oz brazil nuts, chopped to the size of raisins
150 g/5 oz walnuts, finely chopped
75 g/3 oz shelled almonds, finely chopped
125 g/4 oz packet dates, finely chopped
125 g/4 oz dried figs, chopped
75 g/3 oz raisins, washed and dried
175 g/6 oz glacé cherries, each cut in two
75 g/3 oz chopped mixed peel
3 large eggs, beaten
75 g/3 oz light soft brown sugar
75 g/3 oz plain wholemeal flour
1 pinch salt
2 teaspoons lemon juice
½ teaspoon baking powder

1. Grease a 1.2-litre/2-pint metal ring mould. I also think it is worthwhile lining the bottom of the ring. Cut a circle of greaseproof paper the same size as the ring, then cut out the middle, leaving a 2.5-cm/1-inch circle. Lay this in the ring. Preheat the oven to cool, Gas 2, 300°F, 150°C.
2. Place the nuts, fruit and peel in a large mixing bowl and mix well.
3. In another bowl, whisk the eggs and sugar together. Sift the flour into a bowl, adding any residue of bran left in the sieve. Fold the flour, salt, lemon juice and baking powder into the eggs and sugar and pour it into the nut and fruit mixture. Stir very thoroughly then spoon into the metal ring, press down gently and level it all round.
4. Bake for about 1½ hours. While the cake is still hot, slide a knife round the ring to loosen the cake, then leave in the tin until just lukewarm.

Eat as soon as possible. Store in an airtight tin for just 2–3 days.

CHOCOLATE AND RAISIN NUT CAKE

Makes 1 × 18-cm/7-inch round cake

125 g/4 oz butter or block margarine, softened
125 g/4 oz caster sugar
2 medium eggs, beaten
1 tablespoon cocoa powder, sifted
1 tablespoon boiling water
40 g/1½ oz walnuts, finely chopped
40 g/1½ oz raisins, washed, dried and snipped as small as currants
175 g/6 oz self-raising white flour, sifted
A little milk, if necessary

1. Grease and base line an 18-cm/7-inch round cake tin. Preheat the oven to moderate, Gas 4, 350°F, 180°C.
2. In a large mixing bowl, cream the butter or margarine and sugar until pale and fluffy. Beat in the eggs a little at a time, beating well between each addition.
3. Blend the cocoa powder with the boiling water and allow to cool.
4. Fold the walnuts, raisins, cocoa liquid and flour into the egg mixture. The mixture should be soft but not wet. Add a little milk, if necessary, to achieve the correct consistency.
5. Spoon the mixture into the tin and level the surface.
6. Bake for about 1 hour, or until the cake is risen, firm to the touch and shrinking from the sides of the tin. Allow to firm up in the tin for about 10 minutes then turn out, peel off the lining paper and cool on a wire tray.

When cold, wrap in greaseproof paper and store in an airtight tin for 3–4 days, or freeze for up to 3 months.

MADEIRA CAKE

Traditionally this cake is made in a round tin and the top decorated with a large, wafer thin slice of citron peel. Buy the citron peel (it is the pale green one) in a piece from a wholefood shop. Wash all the sugar off, dry it and slice with a very sharp knife.

Makes 1 × 20-cm/8-inch round cake

150 g/5 oz unsalted butter, softened
150 g/5 oz caster sugar
Finely grated rind of 1 large lemon
3 large eggs, beaten
175 g/6 oz plain white flour
2 teaspoons cornflour
1½ teaspoons baking powder
1 pinch salt
1 wafer thin slice citron peel

1. Grease and line the base and sides of a 20-cm/8-inch round cake tin. Preheat the oven to moderate, Gas 4, 350°F, 180°C.
2. In a warm mixing bowl, cream the butter and sugar until pale and creamy and very light. Beat in the grated lemon rind.
3. Beat the eggs into the mixture a little at a time, adding a little of the measured flour if the mixture looks like separating.
4. Sift the flour, cornflour, baking powder and salt into another bowl, and fold into the creamed mixture.
5. Spoon into the cake tin, level off the surface and lay the citron peel on top.
6. Bake for about 1¼ hours, or until the cake is risen, firm to the touch and just beginning to shrink from the sides of the tin. Allow to firm up in the tin for 10 minutes, then turn out onto a wire tray, peel off the lining paper and allow to cool.

Store in an airtight tin for about 1 week, or freeze for up to 3 months.

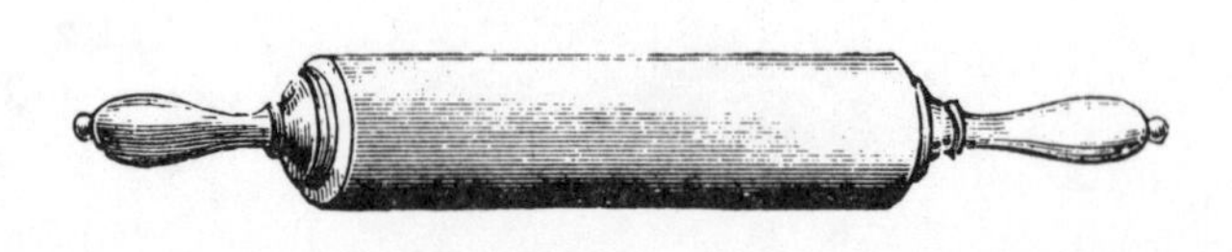

SACHER

This is a version of the famous Austrian cake called 'Sacher-Torte'. The word 'sacher' is always written on the chocolate icing. I understand the cake is named after the pâtissier who created it.

It is helpful to have an icing turntable.

Makes 1 × 20-cm/8-inch cake

150 g/5 oz best quality unsalted butter
150 g/5 oz vanilla sugar *(see page 17)*, **or caster sugar**
3 large eggs, separated
175 g/6 oz best quality plain chocolate, broken into small pieces
150 g/5 oz plain white flour, sifted twice

FOR THE FILLING AND FIRST LAYER OF ICING
6 tablespoons apricot glaze *(see page 248)*, **warmed**
175 g/6 oz best quality plain chocolate, broken into small pieces
5 tablespoons strong black percolated coffee
175 g/6 oz icing sugar, sifted twice
50 g/2 oz milk chocolate

1. Grease and base line a 20-cm/8-inch loose-bottomed cake tin. Preheat the oven to moderate, Gas 4, 350°F, 180°C.
2. In a large bowl, use a hand-held electric mixer to cream the butter and 75 g/3 oz of the vanilla sugar. Beat until they are very pale and fluffy, then add the egg yolks, one at a time, beating hard between each addition.
3. Put the chocolate into a small heatproof bowl set over a pan of simmering water and stir until melted. Whisk this into the mixture.
4. Using a spatula, very gently fold in the flour.
5. In a clean, grease-free bowl, whisk the egg whites until very stiff. Fold in the remaining vanilla sugar and whisk again.
6. Take a clean spatula and stir about 1 dessertspoon of the meringue into the chocolate cake mixture to loosen it. Fold the rest of the meringue in very carefully and spoon the cake mixture into the tin.
7. Bake for about 1 hour 25 minutes, or until the cake is firm, shrinking from the sides of the tin and a skewer inserted in the middle of the cake comes out clean. Leave the cake to firm up in the tin for 10 minutes, then turn it out onto a wire tray, peel off the lining paper and allow to go cold.
8. If the cake has a dome, slice this off with a sharp knife. Turn the cake upside down onto a turntable. This will give you a good flat surface for the icing.
9. Cut the cake in two horizontally. Spread the bottom half with about 2 tablespoons of the apricot glaze and put the top of the cake back on. Brush the remaining glaze all over the top and sides of the cake, as smoothly as you can.
10. To make the icing, melt the plain chocolate with the coffee in a heatproof bowl set over a pan of simmering water. Gradually beat in the icing sugar until it is a smooth, thick spreading consistency. Pour the icing onto the top of the cake and, using a palette knife, ease the icing towards the edge of the cake and down the sides. Try to touch the icing as little as possible. Quickly smooth the sides and leave to set for 2–3 hours.
11. The finishing touch is the wording on top of the cake. Melt the milk chocolate in a heatproof bowl set over hot water. Spoon it into a paper icing cone and snip off a tiny point. Pipe the word 'SACHER' on top of the cake and leave to set.

Store in an airtight tin for 3–4 days, or freeze for up to 3 months.

LEMON CAKE

The combination of natural yoghurt with lemon makes for a good sharp flavour.

Makes 1 × 20-cm/8-inch round cake

175 g/6 oz plain white flour, sifted
2 teaspoons bicarbonate of soda
1 pinch salt
50 g/2 oz tub margarine
275 g/10 oz caster sugar
3 eggs, separated
150 ml/¼ pint natural yoghurt
Grated rind of 1 small lemon
2 tablespoons fresh lemon juice
125 g/4 oz icing sugar, sifted
Finely pared rind of ½ lemon
1 teaspoon caster sugar

1. Grease and base line a 20-cm/8-inch round cake tin. Preheat the oven to moderate, Gas 4, 350°F, 180°C.
2. Sift the flour, bicarbonate of soda and salt into a large mixing bowl. Add the margarine, caster sugar, egg yolks, yoghurt and lemon rind and beat well until very smooth and thick.
3. In a clean grease-free bowl, whisk the egg whites until they stand in peaks. Fold the egg whites carefully into the cake mixture, spoon into the tin and level the surface.
4. Bake for about 1¼ hours, or until the cake is risen, firm to the touch and shrinking from the sides of the tin.
5. Allow to firm up in the tin for 5 minutes, then turn out onto a wire tray, peel off the lining paper and allow to cool.
6. Beat enough of the lemon juice into the icing sugar to achieve a spreadable icing. Take care not to add too much juice as it is very easy to make the icing too thin. Spread the icing on the cooled cake.
7. Cut the pared rind into the thinnest strips you can. Put the strips into a small pan with water just to cover. Bring to the boil and drain, then cover with fresh water. Stir in the sugar and boil for 1–2 minutes until the peel is soft. Drain the peel in a sieve and cool under the cold tap. Pat it dry on kitchen paper and scatter on top of the icing.

Store the undecorated cake in an airtight tin for 3–4 days, or freeze for up to 3 months.

HONEY AND GINGER CAKE

Cakes made with honey are often over-sweet for me. I like this one, however, because the ginger seems to go really well with it.

Makes 1 × 18-cm/7-inch square cake, or 1 × 20-cm/8-inch round cake

225 g/8 oz plain white flour
1 teaspoon bicarbonate of soda
1 teaspoon ground ginger
125 g/4 oz butter or block margarine, cut into pieces
40 g/1½ oz crystallized ginger, finely chopped
1 large egg, beaten
75 g/3 oz clear runny honey, warmed
3 tablespoons ginger wine

FOR THE TOPPING

4 tablespoons ginger wine
2 tablespoons stem ginger syrup
1 piece stem ginger, cut into wafer thin slices

1. Grease and line the base and sides of an 18-cm/7-inch square cake tin, or a 20-cm/8-inch round cake tin. Preheat the oven to moderate, Gas 3, 325°F, 160°C.
2. Sift the flour, bicarbonate of soda and ground ginger into a large mixing bowl. Rub the butter or margarine into the mixture until it resembles breadcrumbs. Stir in the chopped ginger.
3. Take a fork and whisk the egg into the honey. Fold this and the ginger wine into the dry ingredients and mix well. You should have a fairly stiff consistency. Pour into the tin.
4. Bake for about 30 minutes. Leave to firm up in the tin for 5 minutes, then turn out onto a wire tray, peel off the lining paper and leave to get cold.
5. Put the ginger wine and syrup into a small pan and boil until it is golden and syrup-like. Brush this over the top of the cold cake and arrange the slices of ginger round the edge. Allow the syrup to dry, then brush with another coat and leave to set.

Store in an airtight tin for 4–5 days, or freeze for up to 3 months.

CARROT AND ORANGE CAKE

In lots of old recipes you'll find that carrots were used for sweetening and to give added moisture.

Makes 1 × 15- or 18-cm/6- or 7-inch round cake

125 g/4 oz margarine or butter
125 g/4 oz light soft brown sugar
2 large eggs, beaten
75 g/3 oz plain wholewheat flour
75 g/3 oz plain white flour
3 teaspoons baking powder
1 teaspoon cinnamon, or mixed spice
125 g/4 oz grated carrot
Grated rind and juice of ½ large orange
1 tablespoon milk

1. Grease and base line a 15- or 18-cm/6- or 7-inch round baking tin. Preheat the oven to moderate, Gas 3, 325°F, 160°C.
2. In a large mixing bowl, cream the margarine or butter and sugar until pale and fluffy. Add the beaten eggs a little at a time, beating well after each addition.
3. Sift the flours, baking powder and cinnamon into another bowl, adding any residue of bran left in the sieve, and stir in the carrot and orange rind.
4. Fold this into the creamed mixture, adding the orange juice and enough milk to give a dropping consistency. Fill the tin and smooth the surface.
5. Bake for about 1 hour, or until the cake is risen, springy and brown. Allow to firm up in the tin for 10 minutes then turn out onto a wire tray, peel off the lining paper and allow to cool.

Store in an airtight tin for 1 week, or freeze for up to 3 months.

YOGHURT CAKE

Makes 1 × 20-cm/8-inch cake

150 g/5 oz natural yoghurt
Grated rind of 2 small lemons
2 tablespoons fresh lemon juice
2 large eggs, beaten
225 g/8 oz caster sugar
225 g/8 oz self-raising white flour, sifted
½ tablespoon demerara sugar

1. Grease and line the base and sides of a 20-cm/8-inch round cake tin. Preheat the oven to moderate, Gas 4, 350°F, 180°C.
2. Put the yoghurt into a large mixing bowl and add the lemon rind and juice, the eggs and caster sugar. Whisk with an electric mixer until thick and creamy.
3. Fold in the flour with a spatula and pour the mixture into the tin. Sprinkle the top with the demerara sugar.
4. Bake for about 45 minutes until risen and set. Allow to firm up in the tin for about 10 minutes, then loosen the cake by running a knife round the outer edge. Turn out onto a wire tray, peel off the lining paper and allow to cool.

Store in an airtight tin for about 3–4 days, or freeze for up to 3 months.

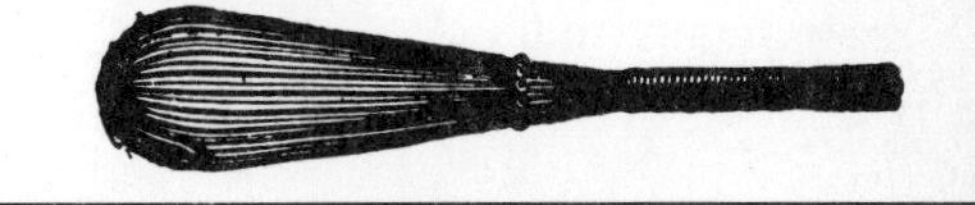

RICE CAKE

Rice cakes seem to have gone out of fashion but there is something rather English about them. They are simple and good and do not need any icings or fillings.

Makes 1 × 20-cm/8-inch round cake

225 g/8 oz tub margarine
225 g/8 oz caster sugar
Grated rind of 1 large lemon
3 large eggs, beaten
200 g/7 oz self-raising white flour
200 g/7 oz ground rice
3 tablespoons lemon juice
A little milk, if necessary

1. Grease and base line a 20-cm/8-inch round cake tin. Preheat the oven to moderate, Gas 3, 325°F, 160°C.
2. In a large mixing bowl, cream the margarine and sugar together until pale and fluffy. Beat in the lemon rind.
3. Gradually beat in the eggs, a little at a time.
4. Sift the flour into the ground rice and stir well. Fold into the creamed mixture and add the lemon juice. If the mixture is rather stiff, add a little milk.
5. Spoon the mixture into the tin and level the surface. Bake for about 1¼ hours, or until the cake is risen and firm and just beginning to shrink from the sides of the tin. Allow to firm up in the tin for 5 minutes, then turn out onto a wire tray, peel off the lining paper and allow to cool.

Store in an airtight tin for 4–5 days, or freeze for up to 3 months.

SEED CAKE

A rich cake with the aromatic and delicious flavour of caraway.

Makes 1 × 18-cm/7-inch square cake

2 teaspoons caraway seeds
225 g/8 oz plain white flour
1 teaspoon baking powder
175 g/6 oz butter or block margarine, softened
175 g/6 oz caster sugar
3 medium eggs, beaten
Grated rind and juice of ½ lemon
1–2 tablespoons milk

1. Grease and base line an 18-cm/7-inch square tin. Preheat the oven to moderate, Gas 4, 350°F, 180°C.
2. Bruise the caraway seeds in a pestle and mortar or in a strong bowl using the end of your rolling pin.
3. Sift the flour and baking powder into a mixing bowl and stir in the caraway seeds.
4. In a large mixing bowl, cream the butter or margarine and sugar until pale and fluffy, then beat in the eggs, a little at a time.
5. Fold in the flour, then add the lemon rind and juice with enough milk to give a dropping consistency.
6. Spoon the mixture into the tin and level it off very carefully.
7. Bake for about 1¼ hours, or until the cake feels firm and is beginning to shrink from the sides of the tin. Cool in the tin for 10 minutes then turn the cake out onto a wire tray, peel off the lining paper and allow to cool.

Store in an airtight tin for 1 week, or freeze for up to 3 months.

POPPY SEED CAKE

I have always liked poppy seeds on bread so I was very pleased to be given this recipe recently. I buy poppy seeds from a wholefood shop – they give a blue tinge to the cake.

Makes 1 × 20-cm/8-inch deep cake

75 g/3 oz poppy seeds
225 ml/8 fl oz skimmed milk
225 g/8 oz butter or block margarine, softened
225 g/8 oz light soft brown sugar
3 medium eggs, separated
225 g/8 oz self-raising wholewheat flour

1. Grease and base line a deep 20-cm/8-inch round cake tin. Preheat the oven to moderate, Gas 4, 350°F, 180°C.
2. Put the poppy seeds into a pan with the milk and bring to the boil. Set aside to cool completely.
3. In a large mixing bowl, beat the butter or margarine and sugar together until pale and fluffy. Add the egg yolks one at a time, beating well between each addition.
4. Sift the flour into a bowl, adding any residue of bran left in the sieve. Fold the flour into the creamed mixture, then stir in the poppy seeds and milk.
5. In a clean, grease-free bowl, whisk the egg whites until stiff and fold these gently into the mixture. Spoon the mixture into the tin and level the surface.
6. Bake for about 1 hour, or until the cake has risen and browned and is beginning to shrink from the sides of the tin. Leave to firm up in the tin for 5–10 minutes, then turn out onto a wire tray, peel off the lining paper and allow to cool.

Store in an airtight tin for up to 1 week, or freeze for up to 3 months.

SPONGE CAKES

CLASSIC VICTORIA SPONGE

Traditionally, the quantities for this recipe were two eggs plus the weight of two eggs in self-raising flour, butter and sugar. The proportion of butter and sugar ensures a rich, close textured cake which keeps well. It is sandwiched together with home-made raspberry jam and the top sprinkled with caster sugar. It is also good filled with a flavoured butter cream and topped with glacé icing.

Makes 1 × 18-cm/7-inch round sandwich

125 g/4 oz butter or margarine, at room temperature
125 g/4 oz caster sugar
2 large eggs, lightly beaten
125 g/4 oz self-raising white flour, sifted
2 heaped tablespoons raspberry jam
Caster sugar for sprinkling

1. Grease and base line two 18-cm/7-inch sandwich tins. Preheat the oven to moderately hot, Gas 5, 375°F, 190°C.
2. In a large mixing bowl, cream the butter and sugar until pale and fluffy, then beat in the eggs, a little at a time.
3. Lastly, fold in the flour as lightly as possible.
4. Pour the mixture evenly into the tins, level and bake for 20–25 minutes until firm and shrinking from the sides of the tin.
5. Allow to firm up in the tin for a minute, then turn out, remove the lining papers and cool on a wire tray.
6. When cold, sandwich the sponges together with the raspberry jam, and sprinkle the top with sugar.

Store in an airtight tin for 3–4 days, or freeze for up to 3 months.

GENOESE SPONGE

This sponge is made in exactly the same way as a fatless sponge (*see page 72*) but is enriched with the addition of melted butter. This type of sponge is often used as the base for iced fancies (*see page 89*). It is then baked in a shallow tin and is therefore suitable for cutting up into shapes which are decorated individually. However, it can also be split and filled, and I always think that whipped cream is the best filling, with perhaps some fresh strawberries sliced in with it.

Makes 1 × 18-cm/7-inch round sponge

3 large eggs, beaten
75 g/3 oz caster sugar
75 g/3 oz plain white flour
50 g/2 oz unsalted butter, melted and cooled

1. Grease and base line an 18-cm/7-inch round cake tin. Preheat the oven to moderate, Gas 4, 350°F, 180°C.
2. In a large mixing bowl, whisk the eggs and sugar together until they have almost doubled in volume and are very thick. A trail left across the surface with the whisk should not sink immediately.
3. Using a nylon sieve, sift about one-third of the flour over the whisked mixture and, using a spatula, fold this in very lightly. Repeat this twice more until all the flour has been incorporated, then quickly pour the melted butter down the side of the bowl and fold this in.
4. Pour the mixture into the tin and bake for about 20–30 minutes until the sponge is firm to the touch and shrinking from the sides of the tin. Leave to firm up in the tin for 5 minutes, then slide a knife round the outer edge of the sponge and turn out onto a wire tray to cool. Peel off the lining paper.

Store the unfilled sponge for 2–3 days in a tin, or freeze for up to 3 months.

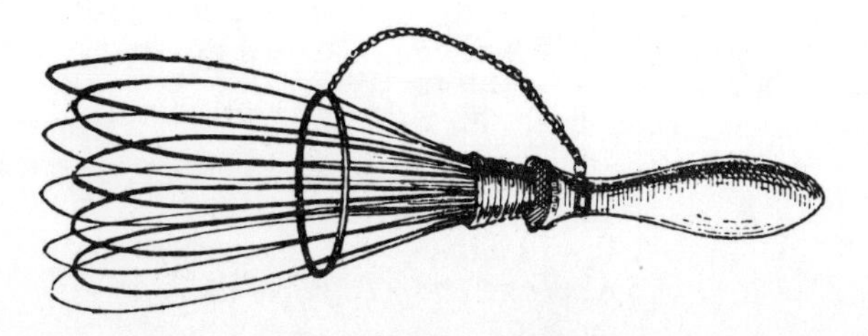

FATLESS FEATHERY SPONGE CAKE

This sponge is made by the whisking method (*see page 57*). Unfilled, the sponge is simple and good. Filled with whipped cream and home-made jam – or fresh or tinned fruit – it is superb. Use it as the base of a glamorous gâteau and you will never buy one again. Cutting the top half of the sponge before you put it on the base, makes the filled sponge much easier to slice.

There is no raising agent in this mixture and plain flour will give a more tender delicate sponge than self-raising flour. Note also that week-old eggs do whip better than really fresh eggs.

This mixture also makes a good sponge flan and sponge drops (*see variations*).

Makes 1 × 20-cm/8-inch sponge

3 large eggs
75 g/3 oz vanilla sugar *(see page 17)*, **or caster sugar**
75 g/3 oz plain white flour
150 ml/¼ pint double or whipping cream
1 tablespoon good raspberry jam

1. Grease and base line a 20-cm/8-inch round tin, about 5–7.5 cm/2–3 inches deep. Preheat the oven to moderate, Gas 3, 325°F, 160°C.
2. Using an electric mixer, whip together the eggs and the sugar until the mixture is very pale, thick and fluffy like marshmallow.
3. Using a sieve, sprinkle approximately one-third of the flour over the surface of the whipped mixture and lightly fold it in, using a flexible rubber spatula or large metal spoon, in a figure of eight movement. Repeat this twice more, cutting through the mixture with the sharp side of the spatula or spoon only, so that you keep the mixture as frothy as possible. Make sure there are no pockets of dry flour left.
4. Pour the mixture into the tin, level the surface and bake for about 40 minutes, or until the sponge is risen and springy to the touch.
5. Allow to cool slightly in the tin. Run a knife round the side of the sponge to loosen it and turn out onto a wire tray to cool. Peel off the lining paper.
6. Split the cold sponge in two horizontally.
7. Whip three-quarters of the cream with a loop whisk. Spread the jam on the bottom sponge and spread the cream over it to a depth of no more than 1 cm/½ inch. Cut the top half of the sponge into sections and lay them on the cream and jam. Put the remaining cream into a piping bag with a star nozzle and pipe stars on each portion of the sponge.

Store the unfilled sponge for 4–5 days, or freeze for up to 3 months.

VARIATIONS

TO MAKE A SPONGE FLAN AND SPONGE DROPS, OR 36 SPONGE DROPS

1 quantity fatless sponge cake mixture *(see left)*

Use exactly the same recipe as for the fatless sponge cake but fill the flan tin to just over half full.

Have ready a baking tray lined with nonstick paper. Use a dessertspoon to drop blobs of the remaining mixture at intervals on the tray.

Bake the flan and the drops in a moderate oven, Gas 3, 325°F, 160°C. The flan will take about 30 minutes and the sponge drops about 13–14 minutes. Sandwich the drops together with a piped swirl of whipped cream and a small teaspoon of jam in the centre or just jam on its own. Alternatively, bake the drops until they are very brown and you'll have very nice crisp biscuits.

SUGGESTED FILLINGS FOR THE FLAN

Green and black grapes, halved and de-pipped

Mandarin oranges and red cherries

Canned pears and fine strips of preserved ginger

TO GLAZE

150 ml/5 fl oz fruit juice (use apple juice over fresh fruit)

1 heaped teaspoon arrowroot powder, or cornflour

Pour the cold fruit juice into a small pan and whisk in the arrowroot or cornflour. Cook carefully over a low heat, stirring all the time for about 2 minutes. Allow to get almost cold then pour over just enough to cover the fruit. Allow to set then decorate with blobs of whipped cream.

TO MAKE SPONGE FINGERS

There are two ways to make sponge fingers – either by piping the mixture onto a baking tray, or by using finger sponge tins. They can be used instead of boudoir biscuits when making a Charlotte Russe.

Makes 36

1 quantity fatless sponge cake mixture *(see page 72)*
Whipped cream (optional)

1. Preheat the oven to moderate, Gas 3, 325°F, 160°C.
2. Either, put the mixture into a piping bag fitted with a 5-mm/¼-inch plain nozzle and pipe 7.5-cm/3-inch long strips onto a baking tray lined with nonstick paper. Use a knife in your left hand to make a clean cut through the sponge mixture. (This method needs a little speed so that the sponge mixture in the bag doesn't start to soften.) Or, well grease finger sponge tins and put a narrow strip of nonstick paper in the bottom of each space. Spoon about 1 dessertspoon of the sponge mixture into each space, pulling it gently to ease it into the tin.
3. Bake for about 12 minutes. Do not allow the fingers to get very brown or they will stick in the tins.
4. Fill the sponge fingers with whipped cream, if liked, or eat them plain with fruit.

Store in an airtight tin for up to 3 days, or freeze for up to 3 months.

ALL-IN-ONE PLAIN SPONGE

Makes 2 × 18-cm/7-inch round sponges

175 g/6 oz self-raising white flour
1½ teaspoons baking powder
175 g/6 oz tub margarine
175 g/6 oz caster sugar
3 large eggs, beaten
2–3 drops vanilla essence
2 tablespoons good raspberry jam

1. Grease and base line two 18-cm/7-inch round sandwich tins. Preheat the oven to moderate, Gas 3, 325°F, 160°C.
2. Sift the flour and baking powder into a large mixing bowl. Add all the remaining ingredients, except the jam, and mix until the mixture is really smooth.
3. Spoon it into the two tins and weigh them to ensure that the mixture is evenly divided. Smooth over each surface and bake for about 20–30 minutes, or until the sponges feel firm to the touch and are just shrinking from the sides of the tin.
4. Allow to firm up in the tins for a few minutes then turn out, peel off the lining papers and cool on wire trays.
5. When cold, sandwich the sponges together with raspberry jam.

Store in an airtight tin for 3–4 days, or freeze for up to 3 months.

RASPBERRY SWISS ROLL

The quality of the jam used is very important in this recipe. The taste of the fruit should be very clear and a world away from the pink glue which passes for jam in some commercial cakes.

Makes 1 × 23-cm/9-inch Swiss roll

3 large eggs
75 g/3 oz vanilla sugar *(see page 17)*, **or caster sugar**
75 g/3 oz plain white flour
Caster sugar for sprinkling
2 tablespoons good raspberry jam, warmed

1. Grease and line the base and sides of a Swiss roll tin measuring 33 × 23 cm/13 × 9 inches. Preheat the oven to fairly hot, Gas 6, 400°F, 200°C.
2. In a slightly warmed bowl, whisk the eggs and sugar together until really thick and fluffy. You should be able to leave a definite trail over the surface with the whisk which does not sink immediately.
3. Using a nylon sieve, sift one-third of the flour over the surface of the creamed mixture. Fold this in lightly with a flexible rubber spatula using a figure of eight movement. Do this twice more and, when all the flour has been incorporated, spoon the mixture into the tin, taking care to get the mixture well into the corners.
4. Bake immediately for about 10 minutes, or until the sponge is firm to the touch and starting to shrink from the sides of the tin.
5. Have ready a piece of greaseproof paper, just larger than the Swiss roll, placed on a clean damp tea towel. Sprinkle this paper lightly with caster sugar.
6. Take the sponge out of the oven and turn it upside down onto the sugared paper. Peel off the lining paper and slice a very narrow strip of sponge off each long end (this is often crisp). Using a palette knife, spread the jam over the sponge to within 1 cm/½ inch of the edges – a thin layer is all that is needed.
7. Just before rolling, take a sharp knife and make a shallow cut across the short end nearest to you, about 2.5 cm/1 inch from the edge. (This slight nick will make rolling the sponge easier.) Use the paper to help you roll up the sponge, starting at the short end nearest to you. Lift it onto a wire tray to cool.

Eat on the day it is made, or freeze for up to 2 months.

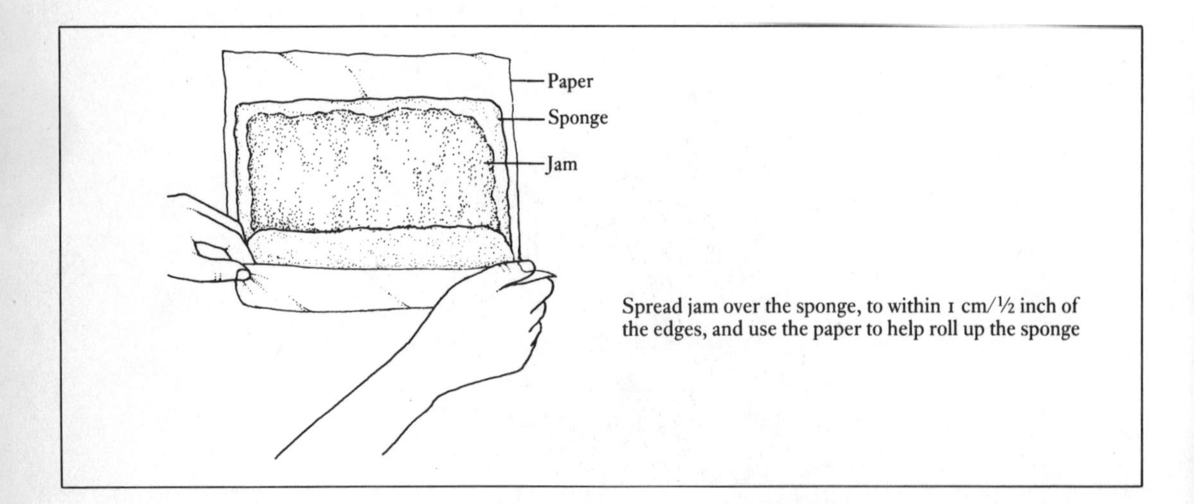

Spread jam over the sponge, to within 1 cm/½ inch of the edges, and use the paper to help roll up the sponge

CHOCOLATE SWISS ROLL

This Swiss roll is filled with a delicious butter cream flavoured with brandy.

Makes 1 × 23-cm/9-inch Swiss roll

3 large eggs
75 g/3 oz caster sugar
75 g/3 oz (bare measure, *see page 12*) **plain white flour**
3 teaspoons cocoa powder

FOR THE FILLING
75 g/3 oz unsalted butter, softened
140 g/4½ oz icing sugar, sifted
2–3 teaspoons brandy

1. Grease and line the base and sides of a large Swiss roll tin measuring 33 × 23 cm/13 × 9 inches. Preheat the oven to fairly hot, Gas 6, 400°F, 200°C.
2. In a large mixing bowl, whisk the eggs and sugar together and continue beating until the mixture is thick and fluffy like marshmallow. A trail left across the surface with the whisk should not sink immediately.
3. In another bowl, stir the flour and cocoa powder together and, using a nylon sieve, sift about one-third of it over the surface of the creamed mixture. Fold this in lightly with a flexible rubber spatula. Do this twice more and, when all the flour and cocoa has been incorporated, spoon the mixture quickly into the tin, taking care to spread it well into the corners.
4. Bake for about 10–12 minutes, or until the sponge is firm to the touch and starting to shrink from the sides of the tin. Slide a knife round the sponge to loosen it.
5. Have ready a piece of greaseproof paper, larger than the Swiss roll, placed on a clean damp tea towel. Sprinkle this paper with caster sugar.
6. Take the sponge out of the oven and turn it upside down onto the sugared paper. Peel off the lining paper and slice a very narrow strip of sponge off each long end. Cover the sponge with the Swiss roll tin and leave to go cold.
7. For the filling, cream the butter until very light then add the icing sugar and brandy and beat well. (Taste the butter cream and add more brandy if you wish.)
8. Lift the tin off the cold sponge and make a shallow cut across the short end nearest to you, about 2.5 cm/1 inch from the edge. (This will make rolling the sponge easier.)
9. Spread the butter cream across the whole of the sponge to within 1 cm/½ inch of the edge all round. Using the greaseproof paper to help you, roll up the sponge starting at the short end nearest to you. Set the sponge on a serving dish with the join underneath.

Eat as soon as possible but will store fairly well for up to 2 days in a tin, or freeze for up to 3 months.

COFFEE AND ALMOND SANDWICH

This is a smaller version of the All-in-one Plain Sponge mixture (*see page 73*).

Makes 1 × 18-cm/7-inch round sandwich

125 g/4 oz self-raising white flour
1 teaspoon baking powder
125 g/4 oz tub margarine
125 g/4 oz caster sugar
2 large eggs, beaten
1 tablespoon coffee granules dissolved in 2 tablespoons hot water and cooled
50 g/2 oz nibbed almonds

FOR THE FILLING
75 g/3 oz butter, softened
175 g/6 oz icing sugar, sifted
1 dessertspoon coffee granules dissolved in 1 dessertspoon hot water
A little milk, if necessary
25 g/1 oz nibbed almonds, toasted

1. Grease and base line two 18-cm/7-inch round sandwich tins. Preheat the oven to moderate, Gas 3, 325°F, 160°C.
2. Sift the flour and baking powder into a large mixing bowl and add the margarine, sugar and eggs. Mix thoroughly then beat in the coffee liquid and the almonds. The mixture should be quite soft so, if needed, add a little water.
3. Spoon the mixture into the tins and weigh them to ensure that the mixture is evenly divided. Level the surface of each tin.
4. Bake for about 25–30 minutes, or until the cakes feel soft and springy to the touch and are just beginning to shrink from the sides of the tins. Remove from the oven and slide a knife round the edge of the cakes to loosen them. Leave in the tins to firm up for about 10 minutes then turn out onto a wire tray, peel off the lining paper and leave to cool.
5. In a large mixing bowl, beat the butter with a wooden spoon, then beat in the icing sugar and coffee liquid. The consistency should be fairly thick, but if it is too thick just add a little milk.
6. Sandwich the cakes together with about half the butter cream. Then spread a layer on top.
7. To toast the almonds, place them on a metal tray and put under a hot grill to brown – watch carefully, they burn easily. Scatter the toasted almonds on top of the cake.

Store in an airtight tin for up to 5 days, or freeze for up to 3 months.

SPONGE SANDWICH USING OIL

The oil, which is used instead of margarine or butter (*see page 10*), gives a good result. The sponges are moist and stay moist. The filling I have suggested is whipped cream and raspberry jam but you could, of course, use a butter cream or just jam on its own.

Makes 1 × 20-cm/8-inch round sandwich

225 g/8 oz self-raising white flour
1 pinch salt
200 g/7 oz caster sugar
150 ml/¼ pint corn oil
150 ml/¼ pint cold water
3 large eggs, separated
3 tablespoons good raspberry jam
150 ml/¼ pint double cream, whipped
Icing sugar for dredging

1. Grease and base line two 20-cm/8-inch sandwich tins. Preheat the oven to moderately hot, Gas 5, 375°F, 190°C.
2. Sift the flour and salt into a large mixing bowl and stir in the sugar.
3. Combine the corn oil and water in a jug and add the egg yolks. Whisk until well blended, then gradually stir into the dry ingredients, using a wooden spoon, until smooth.
4. In a clean, grease-free bowl, whisk the egg whites until they are very stiff. Stir 1 dessertspoon of the whipped egg whites into the batter to slacken the texture, then fold in the remainder carefully but thoroughly.
5. Pour the mixture into the two tins – they should be about two-thirds full – and weigh the tins to ensure the mixture is evenly divided.
6. Bake for 40 minutes, or until the cakes are risen and feel springy to the touch. Run a knife round the edge of each cake to loosen it. Leave to firm up in the tins for about 5 minutes, then turn out onto a wire tray, peel off the lining paper and allow the sponges to cool.
7. Spread the base of one sponge with the jam. Whip the cream and spread over the jam. Top with the remaining sponge and dredge with icing sugar.

Eat the cake on the day it is assembled. Store the unfilled sponges in an airtight tin for 4–5 days, or freeze for up to 3 months.

CHOCOLATE SPONGE SANDWICH

I really do not care for the very deep cake which this will give you if you make the two sponges and sandwich them together. I prefer to make one cake, about 6 cm/2½ inches deep, and six buns with the rest of the mixture. I then split the deeper cake to fill with butter cream.

Makes 1 × 18-cm/7-inch round sandwich, or 1 × 20-cm/8-inch sponge and 6 buns

175 g/6 oz tub margarine
200 g/7 oz caster sugar
3 tablespoons warm water
1½ tablespoons cocoa powder, sifted
3 large eggs, beaten
175 g/6 oz self-raising white flour, sifted

FOR THE BUTTER CREAM
125 g/4 oz butter or block margarine, softened
225 g/8 oz icing sugar, sifted
1–2 teaspoons brandy (optional)
1½ tablespoons cocoa powder, sifted
1½ tablespoons hot water
1 tablespoon milk
A few walnuts or chocolate drops (optional)

1. Grease and base line two 18-cm/7-inch sandwich tins. Or grease and base line one tin and set six paper cases in a bun tin. Preheat the oven to moderately hot, Gas 5, 375°F, 190°C.
2. In a large mixing bowl, cream the margarine and sugar until light and fluffy.
3. In a small bowl, mix the warm water into the cocoa powder until free from lumps. Allow to cool.
4. Beat the cooled cocoa into the creamed mixture and add the eggs a little at a time, beating well between each addition. Add just a little of the measured flour if the mixture looks like separating.
5. Fold in the remaining flour.
6. Either, divide the mixture between the sandwich tins, or fill the paper cases just over half full and spoon the rest of the mixture into one sandwich tin.
7. Level the tops and bake the two sandwich tins for about 25 minutes, or the deeper cake for about 35–40 minutes and the buns for 12–15 minutes.
8. Leave to firm up in the tins for 5 minutes, then turn out onto a wire tray, carefully remove the lining paper and cool completely.
9. To make the butter cream, put the butter or margarine into a bowl and beat to soften, then add the icing sugar and brandy, if using, and beat again.
10. In a small bowl, mix the cocoa powder and hot water and beat this into the icing sugar mixture with enough milk to give a thick consistency. This cream can also be used for piping.
11. Sandwich the two sponges with some of the butter cream and spread the remainder over the top. If you have made the single sponge, slice it horizontally into two. Fill with some of the butter cream and spread the remainder over the top. Smooth the tops and either mark out a design with a fork, or decorate with walnuts or chocolate drops round the edge.

Store the cakes and buns in a tin for 4–5 days, or freeze for up to 3 months.

WHITE SPONGE FLAN

Lining the tin ensures the sponge is easily removed.

Makes 1 × 20-cm/8-inch sponge flan

3 large eggs
75 g/3 oz vanilla sugar *(see page 17)*, **or caster sugar**
75 g/3 oz plain white flour

FOR THE FILLING
1 tablespoon sherry or liqueur
150 ml/5 fl oz double cream
225 g/8 oz ripe strawberries, hulled and halved; raspberries; or grapes, halved and de-pipped
Caster sugar to sweeten

1. Well grease a 20-cm/8-inch metal flan tin with a raised base. Cut a circle of greaseproof paper to fit the raised base and position it in the tin. Cut another circle the same diameter as the ring, fold it in two and cut out most of the centre so that you are left with a narrow ring of greaseproof paper. Lay this in the bottom of the tin. Preheat the oven to moderate, Gas 3, 325°F, 160°C.
2. In a large mixing bowl, beat together the eggs and sugar until very thick and creamy. A trail left across the surface with the whisk should not sink immediately.
3. Using a nylon sieve, sift about one-third of the flour over the surface of the creamed mixture. Fold this in lightly, using a flexible spatula or a large metal spoon. Repeat this twice more and, when all the flour has been incorporated, pour the mixture into the flan tin, filling it to just over halfway. (Use up any remaining mixture by dropping spoonfuls onto a metal baking tray lined with nonstick paper. Bake at the same time as the flan for about 20–25 minutes. Take out when very brown and you will have some very nice biscuits. Store in a tin.)
4. Bake for about 30–40 minutes, or until the sponge is shrinking from the sides of the tin. Remove from the oven and run a knife round the inner edge of the tin to loosen the flan slightly. Leave to firm up in the tin for 10 minutes, then gently ease the flan out and onto a wire tray. Carefully peel off the lining paper and allow to get cold.
5. Set the flan on a serving plate. Put the sherry or liqueur into a small jug with about 2 teaspoons of water and dribble it over the sponge.
6. Whip the cream until it is at the floppy stage and use one third of it to cover the base of the flan. Lay the strawberries, raspberries or grapes in a decorative pattern on the cream and sprinkle a little sugar over the fruit.
7. Whip the remaining cream again and put it into a nylon piping bag fitted with a star nozzle. Decorate the flan with a lattice pattern of whipped cream, or large whirls of cream, all round the edge of the fruit.

Serve on the day the flan is assembled. Store the unfilled flan for 3–4 days, or freeze for up to 3 months.

FATLESS CHOCOLATE SPONGE

Makes 1 × 20-cm/8-inch round sponge

3 large eggs
75 g/3 oz caster sugar
2 teaspoons cocoa powder, sifted
75 g/3 oz (bare measure, *see page 12*) **plain white flour, sifted**

FOR THE FILLING
150 ml/5 fl oz double cream
50 g/2 oz plain chocolate, or 2 flaky milk bars

1. Grease and base line a 20-cm/8-inch cake tin (not a sandwich tin). Preheat the oven to moderate, Gas 3, 325°F, 160°C.
2. In a mixing bowl, beat the eggs and sugar together until very thick and creamy. A trail left across the surface of the mixture with the whisk should not sink immediately.
3. In another bowl, stir the cocoa powder into the flour and, using a nylon sieve, sift one-third over the surface of the creamed mixture. Fold this in lightly, using a flexible rubber spatula or a large metal spoon, in a figure of eight movement.
4. Repeat this twice more and, when all the flour and cocoa has been incorporated, pour the mixture into the tin.
5. Bake for about 40 minutes, or until the sponge is risen, firm to the touch and just shrinking from the sides of the tin. Allow to firm up in the tin for 4–5 minutes then slide a knife carefully around the sponge and turn out onto a wire tray. Peel off the lining paper and allow to cool.

6. To make the filling, whip the cream until it is at the floppy stage.
7. Grate the bar of chocolate on the largest holes of a metal grater, or use a short vegetable knife or loose-headed peeler and scrape chocolate curls off the bar of chocolate. Alternatively, crush the flaky bars.
8. Cut the chocolate sponge in two horizontally and fill with half the cream and most of the grated or crushed chocolate. Whip the remaining cream again until fairly stiff and put it into a nylon piping bag fitted with a small star nozzle. Decorate the top of the sponge with stars of cream all round the edge. Sprinkle the last of the chocolate over the cream stars.

Eat the cream sponge on the day it is assembled. Store the unfilled sponge in a tin for 4–5 days, or freeze for up to 3 months.

ALL-IN-ONE CHOCOLATE SPONGE

Now that we have such soft margarines, it is an easy job to do an all-in mix and get an excellent cake. You will notice that, despite using self-raising flour, extra baking powder is required to make up for the lack of creaming and beating.

This quantity makes two cakes which when sandwiched together make a traditional deep cake. I nearly always just make one cake, and some chocolate buns with the remaining mixture. A good tip is to set quartered walnuts at intervals round the top edge of the cake. The slices are then easy to pick up. Melted chocolate or chocolate-flavoured cake covering can be used to top the cake or buns if you prefer.

Makes 1 × 20-cm/8-inch round sandwich, or 1 × 20-cm/8-inch sponge and 6–8 buns

175 g/6 oz self-raising white flour
1½ teaspoons baking powder
1 teaspoon cocoa powder (not drinking chocolate)
175 g/6 oz caster sugar
175 g/6 oz tub margarine
3 large eggs, beaten
2 tablespoons warm water

FOR THE FILLING AND TOPPING
50 g/2 oz tub margarine
125–175 g/4–6 oz icing sugar, sifted
1 heaped teaspoon cocoa powder (not drinking chocolate)
1 teaspoon hot water
1 teaspoon sherry or liqueur (optional)

TO DECORATE (OPTIONAL)
Walnut pieces

1. Grease and base line two 20-cm/8-inch sandwich tins. Or grease and base line one tin and set 6–8 paper cases in bun tins. Preheat the oven to moderate, Gas 3, 325°F, 160°C.
2. Sift the flour, baking powder and cocoa powder into a large mixing bowl. Add the sugar, margarine, eggs and water and mix well. I like to use a rigid spatula for this job.
3. Either, divide the mixture between the sandwich tins, or fill the paper cases about three-quarters full and spoon the remaining mixture into one sandwich tin.
4. Level the tops and bake the two sandwich tins for 25–30 minutes, or the deeper cake for about 35 minutes and the buns for about 12 minutes.
5. Leave in the tins for 5 minutes, then turn out onto a wire tray, carefully remove the lining paper and cool completely.
6. Put all the ingredients for the filling and topping into a large warmed mixing bowl and beat well until smooth. (If necessary, thicken the mixture by adding more icing sugar, or thin it by adding more water.)
7. Sandwich the two sponges with some of the filling and spread the remainder over the top. If you have made the single sponge, split the cake in two horizontally. Sandwich the halves together with the filling and spread the remainder over the top.
8. Smooth the tops and mark with a skewer or fork in a decorative way. Edge the cake with walnut pieces, if you wish. Decorate the buns by spreading a layer of the chocolate filling on top of each, and top with walnut pieces, if you wish.

Store the cake and buns in an airtight tin for 3–4 days, or freeze for up to 3 months.

CHOCOLATE SPONGE FLAN

Makes 1 × 20-cm/8-inch sponge flan

3 large eggs
75 g/3 oz vanilla sugar *(see page 17)*, **or caster sugar**
2 teaspoons cocoa powder
75 g/3 oz (bare measure, *see page 12*) **plain white flour**

FOR THE FILLING
1 tablespoon rum, sherry or liqueur
1 small can mandarin oranges with juice
150 ml/5 fl oz double cream

1. Well grease a 20-cm/8-inch metal flan tin with a raised base. Cut a circle of greaseproof paper to fit the raised base and position it in the tin. Cut another circle the same diameter as the ring, fold it in two and cut out most of the centre so that you are left with a narrow ring of greaseproof paper. Lay this in the bottom of the tin. Preheat the oven to moderate, Gas 3, 325°F, 160°C.
2. In a large mixing bowl, beat the eggs and sugar together until very thick and creamy. A definite trail left across the surface with the whisk should not sink immediately.
3. Stir the cocoa powder into the flour and, using a nylon sieve, sift about one-third over the surface of the creamed mixture. Fold this in lightly, using a flexible spatula or a large metal spoon. Repeat this twice more until all the flour has been incorporated, then pour the mixture into the flan tin, filling it to just over halfway. (Use up any remaining mixture by dropping spoonfuls onto a baking tray lined with nonstick paper. Bake at the same time as the flan for about 20–25 minutes. Allow them to get very brown. They crisp up on cooling and make very pleasant biscuits.)
4. Bake for about 30–40 minutes, or until the sponge is shrinking from the sides of the tin. Remove from the oven and run a knife round the inner edge of the tin to loosen the flan slightly. Leave to firm up in the tin for 10 minutes, then ease the flan out onto a wire tray, peel off the lining paper and leave to cool.
5. Set the flan on a flat serving plate. Put the rum into a small jug with about 2 teaspoons of the fruit juice and dribble this over the sponge.
6. Whip the cream until it is at the floppy stage and use one-third of it to cover the base of the flan. Drain the mandarin oranges, dry them slightly on kitchen paper and arrange on top of the cream.
7. Whip the remaining cream until fairly stiff and put it into a nylon piping bag fitted with a small star nozzle. Pipe whirls round the edge of the fruit.

Eat on the day the flan is assembled. Store the unfilled flan for 3–4 days in an airtight tin, or freeze for up to 3 months.

COFFEE CREAM SANDWICH

Makes 1 × 18-cm/7-inch round sandwich

175 g/6 oz tub margarine
175 g/6 oz caster sugar
3 medium eggs, beaten
175 g/6 oz self-raising white flour, sifted
1 tablespoon boiling water
2 tablespoons instant coffee granules

FOR THE BUTTER CREAM
175 g/6 oz butter, softened
175 g/6 oz icing sugar, sifted
1 tablespoon instant coffee granules
1 tablespoon boiling water
25 g/1 oz toasted flaked almonds

1. Grease and base line two 18-cm/7-inch round sandwich tins. Preheat the oven to moderately hot, Gas 5, 375°F, 190°C.
2. In a large mixing bowl, cream the margarine and sugar until very light and fluffy. Beat in the eggs a little at a time, adding some of the measured flour if the mixture looks like separating.
3. In a small bowl, dissolve the coffee granules in the boiling water and set aside until cold.
4. Fold the flour into the creamed mixture then add the cooled coffee liquid. Spoon this mixture into the tins – weigh the tins to ensure that the mixture is evenly divided – and level the tops.
5. Bake for about 20 minutes, or until well risen and firm to the touch. Allow to firm up in the tins for 4–5 minutes, then turn out onto a wire tray, peel off the lining paper and allow to cool.
6. To make the butter cream, cream the butter until very soft then beat in the icing sugar.
7. In a small bowl, dissolve the coffee granules in the boiling water and set aside until cold.
8. Beat the cold coffee into the butter cream.
9. Use about two-thirds of the butter cream to sandwich the cakes and thinly cover the top. Use the remainder to fill a small paper icing bag, fitted with a 1-cm/½-inch star nozzle. Pipe stars around the edge of the cake and scatter the toasted almonds all over the top.

Store the decorated cake in an airtight tin for 2–3 days. Freeze, undecorated, for up to 3 months.

BATTENBURG CAKE

This old favourite, coated with almond paste, is at its very best when home-made with real marzipan and good jam. Use the flattish type of loaf tin to get a good long shape. The bread tin is rather too short and deep.

Makes 1 Battenburg Cake about 18 cm/7 inches long and 6 cm/2½ inches square

125 g/4 oz block margarine, softened
125 g/4 oz caster sugar
2 medium eggs, beaten
125 g/4 oz self-raising white flour, sifted
2–3 drops pink food colouring
3 tablespoons raspberry jam

FOR THE MARZIPAN
75 g/3 oz ground almonds
25 g/1 oz fine semolina
75 g/3 oz caster sugar
75 g/3 oz icing sugar, sifted
2–3 drops almond essence
1 small egg, beaten
Extra caster sugar for sprinkling

1. Grease and base line two flattish loaf tins. Preheat the oven to moderate, Gas 4, 350°F, 180°C.
2. In a warm mixing bowl, cream the margarine and sugar until pale and fluffy. Beat in the eggs, a little at a time. Fold in the flour.
3. Weigh half the cake mixture into another bowl, add the pink food colouring to it and stir it through so that the mixture is evenly coloured. Spoon each mixture into a loaf tin.
4. Bake for about 20–25 minutes, or until the cakes are firm and just beginning to shrink from the sides of the tins. Loosen the cakes at the narrow ends. Turn out and cool on a wire tray. Strip off the lining papers.
5. When the cakes are cold, spread a thin layer of jam on the bottom of one and sandwich it to the bottom of the other. Trim the sides of the cake with a sharp knife so that you are left with a neat rectangle. Cut the cake in half lengthways. Turn one half over, spread a thin layer of jam along one side and join the two halves up again.
6. Next, make the marzipan. In a large mixing bowl, stir together the almonds, semolina, sugars and almond essence. Bind with just enough egg to give a firm but not dry marzipan. Knead slightly.
7. Lay a sheet of nonstick paper on a board and dust it with caster sugar. Roll out the marzipan to a rectangle measuring about 18 × 30 cm/7 × 12 inches, depending on the size of the cake. Trim the edges and spread a thin layer of jam over the top of the marzipan.
8. Lay the cake at one end of the marzipan. Use the nonstick paper to help lift the marzipan and wrap it round the cake, pressing it gently so that it adheres. If the marzipan cracks at the corners it is probably just a little too dry. Squeeze the marzipan together again and, if the crack is really obvious, make a fluted pattern with your fingers on each edge. Press the marzipan firmly onto the cake and trim the ends. Place the cake seam-side down. Traditionally a lattice design is scored on the top of the cake – do this with the back of a knife. Sprinkle the top with caster sugar.

Store in an airtight tin for 1 week, or freeze for up to 2 months.

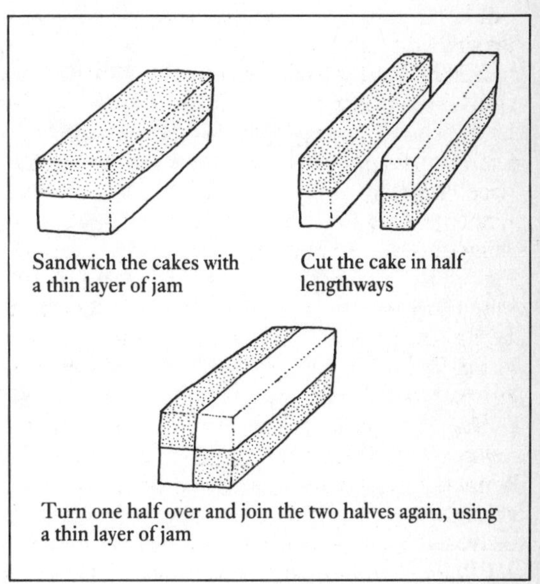

Sandwich the cakes with a thin layer of jam

Cut the cake in half lengthways

Turn one half over and join the two halves again, using a thin layer of jam

MINCEMEAT SPONGE RING

This easy recipe makes a pleasant cake. The ring shape cuts neatly into slices.

Will cut into 24 slices

125 g/4 oz butter or block margarine
125 g/4 oz light soft brown sugar
3 large eggs, beaten
325 g/12 oz fruity mincemeat
200 g/7 oz self-raising brown flour, sifted
About 4 tablespoons milk
Icing sugar for dredging (optional)

1. Grease a 1.2-litre/2-pint ring tin. I also think it is worthwhile lining the bottom of the ring. Cut a circle of greaseproof paper the same size as the ring, then cut out the middle, leaving a 2.5-cm/1-inch circle. Place in the ring tin. Preheat the oven to moderate, Gas 3, 325°F, 160°C.
2. In a large mixing bowl, cream the butter or margarine and sugar until light and fluffy, then beat in the eggs, a little at a time.
3. Stir in the mincemeat and the flour, adding any residue of bran left in the sieve. Gradually add the milk to the mixture to give a soft but not sloppy consistency.
4. Spoon the mixture into the tin and level all round.
5. Bake for about 10 minutes, then reduce the heat to cool, Gas 2, 300°F, 150°C, and bake for 1 hour, until the sponge is risen and firm. (This cake very often cracks on the surface.)
6. Allow the cake to cool a little then slide a knife blade round the cake to loosen it. Turn out onto a wire tray, peel off the lining paper and allow to cool.
7. Dredge the top of the ring with icing sugar, if you wish, either through a sieve or from a perforated flour dredger.

Store in an airtight tin for up to 2 weeks, or freeze for up to 3 months.

VARIATION

MINCEMEAT SPONGE BUNS

Make the mixture as above but spoon into paper cases set in a bun tray. Fill the cases just over half full and bake at Gas 3, 325°F, 160°C for about 15–20 minutes. Dredge the top of the buns with icing sugar, if you wish. Makes about 24.

Store in an airtight tin for 1 week, or freeze for up to 3 months.

COCONUT BATTER CAKE

Creamed coconut is sold in a block in many delicatessens and wholefood shops.

Makes 1 × 20-cm/8-inch sandwich cake

75 g/3 oz solid vegetable fat
75 g/ 3 oz block margarine
175 g/6 oz caster sugar
3 medium eggs, separated
175 g/6 oz self-raising white flour
2 teaspoons baking powder
100 ml/3 fl oz milk
1½ tablespoons vinegar
3–4 drops vanilla essence
75 g/3 oz desiccated coconut
4 tablespoons good apricot jam

FOR THE TOPPING
125 g/4 oz creamed coconut, chopped
100 ml/3 fl oz milk
3 tablespoons natural yoghurt
2 teaspoons icing sugar, sifted
25 g/1 oz toasted coconut *(see page 252)*

1. Grease and base line two 20-cm/8-inch sandwich tins. Preheat the oven to moderate, Gas 4, 350°F, 180°C.
2. In a large mixing bowl, cream together the fat, margarine and caster sugar until very light and fluffy. Beat in the egg yolks, a little at a time.
3. Sift the flour and baking powder into a bowl. Put the milk into a jug and add the vinegar (do not worry that it looks curdled). Fold the flour into the creamed mixture and add the milk and vinegar. Stir in the vanilla essence and the coconut.
4. In a clean, grease-free bowl, whip the egg whites until stiff and fold into the mixture.
5. Pour the batter into the tins – weigh them to ensure that the mixture is evenly divided – and bake for 35–40 minutes. Allow to firm up in the tin for 5 minutes, then turn out onto wire trays, peel off the lining paper and allow to cool.
6. When the cakes are cold, sandwich the two halves together with the apricot jam.
7. To make the topping, put the creamed coconut into a small pan with the milk. Heat gently until dissolved, then allow to get cold.
8. Pour the yoghurt into the coconut mixture and beat or whisk until it is like cream. Stir in the icing sugar. Spread over the top of the sandwich and decorate with a thick border of toasted coconut.

Store the undecorated sponge in an airtight tin for 3–4 days, or freeze for up to 3 months.

LEMON CRUNCH CAKE

This is my variation on a lemon cake recipe which had a lemon syrup poured over the top when it came out of the oven. I always thought it made the cake too soggy. Try it this way for a change.

Makes 2 × 18-cm/7-inch cakes

175 g/6 oz self-raising white flour
1½ teaspoons baking powder
175 g/6 oz tub margarine
175 g/6 oz caster sugar
2 teaspoons finely grated lemon rind
3 large eggs, beaten

TOPPING FOR EACH CAKE
1 large tablespoon fresh lemon juice
125 g/4 oz granulated sugar

1. Grease and base line two 18-cm/7-inch sandwich tins. Preheat the oven to moderate, Gas 3, 325°F, 160°C.
2. Sift the flour and baking powder into a large mixing bowl.
3. Add the margarine, sugar, lemon rind and eggs and beat together with a wooden spoon or a strong spatula.
4. When the mixture is really smooth, spoon it evenly into the tins. Weigh the tins to ensure the mixture is evenly divided.
5. Bake for about 25–30 minutes, or until the cakes are firm to the touch and beginning to shrink from the sides of the tins. Allow to firm up in the tins for 5 minutes, then run a knife round the edge of each cake to loosen it. Turn out onto a wire tray, peel off the lining papers, and allow the sponges to get cold.
6. Mix the toppings for each cake separately. Put the lemon juice into a small bowl and pour in the sugar. Stir just once and immediately pour onto the sponge and level out with a knife. The idea is to get the topping onto the sponge before the sugar dissolves. The lemon juice sinks into the cake and the lemon flavoured sugar crystals stay behind giving a pleasant crunch. Repeat with the second sponge.

Store in an airtight tin for 4–5 days, or freeze for up to 3 months.

SMALL CAKES AND NO-BAKE CAKES

Many of the small cakes in this section can be baked in paper cases set in bun tins. This saves on the washing up and also guarantees a good shape. Freeze them in a rigid plastic box on the day they are made and take them out just a few at a time. They will defrost quickly.

The pastry-based tartlets, with moist fillings, do not freeze quite as well. I always feel they have lost their crispness. I prefer to freeze the raw pastry shells in their baking tins. When frozen I take them out of the tins and keep them in a firm plastic box ready to be filled and baked. They will also bake well without first having to be defrosted.

The no-bake cakes are mostly very sweet so take care to cut them into very small neat pieces.

BUTTERFLY BUNS

A simple old favourite. Serve with either whipped double cream or butter cream.

Makes about 20

150 g/5 oz self-raising white or brown flour
1 teaspoon baking powder
125 g/4 oz light soft brown sugar
125 g/4 oz tub margarine
2 medium eggs, beaten
1 tablespoon warm water

FOR THE FILLING
150 g/5 oz double cream, or butter cream made with 125 g/4 oz sifted icing sugar, 50 g/2 oz tub margarine and 2–3 drops vanilla essence
Sifted icing sugar for dredging

1. Set twenty paper cases in bun trays. Preheat the oven to moderate, Gas 4, 350°F, 180°C.
2. Sift the flour and baking powder into a large mixing bowl.
3. Add the sugar, margarine and warm water and beat with a wooden spoon until smooth and soft. Add the eggs a little at a time, beating well between each addition.
4. Half fill the paper cases and bake for about 15–20 minutes, or until the buns are risen and firm to the touch. Set the buns, in their cases, to cool on wire trays.
5. Cut a small slice from the tops of the cooled buns, cut it in two and set aside. To fill the buns, whip the double cream until fairly firm and spoon or pipe a swirl on top of each bun. If using butter cream, beat the icing sugar, soft margarine and vanilla essence until smooth and soft. Add a minute amount of warm water if needed. Pipe or spoon this mixture on top of each bun.
6. Finish the buns in the traditional way by setting the two reserved halves of sponge at an angle in the cream to look like butterfly wings. Dredge with sifted icing sugar.

Eat on the day they are made. Store the undecorated buns in an airtight tin for up to 4 days, or freeze for up to 3 months.

CHOCOLATE BUTTERFLY BUNS

Makes 7

175 g/6 oz tub margarine
175 g/6 oz caster sugar
175 g/6 oz self-raising flour, sifted
1½ teaspoons baking powder, sifted
3 medium eggs, beaten
1 tablespoon cocoa powder (not drinking chocolate)
2 tablespoons warm water
225 ml/8 fl oz double cream

1. Set sixteen paper cases in bun trays. Preheat the oven to moderate, Gas 4, 350°F, 180°C.
2. Put all the ingredients, except the cream, into a large warm mixing bowl and beat well until smooth.
3. Half fill the paper cases with the mixture and bake for 20–25 minutes, or until firm on top but not dry. Cool in the tins for a minute or two before turning out onto a wire tray.
4. Cut a small slice from the tops of the cooled buns, cut it in two and set aside.
5. To fill the buns, whip the double cream and pipe a generous rosette of cream into the top of each bun. Set the reserved halves of sponge at an angle in the cream to look like butterfly wings.

Store the unfilled buns in an airtight tin for up to 7 days, or freeze for up to 1 month. Freeze the filled buns for 1 week.

SNOWBALLS

These very Scottish buns have to be baked in round-bottomed bun tins to get the correct shape.

Makes about 7

125 g/4 oz self-raising white flour
1 teaspoon baking powder
125 g/4 oz caster sugar
125 g/4 oz tub margarine
2 medium eggs, beaten
1 tablespoon warm water
2–3 drops vanilla essence

FOR THE FILLING
2 heaped tablespoons lemon curd
225 g/8 oz sifted icing sugar
A little warm water
125 g/4 oz desiccated coarse coconut

1. Well grease fourteen round-bottomed bun tins. Preheat the oven to moderate, Gas 4, 350°F, 180°C.
2. To make the buns, sift the flour and baking powder into a large mixing bowl.
3. Beat in all the remaining ingredients until smooth. A very little extra water may be needed to achieve a soft but not sloppy consistency.
4. Half fill the bun tins with the sponge mixture and bake for about 15–20 minutes, or until firm and golden. Allow to firm up slightly, then remove from the tins and cool on wire trays.
5. Spread a little lemon curd on the flat surface of half the buns, and sandwich with the remaining buns.
6. Put the desiccated coconut into a deepish plate. Make a runny glacé icing by mixing the sifted icing sugar with a little water in a small bowl. Pierce each pair of buns, one at a time, on a metal skewer and suspend over the bowl of icing. Brush the runny icing all over the ball in a thin layer.
7. Drop the wet iced bun into the coconut and roll gently until well covered, then set aside to dry.

Store the decorated buns in an airtight tin for up to 4 days. Freeze undecorated for up to 1 month.

FAIRY CAKES

The cornflour used in these cakes is said to make them light and so they are called fairy cakes. The lemon rind gives a lovely flavour.

Makes about 18

125 g/4 oz block margarine, softened
75 g/3 oz caster sugar
75 g/3 oz plain white flour, sifted
75 g/3 oz cornflour, sifted
2 medium eggs, beaten
1 teaspoon baking powder
Grated rind of ½ lemon
A little milk, if necessary

1. Grease eighteen patty tins or set paper baking cases in bun trays. Preheat the oven to fairly hot, Gas 6, 400°F, 200°C.
2. In a mixing bowl, cream the margarine and sugar until light and fluffy.
3. Add the flour and cornflour alternately with the beaten eggs, beating well between each addition. Add the baking powder with the last of the flour.
4. Stir in the lemon rind and extra milk, if necessary, to give a soft consistency.
5. Half fill the tins or cases with the mixture and bake for about 15–20 minutes. Cool on a wire tray.

Store in an airtight tin for up to 1 week, or freeze for up to 1 month.

GINGERBREAD CAKES

Makes 9

9 split almonds
125 g/4 oz plain white or wholemeal flour
½ teaspoon bicarbonate of soda
25 g/1 oz butter or margarine
15 g/½ oz caster sugar
½ teaspoon ground ginger
1 pinch mixed spice
1 heaped tablespoon black treacle, warmed
½ medium egg, or 1 × No. 7 egg, beaten
A little milk

1. Grease nine small patty tins and put half an almond in each. Preheat the oven to moderately hot, Gas 5, 375°F, 190°C.
2. Sift the flour and bicarbonate of soda into a large mixing bowl, adding any residue of bran left

in the sieve if using wholemeal flour. Rub in the butter or margarine.
3. Stir in the sugar and spices and mix well.
4. Add the treacle, beaten egg and just enough milk to give a soft consistency.
5. Half fill the patty tins with the mixture and bake for about 20 minutes, or until the cakes are well risen and firm to the touch. Slide a knife round the cakes to loosen them, turn out and cool on a wire tray. Serve upside down with the almond on top.

Keep very well in an airtight tin for 1 week, or freeze for up to 1 month.

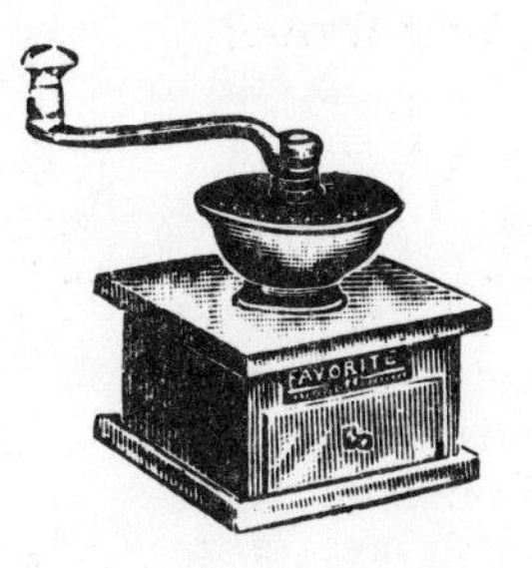

SPICE CAKES

Makes 12

175 g/6 oz plain white flour
1 teaspoon baking powder
125 g/4 oz soft butter
125 g/4 oz caster sugar
2 medium eggs, beaten
1 teaspoon mixed ground cloves, cinnamon, nutmeg
A little milk, if necessary

1. Grease twelve patty tins or line the patty tins with paper baking cases. Preheat the oven to fairly hot, Gas 6, 400°F, 200°C.
2. Sift the flour and baking powder into a mixing bowl.
3. In another bowl, cream the butter and sugar together until pale and fluffy.
4. Beat in the eggs and flour alternately and add the spices with the last spoonful of flour. Add a little milk, if necessary, to get a good dropping consistency.
5. Half fill the tins or paper cases with the mixture and bake for about 15–20 minutes. Cool on a wire tray.

Will keep well in an airtight tin for about 1 week, or freeze for up to 1 month.

NUTTY SPONGE FINGERS

Left plain, these are an excellent accompaniment for ice cream, fruit salad etc. Dressed up with nuts and cream, they are a light cake, very easy to eat.

Makes 10

2 large eggs
75 g/3 oz caster sugar, plus a little extra for dredging
75 g/3 oz plain white flour
2 tablespoons cornflour
50 g/2 oz plain chocolate, broken into small pieces
40 g/1½ oz walnuts, chopped
150 g/5 oz double cream

1. Grease two baking trays and line with nonstick paper. Preheat the oven to moderately hot, Gas 5, 375°F, 190°C.
2. Using an electric mixer if possible, whisk the eggs and the sugar together until very very thick. The mixture should not be at all runny.
3. Mix the flour and cornflour together. Sift this mixture in three batches over the surface of the whipped eggs and sugar, using a spatula to cut and fold it in after each addition. Do not overwork the mixture, but ensure there are no dry pockets of flour at the bottom of the bowl. The consistency should now be like thick marshmallow.
4. Put this mixture into a large piping bag with a 1-cm/½-inch plain piping nozzle and pipe fingers about 10 cm/4 inches long onto the nonstick paper. Dredge lightly with caster sugar.

(If you have got to this stage and the sponge is running, you probably didn't whip the eggs and sugar enough – forget the sponge fingers and put the mixture into a greased and base-lined 20-cm/8-inch cake tin and bake a sponge. Bake at the temperature as above for about 40 minutes.)

5. Bake for about 12–14 minutes. Leave to cool on the trays.
6. Place the nuts in a bowl. Put the chocolate in a heatproof bowl set over a pan of simmering water and stir until melted. Paint a light covering of chocolate on half the sponge fingers, dip them into the nuts and leave to cool.
7. Whip the double cream and spread it on the remaining sponge fingers. Top with the chocolate-coated fingers.

Store the dry sponge fingers in an airtight tin for up to 7 days. Eat the filled fingers within 2–3 hours of filling, or freeze, filled, for up to 2 weeks.

MADELEINES

This simple sponge mixture is baked in the shape of miniature sand castles. I have never seen them decorated any other way than brushed with a light coating of raspberry jam and rolled in coarse coconut, then topped with a piece of red glacé cherry and two green angelica 'leaves'.

Makes about 10

Melted vegetable oil
125 g/4 oz tub margarine
150 g/5 oz caster sugar
2 large eggs, beaten
175 g/6 oz self-raising white or brown flour, sifted
2–3 drops vanilla essence
1 tablespoon hot water
50 g/2 oz desiccated coconut
2 heaped tablespoons raspberry jam, slightly warmed
4–5 red glacé cherries
12 tiny pieces green angelica

1. Using a brush and melted vegetable oil, coat the insides of dariole moulds or castle pudding tins. Put a tiny circle of greaseproof paper in the bottom of each tin. Set the tins on a baking tray. Preheat the oven to fairly hot, Gas 6, 400°F, 200°C.
2. Cream the margarine and sugar in a mixing bowl until light and fluffy.
3. Add the eggs a little at a time, whisking hard with a wire loop-headed whisk.
4. Using a spatula, fold in the flour and vanilla essence and, lastly, the hot water. The consistency should be fairly soft.
5. Three-quarters fill each dariole mould or tin with the sponge mixture and bake for about 15 minutes, or until risen, golden and springy. Allow to firm up for 5 minutes then turn out of the tins onto a wire tray to cool. Peel off the lining paper.
6. Trim the madeleines with a sharp knife so that they stand easily. Put the coconut into a bowl.
7. Spear the cakes one at a time on a fork. Using a pastry brush or a knife, coat the top and sides of each sponge lightly with the jam. Turn the sponges in the coconut until lightly covered.
8. Remove from the fork and stand the sponge upright. Top each madeleine with a piece of red cherry and set a leaf of green angelica either side of it.

Store in an airtight tin for up to 3 days, or freeze for up to 1 month.

FRENCH MADELEINES

You can see these plain sponge cakes in every French pâtisserie. They are very light and are often shaped like shells. Madeleines must not be over-cooked or they will become crisp. Use either madeleine moulds, bun trays or just paper cases.

Makes 25

Melted vegetable oil
125 g/4 oz self-raising white flour (special sponge flour would be excellent)
125 g/4 oz caster sugar
Finely grated rind of 1 lemon
2 medium eggs, beaten
125 g/4 oz unsalted butter, melted
Icing sugar for dredging

1. Grease the moulds or bun trays, putting a film of melted vegetable oil on the tins with a brush to make sure you get into every corner. Preheat the oven to moderately hot, Gas 5, 375°F, 190°C.
2. Sift the flour into a mixing bowl, then stir in the sugar and grated lemon rind.
3. Using a rigid spatula, add the beaten eggs, a little at a time, then gradually fold in the melted butter.
4. Spoon this mixture into the prepared moulds, trays or cases. Do not over-fill – two-thirds full is about right.
5. Bake for about 12 minutes or until they shrink from the sides of the tin. Allow to firm up in the tins, then turn out onto a wire tray to cool. When the buns are cold, dredge each one with a little icing sugar.

Store in an airtight tin for 4–5 days, or freeze for up to 1 month.

SPONGE FANCIES

This sponge base is made with liquid oil instead of butter or margarine (*see page 10*). The quantity will fill a large Swiss roll tin to give a slab of shallow sponge cake very suitable for cutting into small pieces.

A variety of food colourings adds a delicate touch to these very pretty small cakes which can also be used as petits fours.

Makes about 30

225 g/8 oz self-raising white flour
1 pinch salt
200 g/7 oz caster sugar
150 ml/¼ pint corn oil
150 ml/¼ pint cold water
3 large eggs, separated

TO DECORATE
175 g/6 oz apricot jam or glaze (*see page 248*), **warmed**
450 g/1 lb soft marzipan (*see page 248*)
2–3 tablespoons rum or brandy plus 2 tablespoons water, or 4–6 tablespoons water
675 g/1½ lb icing sugar, sifted
Pink, green and yellow food colouring
Almonds, chopped, toasted and flaked, or a few crushed, crystallized rose or violet petals

1. Line a Swiss roll tin with greaseproof paper. Preheat the oven to moderately hot, Gas 5, 375°F, 190°C.
2. Sift the flour and salt into a large mixing bowl and stir in the sugar.
3. Put the oil and water into a jug and whisk in the egg yolks.
4. Gradually stir this mixture into the dry ingredients, then beat well with a wooden spoon until you have a smooth consistency.
5. In a clean, grease-free bowl, whisk the egg whites until they are very stiff indeed then fold them carefully into the batter mixture.
6. Pour the mixture into the tin and bake for about 30 minutes, or until the sponge is well risen, golden in colour and springy to the touch.
7. Turn out the sponge onto a wire tray and leave to cool for several hours before cutting. Peel off the lining paper.
8. Using a sharp knife or sharp metal cutters, cut the cake into small squares, triangles and circles. Use a pastry brush to brush away any loose crumbs.
9. Warm the apricot jam or glaze by standing the jar in a pan of simmering water. While this is heating up, roll out the marzipan very thinly on a board dusted with caster sugar. Cut out pieces the same size as the tops and sides of the little sponges, gathering up the trimmings and rerolling as necessary.
10. Brush the tops and sides of the cakes with the jam and stick on the marzipan to fit.
11. Place the cakes on wire trays set over a metal tray or a laminated work surface.
12. Make up the glacé icing by beating the rum or brandy and water (or all water if you prefer) into the sifted icing sugar to give a pouring consistency. Add the liquid carefully – the icing should coat the back of your spoon. Divide the icing into three bowls and colour each one with 2–3 drops of food colouring. Make the colours very delicate.
13. Using a large spoon, pour the icing over the sponges, allowing it to coat the cakes completely. Coat 10 sponges in each colour. The extra icing will dribble down and can be scraped up and used again.
14. Allow the sponges to almost set and then decorate the tops with tiny amounts of toasted nuts, or crushed rose or violet petals. Leave for several hours. Use a large palette knife to remove the cakes from the wire trays and serve as they are or in pretty paper cases.

Store for 5–6 days in an airtight tin. Freeze the undecorated sponges for up to 1 month. I find that freezing sometimes makes glacé icing sticky.

RASPBERRY AND CREAM SPONGE DROPS

Makes about 15

3 large eggs
75 g/3 oz caster sugar
75 g/3 oz plain white flour

FOR THE FILLING
300 ml/½ pint double cream
4 tablespoons raspberry jam

1. Line one or two baking trays with nonstick paper. Preheat the oven to moderate, Gas 3, 325°F, 160°C.
2. Using an electric mixer or hand whisk, beat the eggs and caster sugar until extremely thick.
3. Use a nylon sieve to sprinkle about one-third of the flour over the surface of the whipped sugar and eggs and, using a flexible spatula, gently fold it into the mixture. Repeat this twice more, gently folding the flour in each time.
4. Drop dessertspoons of this thick mixture onto the baking trays and bake for about 15–20 minutes. Leave to cool on the trays. The drops may feel crisp but will soften when filled.
5. Whip the cream until thick and spoon into a large piping bag fitted with a 1-cm/½-inch star nozzle. Pipe a thick ring of cream on half the sponge rounds and top with a small teaspoon of jam. Cover with the remaining sponges.

Eat the filled sponges within 2–3 hours. Store the unfilled sponge drops in an airtight tin for 3–4 days, or freeze for up to 1 month.

MINCE PIES

Mince pies are nearly always made with a double crust. The addition of cream cheese is not, of course, traditional but it does make for a juicy pie.

Makes 16

225 g/8 oz shortcrust pastry *(see page 28)*
450 g/1 lb mincemeat
125 g/4 oz cream cheese

1. Lightly grease the bun trays. Preheat the oven to fairly hot, Gas 6, 400°F, 200°C.
2. Roll out the pastry thinly on a lightly floured surface and, using a small fluted cutter measuring 6 cm/2½ inches, stamp out sixteen rounds of pastry (these are for the lids). Reroll the trimmings and, using a 9-cm/3½-inch cutter, cut out sixteen rounds for the bottoms.
3. Ease the pastry bottoms into the bun trays. Place a good teaspoon of mincemeat on the pastry and top with a small teaspoon of cream cheese.
4. Dampen the pastry edges and cover with the lids, pressing the edges down to get a good seal. Set aside in a cold place for 10 minutes then, using a pair of scissors, snip one or two holes in the pastry lids.
5. Bake for about 25–30 minutes. Leave in the tins for 10 minutes then transfer to a wire tray to cool.

Store in an airtight tin for up to 1 week. Freeze, uncooked for best results, for up to 1 month.

VARIATIONS

For really crisp mince pies, try baking the pastry bottoms blind (*see page 26*). You can then store them in an airtight tin in quantity. Keep an eye on them during baking and, using the round end of a knife handle, gently pat down any which rise. Fill the empty pastry cases when needed and heat gently if liked before serving, or top with one of the following toppings instead of a pastry lid:

ICED MINCE PIES

Put the mincemeat in the cooked pastry and cover with a light film of white glacé icing. To make the icing, mix a little water with 125 g/4 oz sifted icing sugar to give a runny consistency. Leave to set and serve cold.

MARZIPAN MINCE PIES

Put the mincemeat in the cooked pastry and cover with grated marzipan. Heat gently until the marzipan softens. (A good use for marzipan which has gone hard.) Serve warm.

COVENTRY GOD CAKES

These oddly named triangular pastries are another way of enclosing mincemeat. I prefer them to mince pies, and eaten warm from the oven they are unbeatable.

Makes 8

225 g/8 oz new flaky pastry *(see page 31)*
125 g/4 oz mincemeat (a dryish mincemeat is better and doesn't run out so easily)
1 small egg white, lightly whisked
Granulated sugar for sprinkling

1. Lightly grease a baking tray.
2. On a lightly floured board, roll out the pastry to a rectangle approximately 41 × 20 cm/16 × 8 inches. Cut lengthways into two and cut each strip into 10-cm/4-inch squares (you now have 8 squares).
3. Bearing in mind that the final shape of each pastry is triangular, put a spoonful of mincemeat in one corner of the square (*see diagram below*). Wet the edges of the pastry on the two sides opposite the mincemeat filling, fold over and press firmly to seal.
4. Put the triangles on the baking tray. Make a small slit in the top of each pastry and set the tray aside to chill for 10–15 minutes.
5. Preheat the oven to hot, Gas 7, 425°F, 220°C, and bake the pastries for 20 minutes. Take the pastries out, brush the tops with the egg white and sprinkle on the granulated sugar. Return to the oven and bake for a further 5 minutes. Cool on a wire tray.

Best eaten very fresh but will keep for 5–6 days in an airtight tin. Reheat before use. Freeze for up to 5–6 weeks.

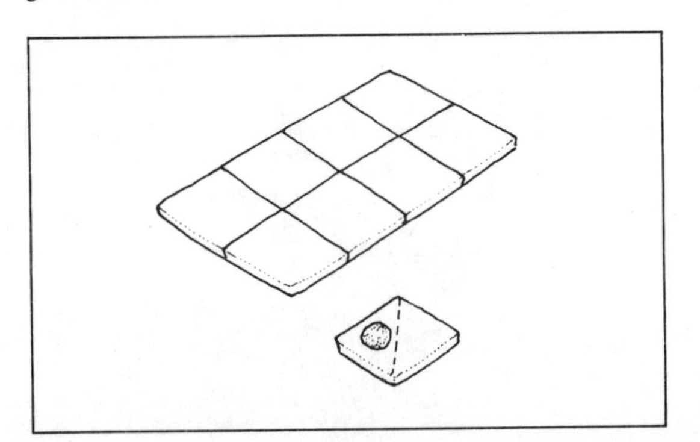

QUEEN CAKES

Proper queen cakes have fallen out of favour because they were baked in little tins of different shapes which were a nuisance to clean, but the modern equivalent in paper cases are not nearly as attractive. However, I often see sets of queen cake tins in antique shops.

The cakes are served bottoms up so that you can see the currants. Butter should be used to get the authentic flavour.

Makes about 18

175 g/6 oz plain white flour, sifted
50 g/2 oz currants, washed and dried
125 g/4 oz butter, softened
125 g/4 oz caster sugar
2 medium eggs, beaten
1 teaspoon baking powder
A little milk, if necessary

1. Grease bun trays or use paper cases set in the bun trays. Preheat the oven to fairly hot, Gas 6, 400°F, 200°C.
2. Stir 1 teaspoon flour into the currants.
3. Cream the butter and sugar together until pale and fluffy.
4. Add the remaining flour and the eggs alternately by degrees, beating well after each addition. Add the baking powder with the last spoonful of flour. Stir in the currants, and a little milk, if necessary, to make a soft consistency.
5. Half fill the tins or paper cases and bake for about 15–20 minutes.
6. Allow to firm up, then ease the cakes out of the tins and cool on wire trays.

Store in an airtight tin for up to 1 week, or freeze for up to 5 weeks.

CREAM HORNS

These always produce gasps of delight. Make sure you use good jam or jelly and fill them at the last minute so that the pastry stays crisp. Although there is a lot of fat in the pastry, I still grease the outside of the cream horn tins.

Makes 10

225 g/8 oz new flaky pastry *(see page 31)*
1 egg white, lightly whisked
2 tablespoons caster sugar
2 tablespoons raspberry jam or redcurrant jelly
225 ml/8 fl oz double cream

1. Lightly grease the outsides of ten cream horn tins.
2. On a lightly floured surface, roll out the pastry to a rectangle 30 × 45 cm/12 × 18 inches. Trim the outer edges and cut the pastry into ten 30-cm/12-inch long strips.
3. Use one strip for each horn tin. Brush the strips with a little water and, starting at the pointed end, wind each strip of pastry round and round the tin, overlapping slightly as it goes (*see below*).

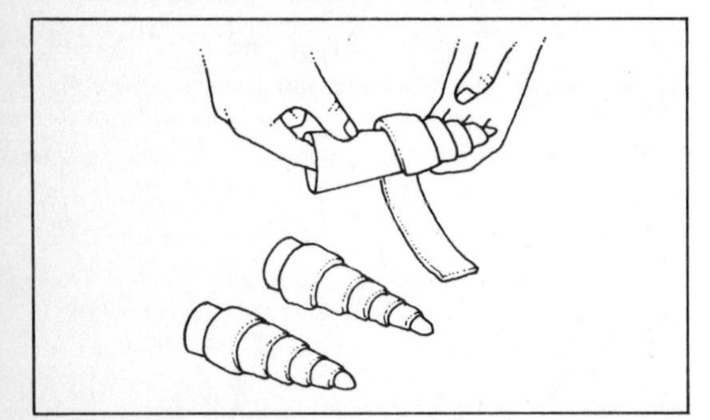

4. Dampen a baking tray by running cold water over it. Shake most of the water off but do not dry. (The steam helps the baking process.) Put the horns, seam side down, on the tray and rest them in the fridge for 15 minutes.
5. Preheat the oven to hot, Gas 7, 425°F, 220°C. Brush the pastry with the egg white and sprinkle with half the caster sugar. Bake for 15–20 minutes. Allow to cool a little and then twist the metal horns out of the pastry cases.
6. When the horns are cold, put a teaspoon of jam or jelly inside each one. Whip the cream with the remaining caster sugar and fill the horns.

Eat on the day they are made. Empty horns keep well in an airtight tin for 1 week, or freeze for up to 2 months.

MAIDS OF HONOUR

There seems to be a dispute about these charmingly named cakes or tartlets. The old recipes were for tarts filled with curd, made from fresh milk and rennet, mixed with almonds, butter, lemon, egg yolks and ground cinnamon. Nowadays, they are made in the following way. They are also sometimes iced and decorated with a cherry.

Makes 14

125 g/4 oz shortcrust pastry *(see page 28)*
25 g/1 oz caster sugar
25 g/1 oz block margarine, softened
50 g/2 oz self-raising white flour, sifted
1 small egg, beaten with a little milk
2 tablespoons raspberry jam

1. Grease fourteen small patty tins. Preheat the oven to hot, Gas 7, 425°F, 220°C.
2. On a lightly floured board, roll out the pastry very thinly and cut out rounds 7.5 cm/3 inches across. Gather up the trimmings, reroll and cut until you have fourteen rounds.
3. Ease the pastry rounds into the tins.
4. In a warm bowl, cream the caster sugar and margarine until pale and fluffy.
5. Stir in the flour and beaten egg and milk mixture alternately. The mixture should be soft so add a minute amount of extra milk if needed.
6. Put a little jam into each pastry case and a good teaspoon of sponge mixture on top. Ease the sponge mixture over the jam to completely seal it. Bake for about 20 minutes. Leave in the tins for about 5 minutes then cool on a wire tray.

Store in an airtight tin for up to 4 days, or freeze for 1 month.

FRUIT BOATS

There is nothing so attractive as fresh fruit in elegant pastry boats gleaming under a bright glaze. The pastry must be a rich one. There must be real confectioner's custard underneath, too. They must also be made on the day they are needed – a daunting set of musts for the home baker, but well worth the effort for a special meal.

Makes 8

125 g/4 oz rich sweet shortcrust pastry *(see page 28)*

FOR THE CONFECTIONER'S CUSTARD (CRÈME PÂTISSIÈRE)
300 ml/½ pint milk
1 vanilla pod
1 medium egg and 1 egg yolk
50 g/2 oz caster sugar
25 g/1 oz plain flour, sifted

TO FILL
450 g/1 lb mixed fruits, fresh or canned *(see below)*

TO GLAZE
4 tablespoons apricot glaze *(see page 248)*
4 tablespoons redcurrant jelly

1. Grease 10-cm/4-inch boat-shaped tins. Preheat the oven to moderately hot, Gas 5, 375°F, 190°C.
2. Roll out the pastry on a lightly floured board and line the tins. Prick the pastry all over. Rest the boats for 10 minutes.
3. Bake the pastry boats for about 12 minutes, or until lightly golden in colour. Take the pastries out of the tins and cool on wire trays.
4. To make the confectioner's custard, heat the milk with the vanilla pod in it, in a small pan. Bring almost to the boil then remove from the heat and allow to infuse for about 20 minutes. Strain the milk through a sieve and into a clean pan. Wash and dry the vanilla pod for re-use.
5. Using a wire whisk, whip together the egg, egg yolk and sugar until pale and creamy. Whisk in the flour until smooth. Reheat the milk again to just below boiling point and pour it onto the egg mixture. Stir well and return the custard to the same pan.
6. Place the pan over a gentle heat, stirring all the time. Bring the custard to the boil, whisking vigorously if any lumps form. Cook for 2–3 minutes, then take off the heat and set the custard aside to cool before using.
7. To assemble the boats, spread a little of the confectioner's custard in the bottom of each boat. Top with whatever fruit you have chosen. (Mixed fruit boats also look attractive.)
8. Put the apricot glaze and redcurrant jelly into two separate heatproof bowls. Set each bowl in a pan of gently simmering water and stir frequently until they are melted. Use apricot for yellow and orange fruits and redcurrant jelly for all the red and purple fruits. Brush over the fruit and allow to set.

Eat on the day they are made. Empty cases will store in an airtight tin for up to 7 days, or freeze for up to 2 months.

SUGGESTED FRUIT

FRESH FRUIT

Grapes – green and black – de-seed after cutting in two

Strawberries – slice down from top in 3–4 slices

Raspberries – leave whole

Cherries – must be very ripe and sweet. Remove stones

Blackcurrants
Redcurrants
Gooseberries
Apricots
Peaches
– Poach in syrup (75 g/3 oz sugar and 300 ml/½ pint water) until soft. Drain very thoroughly

CANNED FRUIT

Use any of the following. Drain them well.

Mandarin oranges
Peaches
Pineapple pieces
Apricots

MACAROONS

Makes 12

175 g/6 oz shortcrust pastry *(see page 28)*
2 tablespoons good jam (I prefer raspberry)
75 g/3 oz ground almonds
50 g/2 oz caster sugar
1–2 drops almond essence
1 × No. 7 egg, beaten

1. Lightly grease a 12-section bun tray. Preheat the oven to hot, Gas 7, 425°F, 220°C.
2. Roll out the shortcrust pastry thinly on a lightly floured board. Using a fluted biscuit cutter, stamp out twelve rounds and line the sections of the tin.
3. Spoon a very small teaspoon of jam into each pastry case.
4. Put the ground almonds, sugar and almond essence into a mixing bowl and add just enough egg to give a wet (not runny) paste – you may not need all the egg.
5. Spoon this almond mixture on top of the jam and spread it to completely seal the jam.
6. Roll out the pastry trimmings, cut very thin strips of pastry and cover each tartlet with a cross.
7. Bake the tartlets for about 20 minutes. Cool on a wire tray.

Store in an airtight tin and eat within 4–5 days, or freeze for up to 2 months.

CHOUX RINGS

I have chosen to make these choux pastry cakes in rings. They look much nicer on the plate than the éclair finger shapes, if you are having them as a dessert. A delicious way to serve them is surrounded with a purée of fresh strawberries – just very lightly sweetened strawberries put through a liquidizer or food processor. Frozen strawberries are perfect for this treatment.

Makes 8

65 g/2½ oz choux pastry *(see page 31)*
150 g/5 oz double cream, whipped
1 teaspoon icing sugar
16 fat ripe strawberries (or any other fruit)
Icing sugar for dredging

1. Line two baking trays with nonstick paper and draw circles on the paper about 7.5 cm/3 inches across. Preheat the oven to hot, Gas 7, 425°F, 220°C.
2. Put the choux pastry into a piping bag fitted with a plain 1-cm/½-inch nozzle, and pipe the choux pastry round the circles, making a neat join.
3. Bake for 15 minutes then reduce the heat to moderately hot, Gas 5, 375°F, 190°C, and bake for a further 25 minutes or until crisp. Allow to cool slightly then slice the rings across very carefully in two and put them back in the oven to dry off.
4. To assemble the rings, fill with the whipped double cream, sweetened with the teaspoon of icing sugar.
5. Allow two fat strawberries for each ring and cut them in quarters. Remove the top of the choux ring and arrange the strawberry quarters around the bottom half. Replace the tops and dredge heavily with icing sugar.

Store the unfilled pastry rings in an airtight tin for up to 7 days, or freeze for up to 2 months. Eat the filled rings on the day they are assembled. The filled rings will not freeze because of the strawberries.

BROWN SUGAR MERINGUES

Use the new fine grain brown sugar for this recipe and not the soft kind. Don't use new-laid eggs.

Makes approximately 16

2 large egg whites
1 pinch cream of tartar
1 pinch salt
125 g/4 oz brown fine grain sugar

FOR THE FILLING
125 g/4 oz plain chocolate, broken into small pieces
50 ml/2 fl oz water
300 ml/½ pint double cream

1. Line baking trays with nonstick paper.
2. Using an electric mixer or hand whisk, whip the egg whites in a clean grease-free bowl. When frothy, add the cream of tartar and the salt and whip at high speed until the whites are very firm indeed. You should be able to turn the bowl upside down and the egg white stay put.
3. Lower the speed to add 2 tablespoons of sugar then whip at high speed again. Continue this way until all the sugar is used up, whipping thoroughly between each addition. The mixture should be thick like marshmallow.
4. Fill a large piping bag fitted with a 1-cm/½-inch star nozzle and pipe the meringues in spirals about 4 cm/1½ inches across onto the baking trays.
5. Bake the meringues in a very low oven, Gas ¼, 225°F, 110°C, for about 3 hours, or until they are dry and crisp. Cool on wire trays.
6. To fill the meringues, put the chocolate and water into a small pan and stir gently over low heat until melted. Remove from the heat and leave to cool.
7. In a clean bowl, whip the cream and gradually add the cooled chocolate mixture. Whip until thick.
8. Sandwich the meringues together with a generous spoonful of chocolate cream.

Store the unfilled meringues in an airtight tin for up to 3 weeks. I also find they store well in a plastic bag which is then tightly fastened with a twist tie. Eat the filled meringues on the day they are assembled. Not suitable for freezing.

WHITE MERINGUES

Vanilla sugar adds a delicate flavour to these meringue fingers. Use eggs which are one week old – they give a much better volume.

Makes approximately 24

2 large egg whites
1 pinch cream of tartar
1 pinch salt
125 g/4 oz vanilla sugar *(see page 17)*, **or caster sugar**

1. Line two baking trays with nonstick paper.
2. Using an electric mixer or electric hand whisk, whisk the egg whites in a large, grease-free mixing bowl until frothy. Add the cream of tartar and salt and continue to whip until the whites are very stiff.
3. Lower the speed and add 2 tablespoons of sugar. Turn up the speed again and beat hard. Continue to add sugar until you have a thick, firm marshmallow mixture.
4. Either spoon the meringue out into rough heaps on the baking trays, or spoon the mixture into a large piping bag fitted with a 1-cm/½-inch star nozzle and pipe 10-cm/4-inch long fingers of meringue onto the baking trays. Keep them as straight as possible.
5. Bake in a very low oven, Gas ¼, 225°F, 110°C, for 3 hours. Cool on a wire tray.

Store for up to 3 weeks in an airtight tin or plastic bag, fastened very tightly. Do not leave lying on an open plate for hours – they will go sticky. Not suitable for freezing.

NAPOLEON HATS

Halfway between a biscuit and a cake, these aptly named hats are fun to make.

Makes 8

FOR THE BISCUITS
50 g/2 oz butter, softened
50 g/2 oz caster sugar
125 g/4 oz plain white flour, sifted
1 pinch baking powder
½ egg, or 1 × No. 7 egg, beaten

FOR THE ALMOND FILLING
50 g/2 oz icing sugar, sifted
25 g/1 oz ground almonds
A little beaten egg

FOR THE ICING
50 g/2 oz icing sugar, sifted
2 teaspoons water

1. Grease a baking tray. Preheat the oven to moderate, Gas 4, 350°F, 180°C.
2. To make the biscuits, cream the butter and sugar together until pale and fluffy. Mix in the flour, baking powder and enough egg to make a stiff dough.
3. Roll out the dough very thinly on a lightly floured surface and stamp out 7.5-cm/3-inch rounds. Gather up the trimmings, reroll and cut until you have eight rounds.
4. To make the almond filling, mix together the icing sugar, almonds and a minute quantity of beaten egg to give a soft paste. Roll into eight balls and put one on each round of biscuit dough (*a*).
5. Moisten the dough at each side of the circle and nip together to form a hat shape. Put the hats on the baking tray.

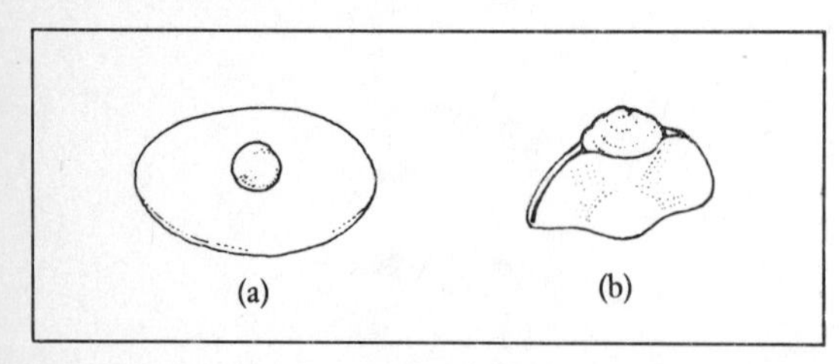

6. Bake for about 20 minutes, then cool on a wire tray.
7. To finish the cakes, mix the icing sugar with enough water to make a smooth icing and coat the top of the almond paste (*b*).

Eat fresh or store in an airtight tin for 2–3 days. Do not freeze.

STRAWBERRY SHORTCAKES

The combination of shortbread biscuit, strawberries and cream makes a delicious cake, and even a very good party dessert.

Makes 9

175 g/6 oz plain white flour, sifted
125 g/4 oz unsalted butter, softened
50 g/2 oz caster sugar
Extra caster sugar for rolling
150 ml/5 fl oz double cream
225 g/8 oz ripe strawberries, quartered
Icing sugar for dredging

1. Line two baking trays with nonstick paper. Preheat the oven to cool, Gas 2, 300°F, 150°C.
2. Warm the mixing bowl of an electric mixing machine, put the flour, butter and sugar in the bowl and the beater in the slot. Beat slowly at first, then a little faster until all the ingredients come together in a soft malleable paste. (If you have no mixing machine, rub the butter into the flour and, still using your hands, work all the ingredients together.)
3. Dust the work surface with caster sugar and roll out the shortcake mixture. Using a 7.5-cm/3-inch cutter, stamp out nine rounds. Reroll the trimmings and, using a 5-cm/2-inch cutter, stamp out nine smaller rounds.
4. Lay the rounds on the baking trays, and chill for 10 minutes then bake for about 30 minutes.
5. To assemble the cakes, whip the double cream with a little icing sugar and put it into a piping bag fitted with a medium-sized star nozzle.
6. Pipe a circle of cream round each large biscuit. Lay the quartered strawberries round the edge, pointed ends towards the centre.
7. Lay the smaller shortbread biscuits on a tray and dredge them with icing sugar. Top each cake with a smaller biscuit to show off the cream and the strawberries.

Eat on the day they are made. The dry biscuits store well in an airtight tin for 10–12 days, or freeze for up to 2 months.

VARIATION

To serve as a pudding, liquidize 225 g/8 oz fresh or frozen strawberries and sweeten with 25 g/1 oz caster sugar. Serve this as a sauce with the assembled shortcakes.

Keeps for 2–4 days in the fridge, or freeze for up to 1 month.

CHOCOLATE BOXES

These are very impressive special occasion cakes made with a base of Genoese sponge. Make your own chocolate squares or buy them from a specialist chocolate shop.

Makes about 9

FOR THE SPONGE
2 medium eggs
65 g/2½ oz caster sugar
50 g/2 oz plain flour, sifted
25 g/1 oz butter, melted

FOR THE CHOCOLATE SQUARES
150 g/5 oz plain chocolate, broken into small pieces

FOR THE CHOCOLATE BUTTER CREAM
50 g/2 oz butter, softened
125 g/4 oz icing sugar, sifted
2 tablespoons cocoa powder, sifted
1 tablespoon hot water
1–2 tablespoons cream (double or single), if necessary

1. Grease and base line an 18-cm/7-inch square shallow tin. Preheat the oven to moderate, Gas 4, 350°F, 180°C.
2. First, make the sponge. Put the eggs and sugar into a medium-sized mixing bowl and, using an electric hand whisk, whip until very thick.
3. Fold the flour and melted butter alternately into the mixture. Pour into the tin.
4. Bake for about 35 minutes when the sponge should be springy and just beginning to shrink from the sides of the tin. Cool on a wire tray. When cooled, cut nine pieces each about 4 cm/1½ inches square. (There will be some sponge left over – use in a trifle or to make Sponge Fancies, *see page 89*.)
5. To make the chocolate squares, put the chocolate into a small heatproof bowl set over a pan of gently simmering water and stir until melted.
6. Pin a sheet of greaseproof paper on a board and mark out a square measuring 30 × 30 cm/12 × 12 inches. Pour the melted chocolate inside the square and, using a palette knife, carefully spread the chocolate to fit the square. A gentle bang of the board, by lifting it up a few inches and dropping it, often gives a smooth result.
7. Allow the chocolate to set, but not too hard, then trim the edges and mark out the chocolate into 36 × 4-cm/1½-inch squares.
8. To make the butter cream, cream together the butter and icing sugar. In another bowl, blend the cocoa powder with the hot water and allow to cool. Then beat it into the butter and sugar mixture. Add the cream to this mixture only if necessary – the texture of the butter cream should be fairly firm.
9. To assemble the boxes, spread a layer of chocolate butter cream over the four sides of each piece of sponge and stick a chocolate square on each side. Handle the chocolate as little as possible.
10. To finish off the top of each box, either put the butter cream in a piping bag fitted with a small star nozzle and pipe 3 rows of four stars, or spoon a little butter cream on the top of each box and top with a piece of fruit or toasted nuts.

Keep fairly well in an airtight tin for 2–3 days. Freeze if you have to, but use within 2 weeks.

CHOCOLATE CUP CAKES

An exotic cake – a chocolate cup holding a liqueur-flavoured mixture, topped with cream and chocolate mousse.

Makes 6

225 g/8 oz plain chocolate, broken into small pieces
5 sponge fingers *(see page 73)*, **or boudoir biscuits**
5–6 teaspoons brandy or cherry brandy
1 × 75-g/3-oz carton chocolate mousse
3 tablespoons double cream

1. Have ready a small sheet of nonstick paper. Put the chocolate into a small heatproof bowl set over a pan of simmering water and stir until melted. Use aluminium foil cases about 7.5 cm/3 inches across and 5 cm/2 inches deep. Put a teaspoon of melted chocolate in the bottom of each case and, using an artist's brush, work the chocolate across the bottom and up the sides. Turn upside down onto the nonstick paper to dry.
2. Give each case a second coating of chocolate. Leave to set for 30 minutes, then slip the foil cases away and leave the chocolate cups in a cool place.
3. In a small bowl, break up the sponge fingers or boudoir biscuits into very small pieces and pour in the brandy or cherry brandy. Mix until the biscuits are soft but not liquid. Put a good teaspoon of this mixture in the bottom of each chocolate cup and spoon a layer of chocolate mousse on top of each.
4. Whip the double cream with a wire whisk and spoon a little on each cup.

Eat on the day they are made. The empty chocolate cups will keep for 3–4 days in an airtight tin.

GINGER DROPS

These light buns are halfway to being biscuits.

Makes 20

125 g/4 oz block margarine, softened
125 g/4 oz caster sugar
½ large beaten egg
125 g/4 oz self-raising white or brown flour
2 teaspoons ground ginger

1. Line two baking trays with nonstick paper. Preheat the oven to slow, Gas 1, 275°F, 140°C.
2. In a medium-sized mixing bowl, cream the margarine and the sugar together until pale and fluffy, then beat in the egg.
3. Sift in the flour and ginger and mix to a stiffish dough. Add a minute amount of extra egg if the dough is too stiff.
4. Slightly dampen your hands and roll out the mixture into balls about the size of a walnut. Set the balls well apart on the baking trays and press down on each with the back of a fork.
5. Bake for about 40 minutes, or until risen and golden, then cool on a wire tray.

Store in an airtight tin for 1 week, or freeze for up to 3 months.

COCONUT TOWERS

Still a very popular sweetie-cake. I have tried shaping them in containers such as egg cups and other tins but they never come out very easily.

Makes 14

5 tablespoons condensed milk
225 g/8 oz coarse desiccated coconut (plus a little extra)
1 teaspoon vanilla essence

1. Grease a baking tray. Preheat the oven to moderate, Gas 3, 325°F, 160°C.
2. Place the ingredients in a mixing bowl and mix together, adding a little more coconut if the mixture looks sticky.
3. Using a spoon, drop small heaps of the mixture onto the baking tray and shape each into a small tower with your fingers.
4. Bake for 10 minutes, or until the coconut is golden brown on top.

Will keep fairly well in an airtight tin for 4–5 days, or freeze for up to 2 months.

FUNNY CHEESEBURGERS

Based on Rice Krispies, these are fun cakes for a child's party. Make up the burgers on the day they are needed.

Makes 6

25 g/1 oz caster sugar
25 g/1 oz golden syrup (about 1 tablespoon)
50 g/2 oz block margarine
50 g/2 oz Rice Krispies
Extra caster sugar

FOR THE FILLING
175 g/6 oz soft marzipan *(see page 248)*
2 tablespoons red jam or jelly
4 green glacé cherries, halved
2 tablespoons sesame seeds

1. In a pan, melt the sugar, syrup and margarine over medium heat until almost boiling. Take the pan off the heat and stir in the Rice Krispies.
2. Line twelve round-bottomed patty tins with foil and press the Rice Krispie mixture in firmly. Flatten the tops and leave to set for about 20 minutes.
3. Dust the working surface with a little caster sugar and roll out the marzipan very thinly. Cut it into six 5-cm/2-inch squares.
4. Ease the buns out of the tins. Place a square of marzipan on six of them so that it hangs over one edge and top with a spoonful of jam or jelly and a green cherry. Cover each with the remaining buns and sprinkle with sesame seeds.

Eat on the day they are made, or freeze for up to 1 month.

AMERICAN CHOCOLATE BROWNIES

All brownie recipes which I have tried sink a little in the middle but the chewy texture is very pleasant.

Will cut into 9 squares

50 g/2 oz plain chocolate, broken into pieces
125 g/4 oz plain white flour
1 small teaspoon baking powder
75 g/3 oz block margarine, softened
50 g/2 oz caster sugar
1 medium egg, beaten
50 g/2 oz walnuts, chopped
A little milk, if necessary

1. Grease and base line an 18-cm/7-inch square cake tin. Preheat the oven to moderate, Gas 4, 350°F, 180°C.
2. Put the chocolate into a small heatproof bowl set over a pan of simmering water. Stir gently until melted then remove from the heat.
3. Sift the flour and baking powder into a mixing bowl.
4. In another bowl, cream the margarine and sugar until soft and fluffy then beat in the egg, a little at a time. Stir in the melted chocolate.
5. Lightly fold in the flour mixture and the walnuts and add enough milk to get a soft dropping consistency.
6. Pour into the tin and smooth over a little, but make a slight hollow in the centre.
7. Bake for about 35 minutes until the cake is beginning to shrink from the sides of the tin. Cool a little, then cut into squares while the cake is still warm. Leave in the tin to cool then turn out onto a wire tray and peel off the lining paper.

Store in an airtight tin for about 4 days, or freeze for up to 3 months.

FLY CEMETERY

This simple fruit slice used to be called fly cake. The addition of the custard is my idea as it holds the currants in place.

Will cut into 9 squares

225 g/8 oz shortcrust pastry *(see page 28)*
125 g/4 oz currants, washed and dried
2 fat pinches ground cinnamon
25 g/1 oz granulated sugar
4–5 tablespoons fairly thick cooked custard (the ordinary packet variety)
25 g/1 oz butter, cut into small pieces
A little milk
Extra sugar for sprinkling

1. Divide the pastry in two. Roll out one half on a lightly floured surface to fit a shallow, greased 18 × 18-cm/7 × 7-inch tin. Roll it so that the pastry comes up the sides slightly. Preheat the oven to hot, Gas 8, 450°F, 230°C.
2. Put the currants, cinnamon and sugar into a mixing bowl with enough custard to make a sticky mixture and stir well.
3. Spread this mixture evenly in the tin on top of the pastry and dot with the butter.
4. Roll out the remaining pastry to fit the square exactly. Moisten the joining edges, put the top on and seal the edges. Use a fork to mark and seal the edges of the pastry all round.
5. Score the surface of the pastry very lightly and make a couple of steam holes in the top. Brush with the milk and sprinkle with sugar.
6. Bake for 20–25 minutes. Cool in the tin then transfer to a wire tray. Cut into nine squares when cold.

Store in an airtight tin for up to 5 days. Freezes fairly well for up to 2 months. The pastry goes a bit soft but of course it could be re-heated.

NO-BAKE CAKES

Many of the no-bake cakes are based on crushed biscuits. If you are using a food processor to make the biscuit crumbs, try to stop the machine before the crumbs are reduced to powder because I think the paste-like quality of some no-bake cakes is because the crumbs were far too fine. In fact, I rather like to see the uneven bits of biscuit in the mixture, but you can only achieve this by crushing the biscuits with a rolling pin. I do mine in a roasting tin; the depth of the tin keeps the crumbs from scattering and I can shake the tin and the big pieces of biscuit come to the surface. I also have a rolling pin which fits into my roasting tin.

No-bake cakes are very sweet and since most of the ingredients, like chocolate, biscuits and dried fruit, are sweet too it is often possible to cut down the quantity of actual sugar added. Cut them into thin pieces – much smaller than you would cut a cake.

DATE SLICES

Will cut into 24 bars

125 g/4 oz block margarine
50 g/2 oz light soft brown sugar
75 g/3 oz dates, finely chopped
75 g/3 oz Rice Krispies
125 g/4 oz plain chocolate, broken into small pieces

1. Grease and base line a Swiss roll tin measuring 28 × 18 cm/11 × 7 inches.
2. Put the margarine, sugar and dates into a roomy pan and heat gently until soft. Take the pan off the heat.
3. Stir in the Rice Krispies and mix well to distribute the dates.
4. Turn the mixture out into the tin and press down evenly.
5. Put the chocolate into a small heatproof bowl set over a pan of simmering water and stir until melted. Quickly spread it over the Rice Krispie mixture and leave to set. When cold, turn out and slice with a sharp knife.

Will keep well in an airtight tin for 4–5 days. Do not freeze.

GINGER BISCUIT SLICE

This is an old favourite. Serve as a cake or as a dessert. Start the day before.

Will cut into 10 slices

300 ml/½ pint double cream
1 small piece of stem ginger, finely chopped
Stem ginger syrup
225 g/8 oz ginger biscuits (not too small)

1. The day before the slice is needed, put half the cream into a bowl with a little of the ginger syrup and whip until firm.
2. Use this cream to sandwich together the ginger biscuits in a long roll. Put the roll on a serving plate and leave it covered in the fridge overnight.
3. Next day, whip the remaining cream and smooth it all over the ginger roll. Mark a bark pattern on the top, and sprinkle on the finely chopped ginger. Chill.
4. To serve, cut in thin diagonal slices, using a very sharp knife, with extra pouring cream, if liked.

Best eaten the day it is made but will keep fairly well in the fridge for 2 days. Not suitable for freezing.

MARS BAR CRUNCHIES

Will cut into 24 bars

75 g/3 oz butter or block margarine
3 Mars bars (normal size), thinly sliced
3 large tea cups of Rice Krispies
125 g/4 oz chocolate flavour cake covering

1. Grease and base line a Swiss roll tin measuring about 28 × 18 cm/11 × 7 inches.
2. In a roomy, heavy-based pan, gently melt the butter or margarine. Add the Mars bar pieces and stir until no lumps are left.
3. Take the pan off the heat and stir in the Rice Krispies, adding more if the mixture will take it.
4. Spread the mixture in the tin, pressing down evenly with the flat of a knife.
5. Melt the cake covering in a heatproof bowl set over a pan of simmering water. Quickly spread over the Rice Krispie mixture and leave to set. Cut into bars when cold.

Will keep for 4–5 days in an airtight tin. Do not freeze – the Rice Krispies go soft on thawing.

CHOCOLATE CAKE

Dates and cherries add to the calories in this biscuit-based cake.

Will cut into about 24 pieces

225 g/8 oz butter or block margarine
75 g/3 oz light soft brown sugar
3 tablespoons golden syrup
5 tablespoons cocoa powder (not drinking chocolate)
325 g/12 oz digestive biscuits
50 g/2 oz stoned dates, finely chopped
50 g/2 oz glacé cherries, finely chopped
25 g/1 oz chopped walnuts
225 g/8 oz plain chocolate, broken into small pieces

1. Grease and base line a Swiss roll tin measuring 30 × 20 cm/12 × 8 inches.
2. In a roomy, heavy-based pan, melt the butter or margarine, sugar and syrup. Sift the cocoa powder into the pan and stir until smooth.
3. Crush the digestive biscuits in a strong plastic bag with a rolling pin. (You could crush them in a food processor but stop before the biscuits are reduced to powder.)
4. Stir the biscuits, dates, cherries and walnuts into the butter mixture and mix well so that they are well coated. Turn into the Swiss roll tin, flatten with a palette knife and leave to set.
5. Put the chocolate into a heatproof bowl set over a pan of simmering water and stir until melted. Spread the chocolate over the biscuit mixture and leave in the fridge to set. Turn out and cut with a sharp knife. Keep in a tin in the fridge to prevent it from going sticky.

Will keep in good condition in the fridge for 1 week, or freeze for up to 4–5 weeks.

NUTTY SLACK

This biscuit-based recipe dates from the days when biscuits were sold, not in packets, but from rows of tin boxes with lids. You could always buy broken biscuits fairly cheaply. I wonder if coal merchants still sell nutty slack!

Will cut into 24 small pieces

75 g/3 oz block margarine
2 tablespoons golden syrup
1 tablespoon cocoa powder, sifted
1 tablespoon caster sugar
225 g/8 oz broken biscuits (marie or digestive biscuits are suitable)
40 g/1½ oz walnuts, chopped
75 g/3 oz plain chocolate, broken into small pieces

1. Generously grease then base line a Swiss roll tin measuring 28 × 18 cm/11 × 7 inches.
2. Put the margarine, syrup, cocoa powder and sugar into a roomy, heavy-based pan and melt gently.
3. Meanwhile, crush the biscuits in a strong plastic bag with a rolling pin. Do not be too efficient and reduce them to a powder.
4. Take the pan off the heat, and stir in the biscuits and the nuts. Stir well so that the crumbs are well coated. Turn the mixture into the tin, smooth down and level.
5. Put the chocolate into a small heatproof bowl set over a pan of simmering water and stir until melted. Quickly spread the chocolate over the mixture in the tin and leave to set. When it is cold, cut the slice into twenty-four pieces with a sharp knife.

Store in an airtight tin for 4–5 days, or freeze for up to 2 months.

PEANUT CRUNCH

Crunchy peanut butter is the basis of this no-bake biscuit slice.

Will cut into 12 small bars

50 g/2 oz butter
2 tablespoons golden syrup
25 g/1 oz caster sugar
4 tablespoons crunchy peanut butter
175 g/6 oz digestive biscuits
50 g/2 oz plain chocolate, broken into small pieces

1. Grease and base line a flat tin measuring about 18 × 18 cm/7 × 7 inches.
2. In a roomy pan, melt the butter, syrup, sugar and peanut butter.
3. Meanwhile, crush the digestive biscuits in a strong plastic bag with a rolling pin. Do not be too efficient and reduce them to a powder.
4. Take the pan off the heat and stir in the digestive biscuits. If the mixture looks wet, add more crushed biscuits. Spread the biscuit mixture in the tin, smooth down and level.
5. Put the chocolate into a small heatproof bowl set over a pan of simmering water and stir until melted. Spread over the biscuit mixture and leave to set. Cut with a sharp knife into twelve small bars.

Store in an airtight tin for up to 1 week. Do not freeze.

MARZIPAN FANCIES

These marzipan log cakes should be cut small. They also make good sweets but of course should be cut even smaller, and the rum omitted if making for children.

Will cut into about 15 small or 30 very small logs

225 g/8 oz soft plain cake crumbs
2 teaspoons redcurrant jelly or red jam
2–3 teaspoons rum
175 g/6 oz soft marzipan *(see page 248)*

1. Mix the cake crumbs with the jelly or jam and rum to a soft, but not wet, consistency. Use more crumbs or plain white flour to roll the mixture into a long sausage about as thick as a cigar. Divide the sausage into three pieces.
2. Roll out the marzipan into an oblong, 9 mm/⅜ inch thick. Lay one piece of rum-flavoured sausage along the length of the strip about 4 cm/1½ inches in from the edge. Roll the marzipan over the 'sausage', moisten one long edge where it joins on the other side and enclose the marzipan tightly. Cut off the roll formed and repeat with the other two pieces of 'sausage'.
3. Set the rolls aside in a cool place to firm up, then cut each into log shapes, using slanting cuts. Serve in small paper cases.

Store in an airtight tin for about 4–5 days, or freeze for up to 1 month.

CRUNCHY BAKING

Home-made biscuits are cheap and easy to make but they do need a lot of oven space. However, with a little balancing, you can rig up an extra shelf when needed. Just position a tiny jar at each of the four corners of a large baking tray and balance another baking tray on top. I do this regularly so I know it works.

Many recipes which require the dough to be rolled out and cut into shapes are easy to adapt to the fridge method of chilling the dough. Either shape the dough into a fat sausage shape or press into a tin to achieve a block. The hardened dough is then sliced very finely into the required thickness. The biscuits won't have a perfect shape but it does save time.

To take the guesswork out of baking biscuits, I nearly always use nonstick paper to line my trays. With a careful wipe, the paper can be used two or three times.

Store your biscuits in airtight tins as soon as they are cold. I am not convinced that plastic storage boxes are quite as good as my old tins. If the tin lid is not a tight fit, use a pad of kitchen paper over the rim before the lid goes on. If you have left your biscuits on a plate and they have softened, five minutes in a hot oven will revive them.

I do not think there is much to be gained by freezing cooked biscuits. A lot of them would be soft on thawing. I do, however, think that freezing the uncooked dough is a good idea. Double the amount you are making and put one quantity of dough in the freezer for future use.

AYRSHIRE OAT CAKES

Real oat cakes are always cut in 'farls' – the dough is rolled into circles of about 15 cm/6 inches diameter and each circle is cut into three even-sized triangles.

Serve them with good butter and cheese and a stick of crisp celery for an excellent light lunch.

Makes about 15

225 g/8 oz medium oatmeal
2 fat pinches salt
2 fat pinches bicarbonate of soda
2 tablespoons melted lard or fat (bacon fat if you have it)
Warm water to mix
Extra oatmeal for rolling

1. Add the dry ingredients to the melted lard or fat in a mixing bowl and mix to a softish dough with warm water.
2. Sprinkle oatmeal on a board and roll out the dough very thinly into rounds measuring 15 cm/6 inches across. Cut each round into three triangles. Gather up the trimmings, reroll and cut.
3. Transfer the oat cakes to a hot girdle or a heavy frying pan on the hob. I use a fish slice to do this.
4. Bake the oat cakes until the edges start to curl up. Handle them carefully as they are very fragile. Crisp the other side under a hot grill. Try to avoid browning the oat cakes as the flavour will be altered. Cool on wire trays.

Store in an airtight tin.

BRAN BISCUITS

A very good biscuit for cheese. Reduce the bran to crumbs in a food processor or by putting it into a thick polythene bag and crushing it with a rolling pin.

Makes about 24

125 g/4 oz plain wholewheat flour
1 teaspoon baking powder
50 g/2 oz bran breakfast cereal
75 g/3 oz caster sugar
125 g/4 oz butter or block margarine, cut into pieces
4 drops vanilla essence
Milk to mix

1. Line baking trays with nonstick paper. Preheat the oven to moderately hot, Gas 5, 375°F, 190°C.
2. Sift the flour into a mixing bowl, adding any residue of bran left in the sieve, and add all the dry ingredients. Rub in the butter or margarine.
3. Stir in the vanilla essence and enough milk to make a stiffish dough. Knead lightly in the bowl.
4. Turn out the dough on a lightly floured board and roll out as thinly as possible. Using a biscuit cutter, stamp out rounds about 5 cm/2 inches across, or cut round a small plate to give circles of 15–18 cm/6–7 inches across, then cut into wedges. Gather up the trimmings, reroll and cut.
5. Slide the rounds onto the trays and bake for about 15 minutes, or until the biscuits are a darker shade of brown all over. Cool on wire trays.

Store in airtight tins.

SAVOURY CELERY BISCUITS

Celery seeds give these biscuits their distinctive flavour. They are rather hard seeds so bruise them in a mortar and pestle, or crush them with the end of your rolling pin in a strong bowl. These biscuits are good with cheese.

Makes about 35

225 g/8 oz plain white or wholewheat flour
50 g/2 oz butter, cut into pieces
Salt and pepper
2 teaspoons celery seed, crushed
Single cream or milk to mix

1. Line two or three baking trays with nonstick paper. Preheat the oven to fairly hot, Gas 6, 400°F, 200°C.
2. Sift the flour into a mixing bowl, adding any residue of bran left in the sieve if using wholewheat flour, and rub in the butter. Alternatively, process the ingredients in a food processor and return the mixture to a mixing bowl.
3. Add the salt and pepper and the celery seeds and mix with enough cream or milk to make a stiffish dough.
4. Roll out the dough very thinly on a floured board to about 3 mm/⅛ inch thick and stamp out 5-cm/2-inch rounds. Gather up the trimmings, reroll and cut.
5. Lay the rounds on the trays and bake for about 15 minutes, or until the biscuits are lightly browned. Cool the biscuits on wire trays.

Store in airtight tins.

CHEESE STRAWS

This charming name is given to biscuits cut like thickish matchsticks. It is almost a tradition to serve them in groups of three or four threaded through rings of the same mixture. If you have small fancy biscuit cutters you can make quite a boxful in no time at all. Otherwise, just cut the mixture into 2½-cm/1-inch squares.

Makes about 325 g/12 oz

175 g/6 oz plain white or wholewheat flour
¼ teaspoon mustard powder
¼ teaspoon salt
1 fat pinch cayenne pepper
75 g/3 oz block margarine, cut into pieces
75 g/3 oz finely grated and dried cheese* (Parmesan and Cheddar have a good strong flavour)
1 medium egg yolk
4 teaspoons water
Paprika pepper (optional)

* *Some cheese is very waxy and will dry out slightly if spread on kitchen paper for 1–2 hours before it is needed.*

1. Line two baking trays with nonstick paper. Preheat the oven to fairly hot, Gas 6, 400°F, 200°C.
2. Sift the flour, mustard, salt and cayenne pepper into a large mixing bowl, adding any residue of bran left in the sieve if using wholewheat flour. Rub in the margarine then add the cheese. Alternatively, process the ingredients in a food processor then tip the mixture back into the bowl.
3. Mix to a fairly firm dough with the egg yolk and water. Turn out the dough on a lightly floured board and roll it to a thickness of about 5 mm/¼ inch. Aim to cut the straws about 7.5 cm/3 inches long. Cut out the rest of the biscuits in whatever shape you like, including the small rings to hold the cheese straws. (I use a cutter 2.5 cm/1 inch in diameter and I cut the centres out with a well-washed metal lipstick tube.) Gather up the trimmings, reroll and cut.
4. Lay the biscuits on the trays and bake for about 12–15 minutes until they are light golden in colour. Allow the biscuits to firm up, then cool on wire trays. Dip the ends of some of the cheese straws in paprika pepper, if liked.

Store in airtight tins.

CHEESY PARMESAN SQUARES

Makes about 40

175 g/6 oz plain wholemeal flour
¼ teaspoon salt
¼ teaspoon mustard powder
1 fat pinch cayenne pepper
75 g/3 oz block margarine, cut into small pieces
75 g/3 oz Parmesan cheese, grated
1 medium egg yolk
3 teaspoons iced water

1. Sift the flour, salt, mustard and cayenne pepper into a mixing bowl, adding any residue of bran left in the sieve. Rub in the margarine. Stir in the Parmesan cheese.
2. Mix to a firm dough with the egg yolk and water, then set the dough to rest for 20 minutes.
3. Line two or three baking trays with nonstick paper. Preheat the oven to hot, Gas 7, 425°F, 220°C.
4. Turn out the dough on a lightly floured board and roll it as thinly as possible. Cut into 4-cm/1½-inch squares. Gather up the trimmings, reroll and cut.
5. Lay the squares on the trays and bake for about 12 minutes, or until the biscuits are golden in colour all over. Cool on wire trays.

Store in an airtight tin.

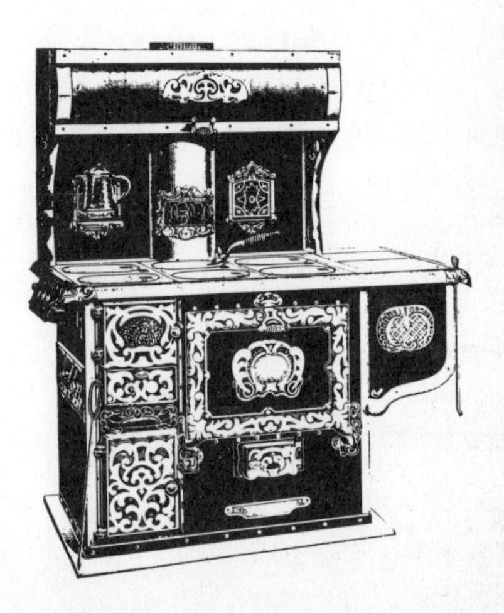

CHEESY COCONUT SAVOURIES

These savouries have a very unusual and different flavour. The recipe was given to me years ago and has proved popular ever since. Serve hot or cold.

Makes about 14

50 g/2 oz coarse coconut
125 g/4 oz strongly flavoured Cheddar cheese, grated
50 g/2 oz plain white flour
1 pinch each cayenne pepper, salt and cinnamon
1 medium egg, separated

1. Spread the coconut in the bottom of a grill pan and toast very lightly. Set aside to cool.
2. Line two baking trays with nonstick paper. Preheat the oven to fairly hot, Gas 6, 400°F, 200°C.
3. Put the cheese into a mixing bowl. Sift in the flour, cayenne pepper, salt and cinnamon, add the toasted coconut and egg yolk and mix very well.
4. In a clean, grease-free bowl, whisk the egg white until snowy and gently fold into the cheese mixture.
5. Form teaspoons of the mixture into tiny pyramids on the trays and bake for 6–8 minutes until lightly brown in colour. If eating cold, cool on wire trays.

Store in an airtight tin.

CHEESE AND TOMATO BISCUITS

These biscuits are very nice sandwiched with a cheese spread.

Makes about 20

125 g/4 oz plain white or wholemeal flour
1 pinch mustard powder
50 g/2 oz butter or block margarine, cut into pieces
50 g/2 oz strongly flavoured cheese, grated
2 tablespoons tomato sauce
Water to mix

1. Line two baking trays with nonstick paper. Preheat the oven to fairly hot, Gas 6, 400°F, 200°C.
2. Sift the flour and mustard powder into a large mixing bowl, adding any residue of bran left in the sieve, and rub in the butter or margarine. Add the cheese and the tomato sauce and mix with enough water to make a stiffish dough.
3. Turn out the dough on a lightly floured board and roll it very thin. Cut into small rounds.
4. Lay the rounds on the trays and bake for 10–15 minutes until the biscuits are golden in colour. Cool on wire trays.

Store in an airtight tin.

WHOLEWHEAT SAVOURIES

The combination of good butter and nutty wholewheat flour gives these biscuits an excellent flavour. They are topped with sesame seeds.

Makes about 28

125 g/4 oz plain wholewheat flour
125 g/4 oz plain white flour
125 g/4 oz unsalted butter, cut into small pieces
125 g/4 oz cheese, grated (include 1 teaspoon Parmesan if you can)
3 tablespoons cold water
1 small egg, beaten
3 tablespoons sesame seeds

1. Line two baking trays with nonstick paper. Preheat the oven to moderately hot, Gas 5, 375°F, 190°C.
2. Sift the flours into a mixing bowl, adding any residue of bran left in the sieve, and rub in the butter. Stir in the cheese.
3. Mix with the water to make a firm dough and knead slightly to get rid of cracks.
4. Turn out the dough on a lightly floured board and roll very thinly. Cut out 5-cm/2-inch rounds, gather up the trimmings, reroll and cut.
5. Brush the top of each biscuit with the beaten egg and sprinkle the sesame seeds all over.
6. Lay the rounds on the trays and bake for 10–12 minutes. Cool on wire trays.

Store in an airtight tin.

WHOLEMEAL NIBBLES

These very simple small biscuits are suitable for serving with a variety of savoury toppings to go with drinks before a meal. Pâté, cream cheese with chives, meat and fish spreads are all suitable. Decorate with tiny pieces of parsley, cucumber, tomato, radish etc. Add the savoury spreads just before serving or the biscuits will go soft.

Makes about 30

125 g/4 oz plain wholemeal flour
½ teaspoon baking powder
Salt and pepper
25 g/1 oz lard or solid vegetable oil
Milk to mix

1. Line one or two baking trays with nonstick paper. Preheat the oven to moderate, Gas 4, 350°F, 180°C.
2. Sift the flour into a mixing bowl, adding any residue of bran left in the sieve, and stir in the baking powder, salt and pepper.
3. Rub in the lard or solid vegetable oil and mix with enough milk to form a stiff dough.
4. Turn out the dough on a lightly floured board and roll it as thin as possible. Cut out small shapes and squares. Gather up the trimmings, reroll and cut. Prick the biscuits all over with a sharp fork.
5. Lay the biscuits on the trays and bake for about 12–15 minutes. Cool on wire trays.

Store in an airtight tin.

FLORENTINES

Makes about 15 medium-sized ones or 30 tiny ones

50 g/2 oz unsalted or lightly salted butter
50 g/2 oz caster sugar
50 g/2 oz mixed walnuts and almonds, finely chopped
15 g/½ oz sultanas, washed, dried and finely chopped (use scissors)
15 g/½ oz candied orange peel, finely chopped
15 g/½ oz red glacé cherries, finely chopped
75 g/3 oz plain chocolate, broken into small pieces

1. Line baking trays with nonstick paper. Preheat the oven to moderate, Gas 4, 350°F, 180°C.
2. Melt the butter in a roomy pan, then add the sugar. Boil this mixture for 1 minute then take the pan off the heat and add all the remaining ingredients except the chocolate and stir well.
3. Place teaspoons of the mixture well apart on the trays and bake for 10 minutes until the biscuits are a rich golden brown in colour.
4. Take the trays out of the oven and, using a knife, coax the biscuits into a round shape. Leave on the trays to become firm and cold, then remove to wire trays.
5. Put the chocolate into a small heatproof bowl set over a pan of simmering water, and stir until melted. Spread the underside of each biscuit with the melted chocolate, making a wavy pattern in it with a fork. Leave to set.

Store in airtight tins in single layers, separating each layer with a strip of foil.

BOUNTY MACAROONS

Macaroons used to be baked on edible rice paper which stuck to the bottom of each biscuit. Nowadays, nonstick paper which is treated with silicone makes the job much easier and the macaroons lift easily off the trays.

I use coarse coconut for these biscuits and I buy it loose as prepacked coconut is often very fine.

Makes about 16

2 large egg whites
1 dessertspoon cornflour
125 g/4 oz caster sugar
150 g/5 oz desiccated coconut
2 drops vanilla essence
15 g/½ oz flaked almonds

1. Line two baking trays with nonstick paper. Preheat the oven to moderate, Gas 4, 350°F, 180°C.
2. In a large, grease-free mixing bowl, whisk the egg whites until they are at the frothy stage.
3. Stir in the cornflour, sugar, coconut and vanilla essence and mix well.
4. Place heaped teaspoons of the mixture onto the trays, allowing room for the biscuits to spread a little. Put a flaked almond in the centre of each macaroon.
5. Bake for about 20 minutes, or until a good brown colour all over. Allow the macaroons to firm up, then cool on wire trays.

Store in an airtight tin.

COCONUT AND CHOCOLATE CHIP BISCUITS

Chocolate chips or polka dots can be found in packets on the 'baking ingredients' shelves in supermarkets. If you cannot find them, just chop up chocolate drops.

Makes 24

225 g/8 oz plain white or wholewheat flour
2 teaspoons baking powder
75 g/3 oz caster sugar
75 g/3 oz butter or block margarine, cut into small pieces
50 g/2 oz chocolate chips, finely chopped
25 g/1 oz desiccated coconut
1 large egg, beaten

1. Line two or three baking trays with nonstick paper. Preheat the oven to moderate, Gas 4, 350°F, 180°C.
2. Sift the flour and baking powder into a large mixing bowl, adding any residue of bran left in the sieve, and stir in the sugar. Rub in the butter or margarine.
3. Stir in the chocolate chips, coconut and lastly the egg, and mix to a soft dough.
4. Turn out the dough on a lightly floured board. Roll it out as thinly as possible and stamp out rounds 5 cm/2 inches across. Gather up the trimmings, reroll and cut.
5. Lay the rounds on the trays and bake for about 15–20 minutes.
6. Allow the biscuits to firm up, then cool on wire trays.

Store in airtight tins.

CHOCOLATE AND VANILLA WHIRLS

These biscuits are always popular with children as they like to try to unwind them.

Makes about 20

125 g/4 oz block margarine, cut into pieces
225 g/8 oz plain white flour, sifted
150 g/5 oz caster sugar
1 medium egg, beaten
25 g/1 oz cocoa powder, sifted
1 teaspoon vanilla essence

1. Line two baking trays with nonstick paper.
2. In a mixing bowl, rub the margarine into the flour. Stir in the sugar and enough egg to make a smooth dough. Divide the dough in two and put half into another bowl.
3. Add the cocoa powder to one bowl and work it into the dough until smooth. Add the vanilla essence to the other bowl and work it into the dough.
4. Turn out each piece of dough onto a lightly floured board and roll each to an oblong 20 × 25 cm/8 × 10 inches long. Put the vanilla strip on top of the chocolate strip and press down gently. Roll up the two doughs together from the long end like a Swiss roll. Put the roll in the fridge to firm up.
5. Preheat the oven to fairly hot, Gas 6, 400°F, 200°C. Using a sharp knife, slice 5-mm/¼-inch biscuits from the roll and lay them, cut side up, on the trays.
6. Bake for about 15 minutes, then cool on wire trays.

Store in an airtight tin.

ORANGEY CHOCOLATE BISCUITS

I have never really liked chocolate biscuits made with cocoa powder. This recipe uses real chocolate with orange juice and orange rind and the results are excellent.

Makes about 15

75 g/3 oz plain chocolate, broken into small pieces
Juice of 1 orange (or 2 small oranges)
225 g/8 oz plain white or wholemeal flour, sifted and residue of bran from sieve added
2 teaspoons baking powder
150 g/5 oz block margarine, softened
Grated rind of 1 orange (or 2 small oranges)
Icing sugar for sprinkling (optional)

FOR THE FILLING
175 g/6 oz icing sugar, sifted
50 g/2 oz block margarine, softened

1. Line two baking trays with nonstick paper. Preheat the oven to moderate, Gas 4, 350°F, 180°C.
2. Put the chocolate pieces into a small heatproof bowl set over a pan of simmering water. Stir until melted, then add 1 teaspoon of the orange juice to loosen the mixture.
3. Put the liquid chocolate into a large mixing bowl. Add the flour, baking powder, margarine and almost all the grated orange rind (set aside 1 teaspoon of rind for the filling). Beat these ingredients together with just enough of the orange juice to form a stiff paste. If it is too soft, add a little flour.
4. Turn out the paste onto a lightly floured board and roll it to a thickness of 5 mm/¼ inch. Using a 5-cm/2-inch cutter, cut into rounds. Gather up the trimmings, reroll and cut.
5. Lay the rounds on the trays and bake for about 20 minutes. Allow the biscuits to firm up, then cool on wire trays. Store in an airtight tin until ready to serve.
6. Just before serving, make the filling. Put the icing sugar, margarine and reserved teaspoon of grated orange rind into a mixing bowl and add just a little of the orange juice to make a spreadable paste.
7. Sandwich the biscuits together with the butter cream. A dusting of icing sugar looks nice, too.

ALMOND RICE BISCUITS

Makes about 20

125 g/4 oz plain white flour
15 g/½ oz cornflour
½ teaspoon bicarbonate of soda
75 g/3 oz lard or solid vegetable oil
75 g/3 oz caster sugar
1 small egg, beaten
1 tablespoon cold water
4 drops almond essence
25 g/1 oz ground rice
15 g/½ oz flaked almonds

TO GLAZE
50 g/2 oz caster sugar
4 tablespoons water

1. Line two baking trays with nonstick paper. Preheat the oven to moderate, Gas 4, 350°F, 180°C.
2. Sift the flour, cornflour and bicarbonate of soda into a mixing bowl. Rub in the fat.
3. Stir in the caster sugar, egg, 1 tablespoon water, almond essence and ground rice, and mix to a smooth dough.
4. Take the mixture up in teaspoons and, with dampened hands, roll into small balls. Place the biscuit balls well apart on the trays and flatten each one slightly with the back of a fork dipped in cold water and shaken.
5. Now prepare the glaze. Put the sugar and water into a small pan over a low heat and stir until the sugar dissolves, then boil the syrup gently for 2 minutes. Using a pastry brush, paint the syrup over the surface of each biscuit and decorate with a flaked almond.
6. Bake for about 20 minutes, then cool on wire trays.

Store in an airtight tin.

ORANGE CRUNCH

A crunchy, buttery biscuit with the taste of orange. Leave the orange rind on a piece of kitchen paper for a couple of hours to dry it off slightly.

Makes about 20

150 g/5 oz self-raising white flour
50 g/2 oz caster sugar
125 g/4 oz butter, cut into pieces
Finely grated rind of 1 orange
Extra caster sugar for sprinkling

1. Line two baking trays with nonstick paper. Preheat the oven to moderate, Gas 4, 350°F, 180°C.
2. Sift the flour into a mixing bowl. Add the sugar and rub in the butter.
3. Add the grated orange rind and work the mixture until it forms a dough.
4. Roll the mixture into small balls about 2.5 cm/1 inch diameter. Lay the balls about 5 cm/2 inches apart on the baking trays and flatten each ball slightly with the back of a fork dipped in cold water and shaken.
5. Bake for 10–12 minutes until pale gold in colour. Sprinkle with caster sugar while still hot then cool on wire trays.

Store in an airtight tin.

BELGIAN BISCUITS

Makes about 14

125 g/4 oz plain white or wholemeal flour
25 g/1 oz cornflour
60 g/2½ oz block margarine, cut into small pieces
40 g/1½ oz caster sugar
1 medium egg yolk

TO DECORATE
Lemon curd or jam
Icing sugar

1. Line two baking trays with nonstick paper. Preheat the oven to fairly hot, Gas 6, 400°F, 200°C.
2. Sift the flour and cornflour into a mixing bowl, adding any residue of bran left in the sieve if using wholemeal flour, and rub in the margarine.
3. Stir in the sugar and, using a knife, mix in the egg yolk to make a soft dough.
4. Turn out the dough on a lightly floured board and roll it to a thickness of about 5 mm/¼ inch. Using a 5-cm/2-inch cutter, cut an equal number of rounds and circles. Using a smaller cutter, take the centres out of the circles. Gather up the trimmings and centres, reroll and cut.
5. Lay the rounds and circles on the trays and bake for about 15 minutes.
6. Allow the biscuits to firm up, then cool on wire trays. Store in an airtight tin until needed.
7. To serve, spread a light coating of lemon curd or jam on the rounds. Top each one with a circle biscuit and dust on a little icing sugar.

BISCUIT STARS

You can use an electric mixer for these biscuits, but if your margarine is soft enough they are easily made by hand. They are often also called Viennese biscuits and another way of serving them is to pipe spirals of the mixture into paper cases (set in bun tins for support), leaving a small dent in the centre of each. Before serving, this dent is filled with a spot of red jam or jelly and the whole dusted with icing sugar from a dredger.

Makes about 30

225 g/8 oz block margarine, softened
50 g/2 oz icing sugar
225 g/8 oz plain white flour or half white and half wholewheat flour
2–3 drops vanilla essence

TO DECORATE (OPTIONAL)
Red glacé cherries, finely chopped

1. Line two baking trays with nonstick paper. Preheat the oven to cool, Gas 2, 300°F, 150°C.
2. Cream the margarine in a large mixing bowl until soft and fluffy.
3. Sift in the icing sugar and beat again. Sift in the flour, adding any residue of bran left in the sieve if using wholewheat flour, and continue beating until smooth, then add the vanilla essence and mix well.
4. Prepare a large piping bag with a large star nozzle and scrape the mixture into the bag. Pipe star shapes onto the trays and top each star with a tiny piece of glacé cherry, if you wish.
5. Bake for about 25 minutes, or until the biscuits are golden in colour. Allow the biscuits to firm up, then cool on wire trays.

Store in an airtight tin.

NUTTY MERINGUE BISCUITS

These ingredients will make quite a large quantity of lovely little crunchy biscuits. It is important to use an electric mixer to get the meringue very thick and firm.

Makes about 30

125 g/4 oz flaked almonds
2 large egg whites
1 pinch salt
1 pinch cream of tartar
125 g/4 oz vanilla sugar *(see page 17)*

1. Spread the flaked almonds in the bottom of a grill pan and toast them until golden in colour. Watch carefully – they burn easily. Cool them and then place in a thick plastic freezer bag and hit them with a hammer. When they are all reduced to very small pieces, pour them into a wide, shallow dish.
2. Line three baking trays with nonstick paper.
3. Using an electric mixer, whip the egg whites until they are frothy. Add the salt and cream of tartar and continue to whip until the mixture is like firm white snow.
4. With the machine still running, start adding the sugar – about 1 tablespoon at a time. Continue beating until all the sugar is added. You should end up with a very white shiny fluff.
5. Scoop up 1 heaped teaspoon at a time of this mixture and drop into the dish of nuts. Toss carefully so that each meringue has a good coating. Try not to touch the meringue itself or let it touch the dish before it is coated with nuts.
6. Place the meringues well apart on the baking trays and bake in a slow oven, Gas 1, 275°F, 140°C, for about 1 hour, or until they are really well toasted. Cool on wire trays.

Store in airtight tins.

PARKIN BISCUITS

Black treacle gives a strong flavour to these ginger biscuits.

Makes 24

225 g/8 oz plain white flour
2 teaspoons ground ginger
125 g/4 oz dark soft brown sugar
125 g/4 oz block margarine
4 tablespoons black treacle
15 g/½ oz flaked almonds

1. Line two baking trays with nonstick paper. Preheat the oven to moderate, Gas 4, 350°F, 180°C.
2. Sift the flour and ground ginger into a mixing bowl and add the sugar.
3. Melt the margarine and black treacle in a small pan over a low heat. Remove from the heat and pour into the dry mixture. Mix well to a stiffish dough.
4. Turn out the dough on a lightly floured board and knead very slightly. Roll it out to 5 mm/¼ inch thick and cut into rounds about 5 cm/2 inches in diameter. Gather up the trimmings, reroll and cut.
5. Put a flaked almond on top of each biscuit and lay the biscuits on the trays.
6. Bake for about 12–14 minutes. Allow the biscuits to firm up, then cool on wire trays.

Store in an airtight tin.

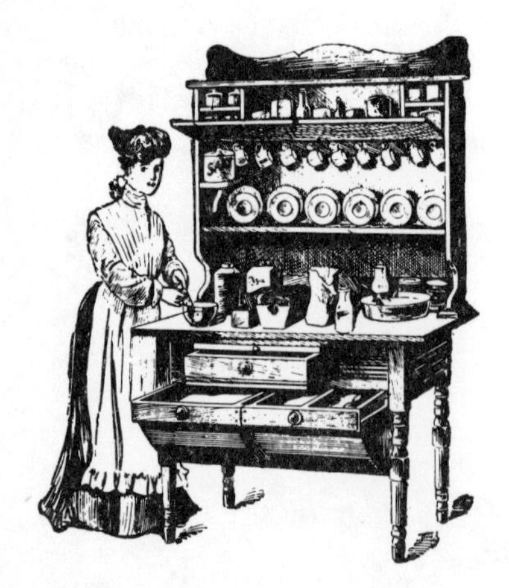

GINGERBREAD BOYS AND GIRLS

Makes about 4, depending on the size of cutter

175 g/6 oz self-raising white or wholewheat flour
1 pinch salt
1 teaspoon ground ginger
50 g/2 oz golden syrup
25 g/1 oz margarine
15 g/½ oz caster sugar
1 small egg, beaten
25 g/1 oz currants, washed and dried
125 g/4 oz soft marzipan *(see page 248)*:
50 g/2 oz coloured green
50 g/2 oz coloured pink
1 teaspoon jam

1. Line a baking tray with nonstick paper. Preheat the oven to moderate, Gas 4, 350°F, 180°C.
2. Sift the flour, salt and ground ginger into a mixing bowl, adding any residue of bran left in the sieve if using wholewheat flour.
3. In a small heavy pan, melt the syrup, margarine and sugar over a low heat. Stir until the sugar dissolves.
4. Pour the syrup mixture into the flour mixture, add the egg and mix well to a stiffish dough.
5. Turn out the dough on a lightly floured board and roll it out fairly thin. Using a gingerbread man cutter, stamp out the figures. Gather up the trimmings, reroll and cut.
6. Put the shapes on the tray and fix currants for eyes, nose and mouth.
7. Bake for 15–20 minutes. Cool on a wire tray.
8. To trim the finished figures, roll out the coloured marzipan and make bows and skirts according to the size of the figures. Give the boys green bow ties and the girls pink skirts (*see below*). Stick them on with a spot of jam.

Store in an airtight tin.

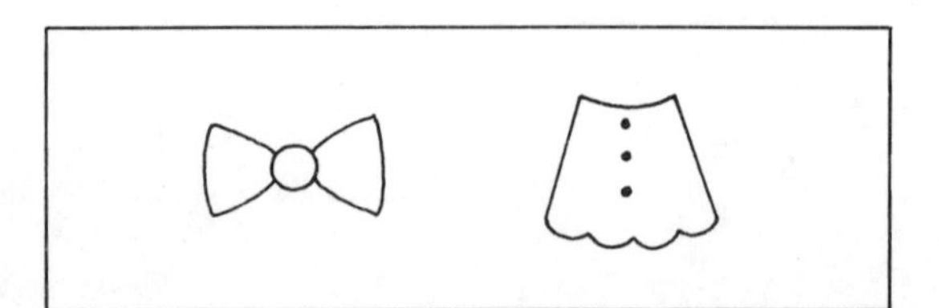

MRS MOFFAT'S GINGER CRISPS

This is a very economical recipe giving 325 g/12 oz biscuits.

Makes about 40

225 g/8 oz plain white or wholemeal flour
1 teaspoon ground ginger
1 teaspoon bicarbonate of soda
25 g/1 oz light soft brown sugar
125 g/4 oz golden syrup
50 g/2 oz butter or margarine

1. Grease and line the base and long sides of a 450-g/1-lb loaf tin. This will help to get the mixture out of the tin.
2. Sift the flour, ground ginger and bicarbonate of soda into a large mixing bowl, adding any residue of bran left in the sieve if using wholemeal flour. Stir in the sugar.
3. Put a small pan on the scales, weigh it and then weigh the syrup into it. Add the butter or margarine to the syrup in the pan and melt over a low heat.
4. Add the melted mixture to the dry ingredients and mix well.
5. Press this soft, wax-like mixture into the tin. Level it off and leave in the fridge for about 1½ hours until it hardens.
6. Slide a knife down the short sides of the loaf tin and, using the greaseproof paper, lift the block out.
7. Line two or three baking trays with nonstick paper. Preheat the oven to moderate, Gas 3, 325°F, 160°C.
8. Using a very sharp knife, shave off very thin biscuits from the block. Lay the biscuits on the trays and bake for about 12 minutes, or until the biscuits are well browned. Leave on the baking trays to become firm and cold.

Store in an airtight tin.

GINGER SHORTBREAD BARS

The topping for these biscuits goes on after they have been baked and cooled.

Makes 32 bars

FOR THE BASE
125 g/4 oz butter, softened
50 g/2 oz caster sugar
125 g/4 oz self-raising white flour, sifted
1 heaped teaspoon ground ginger

FOR THE TOPPING
4 generous tablespoons icing sugar, sifted
50 g/2 oz butter
3 teaspoons golden syrup

1. Generously grease an 18 × 28-cm/7 × 11-inch baking tin. Preheat the oven to moderate, Gas 4, 350°F, 180°C.
2. First make the base. In a mixing bowl, cream the butter and sugar really well. Fold in the flour and the ground ginger. Press the mixture into the tin and level off.
3. Bake for about 20 minutes, or until the shortbread is golden in colour. Remove from the oven and allow to cool in the tin.
4. To make the topping, combine the icing sugar, butter and syrup in a small, heavy-based pan.
5. Stir over a low heat until the sugar has dissolved, then bring to a steady boil and continue boiling until the soft ball stage is reached (*see page 216*).
6. Pour the caramel topping over the shortbread in the tin and leave it to cool and set. Turn out the block and cut into neat bars.

Store in an airtight tin.

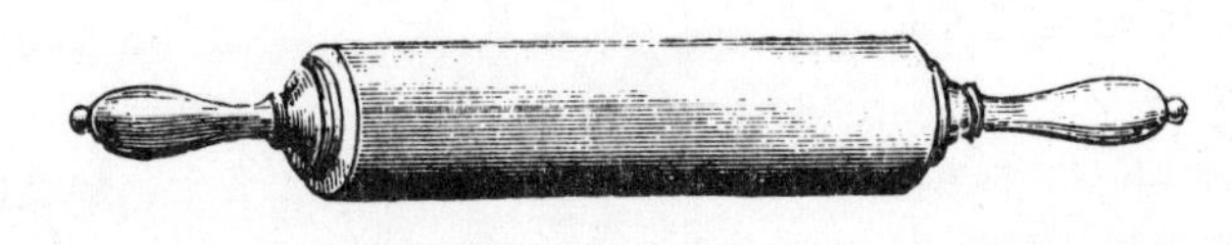

GINGER DROPS

Makes about 20

125 g/4 oz self-raising white flour
1–2 teaspoons ground ginger
1 teaspoon bicarbonate of soda
40 g/1½ oz caster sugar
50 g/2 oz butter or block margarine, cut into pieces
2 tablespoons golden syrup

1. Line two baking trays with nonstick paper. Preheat the oven to moderately hot, Gas 5, 375°F, 190°C.
2. Sift the flour, ground ginger and bicarbonate of soda into a mixing bowl and stir in the sugar.
3. Rub in the butter or margarine as you would for pastry, then add the syrup (stand the tin in hot water for half an hour to make the syrup runny).
4. Mix well until you have a fairly stiff paste, then roll the paste into balls about the size of a large marble.
5. Lay the balls well apart on the trays and flatten each one slightly with the back of a fork dipped in cold water and shaken.
6. Bake for about 12–15 minutes. Allow the biscuits to firm up, then transfer to wire trays to become crisp and cool.

Store in an airtight tin.

GINGERED SHORTBREAD ROUNDELS

The ground ginger gives a nice edge to the shortbread flavour.

Makes about 22

125 g/4 oz block margarine, softened
125 g/4 oz caster sugar
½ medium egg, beaten
125 g/4 oz self-raising white flour
2 teaspoons ground ginger

1. Line a baking tray with nonstick paper. Preheat the oven to slow, Gas 1, 275°F, 140°C.
2. In a mixing bowl, cream the margarine with the sugar. Beat in the egg.
3. Sift the flour and ground ginger into the mixture and work into a stiff dough.
4. Form the dough into small balls about the size of a large marble. Lay the balls well apart on the tray and flatten each ball slightly with the back of a fork dipped in cold water and shaken.
5. Bake for about 30 minutes. Allow the biscuits to firm up, then cool on wire trays.

Store in airtight tins.

ROSEMARY SHORTCAKES

If you have never tasted rosemary you are in for a pleasant surprise. It goes really well in this buttery biscuit.

Makes about 20

125 g/4 oz unsalted butter, softened
125 g/4 oz caster sugar
175 g/6 oz plain white flour, sifted
2 fat pinches finely snipped fresh rosemary needles, or 1 fat pinch dried rosemary
Extra caster sugar for rolling

1. Put all the ingredients into the bowl of an electric mixer. Use the beater to reduce the mixture to crumbs and continue beating until it forms a ball. If you wish to do this by hand, cut the butter into small pieces. Using a knife, work it into the other ingredients, then use your hands to knead the mixture until it is smooth. If the butter is rather firm, it helps to warm the mixing bowl.
2. Shape the dough into a fat sausage shape about 4 cm/1½ inches thick. Roll it smooth in a little caster sugar then leave in the fridge for 2 hours to firm up.
3. Line two baking trays with nonstick paper. Preheat the oven to slow, Gas 2, 300°F, 150°C.
4. Using a sharp knife, cut thin slices off the roll and lay them on the trays. Bake for about 20–30 minutes. Allow the biscuits to firm up, then cool on wire trays.

Store in airtight tins.

SHORTBREAD THINS

This method of biscuit-making works for many recipes which suggest rolling and cutting shapes. Your circles may not be perfect but you do get thin biscuits. You need to use an electric mixer.

Makes about 40

225 g/8 oz unsalted butter, at room temperature (softish)
325 g/12 oz plain white flour, sifted
125 g/4 oz caster sugar
Extra caster sugar for sprinkling

1. Warm the bowl of the electric mixer by pouring in some boiling water. Pour the water away and dry the bowl.
2. Put the butter, flour and sugar into the bowl and, using the beater slowly at first then a little faster, blend until the mixture resembles damp breadcrumbs. If you wish to do this by hand, cut the butter into small pieces and rub it into the flour and sugar as swiftly as possible.
3. Using your hands, form the crumbs into two fat sausage shapes. Work the mixture as little as possible and make the sausages about 4 cm/1½ inches thick. Roll them smooth in a little caster sugar then leave in the fridge to firm up.
4. Line two baking trays with nonstick paper. Preheat the oven to cool, Gas 2, 300°F, 150°C.
5. Using a very sharp knife, cut thin slices from each roll and lay them carefully on the trays. The biscuits do not spread much so you can lay them close together. If the biscuits have a slight curl, just leave them to flatten out in the oven.
6. Bake for about 30 minutes, or until the biscuits are lightly browned. Do not over-bake.
7. Remove from the oven and dredge the hot biscuits with caster sugar. Allow to firm up, then slide onto wire trays to cool.

Store in airtight tins.

VARIATIONS

Replace white flour with wholewheat for a delicious nutty flavour.

Flavour half the mixture with 1 teaspoon finely chopped fresh rosemary needles, or ½ teaspoon dried rosemary. Add at step 3. Leave the other half plain.

Flavour half the mixture with ½ teaspoon crushed caraway seed. Crush the seed either in a mortar and pestle or in a strong bowl with a rolling pin. Add at step 3. Leave the other half plain.

PETTICOAT TAILS

The name comes from the shape of the biscuit – like a petticoat skirt. They are not as thick as shortbread.

Makes about 26 pieces

1 quantity shortbread dough as for Shortbread Thins ***(left)***

1. Make the dough as described. Divide the dough into two pieces.
2. Roll out the pieces evenly in a little caster sugar to make two circles about 20 cm/8 inches across. Use a pan lid or a plate to make the circles even.
3. Line baking trays with nonstick paper. Preheat the oven to cool, Gas 2, 300°F, 150°C.
4. Lay the circles on the trays and, using a 5-cm/2-inch cutter, cut a hole in the centre of each. Cut the circles into even-sized pieces, prick each piece with a fork and crimp the outside edge (see below).

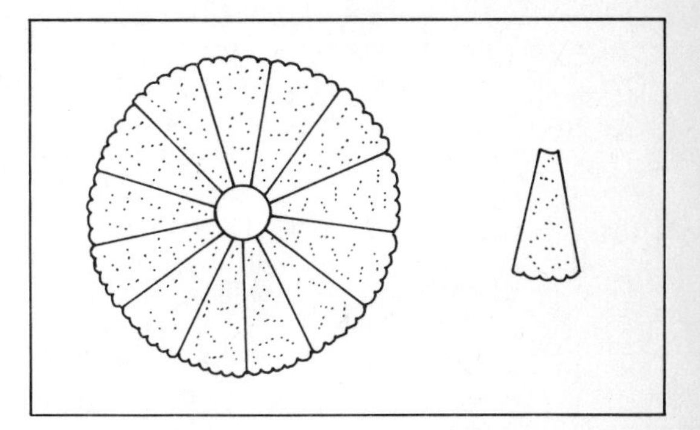

5. Bake for about 30 minutes, or until the biscuits are evenly gold in colour. Allow the biscuits to firm up, then cool on wire trays.

Store in airtight tins.

SHORTBREAD IN A MOULD

A 'cake' of shortbread is very traditional in Scotland and is a popular gift at Hogmanay. It should be fairly thick – anything from 1 cm/½ inch to 2.5 cm/1 inch. One way to achieve this is to use a wooden mould. This is a carved block of wood, often with a thistle picked out and a pretty curved border. A good shortbread mould should be deeply and smoothly cut. Old ones are now being collected, but some new ones are far too shallow and the pattern sometimes disappears during baking.

Makes a 'cake' about 23 cm/9 inches across

1 quantity shortbread dough as for Shortbread Thins *(see page 115)*

1. Dust the shortbread mould with flour and knock it carefully on its side to remove the surplus flour.
2. Make the dough as in the recipe on page 115. Take up the ball of uncooked dough and press and roll it across the carved mould, working the dough into each decorative pattern. Use a rolling pin to get a smooth surface. Gather up all the trimmings and set aside to be rerolled and cut later into biscuits.
3. The next step is sometimes tricky. First, grease a baking tray and line it with nonstick paper. Invert this over the top of the mould. Lift the two together, swiftly turn them upside down and see if the patterned 'cake' of raw shortbread has dropped. Three cheers to you if it does so first time! You may have to spread-eagle your hand over the dough, lift the mould and tap it gently on its side to help the dough out.
4. Bake in a cool oven, Gas 2, 300°F, 150°C, for up to 1 hour depending on the thickness of the dough. The 'cake' should be an even gold colour.
5. Allow to cool, then slide the 'cake' onto a wire tray to get cold.

Store in an airtight tin.

VARIATION

SHORTBREAD IN A 'CAKE' – WITHOUT A MOULD

Sometimes the 'cake' is lightly scored with a knife before it goes into the oven. About eight sections is enough.

1. Make the dough as in the recipe for Shortbread Thins on page 115. Turn out the dough on a flat surface dusted with a little caster sugar or flour. Try to get an even thickness, then use a pan lid as a giant cutter to make the 'cake'. Gather up all the trimmings and set aside to be rerolled and cut later into biscuits.
2. Line a baking tray with nonstick paper. Using a large fish slice or removable base of a quiche tin, transfer the circle of dough to the tray.
3. To prevent the shortbread from rising, it is customary to puncture it all over with a fork or skewer. With care this can look quite decorative. Finally, pinch the outer edge of the cake into a decorative border.
4. Bake in a cool oven, Gas 2, 300°F, 150°C, for up to 1 hour when it should be an even gold colour.
5. Allow to cool, then slide the 'cake' onto a wire tray to get cold.

Store in an airtight tin.

BRANDY ROLLS

Keep the unfilled rolls in an airtight tin, then fill them with brandy-flavoured cream just before serving.

Makes about 24

125 g/4 oz golden syrup
125 g/4 oz unsalted or lightly salted butter
125 g/4 oz caster sugar
75 g/3 oz plain white flour, sifted
½ teaspoon ground ginger
¼ teaspoon cinnamon

FOR THE FILLING
5 fl oz/¼ pint double cream, whipped and flavoured with 3 teaspoons of brandy

1. Put a small pan on the scales, weigh it and then weigh the syrup into it.
2. Add the butter and sugar and melt over a low heat.
3. Remove the pan from the heat and add the flour, ground ginger and cinnamon. Stir well and allow the mixture to become cold.
4. Line a baking tray with nonstick paper. Preheat the oven to moderate, Gas 4, 350°F, 180°C.
5. Place small teaspoons of the mixture very well apart on the tray (they will spread out to the size of a small saucer), and bake for 8–12 minutes until a good brown colour.
6. Very lightly grease the handle of a clean wooden spoon. Using a small egg slice, lift each biscuit off the tray and, while it is still warm, curl it round the spoon handle. Place the rolled biscuits to cool on wire trays. If the biscuits are cooling too quickly to curl, you can return them to the oven for 1–2 minutes to soften up again.
7. When the rolls are cold, and just before serving, fill each end with brandy cream using a piping bag with a 1-cm/½-inch star nozzle.

Store the unfilled biscuits in an airtight tin.

RICH VANILLA CRISPS

This is an ideal biscuit to go with exotic ices or fruit salads. Because of the high proportion of butter to flour, they are very fragile.

Makes 40

225 g/8 oz butter, softened
225 g/8 oz vanilla sugar *(see page 17)*
1 small egg, beaten
1 tablespoon milk
5–6 drops vanilla essence
A squeeze of lemon juice
300 g/10 oz self-raising white flour, sifted
2 tablespoons water
25 g/1 oz demerara sugar

1. In a large mixing bowl, cream the butter and sugar until really fluffy.
2. Beat in the egg, milk, essence and lemon juice.
3. Using a spatula, fold in the flour and mix well. The dough should be fairly firm.
4. Knead the dough in the bowl and divide the mixture in two. Shape each piece into a fat sausage about 4 cm/1½ inches across. Brush the sausages with the water and roll them in the demerara sugar, coating them thickly. Set aside for 2 hours to firm up, preferably in the fridge.
5. Line two baking trays with nonstick paper. Preheat the oven to moderate, Gas 4, 350°F, 180°C.
6. Using a sharp knife, cut the thinnest possible slices off each roll and lay them on the trays.
7. Bake for about 8–10 minutes, or until the biscuits are golden in colour. Allow to firm up, then cool on wire trays.

Store in an airtight tin.

VARIATION

Roll the biscuit dough in 40 g/1½ oz very finely chopped walnuts instead of sugar.

CATS TONGUES/LANGUES DE CHAT

Very elegant, light, crisp biscuits, ideal for serving with ice cream and soft puddings. It is not easy to get a very even shape like the commercial ones but these taste better and cost much less.

Makes 20

50 g/2 oz caster sugar
50 g/2 oz unsalted butter, very soft
2 large egg whites
50 g/2 oz plain white flour
2 drops vanilla essence

1. Line two baking trays with nonstick paper. Preheat the oven to moderately hot, Gas 5, 375°F, 190°C.
2. In a large mixing bowl, beat the sugar into the butter and gradually beat in the egg whites a little at a time.
3. Sift the flour into the mixture, add the vanilla essence and fold in very gently.
4. You can just drop teaspoons of the mixture onto the trays, keeping them well apart. However, the traditional shape is a rough oval or 'tongue'. To make these, put the mixture into a piping bag with a 5-mm/¼-inch plain nozzle. Pipe 5-cm/2-inch lengths evenly over the trays.
5. Bake for 6–8 minutes, or until pale gold in colour with a characteristic brown edging. Cool on wire trays.

Store in an airtight tin.

CRUNCHY PEANUT BUTTER BISCUITS

Makes about 30

75 g/3 oz butter or block margarine, softened
50 g/2 oz light soft brown sugar
125 g/4 oz caster sugar
1 medium egg, beaten
4 tablespoons crunchy peanut butter
175 g/6 oz plain white or wholemeal flour
1 teaspoon bicarbonate of soda
1 tablespoon milk

1. Line two baking trays with nonstick paper. Preheat the oven to fairly hot, Gas 6, 400°F, 200°C.
2. In a large mixing bowl, cream together the butter or margarine, and the two sugars.
3. Add the egg a little at a time, beating well after each addition, then beat in the peanut butter.
4. Sift the flour and bicarbonate of soda into a large mixing bowl, adding any residue of bran left in the sieve if using wholemeal flour.
5. Fold the flour into the creamed mixture, add the milk and beat. Add a little more milk, if necessary, to achieve a soft dropping consistency.
6. Place teaspoons of the mixture about 7.5 cm/3 inches apart on the trays and flatten each one with the back of a fork dipped in cold water and shaken.
7. Bake for about 10–15 minutes. Allow the biscuits to firm up on the tray, then turn out onto wire trays to cool.

Store in airtight tins.

HAZELNUT BISCUITS

Makes about 36 small bars

225 g/8 oz plain white or wholewheat flour
125 g/4 oz block margarine, cut into small pieces
150 g/5 oz caster sugar
125 g/4 oz ground hazelnuts
1 large egg, beaten

1. Sift the flour into a mixing bowl, adding any residue of bran left in the sieve if using wholewheat flour, and rub in the margarine.
2. Stir in the sugar and the ground hazelnuts and mix in the egg to make a smooth soft dough.
3. Grease and line the base and long sides of a 450-g/1-lb loaf tin. This will help to get the mixture out of the tin.
4. Press the dough into the tin and level off. Leave in the fridge for 1½–2 hours to firm up.
5. Slide a knife down the unlined sides of the loaf tin and, using the greaseproof paper, lift the block out.
6. Line two baking trays with nonstick paper. Preheat the oven to fairly hot, Gas 6, 400°F, 200°C.
7. Using a sharp knife, cut very thin slices off the block and lay them on the trays. Bake for about 15 minutes, or until the biscuits are nicely browned. Allow to firm up, then cool on wire trays.

Store in airtight tins.

PIPED WHIRLS

These biscuits are very swiftly mixed if you have an electric mixer. However, if the margarine is really soft they are also easy to make by hand.

Makes about 32

225 g/8 oz plain white or wholewheat flour, sifted
225 g/8 oz block margarine, softened
50 g/2 oz icing sugar, sifted

TO DECORATE (OPTIONAL)
Red glacé cherries, chopped

1. Line two baking trays with nonstick paper. Preheat the oven to cool, Gas 2, 300°F, 150°C.
2. Sift the flour into a large mixing bowl, adding any residue of bran left in the sieve if using wholewheat flour, and add the margarine and sugar. Using an electric mixer, beat together until smooth.
3. Scrape the soft mixture into a large piping bag with a large star nozzle and pipe small stars onto the trays. If liked, top each star with a small piece of glacé cherry.
4. Bake for about 25 minutes, or until the biscuits are golden in colour. Cool on wire trays.

Store in an airtight tin.

GARIBALDI SQUARES

I cannot imagine why these biscuits are named after a famous Italian Statesman. They are much improved if you can chop the currants quite small – a food processor would do the job in seconds.

Makes about 24

125 g/4 oz self-raising white or wholewheat flour
25 g/1 oz butter
25 g/1 oz caster sugar
A little milk to mix
50 g/2 oz small currants, washed, dried and finely chopped

1. Line two baking trays with nonstick paper. Preheat the oven to fairly hot, Gas 6, 400°F, 200°C.
2. Sift the flour into a large mixing bowl, adding any residue of bran left in the sieve if using wholewheat flour, and rub in the butter. Stir in the sugar and add just enough milk to make a stiff dough.
3. Turn out the dough on a lightly floured surface and roll it very thinly until you have an oblong, 20 × 30 cm/8 × 12 inches, about 3 mm/⅛ inch thick.
4. Sprinkle the currants on one half of the dough and lightly brush the unfruited half with a little milk. Bring the unfruited side up to cover the fruited dough.
5. Roll out the sandwich again until it is very thin. Trim the edges and cut into 4-cm/1½-inch squares. Brush the squares lightly with milk and transfer to the baking trays.
6. Bake for about 15 minutes, or until the biscuits are nicely browned. Cool on wire trays.

Store in an airtight tin.

LEMON PALMIERS

This odd name belongs to a type of biscuit made from puff pastry. Bought frozen puff pastry can also be used; defrost according to the instructions on the packet.

Makes about 24

225 g/8 oz rough puff pastry *(see page 33)*, **or frozen puff pastry, defrosted**
Grated rind of ½ lemon
Caster sugar for sprinkling

FOR THE ICING
2 teaspoons fresh lemon juice
125 g/4 oz icing sugar, sifted

1. Grease two or three baking trays. Preheat the oven to hot, Gas 7, 425°F, 220°C.
2. Roll out the pastry on a lightly floured board to a rectangle measuring 30 × 36 cm/12 × 14 inches. The pastry must be very thin.
3. Wet a pastry brush and lightly brush down the centre of the rectangle. Sprinkle the lemon rind over this wet strip, followed by a sprinkling of sugar.
4. Trim the edges of the pastry and fold each long edge to the centre. Press gently, and bring each folded outside edge to the centre again. You should now have a tightly folded long strip of pastry about 6 cm/2½ inches wide.

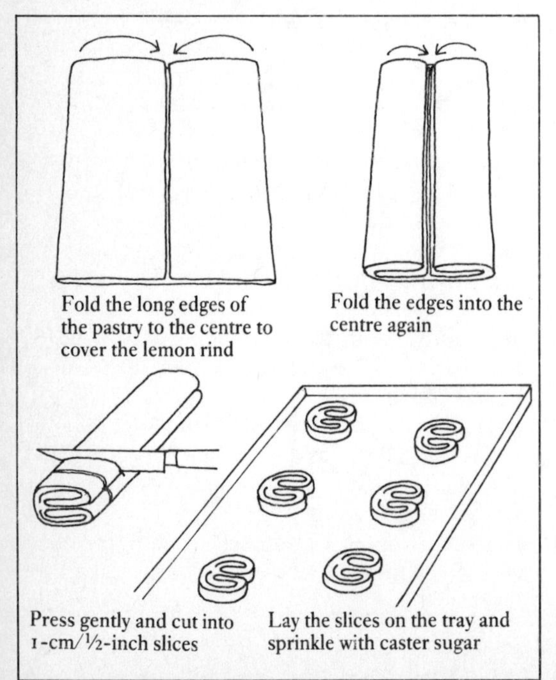
Fold the long edges of the pastry to the centre to cover the lemon rind
Fold the edges into the centre again
Press gently and cut into 1-cm/½-inch slices
Lay the slices on the tray and sprinkle with caster sugar

5. Press the pastry gently and cut into 1-cm/½-inch slices. Lay the slices, cut side up, well apart on the trays and sprinkle a little caster sugar over the cut surfaces.
6. Bake for about 12–15 minutes until the palmiers are brown and crunchy. Turn them over halfway through the baking time so that each side is well browned. Cool on wire trays.
7. When the palmiers are cold, make up the icing using the lemon juice and icing sugar. Add just enough water to get a thick icing which will run.
8. Put the icing into a paper cone (*see page 243*). Cut a tiny piece off the point and dribble the icing over the biscuits in a zigzag pattern.* Allow to set.

Store in airtight tins.

* *You can also do this sort of icing using a small plastic bag. Cut a tiny piece off one corner, fill the bag with icing and push the icing down to the corner. Twist the open end of the bag as you work.*

CARAWAY SEED BISCUITS

I am always sorry to hear someone say they hate the flavour of caraway. Used with care, caraway seeds impart a distinctive and aromatic flavour as in these delicious biscuits. The seeds are very hard so crush them in a mortar and pestle or use the end of your rolling pin in a heavy bowl.

Makes about 24

125 g/4 oz plain white or wholewheat flour
50 g/2 oz caster sugar
1 teaspoon caraway seeds, crushed
50 g/2 oz butter or margarine, cut into pieces
2 teaspoons finely grated lemon rind
1 medium egg yolk

1. Sift the flour into a mixing bowl, adding any residue of bran left in the sieve if using wholewheat flour. Add the sugar and caraway seeds and rub in the butter or margarine. Add the lemon rind and enough of the egg yolk to make a soft dough.
2. Form the dough into a sausage shape about 5 cm/2 inches thick. Roll the sausage in a little flour and leave it in the fridge to firm up.
3. Line two baking trays with nonstick paper. Preheat the oven to moderate, Gas 4, 350°F, 180°C.
4. Cut thin slices off the roll and lay them on the trays.
5. Bake for about 10 minutes, or until golden in colour. Allow the biscuits to firm up, then transfer them to a wire tray until they are cold and crisp.

Store in an airtight tin.

HONEY AND SESAME SEED FLAPJACKS

Try this old-fashioned favourite under a new guise – with sesame and sunflower seeds. Their increasing use has added to the range of flavours in baking. The seeds are excellent plain but toasting them briefly under a hot grill intensifies their taste.

Makes about 36 small bars

2 tablespoons sunflower seeds
75 g/3 oz sesame seeds
175 g/6 oz block margarine
3 tablespoons runny honey
75 g/3 oz light soft brown sugar
75 g/3 oz coarse desiccated coconut
175 g/6 oz rolled oats

1. Grease a 23 × 30-cm/9 × 12-inch tin and line it with nonstick paper. Preheat the oven to moderate, Gas 3, 325°F, 160°C.
2. Spread the sunflower seeds in a grill pan and toast them slightly. Watch carefully – they burn easily. Do the same with the sesame seeds.
3. In a large pan, melt the margarine, honey and sugar. Stir in all the other ingredients and mix well, then take the pan off the heat.
4. Spread the mixture carefully and evenly in the tin, using a palette knife to level it off.
5. Bake for about 20–25 minutes, or until the biscuits are nicely browned.
6. Remove from the oven and mark into bars while still warm. Leave the flapjack until it firms up then take out of the tin while it is still warm and cut into bars. Cool on wire trays.

Store in an airtight tin.

MUESLI DROPS

Use any kind of muesli for these biscuits.

Makes about 35

125 g/4 oz muesli
75 g/3 oz self-raising brown or white flour
125 g/4 oz light soft brown sugar
125 g/4 oz block margarine, softened
1 small egg, beaten

1. Line two baking trays with nonstick paper. Preheat the oven to moderate, Gas 4, 350°F, 180°C.
2. Put the muesli in a mixing bowl. Cut up the dried fruit with scissors and chop the nuts very finely.
3. Add all the remaining ingredients except the egg, mix well and add just enough egg to the mixture to make a stiffish dough.
4. Form the mixture into balls about the size of a walnut. Wet your hands slightly to help you. Place the balls well apart on the trays and flatten each ball slightly with the back of a fork dipped in cold water and shaken.
5. Bake for about 15 minutes, or until the biscuits are well browned. Allow the biscuits to firm up, then cool on wire trays.

Store in airtight tins.

RICE KRISPIE DROPS

I think this recipe was sent to me by a viewer and the basic biscuit mixture was rolled in crushed cornflakes. However, I prefer them rolled in Rice Krispies.

Makes about 30

150 g/5 oz block margarine
150 g/5 oz caster sugar
175 g/6 oz self-raising white flour
1 medium egg, beaten
50 g/2 oz sultanas, washed, dried and finely chopped (use scissors)
50–75 g/2–3 oz Rice Krispies

1. Line two baking trays with nonstick paper. Preheat the oven to moderate, Gas 3, 325°F, 160°C.
2. In a roomy pan, melt the margarine and sugar over a low heat.
3. Take the pan off the heat and stir in the flour, egg and sultanas. Mix well; the mixture should be quite soft. Allow to cool a little.
4. Put the Rice Krispies into a wide shallow dish and, using a teaspoon, drop four or five small balls of the biscuit mixture into the dish. Toss the balls so that each is well coated. Try not to touch the sticky mixture.
5. Lay the coated balls on the trays, allowing room for them to spread, and flatten each ball slightly with the back of a fork dipped in cold water and shaken.
6. Bake for 15–20 minutes until the biscuits are golden in colour. Allow the biscuits to firm up, then cool on wire trays.

Store in airtight tins.

ROLLED OATY CRUNCH

The demerara sugar blends well with the oats for an easy biscuit. Put the All Bran in a thick polythene bag and crush it with a rolling pin.

Makes about 20 bars

125 g/4 oz porridge oats
15 g/½ oz All Bran, finely crushed
75 g/3 oz demerara sugar
1 fat pinch ground ginger
125 g/4 oz block margarine

1. Grease and line the base and sides of a small shallow baking tin, 18 × 28 cm/7 × 11 inches. Preheat the oven to moderately hot, Gas 5, 375°F, 190°C.
2. Put the oats, All Bran, sugar and ground ginger into a mixing bowl and mix well.
3. In a small pan, melt the margarine and pour this into the mixture. Mix very thoroughly.
4. Press the mixture fairly firmly into the lined tin and smooth it over.
5. Bake for about 15 minutes, or until the slab is an even brown colour all over.
6. Mark the biscuits into even bars or squares while still warm. Leave in the tin until cold and firm then break into pieces.

Store in airtight tins.

WALNUT AND CARDAMOM ROUNDS

Makes about 30

75 g/3 oz icing sugar
225 g/8 oz plain white or wholewheat flour
225 g/8 oz butter, softened and cut into pieces
50 g/2 oz walnuts, very finely chopped
3–4 drops vanilla essence
½ teaspoon ground cardamom
Extra icing sugar for dredging

1. Line two baking trays with nonstick paper. Preheat the oven to moderate, Gas 4, 350°F, 180°C.
2. Sift the icing sugar and flour into a mixing bowl, adding any residue of bran left in the sieve if using wholewheat flour. Add all the other ingredients.
3. Using a spatula or long-bladed knife, work the ingredients together and, finally, knead the dough briefly with your hand to get it smooth. Shape the dough into balls about the size of a walnut and set them well apart on the trays.
4. Bake for about 20 minutes. Allow the biscuits to firm up, then cool on wire trays.
5. Just before serving, dredge or sieve each biscuit with icing sugar.

Store the biscuits in an airtight tin.

BAKED PUDDINGS

Puddings, afters, desserts – whatever you call them, we in Britain excel in the quality and variety of our traditional recipes. There are hundreds of puddings, based on bread, pastry, fruit and cream, that are now reappearing on many restaurant and hotel menus.

When Michael Quinn, former Head Chef of the Ritz Hotel in London, joined me on Farmhouse Kitchen *he told me he had used three of our recipes in his menus. When I was at the hotel, rehearsing for the programme, he showed me the Ritz version of Bread and Butter Pudding. It was very ritzy and tasted wonderfully rich. He had made it in individual small soufflé dishes, the custard had cream in it and the raisins were plump and soaked in rum. The top of the pudding was nicely crusted and golden and an artistic group of raisins sat on one side.*

From the simple rice pudding to the more elaborate mille feuilles, it's good to see these well-loved favourites coming back.

FRUIT CRUMBLE

Fruit crumbles must be about the most popular of all family puddings. Freshly made with fresh fruit they are at their best, and even when made with canned fruit they are cheap and good. The topping ingredients can also be varied. Two golden rules – drain off most of the fruit juice – soggy crumble is not pleasant, and do not press the crumble down hard so that it becomes like pastry.

A note about frozen fruit: some fruit, like gooseberries, blackcurrants, redcurrants, damsons, and sometimes plums, develop a tougher skin in the freezer and take extra time to cook.

BASIC CRUMBLE MIXTURE

Serves 4

75 g/3 oz plain wholewheat flour
25 g/1 oz rolled oats
65 g/2½ oz butter or block margarine, cut into pieces
65 g/2½ oz light soft brown sugar

1. Stir the flour and oats together in a mixing bowl, adding any residue of bran left in the sieve.
2. Rub in the butter or margarine until the mixture resembles breadcrumbs.
3. Stir in the sugar and sprinkle over the cooked fruit (*see right*).

VARIATIONS

COCONUT CRUMBLE

50 g/2 oz plain wholewheat flour
40 g/1½ oz rolled oats
15 g/½ oz desiccated coconut
65 g/2½ oz butter or block margarine, cut into pieces
65 g/2½ oz light soft brown sugar

Mix as above, adding the coconut to the flour and oats.

MUESLI CRUMBLE

50 g/2 oz plain wholewheat flour
50 g/2 oz muesli mixture
65 g/2½ oz butter or block margarine, cut into pieces
65 g/2½ oz light soft brown sugar

Mix as for the basic crumble.

NUTTY CRUMBLE

75 g/3 oz plain wholewheat flour
50 g/2 oz rolled oats
50 g/2 oz butter or block margarine, cut into pieces
50 g/2 oz sunflower seeds
25 g/1 oz chopped walnuts
40 g/1½ oz demerara sugar
3 tablespoons sunflower oil

Mix as above, adding all the remaining ingredients after rubbing in the butter.

FRUIT MIXTURES

SPICED APPLE

450 g/1 lb Bramley cooking apples, peeled, cored and sliced
2 dessertspoons light soft brown sugar
2–3 tablespoons water
¼ teaspoon ground cloves

1. Put all the ingredients into a pan, cover and cook over a gentle heat, shaking from time to time. When the apples are just beginning to soften, remove the pan from the heat. Drain away most of the juice and spread the fruit in the bottom of a heatproof dish.
2. Sprinkle over one of the crumbles (*see above*) and bake in a moderate oven, Gas 4, 350°F, 180°C, for about 25 minutes, or until the topping is beginning to darken and is slightly crisp.

RHUBARB AND GINGER

675 g/1½ lb rhubarb, wiped and cut into 1-cm/½-inch pieces
75 g/3 oz caster sugar
1 tablespoon water
½ teaspoon ground ginger

Cook as for Spiced Apple.

GOOSEBERRY

450 g/1 lb gooseberries, washed, topped and tailed
75 g/3 oz caster sugar

Cook as above.

FIG AND APPLE

225 g/8 oz Bramley cooking apples, peeled, cored and sliced
125 g/4 oz dried figs, finely chopped
150 ml/¼ pint water

Cook as above.

BLACKCURRANT AND APPLE

450 g/1 lb blackcurrants, washed and stalked
75 g/3 oz cooked apples
50 g/2 oz caster sugar

You do not need to pre-cook the blackcurrants. Just spread them out in the bottom of the baking dish, sprinkle with sugar then the apples, followed by the crumble ingredients.

The basic crumble mixtures freeze well.

APPLE CHARLOTTE

A charlotte tin, which is what should be used to make this pudding, is a bit like a pudding basin only bigger. If you are using one, you will need to make up this recipe adding half as much again.

Serves 4

675 g/1½ lb apples (eating and baking mixed), peeled, cored and sliced
25 g/1 oz caster sugar
25 g/1 oz butter
6–7 large slices thin-cut bread, crusts removed
75 g/3 oz melted butter
1 medium egg yolk

1. Put the apples, sugar and butter into a pan and cook, covered, over a low heat until the apples are soft. Mash the apples to a very thick firm purée, and cook to evaporate as much liquid as possible. Set aside to cool.
2. Preheat the oven to fairly hot, Gas 6, 400°F, 200°C.
3. Cut the sliced bread in long strips to line a 600-ml/1-pint pudding basin, reserving some strips for the top. Brush the bread on both sides with the melted butter and line the basin carefully. Do not leave any gaps.
4. Mix the egg yolk into the cooled apples and put the mixture into the bread-lined basin. Fit the reserved buttered strips of bread on top of the fruit. Find a saucer which fits into the top of the basin and weigh this down with something heavy which will not burn – a weight, or a stone wrapped in foil.
5. Stand the bowl on a baking tray and bake for about 40 minutes. About 10 minutes before the end of cooking time, take the weight and saucer off to allow the top to crisp and brown. Invert onto a warm plate and serve with chilled pouring cream.

Will keep for 2–3 days in the fridge. Do not freeze.

APPLE PIE

This is an everyday fruit pie with pastry top and bottom. I much prefer our own Bramley cooking apples but many people, influenced by French flans and tarts, prefer dessert apples for a subtle flavour. The pie is good hot as a pudding or cold with a slice of cheese in the Yorkshire tradition.

Serves 8–10

325 g/12 oz shortcrust pastry *(see page 28)*
675 g/1½ lb thinly peeled, cored and sliced (not too finely) apples, cooked and sweetened
3 tablespoons milk

1. Set the oven to hot, Gas 7, 425°F, 220°C, and put a baking tray in to heat up. Grease a 25-cm/10-inch metal pie plate.
2. Divide the pastry in two. On a lightly floured surface, roll out each piece of pastry big enough to cover the plate. Wrap one piece of pastry round the rolling pin and lower it centrally onto the plate. Press into shape and, using the back of a knife, trim off any surplus pastry.
3. Drain any juice from the apples and pile them on the pastry base.
4. Moisten the edge of the pastry base and cover with the remaining piece of pastry, using the rolling pin to support it as before. Using a fork, press the edges together and trim off any surplus pastry. Brush the top of the pie with milk and cut two steam holes.
5. Put the pie plate on the preheated baking tray in the oven. Reduce the heat to fairly hot, Gas 6, 400°F, 200°C, and bake for about 30–45 minutes, or until the pie is lightly browned.

Eat at its best on the day it is made, or store in the fridge for 2–3 days. Not suitable for freezing.

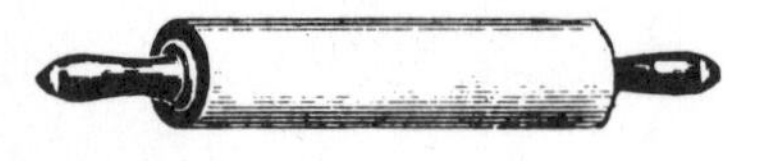

APPLE OR MINCEMEAT SPONGE PUDDING

It is so much easier to make up one big batch of the sponge topping that I usually make two puddings – one with apples and the other with mincemeat – and put one in the freezer. Alternatively, you could use half the sponge topping to make half a dozen buns.

Makes 2 puddings and each serves 4

675 g/1½ lb Bramley cooking apples, peeled, cored and sliced
40 g/1½ oz granulated sugar, or to taste
325 g/12 oz mincemeat

FOR THE SPONGE
175 g/6 oz tub margarine
175 g/6 oz caster sugar
175 g/6 oz self-raising white or wholewheat flour, sifted
1 teaspoon baking powder, sifted
3 medium eggs, beaten
A little milk, if necessary

1. Preheat the oven to moderate, Gas 3, 325°F, 160°C.
2. Put the apples and sugar into a pan with 2 tablespoons water, cover and cook until just starting to soften. Remove from the heat and drain. Spread in the bottom of a 600-ml/1-pint pie dish.
3. Place the mincemeat in the bottom of another 600-ml/1-pint pie dish.
4. Put all the sponge ingredients into a large mixing bowl and beat together for 2 minutes. The mixture should be soft but not wet. Add a little cold milk if necessary.
5. Drop the sponge mixture in blobs over the fruit in the dishes and level it off. The sponge mixture should be about 2-cm/¾-inch deep.
6. Set the pie dishes in a roasting tin with hot water coming halfway up the sides of the tin. (This will prevent the fruit from boiling and spoiling.)
7. Bake for about 40–45 minutes. Reduce the heat slightly if the sponge is getting too brown on top. Check that the sponge is fully cooked by touching the top with your fingers – it should be easy to detect if there is still a wobble underneath.

Eat while warm or store in a fridge for 3–4 days. Freeze uncooked for up to 2 months.

VARIATION

TO MAKE SIX BUNS INSTEAD OF A SECOND PUDDING

1. Set paper bun cases in bun trays.
2. Spoon the sponge mixture into the paper cases* – 2 good teaspoons in each.
3. Bake at the same temperature for 12–15 minutes or until risen, firm and brown.

* *If liked, add 40 g/1½ oz currants or nuts to the remaining sponge mixture before spooning it into the paper cases.*

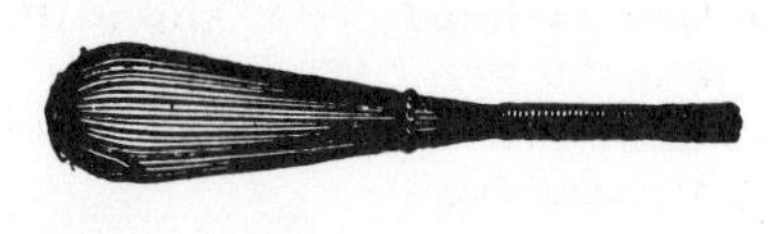

LEMON SURPRISE

This is an old and simple lemon pudding. The surprise is that during cooking it separates into a lemony custard with a light sponge on top.

Serves 4

50 g/2 oz very soft butter
125 g/4 oz caster sugar
2 large eggs, separated
Grated rind of 1 lemon
3 tablespoons lemon juice
50 g/2 oz self-raising white flour, sifted
Just over 300 ml/½ pint milk (about 2 tablespoons more)

1. Put some hot water into a roasting tin – about 1 cm/½ inch deep. Set the oven to moderate, Gas 3, 325°F, 160°C, and put the tin in to heat up.
2. In a large mixing bowl, beat the butter and sugar together until pale and fluffy. Beat in the egg yolks and lemon rind, then stir in the lemon juice and the flour. Slowly mix in the milk to make a fairly thick batter.
3. In a clean, grease-free bowl, whisk the egg whites until they are very stiff, then fold them into the batter mixture.
4. Turn into a 900-ml/1½-pint buttered pie dish. Put the dish carefully into the roasting tin in the oven and bake for about 45 minutes, or until the sponge is firm on top and golden.

Serve as soon as possible. Do not freeze.

CLAFOUTIS

This strange name belongs to a fruity French pudding tart usually made with cherries. I have replaced the original batter mixture with a rich custard. Almost any fruit can be used but sweet black cherries, grapes or fresh whole raspberries are nice because the custard can run in and around each piece of fruit.

Serves 8

1 pre-baked 20-cm/8-inch shallow shortcrust pastry shell *(see page 29)*
4 medium eggs
300 ml/½ pint milk
125 g/4 oz caster sugar
2 tablespoons orange liqueur (Cointreau or Grand Marnier)
225 g/8 oz fruit – black cherries, pitted; grapes, stoned; or whole raspberries

1. Preheat the oven to cool, Gas 2, 300°F, 150°C. Set the pastry shell on a flat, ovenproof serving dish.
2. In a large mixing bowl, beat the eggs, milk and sugar together. Stir in the liqueur and whisk again. Make sure the sugar has dissolved.
3. Arrange the fruit in the pastry case and strain the custard through a nylon sieve over it. (You may have a little custard over.)
4. Bake for about 30 minutes, or until the custard is set.

Eat on the day the tart is made, or store the cooked pastry shell in an airtight tin for 4 days, or the uncooked shell in the freezer for about 1 month.

QUEEN OF PUDDINGS

This is the best of all the breadcrumb-based puddings. It is light and delicate and even more special if you use some home-made strawberry or raspberry jam. I remember clearly the first time we made this at school; my chum and I scoffed the lot before we got home!

Serves 4–5

450 ml/¾ pint milk
25 g/1 oz butter
Grated rind of 1 small lemon
125 g/4 oz caster sugar
75 g/3 oz fresh breadcrumbs
2 medium eggs, separated
50 g/2 oz good strawberry or raspberry jam

1. Lightly butter a 1.2-litre/2-pint pie dish. Preheat the oven to moderate, Gas 4, 350°F, 180°C.
2. Put the milk into a large pan and bring to boiling point. Remove from the heat and stir in the butter, lemon rind and 25 g/1 oz of the sugar.
3. Beat the egg yolks and add to the mixture with the breadcrumbs. Set this aside for 10 minutes.
4. Pour the mixture into the pie dish and bake for about 20 minutes, or until set. Remove from the oven.
5. Spread the jam carefully over the set custard.
6. In a clean, grease-free bowl, whisk the egg whites until stiff and fold in the remaining sugar. Spread this over the top of the pudding, making sure no gaps remain.
7. Reduce the heat to slow, Gas 1, 275°F, 140°C, and bake for a further 15 minutes, or until the meringue is just turning golden.

Eat at once. Not suitable for freezing.

CARAMEL QUEEN

This pudding is loosely based on the recipe for Queen of Puddings (*left*). Its lovely caramel flavour is particularly nice.

Serves 6

125 g/4 oz golden syrup
15 g/½ oz butter
300 ml/½ pint milk
50 g/2 oz fresh white breadcrumbs
2 large eggs, separated
2–3 drops vanilla essence
1 pinch cream of tartar
125 g/4 oz caster sugar

1. Grease a deep 1.2-litre/2-pint casserole dish. Preheat the oven to moderate, Gas 3, 325°F, 160°C.
2. In a heavy based pan, cook the syrup and butter until the mixture is a deep golden brown in colour.
3. Add the milk slowly, stirring all the time.
4. Put the breadcrumbs into a large heatproof jug and pour the flavoured milk over them. Set aside to cool.
5. Beat the egg yolks into the mixture and add the vanilla essence.
6. Pour the custard into the casserole dish and bake for about 30 minutes or until set. Allow to cool.
7. In a large grease free bowl, whisk the egg whites with the cream of tartar until they are very stiff. Continue whisking and add the caster sugar, 1 tablespoon at a time. You will now have a good stiff meringue.
8. Pile the meringue into a large piping bag with a star nozzle and pipe a lattice design over the cooled custard.
9. Bake in a low oven, Gas ½, 250°F, 120°C, for about 30 minutes. Serve warm or chilled.

Will keep in the fridge for 3–4 days but meringue goes soft. Not suitable for freezing.

BREAD AND BUTTER PUDDING

One of the most famous and popular puddings. It can be made very rich by using half milk and half single cream for the custard, and adding mixed peel to the dried fruit. It is also very good made with spiced tea bread instead of plain bread as the base.

Serves 6

6–8 slices of bread, well buttered, cut into strips or squares, and triangles
75 g/3 oz granulated sugar
150 g/5 oz raisins, or any mixed dried fruit
1 teaspoon ground cinnamon
3 large eggs, beaten
600 ml/1 pint milk
25 g/1 oz demerara sugar

1. Butter a fairly deep baking dish. It is easier to cut the bread to fit if the tin is oblong or square.
2. Fit a layer of bread in the bottom of the dish and sprinkle with the granulated sugar, raisins and cinnamon. Continue to fill the dish – you will probably have three layers. Top with a layer of bread cut into triangles and lay the pieces to give a tiled effect, overlapping in a decorative way.
3. Whisk the eggs into the milk and pour over the pudding. Leave it to soak in for about 10 minutes.
4. Preheat the oven to moderate, Gas 4, 350°F, 180°C.
5. Sprinkle the demerara sugar over the top of the pudding. Place the dish on a baking tray and bake for about 45 minutes, or until the custard is set and the top is brown and crusty.

Store in the fridge for up to 2 days. Do not freeze.

BAKED RICE PUDDING

Traditional rice pudding is baked long and slowly in a moderate oven. You can hasten things along by first boiling the rice in water and draining it, and then adding the milk to continue cooking in the oven. However, you will not get that rich and thick texture which most people like. A good brown caramelized top is essential, too, so that everyone can have a share! Use a large pie or baking dish as you have to stir this pudding a couple of times and need the dish to be deep and not brimming over.

Serves 4–5

25 g/1 oz butter or margarine
50 g/2 oz round pudding rice
25 g/1 oz caster sugar
600 ml/1 pint milk

1. Using a little of the butter or margarine, butter a deep pie dish or baking dish which will hold 1 litre/1½ pints. Preheat the oven to moderate, Gas 3, 325°F, 160°C.
2. Put the rice into a sieve and rinse it under a running tap, then put it into the dish with the sugar and milk. Stir until all the sugar has dissolved. Add the remaining butter.
3. Put the baking dish on a metal baking tray and bake for about 1¾ hours, or until the rice is soft and the top nicely browned. Stir two or three times in the first hour. Once the skin has formed, slide your stirring spoon carefully under it in order to keep it intact. You may have to add a little milk.
4. Serve hot or cold with pouring milk or with fruit – stewed apples, rhubarb etc.

Store in the fridge for 2–3 days. Not suitable for freezing.

MINCEMEAT FLAN

This is a good mixture if, like me, you do not care for too much mincemeat at one time.

Serves 8

1 pre-baked 18–20-cm/7–8-inch shortcrust pastry shell *(see page 29)*
225 g/8 oz cottage cheese
225 g/8 oz mincemeat
2 large eggs, separated
75 g/3 oz caster sugar
Grated rind of 1 lemon

1. Put the baked pastry shell on a heatproof plate or baking tray. Preheat the oven to moderate, Gas 4, 350°F, 180°C.
2. Put the cottage cheese in a food processor and beat until smooth, or beat by hand. Mix 50 g/2 oz of the cottage cheese with the mincemeat and spread in the pastry shell.
3. In a large mixing bowl, beat the egg yolks with 25 g/1 oz of sugar. Stir in the remaining cottage cheese and the lemon rind and set aside.
4. In a clean, grease-free bowl, whip the egg whites until they are stiff. Fold half the egg whites into the cottage cheese and lemon rind mixture and spread this over the mincemeat.
5. Stir the remaining sugar into the remaining whipped egg whites and whip again until stiff. Spread this meringue all over the top of the flan, making sure there are no gaps.
6. Bake for about 30 minutes, when the meringue should be golden tipped and lightly crisp.

Serve warm on the day it is made. It can be stored in the fridge for 1 day but becomes a bit runny. Store the cooked pastry shell in an airtight tin for up to 4 days, or freeze the uncooked pastry shell for up to 1 month.

BUTTERSCOTCH FLAN

This is a rich, firm custard with a good caramel flavour.

Serves 8

1 pre-baked 20-cm/8-inch shortcrust pastry shell *(see page 29)*
50 g/2 oz butter
200 g/7 oz demerara sugar
600 ml/1 pint milk
2 teaspoons cornflour
2 large eggs, beaten
40 g/1½ oz plain chocolate, broken into pieces

1. Put the baked pastry shell on a serving plate.
2. Melt the butter and sugar in a roomy pan and set aside.
3. In a heavy based pan, heat the milk gently.
4. In a mixing bowl, beat the cornflour into the eggs, using a wire loop whisk, then whisk the egg mixture into the hot milk. Simmer until the custard thickens, stirring with a wooden spoon.
5. Pour the custard into the melted butter and sugar and stir well. Pour into the pastry shell and leave to set for about 30 minutes. (If the pastry shell is too shallow to take all the mixture, pour the extra into one or two glass serving dishes.)
6. Put the chocolate into a small heatproof bowl set over a pan of simmering water and stir until melted. Pour the melted chocolate into a paper icing bag, snip off the point and dribble a zigzag design all over the flan filling. Alternatively, you could try your hand at piping the word 'BUTTER-SCOTCH'.

Eat within 2 days. Store the cooked pastry shell in an airtight tin for up to 4 days, or freeze the uncooked pastry shell for up to 1 month.

YORKSHIRE PUDDING

Everybody knows that Yorkshire puddings go with roast beef, but it wasn't until I came to live in Yorkshire that I heard of Yorkshire puddings with a sweet sauce. The idea is to eat half the pudding with the main course and the remainder with a sauce made from golden syrup and lemon juice. I asked about the salt, which is usually put into savoury puddings, and was told to add just a pinch. It is essential to have a very, very hot oven so that the puddings start to rise the minute they go in.

Makes 12–14 small puddings

125 g/4 oz plain white flour
1 pinch salt
1 large egg
150 ml/¼ pint milk and 150 ml/¼ pint water, mixed
Cooking fat

FOR THE SAUCE
125 g/4 oz golden syrup
Juice of ½ lemon (1–2 tablespoons)

1. Sift the flour and salt into a mixing bowl.
2. Beat in the egg and enough milk and water mix to give the beating consistency of thick cream. Set this mixture aside for about 30 minutes.
3. Preheat the oven to very hot, Gas 8, 450°F, 230°C.
4. Prepare small individual bun tins, or tins set in a tray, by putting a small knob of fat in each. Put the trays in the oven until the fat is smoking hot.
5. Beat the remaining milk and water into the batter mixture and pour about 2 tablespoons into each bun tin. Bake for 15–20 minutes, or until the puddings are crisp and brown.
6. Meanwhile, make the sauce. Put a small pan on the scales, weigh it and then weigh the syrup into it. Melt the syrup slowly over a low heat, and add the lemon juice to taste.
7. Serve poured over the hot puddings.

Eat immediately. Not suitable for freezing.

BRANDY SNAP GINGER BASKETS

These crunchy baskets have a delicate texture, and filled with cream and preserved ginger make a very delicious dessert.

Makes about 14

125 g/4 oz butter
125 g/4 oz granulated sugar
125 g/4 oz golden syrup
Juice of ½ lemon
125 g/4 oz plain white flour
½ teaspoon ground ginger

FOR THE FILLING
150 ml/¼ pint single cream
150 ml/¼ pint double cream
2 tablespoons brandy
125 g/4 oz preserved ginger, chopped

1. Line baking trays with nonstick paper. Well grease the outside of an upturned cup. Preheat the oven to moderate, Gas 4, 350°F, 180°C.
2. Put the butter, sugar, syrup and lemon juice into a roomy pan and heat gently until melted, but not too hot.
3. Remove the pan from the heat and sift in the flour and ground ginger. Stir well.
4. Drop heaped teaspoons of the mixture onto the baking trays, keeping them about 15 cm/6 inches apart as they spread out to the size of small saucers.
5. Bake for about 8–10 minutes until brown and bubbly.
6. Allow to cool very slightly, then, using an egg slice, lift a biscuit off the tray and mould it over the upturned cup to form a basket shape. Remove from the cup and place on a baking tray to cool and crisp up. Repeat this process with the remaining biscuits. If the biscuits become too hard to shape, put them back into the oven for a minute or two to soften up.
7. When ready to serve, whip the two creams with the brandy and stir in the ginger. Spoon the cream into each basket and serve with a little of the preserved ginger syrup trickled over the filled baskets.

Eat on the same day. The unfilled baskets will store in an airtight tin for up to 4 days. Not suitable for freezing.

RASPBERRY MILLE FEUILLES

This famous dessert is not difficult to make. What is difficult is serving it neatly – as all the filling tends to squash out when you cut it. I have solved this problem by partially freezing the pudding, slicing it in its frozen state then re-assembling it on the serving plate.

Serves 6

225 g/8 oz new flaky pastry *(see page 31)*,
or 225 g/8 oz frozen puff pastry, defrosted
125 g/4 oz icing sugar, sifted
1 tablespoon water
1 tablespoon redcurrant jelly
40 g/1½ oz walnuts, chopped

FOR THE FILLING
150 ml/¼ pint double cream
3 tablespoons single cream
2 teaspoons caster sugar
225 g/8 oz fresh raspberries, or 225 g/8 oz frozen raspberries, defrosted and drained

1. Grease and wet a large baking tray. Put a mixing bowl in the fridge to chill.
2. On a lightly floured board, roll out the pastry evenly to a large rectangle about 28 × 30 cm/11 × 12 inches. Place the pastry carefully on the baking tray and, using a sharp fork, prick the pastry all over. Chill for 30 minutes.
3. Preheat the oven to hot, Gas 7, 425°F, 220°C. Bake the pastry for about 15 minutes. To make sure both sides are evenly brown, turn the pastry over for the last 5 minutes of baking time. Cool on a wire tray.
4. Trim the cooled pastry and cut lengthways into three.
5. Next, ice the top layer of the dessert with a traditional feather design. Mix the icing sugar with just enough water to make a smooth coating consistency. Pick a very flat slice of pastry and carefully and smoothly spread the icing over one side of it.
6. Using a fork, beat the redcurrant jelly and put it into a small paper icing bag. Cut a tiny point off the paper cone and pipe lines of jelly diagonally over the icing, about 2.5 cm/1 inch apart. While the icing is still wet, draw a skewer, or the back of a knife, alternately backwards and forwards diagonally across the lines of jelly at about 2.5-cm/

1-inch intervals, to create a 'feathered' pattern. Clean the icing from your skewer after each stroke. Sprinkle the chopped walnuts round the outside edge to make a border. Leave to set.
7. To assemble the mille feuilles, whip the two creams together in the chilled bowl. Add the sugar and whip again. Spread half this cream over one of the pastry strips and top with half the raspberries. Cover with the middle layer of pastry and top this with the remaining cream and raspberries. Cover with the iced and decorated top pastry layer.

Serve chilled and eat on the day it is assembled – the pastry will go soft otherwise. The pastry strips store well in an airtight tin for up to 1 week, or freeze for up to 2 months.

ICE CREAM OR PUDDING SAUCES

CHOCOLATE SAUCE

Wonderful over fresh juicy pears. Serve hot or cold.

300 ml/½ pint double cream
1 tablespoon brandy
1 tablespoon strong instant coffee
225 g/8 oz plain chocolate, broken into small pieces

1. Put the cream, brandy and coffee into a small pan and heat to boiling point.
2. Take off the heat, add the pieces of chocolate and stir until melted.

Store in the fridge for up to 2 days. To reheat, stand the jug of sauce in a pan of hot water and stir. Not suitable for freezing.

FUDGE SAUCE

Excellent over vanilla ice cream. Serve hot or cold.

75 g/3 oz soft brown sugar
150 ml/¼ pint evaporated milk
125 g/4 oz plain chocolate, broken into small pieces
40 g/1½ oz butter
2–3 drops vanilla essence

1. In a heavy based pan, mix the sugar and the evaporated milk. Stir this over a low heat until the sugar is completely dissolved, then bring the mixture to a boil and boil for 1–2 minutes.
2. Take off the heat, add the chocolate, butter and essence and stir until dissolved.

Store in the fridge for up to 2 days. To reheat, stand the jug of sauce in a pan of hot water and stir. Not suitable for freezing.

MELBA SAUCE

Peach Melba is the famous dessert for which this simple sauce was invented. Put ½ fresh skinned peach into a glass dish, top with a scoop of vanilla ice cream and pour on the Melba sauce.

Raspberries, fresh or frozen
Icing sugar, sifted, to taste

1. Sieve the raspberries to make a purée. The sieve must be fine to trap the seeds.
2. Beat the icing sugar into the purée, 1 teaspoon at a time. Take care to keep the sharp flavour.

Store in the fridge for 2–3 days, or freeze for up to 1 month.

MERINGUES, GÂTEAUX AND CHEESECAKES

For a special occasion or a dinner party, meringues, gâteaux or cheesecakes seldom fail to please and can be as simple or elaborate as you care to make them.

I always feel the quality of a good meringue is lost if it is served with heavily sweetened fruit. I much prefer a sauce which is sharp and if possible fresh. Something I often do is serve meringues, either small or as a gâteau filled with unsweetened cream, with a sauce made of gooseberries which have been cooked very lightly, sweetened and liquidized to a thin purée. Or make the sauce with raspberries or strawberries – just liquidize and sweeten them.

It seems to me there are two kinds of gâteaux offered in restaurants – the solid leaden cake smothered in cream and decorated with two or three bits of fruit, or the aerated sponge which is very light, but also tasteless, and again smothered in cream. However, by using a fatless sponge for the base you will already have good flavour, and if you fill the gâteau with good quality fruit and flavour the cream with a liqueur which complements the fruit you will have a respectable gâteau.

Cheesecakes also can be leaden disasters. If you are not using real cream cheese, which will give a rich and buttery taste, I think it is very important to flavour whatever you are using. When crushing biscuits for the base try to avoid getting the crumbs too fine, which will make the texture very cloying instead of crunchy as it should be.

MERINGUES

Meringues are very easy to make if you obey three rules:

1. Use a gleaming clean bowl. The merest spot of grease or oil will stop the egg whites working properly.

2. Use eggs which are over 1 week old. Fresh egg whites do not whip well.

3. Whip the egg whites until they are so stiff and firm that the bowl can be turned upside down without them falling out. An electric whisk makes an easy job of whisking the egg whites.

BASIC MERINGUE

Makes 12–14

2 large egg whites
1 pinch salt
1 fat pinch cream of tartar
125 g/4 oz caster sugar*

* *Alternatively, use demerara sugar which you have reduced to the consistency of caster sugar in an electric (coffee) grinder. The flavour is delicious.*

1. Line baking trays with nonstick paper or foil.
2. Put the egg whites into a large, clean, grease-free mixing bowl and whisk until they are frothy. Add the salt and cream of tartar and continue whipping until the whites are really stiff.
3. Add the sugar 1 tablespoon at a time, whisking between each addition. The mixture should be thick and glossy and so stiff that you could easily cut it with a knife.
4. Put the meringue mixture into a large piping bag fitted with a 1-cm/½-inch star nozzle, and pipe the shapes required onto the baking trays (*see right*).
5. Bake the meringues in a very low oven, Gas ¼, 225°F, 110°C, for a minimum of 1½ hours. (Ideally, meringues should be baked very, very slowly for 3 hours so that the mixture is extremely dry.)
6. Cool the meringues on wire trays. When the meringues are cold, immediately put them into an airtight tin or a tightly fastened plastic bag.
7. When the meringues are filled, eat within 2 hours, or longer if you really enjoy quite sticky meringues.

MERINGUE SHAPES

SMALL ROUND MERINGUES

Makes 16

Suitable for putting together with whipped cream. Squeeze the piping bag until you get the size of meringue required and pull the nozzle away quickly to give a nice point on the meringue. You can pipe them fairly close together on the baking tray since they do not spread much in baking. When cold, sandwich them in pairs with thick cream. Alternatively, coat the flat bottom of each meringue in melted chocolate and leave to set before sandwiching with whipped cream.

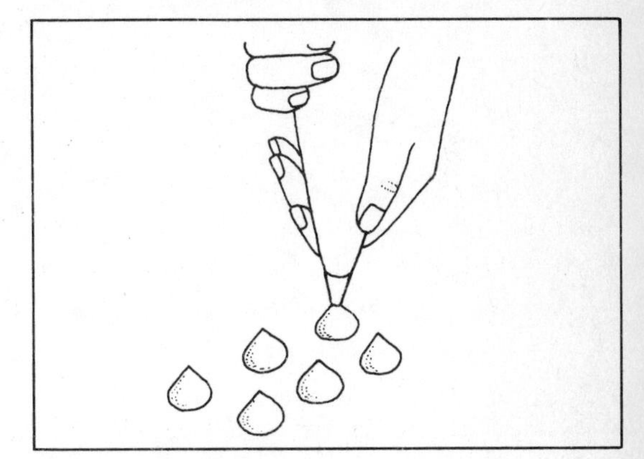

MERINGUE BASKETS

Makes 10

Pipe a solid, circular base of meringue, about 5 cm/2 inches across. Then pipe round the edge to make a small wall. With practice you will be able to do this in one movement. From the full quantity of meringue you should get 10 baskets. Fill with fresh whipped cream and fruit – strawberries, raspberries or grapes, or a mixture of fresh or canned fruit. A particular favourite of mine is home-made lemon curd folded into whipped cream.

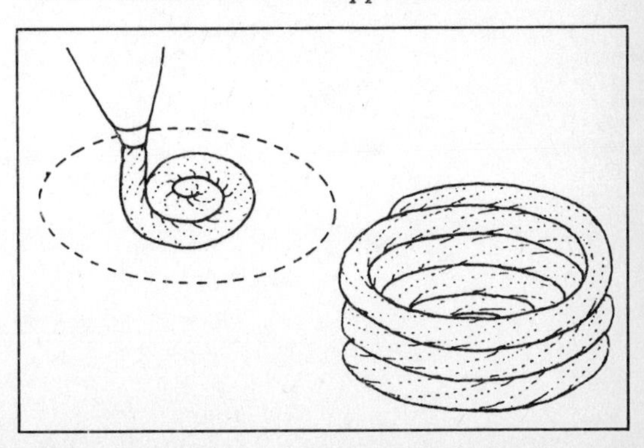

MERINGUE GÂTEAU

Draw three 20-cm/8-inch circles on nonstick paper or foil. Divide the meringue mixture roughly into three lots and, using the pencilled rings as a guide, spread the mixture into them with a knife. For a decorative top layer, put the meringue into a piping bag fitted with a 1-cm/½-inch star nozzle and, starting in the centre, pipe round and round until you meet the pencilled edge. This gives you a top layer of 'stars' which join together in the oven. When cooked and cold, sandwich the three layers with whipped cream and fruit or a chocolate cream filling (*see page 251*).

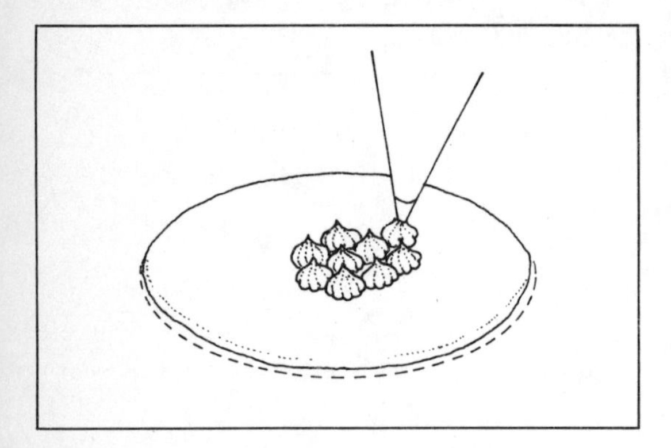

MERINGUE CASKET

Instead of a round meringue gâteau, try this shape – it is very much easier to slice. Draw a 13 × 23-cm/5 × 9-inch oblong shape onto nonstick paper or foil. Pipe zigzags of meringue to fill the oblong, then, using a 1-cm/½-inch star nozzle, pipe stars all around the edge on top of the base. When cooked and cold, fill the casket with fruit or fruit and cream.

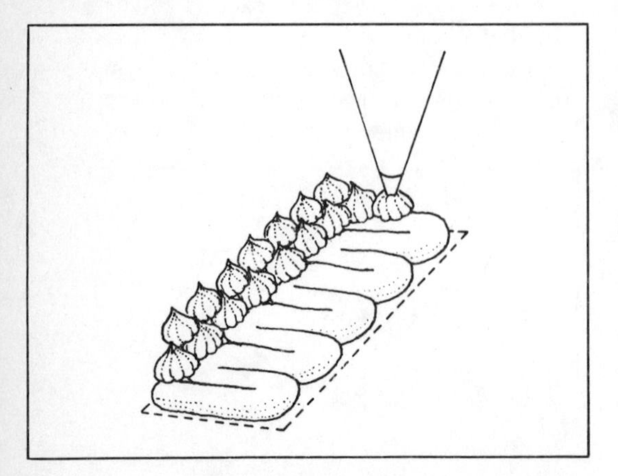

PAVLOVA

This is a huge pavlova for a party. The texture should be crisp on the outside and soft inside, which the cornflour and vinegar help to achieve. Vary the fruit according to the season. I rather like mixed fruit with lots of colour, or just all one fruit like strawberries, or black and green grapes, halved and de-seeded.

Serves 12

6 large egg whites
1 pinch salt
325 g/12 oz caster sugar
1½ teaspoons cornflour
1½ teaspoons vanilla essence
1½ teaspoons vinegar
300 ml/½ pint double cream, whipped
Fresh fruit: strawberries, raspberries, grapes, passion fruit etc.

1. Line a large baking tray with nonstick paper and draw on it a circle 22–23 cm/8–9 inches across, using a dinner plate to help. Preheat the oven to slow, Gas 1, 275°F, 140°C.
2. Put the egg whites and salt into an electric mixer and whip at high speed until the egg whites are very stiff, or whip with a large loop whisk.
3. With the machine running, add the sugar, 2 tablespoons at a time, whipping well between each addition, until all the sugar is incorporated. The mixture should be very stiff.
4. Take the bowl away from the machine and quickly fold in the cornflour, vanilla essence and vinegar.
5. Pile the meringue into the circle on the baking tray, making the sides higher than the centre. Use a skewer to make swirls all round and pull the meringue out in little peaks.
6. Bake for about 1–1½ hours, when the outside should be crisp and the inside soft.
7. Allow to cool, then lift gently onto a large serving plate or tray.
8. Just before serving, pile the whipped cream into the centre of the meringue and cover with the fruit. Serve cut in wedges.

Eat on the day it is assembled. Do not freeze.

HAZELNUT AND RASPBERRY MERINGUE

A wonderful combination of flavours and textures. Don't worry if the meringue bases look cracked and uneven – the finished dish tastes delicious.

Serves 6–8

3 large egg whites
1 pinch salt
175 g/6 oz granulated sugar
40 g/1½ oz ground rice or fine semolina
75 g/3 oz ground hazelnuts

FOR THE FILLING AND DECORATION
300 ml/½ pint double cream
225 g/8 oz raspberries, drained
50 g/2 oz hazelnuts, chopped
8 whole hazelnuts
15 g/½ oz plain chocolate, grated

1. Line the base and sides of two 18-cm/7-inch sandwich tins with nonstick paper. Preheat the oven to moderate, Gas 4, 350°F, 180°C.
2. Put the egg whites and salt into a large, clean, grease-free mixing bowl and whip until they are really stiff. Sprinkle half the sugar over and whisk again.
3. In another bowl, mix the remaining sugar with the ground rice or semolina and ground hazelnuts and fold this into the egg whites.
4. Divide this mixture between the two tins, level it off and bake for 25–30 minutes until crisp. Turn the meringues out and cool on a wire tray. Peel off the lining paper.
5. Whip the double cream until firm and spread a generous layer on one meringue. Spoon the raspberries over the cream then top with the other meringue. Spread a little whipped cream in a thin layer round the sides of the meringues and pat the chopped nuts into it.
6. Scrape the remaining cream down the bowl, whip again and fill a piping bag fitted with a star nozzle. Pipe eight whirls of cream round the top of the meringue and top each with a whole hazelnut. Scatter the grated chocolate over each whirl of cream.

Eat on the day the gâteau is assembled. The bases store well in airtight tins for up to 6 days. The whole gâteau freezes very well and, because the texture is light, it defrosts easily.

GÂTEAUX AND SPONGE DESSERTS

ROCKY RUM GÂTEAU

The contrast of the crunchy toffee and the soft rum-soaked sponge is delightful.

Serves 12

FOR THE SPONGE
3 large eggs
75 g/3 oz vanilla sugar *(see page 17)*
75 g/3 oz plain white flour

FOR THE FILLING AND TOPPING
175 g/6 oz peanut brittle
150 ml/¼ pint double cream
125 ml/4 fl oz rum
125 ml/4 fl oz water

1. Grease a round tin, 20 cm/8 inches across and 7.5 cm/3 inches deep, and put a circle of greaseproof paper in the base. Preheat the oven to moderate, Gas 3, 325°F, 160°C.
2. Using an electric mixer or electric hand whisk, whisk together the eggs and sugar until they are very, very thick and pale. This will take about 5 minutes at high speed.
3. Using a sieve, sprinkle about one-third of the flour over the egg mixture. Fold this in carefully and quickly with a spatula. Repeat this twice, when you should have a very firm, fluffy mixture.
4. Pour the mixture into the tin and bake immediately for about 40 minutes, or until the sponge is well risen and just starting to shrink from the sides of the tin.
5. Take out of the oven and allow to cool for about 10 minutes. (The sponge often sinks a bit in the middle.) Run a knife round the cake to loosen it, then turn it out onto a wire tray, peel off the lining paper and cool.
6. Break up the peanut brittle by putting it in a very strong plastic bag and crushing it with a rolling pin or hammer. (Leave it nicely dotted with crunchy pieces of nut and toffee.)
7. Whip the double cream until it is quite thick.
8. Cut the cooled sponge into two layers and put the bottom layer on a flat serving plate. Mix the rum with the water and use about half to sprinkle

this layer very thoroughly so that it is really moistened.

9. Spread half the whipped cream over the bottom layer. Cover with the other sponge and again drench the dry sponge with the rum and water mixture. Spread the remaining cream all over the top and sides of the gâteau – this does not need to be very tidy. Cover the creamed top and sides with the peanut brittle powder and chunky pieces.

Serve on the day the gâteau is assembled, but will keep fairly well for 2 days in a fridge. Freezes well for up to 1 month.

CHOCOLATE AND MARASCHINO GÂTEAU

You could say that this is my version of the famous Black Forest Gâteau. I use a fatless chocolate sponge base which I much prefer to cake. The cherries are the kind you buy to put in cocktails and have a maraschino flavour. Their firm texture contrasts beautifully with the soft texture of the gâteau. Look for a jar of red cherries in a clear pinkish rather than dark red liquid. They are both fine but the dark red syrup makes the cream go a funny colour, although the taste is unaltered. If you can get the maraschino liqueur with which to soak the sponge, so much the better. If not, use a good sherry.

Serves 12

FOR THE FATLESS CHOCOLATE SPONGE

3 large eggs
75 g/3 oz caster sugar
2 teaspoons cocoa powder, sifted (not drinking chocolate)
75 g/3 oz plain white flour

FOR THE FILLING AND COVERING

125 ml/4 fl oz maraschino liqueur or sherry
125 ml/4 fl oz water
125 ml/4 fl oz syrup from cherries
300 ml/½ pint double cream
1 single portion carton of chocolate mousse (about 2–3 tablespoons)
225 g/8 oz jar maraschino-flavoured red cherries in syrup, drained and cut in half

CHOCOLATE CARAQUE TO DECORATE

50 g/2 oz best quality plain chocolate, broken into small pieces
A little salad oil
Extra whipped cream (optional)

1. Grease and base line a 20-cm/8-inch cake tin with sides about 7.5 cm/3 inches deep. Preheat the oven to moderate, Gas 3, 325°F, 160°C.
2. Using an electric mixer or an electric hand whisk, whip the eggs and sugar until they have increased in volume and are very, very thick and fluffy.
3. Mix the cocoa powder and flour and, using a sieve, sprinkle about one-third of the flour mixture over the whipped eggs and sugar. Fold this in carefully, using a spatula and a figure of eight movement and sliding the spatula to the bottom of the bowl so that no dry flour is left. Repeat this twice, taking care to cut through the mixture with the sharp edge of the spatula to keep the mixture as fluffy as possible.
4. Pour this mixture into the tin and bake for about 40 minutes, or until the sponge is risen, firm to the touch and beginning to shrink from the sides of the tin.
5. Leave in the tin for about 10 minutes, then slide a knife carefully round the sponge and turn it out onto your open hand. Peel off the lining paper and turn the sponge over again and onto a wire tray to cool. The sponge sometimes sinks in the centre.
6. To fill the gâteau, select a large serving plate, as flat as possible. Slice the cold sponge horizontally into three layers and place the bottom slice on the serving plate.
7. In a jug, mix the liqueur, water and syrup and pour about one-third of this mixture over the sponge on the plate. Aim to stop pouring before the liquid starts oozing out of the sponge.
8. Whip the cream to the floppy stage and spread 2 generous tablespoons on the sponge. Do this carefully as the sponge will be very soft. Spread about half the chocolate mousse on top of the cream, and top this with half the cherries.
9. Put the middle slice of sponge in position and repeat the layers of liquid, cream and mousse, and top with the remaining cherries.
10. Put the top layer of sponge on and pour over the remaining liquid (you may have to add a little extra at this point). Press the sponge down carefully.
11. Whip the remaining cream again, if necessary, and, using a wide palette knife, mask the whole of the gâteau. It does not need to be very smooth – as long as you achieve a thin layer of cream all over. Set the gâteau aside to firm up, in a fridge if possible.
12. Meanwhile, make the chocolate caraque (curls) to decorate the gâteau. (You can cut a corner at this point by surrounding the sides of the gâteau with thin rectangles or squares of plain

chocolate – some specialist chocolate shops sell these. Large chocolate drops can also look attractive.) Put the chocolate into a small heatproof bowl set over a pan of simmering water and stir until melted. A flat hard surface is needed now – marble is ideal but I use a large laminated chopping board. Wipe the surface lightly with a tissue dipped in vegetable oil. Pour the melted chocolate over this surface and spread it out fairly thinly. Leave to set until no longer sticky to the touch.

13. To make long curls, hold a sharp knife at an angle and push the blade away from yourself across the surface of the chocolate. (Some people use a clean wallpaper stripper for this job and the movement is somewhat similar.) If the chocolate shatters into crumbs, it is too hard: soften it up again by leaving the board in a warm room. If the chocolate just gathers up the knife, it is too soft: leave it to set a little longer.

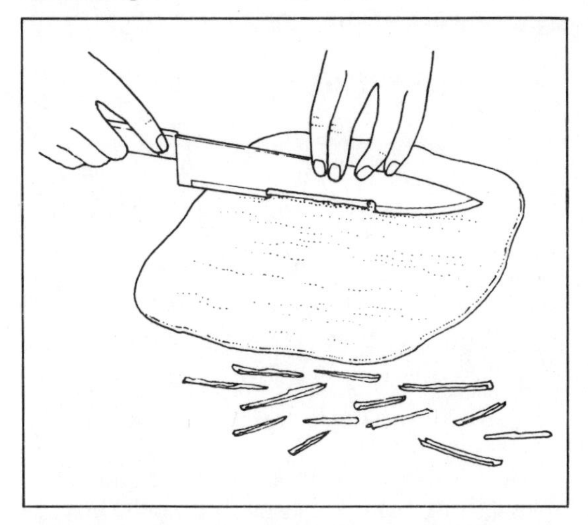

14. Drop the chocolate curls straight onto the gâteau. (I like to pile them up on top.) Cover the sides of the gâteau using the chocolate crumbs. You can, if you like, finish the top with whirls of whipped cream, using a piping bag fitted with a 1-cm/½-inch star nozzle. Chill before serving.

Eat on the day the gâteau is assembled, or freeze for up to 1 month. Store the unfilled sponge in an airtight tin for up to 4 days, or freeze for up to 1 month.

MANDARIN AND GRAPE FLAN

Serves 8

A little solid vegetable oil, melted
3 large eggs
75 g/3 oz vanilla sugar *(see page 17)*
75 g/3 oz plain white flour, sifted
2 tablespoons sherry
1 small can mandarin oranges, drained
125 g/4 oz seedless green grapes, or halved and de-seeded green grapes
2 tablespoons redcurrant jelly
150 ml/¼ pint double cream (optional)

1. Use the melted vegetable oil to grease a 20-cm/8-inch shallow flan ring with a raised base. Cut two circles of greaseproof paper and fit one to the raised base. Cut the centre out of the other circle so that you are left with a narrow band of paper, and lay this in the bottom of the flan ring. Preheat the oven to moderate, Gas 3, 325°F, 160°C.
2. Using an electric mixer or hand held mixer, whip the eggs and sugar together until you have a billowy mass of fluff. (It will take a good 5 minutes with a machine and 10–15 minutes by hand.)
3. Using a sieve, sprinkle about one-third of the flour over the egg mixture and fold this in carefully and quickly with a spatula. Repeat this twice, when you should have a very firm fluffy mixture.
4. Fill the flan ring about three-quarters full with the mixture and set the flan on a baking tray before putting it into the oven.* Bake for about 30 minutes.
5. Allow the flan to cool a little then run a knife round the outer and inner circles to release it. Peel off the lining paper and cool on a wire tray.
6. When cold, set the flan on a flat serving plate. Put the sherry in a small jug and dribble it over the flan. Arrange the fruit in a neat pattern, packing it very tightly.
7. Melt the redcurrant jelly in a small bowl in a pan of simmering water. Brush the jelly over the fruit making sure to get into all the corners. Allow to set, then decorate with whipped cream if you wish.

Eat on the day the flan is assembled. I do not like this frozen. The unfilled sponge flan will keep in an airtight tin for 1 week, or freeze for up to 1 month.

* *To use up any remaining mixture, drop blobs well apart onto two baking trays lined with nonstick paper, and bake for about 20 minutes or until they are brown. Leave to crisp up for 5–10 minutes. Store in an airtight tin.*

STRAWBERRY SHORTCAKE LAYER

This attractive dessert can be made with plain shortbread (*see page 96*) but I have used ground hazelnuts to give a really lovely flavour.

Serves 8

140 g/4½ oz plain white flour, sifted
1 pinch salt
85 g/3¼ oz butter, softened
60 g/2¼ oz caster sugar
75 g/3 oz ground hazelnuts
150 ml/¼ pint double cream
225 g/8 oz fresh strawberries or raspberries, hulled and wiped
Icing sugar
8 small strawberries or raspberries, with hulls intact and wiped

1. Using the slow speed of an electric mixer, bind together the flour, salt, butter, caster sugar and hazelnuts until a crumbly paste. Or blend by hand.
2. Using your hand, knead the shortbread in the bowl until it comes together. Cut the pastry into three pieces, knead briefly and set aside to chill and rest for 30 minutes – preferably in the fridge.
3. Line a baking tray with nonstick paper. Preheat the oven to moderate, Gas 3, 325°F, 160°C. Remove the pastry from the fridge and allow the pieces to soften up slightly.
4. Roll each piece out on a lightly floured surface to a circle about 18 cm/7 inches across and trim each circle neatly, using a plate or pan lid as a guide. Slide each circle onto the baking tray.
5. Bake for about 20 minutes, or until golden in colour. Allow to cool and crisp up.
6. When ready to serve, whip the cream until it is firm then put it into a piping bag fitted with a 1-cm/½-inch star nozzle. Slice the 225 g/8 oz strawberries or raspberries in two lengthways.
7. Lay one layer of hazelnut shortcake on a large flat plate and pipe or spread with half the cream. Top with half the strawberries, arranging the pointed ends outwards around the edge.
8. Put the middle shortcake in place and layer with the cream and strawberries.
9. Finally, top with the remaining shortbread and dredge with icing sugar. Lay the 8 small unhulled strawberries or raspberries around the edge.

Serve within 2 hours. Do not freeze. The cooked and cooled shortcakes will keep well for 4–5 days stored in an airtight tin.

MY TRIFLE

I always make trifle with raspberries and my own recipe fatless sponge. I don't make it in a deep bowl because I find it easier to serve from a flattish dish, and I'm not fond of sherry covering the flavour of my home-grown raspberries either!

Serves 8

Half a 20-cm/8-inch fatless sponge *(see page 72)*
450 g/1 lb raspberries, fresh or frozen
25 g/1 oz caster sugar
300 ml/½ pint single cream
1 teaspoon cornflour
3 medium egg yolks
25 g/1 oz caster sugar
1–2 drops vanilla essence
25 g/1 oz flaked almonds
150 ml/¼ pint double cream
2 medium egg whites

1. Cut the sponge horizontally and lay the pieces in the bottom of a 1.7-litre/3-pint flattish dish.
2. Reserve about 10 perfect raspberries. Put the remainder in a pan with 2–3 tablespoons of water and 25 g/1 oz sugar (no water is needed with frozen raspberries). Heat just a little to draw some juice, then remove from the heat and allow the raspberries to cool.
3. While the raspberries are cooling, make the custard. Put the single cream in a small pan and heat gently.
4. In a small basin, mix together the cornflour and the egg yolks with the sugar and vanilla essence. When this is smooth, pour some of the hot cream into the basin. Stir well, then pour the mixture into the cream in the pan, return the pan to the heat and stir until the custard thickens. Set aside.
5. Drain the raspberries and spread them over the sponge base. Pour enough of the raspberry juice over to make the sponge very wet, but not swimming. Scatter the flaked almonds on top.
6. Pour the custard over the fruit and leave in a cool place to set.
7. When the trifle is cold, whip the double cream to the floppy stage. In a clean, grease-free bowl, whisk the egg whites until they are fairly firm then fold them into the cream. Pile this cream on top of the trifle.
8. Just before serving, decorate the top of the trifle with the reserved raspberries.

Best eaten fresh. Do not freeze.

CHEESECAKES

There are two main types of cheesecake. The original cheesecake is the baked type on a sponge base. It is almost cake-like in texture and is very rich indeed. Its origins are said to be German or Austrian. The other type, probably the more popular, came from America. It is a much lighter cheesecake, often set with gelatine and has a biscuit base. Both types freeze well and are a good standby if you're having a party. It is best to freeze them undecorated, adding the finishing touches at the last minute.

BAKED CHEESECAKES

A baked cheesecake is cooked in two stages. The thin sponge base is baked first and allowed to cool, then the cheesecake topping is added and the whole thing baked again.

GINGER AND WALNUT CHEESECAKE

Serves 10–12

FOR THE SPONGE BASE
50 g/2 oz soft butter or margarine
50 g/2 oz caster sugar
1 small egg, beaten
50 g/2 oz self-raising white or brown flour, sifted and residue of bran left in the sieve added

FOR THE FILLING
150 ml/ ¼ pint sour cream
125 g/4 oz cream cheese, softened
125 g/4 oz cottage cheese
225 g/8 oz curd cheese
2 medium eggs, beaten
50 g/2 oz caster sugar
75 g/3 oz chopped walnuts
3 pieces stem ginger, drained and chopped

TO DECORATE
10 whole walnuts
Slivers of stem ginger
2 teaspoons ginger syrup

1. Grease and base line a 20-cm/8-inch loose-bottomed round tin. Preheat the oven to moderately hot, Gas 5, 375°F, 190°C.
2. To make the sponge base, beat together the butter, sugar, egg and flour in a mixing bowl. When the mixture is smooth, spread and level it in the bottom of the tin.
3. Bake for about 20 minutes until golden in colour. Leave to cool in the tin.
4. To make the filling, beat the cream and cheeses together either in a liquidizer or food processor. Or this can easily be done by hand if they are all softened and at room temperature; the cottage cheese will need to be either sieved or mashed thoroughly. Add the eggs and caster sugar and process again until smooth. Or beat in by hand until smooth.
5. Stir in the chopped walnuts and ginger and pour this mixture on top of the cooked sponge base. Reduce the heat to moderate, Gas 4, 350°F, 180°C, and bake for a further 30 minutes, or until just set.
6. Leave in the tin to become cold, then stand the tin on a small pudding basin and ease the sides of the tin down. Slide the cheesecake onto a serving plate, removing the lining paper as you do so. Decorate with the whole walnuts and slivers of ginger. Just before serving, brush the ginger syrup all over the surface to glaze.

Will keep in the fridge fairly well for 2 days, or freeze for up to 1 month.

BLACKCURRANT CHEESECAKE

Of all the fruits, I think that blackcurrants go best with cheesecake.

Serves 8–10

Sponge base as for Ginger and Walnut Cheesecake *(see page 141)*

FOR THE TOPPING
125 g/4 oz fresh or frozen blackcurrants, drained
25 g/1 oz plain white flour
75 g/3 oz caster sugar
OR
½ × 400-g/14-oz can blackcurrant pie filling

FOR THE FILLING
225 g/8 oz curd cheese
125 g/4 oz cream cheese
125 g/4 oz cottage cheese
50 g/2 oz caster sugar
2 medium eggs, beaten
150 ml/¼ pint sour cream
150 ml/¼ pint double cream

1. Prepare the tin and make and bake the sponge base as for Ginger and Walnut Cheesecake. Leave to cool in the tin.
2. Meanwhile, make the topping. If using the fresh or frozen blackcurrants, place them with the flour and caster sugar in a small pan over a low heat and cook, stirring, until you have a thick jam-like purée. You may need to add a little water. Allow to cool.
3. Beat all the ingredients for the filling, except the double cream, by hand or in a food processor or liquidizer, until very smooth.
4. Pour the filling on top of the cooked sponge base and bake in a moderate oven, Gas 4, 350°F, 180°C, for 30 minutes, or until just set.
5. Leave in the tin to become cold, then stand the tin on a pudding basin and ease the sides of the tin down. Slide the cheesecake onto a serving plate, removing the lining paper as you do so.
6. Whip the cream until firm, place it in a piping bag and pipe a thick border round the edge of the cheesecake.
7. Just before serving, put the cooled blackcurrants, or blackcurrant pie filling, in the centre of the cheesecake (otherwise they will stain the cream). Level off carefully. Serve chilled.

Eat on the day the cheesecake is assembled. Not suitable for freezing.

NO-BAKE CHEESECAKES

No-bake cheesecakes consist of a biscuit crumb base, topped with a creamy filling, usually set by gelatine.

STRAWBERRY PARADISE CHEESECAKE

Serves 8–10

FOR THE BISCUIT CRUMB BASE
225 g/8 oz digestive biscuits
75 g/3 oz butter
1 tablespoon golden syrup

FOR THE FILLING
3 tablespoons hot water
15-g/½-oz packet powdered gelatine
225 g/8 oz cream cheese, softened
225 g/8 oz curd cheese
75 g/3 oz icing sugar, sifted
1 tablespoon lemon juice
150 ml/¼ pint natural yoghurt
225 g/8 oz strawberries, hulled, wiped and puréed (if using frozen strawberries, drain very well in a sieve before puréeing)
2 large egg whites

TO DECORATE
8 small strawberries, hulled and wiped

1. Grease and base line a deep 20-cm/8-inch loose-bottomed round tin.
2. To make the biscuit crumb base, crush the biscuits by putting them into a thick plastic bag and beating with a rolling pin.
3. In a roomy pan, melt the butter and the syrup over a low heat. Stir in the biscuit crumbs and continue stirring until they are thoroughly moistened with the butter and syrup. Press the crumbs in an even layer in the bottom of the tin and allow to cool.
4. Put the hot water into a small bowl, sprinkle the gelatine on and leave to dissolve. Allow to cool.
5. To make the filling, put all the filling ingredients, including the cooled gelatine but excluding the egg whites, into a food processor or liquidizer and beat until smooth. Or, see that everything is at room temperature and beat by hand until smooth.
6. In a clean, grease-free bowl, whip the egg whites until very firm. Fold these into the cheese mixture.

7. Pour the filling into the tin on top of the biscuit base and leave in a cool place to set.
8. When the cheesecake has set, stand the tin on a pudding basin and ease the sides of the tin down. Slide the cheesecake onto a serving plate, removing the lining paper as you do so. Chill in the fridge.
9. Just before serving, decorate the top with the small, whole strawberries.

The undecorated cheesecake will store for 2–3 days in a fridge, or freeze for up to 1 month.

HAZELNUT AND ORANGE LOW-FAT CHEESECAKE

Serves 6–8

FOR THE BISCUIT CRUMB BASE
150 g/5 oz ginger or digestive biscuits
25 g/1 oz butter

FOR THE FILLING
1 large orange
325 g/12 oz low-fat cottage cheese
75 g/3 oz hazelnuts, chopped
75 g/3 oz raisins, soaked in hot water and drained
1 tablespoon thin honey
15-g/½-oz packet powdered gelatine
2 tablespoons water
2 teaspoons caster sugar
2 large egg whites

1. Grease and base line a 20-cm/8-inch loose-bottomed round tin.
2. Crush the biscuits by putting them into a thick plastic bag and beating with a rolling pin.
3. In a roomy pan, melt the butter and stir in the biscuits. Press the crumbs in an even layer in the bottom of the tin and allow to cool.
4. Grate the peel off the orange. Cut the orange in two and cut a wafer thin slice from each half. Squeeze the juice from the halves.
5. Liquidize the cottage cheese with the orange juice. Stir in the nuts and raisins and set aside.
6. Put the honey into a small bowl, sprinkle the gelatine over and set the bowl in hot water over a low heat. Stir until dissolved then allow to cool.
7. While the gelatine and honey mixture is cooling, put the two slices of orange into a small pan with about 2 tablespoons water and the sugar. Cook gently until the slices go transparent then lift them onto a plate to dry.
8. Stir the gelatine mixture into the cottage cheese along with the orange rind.
9. In a clean, grease-free bowl, whip the egg whites until very stiff and fold into the mixture. Pour this over the biscuit base and leave to set.
10. When the cheesecake has set, stand the tin on a pudding basin and ease the sides of the tin down. Slide the cheesecake onto a serving plate, removing the lining paper as you do so. Chill.
11. Just before serving, cut each slice of orange in half and decorate the top of the cheesecake.

The undecorated cheesecake will keep for 2–3 days in a fridge, or freeze for up to 1 month.

RASPBERRY BRITTLE CHEESECAKE

Serves 8–10

Biscuit crumb base as for Strawberry Paradise Cheesecake *(see page 142)*

FOR THE FILLING

3 tablespoons hot water
15-g/½-oz packet powdered gelatine
225 g/8 oz fresh or frozen raspberries, drained
225 g/8 oz cream cheese, softened
225 g/8 oz curd cheese
75 g/3 oz icing sugar
1 tablespoon lemon juice
150 ml/¼ pint natural yoghurt
2 medium egg whites

TO DECORATE

75 g/3 oz peanut brittle, crushed
Extra raspberries

1. Prepare the tin and make the biscuit crumb base as for Strawberry Paradise Cheesecake. Leave to cool.
2. Put the hot water into a small bowl, sprinkle the gelatine on and leave to dissolve. Allow to cool.
3. To make the filling, lay the 225 g/8 oz raspberries on top of the cooled biscuit crumb base.
4. Put all the remaining filling ingredients, including the cooled gelatine but excluding the egg whites, into a food processor or liquidizer and beat until smooth. Or, see that everything is at room temperature and beat by hand until smooth.
5. In a clean, grease-free bowl, whip the egg whites until very firm. Fold into the cheese mixture.
6. Pour the filling over the raspberries and leave to set.
7. When the cheesecake has set, stand the tin on a pudding basin and ease the sides of the tin down. Slide the cheesecake onto a serving plate, removing the lining paper as you do so. Chill in the fridge.
8. Just before serving, decorate the top of the cheesecake with a border of peanut brittle, and a few raspberries in the centre.

The undecorated cheesecake will store for 2–3 days in a fridge, or freeze for up to 1 month.

ORANGE CHEESECAKE

Because there is no gelatine in this cheesecake it does not set very firmly. I use the frozen concentrated orange juice.

Serves 4–5

FOR THE BISCUIT CRUMB BASE

50 g/2 oz butter
125 g/4 oz ginger biscuits

FOR THE FILLING

65 g/2½ oz caster sugar
75 ml/3 fl oz concentrated orange juice
275 g/10 oz cream cheese

TO DECORATE

1 × 50-g/2-oz bar of chocolate

1. Put a 20-cm/8-inch flan ring on a flat serving plate (or use a 20-cm/8-inch loose-bottomed round tin).
2. Crush the biscuits by putting them into a thick plastic bag and beating with a rolling pin.
3. In a roomy pan, melt the butter and stir in the biscuits. Mix well then press the crumbs into the flan ring and leave to set.
4. To make the filling, stir the sugar into the orange juice and stir until dissolved.
5. Beat the cream cheese in a large mixing bowl and very gradually mix in the sweetened orange juice. When it is all incorporated, pour the mixture over the biscuit base and leave in the fridge to set.
6. Decorate with curls of chocolate. To make these, use a loose head vegetable peeler and peel curls of chocolate off the edge of the block. Drop the curls directly onto the cheesecake or onto a sheet of greaseproof paper.

Store in a fridge and eat within 2 days, or freeze for up to 1 month.

TEA BREADS, SLICING LOAVES AND SCONES

As a Scot, I have a great liking for tea breads of all kinds and Scottish bakers produce a wide variety of these tea-time treats. The recipes here are for both sweet and savoury breads and I always find it useful to have one or two handy in the freezer.

There are also some good recipes for the ever popular slicing loaf. It keeps well in a tin and can be eaten like a cake or sliced and buttered, or even used for luxury toast.

I have tried to give good advice on the making of the simple scone – not as simple as it sounds. It is all too easy to bake biscuit-like scones which are far too short in texture. A good scone should be soft inside and just a little crisp on the outside.

TEA BREADS

COUNTRY TEA BREAD

This little loaf is sweetened with honey and has a lovely nutty topping. Serve it sliced and buttered. Start the night before.

Makes 1 × 450-g/1-lb loaf

150 g/5 oz sultanas
50 g/2 oz currants
25 g/1 oz red glacé cherries, finely chopped
5 tablespoons clear runny honey
150 ml/¼ pint cold tea (not too strong)
1 medium egg, beaten
225 g/8 oz self-raising white flour, sifted
25 g/1 oz butter, melted
25 g/1 oz demerara sugar
25 g/1 oz walnuts, chopped

1. Place the fruit in a large mixing bowl, pour in 4 tablespoons honey and the cold tea and leave overnight.
2. Next day, fold in the egg, flour and melted butter.
3. Grease and line the base and sides of a 450-g/1-lb loaf tin. Preheat the oven to moderate, Gas 4, 350°F, 180°C.
4. Spoon the mixture into the tin and bake for about 50 minutes. Remove from the oven, brush the top with the remaining honey and sprinkle on the sugar and walnuts. Return the loaf to the oven and bake for a further 15 minutes. Leave to firm up in the tin for 5 minutes then turn out onto a wire tray, peel off the lining paper and allow to cool.

Store in an airtight tin for 3–4 days, or freeze for up to 3 months.

CARROT TEA BREAD

Makes 1 × 450-g/1-lb loaf

175 g/6 oz plain wholemeal flour
1 teaspoon ground cinnamon
1 pinch salt
2 teaspoons baking powder
125 g/4 oz grated carrot
125 g/4 oz tub margarine
125 g/4 oz light soft brown sugar
Grated rind of ½ large orange
2 large eggs
50 g/2 oz walnuts, finely chopped
A little milk

1. Grease and line the base and sides of a 450-g/1-lb loaf tin. Preheat the oven to moderate, Gas 3, 325°F, 160°C.
2. Sift the flour, cinnamon, salt and baking powder into a mixing bowl, adding any residue of bran left in the sieve. Stir in the grated carrot and mix well.
3. In a large mixing bowl, cream the margarine and sugar until pale and fluffy. Beat in the orange rind.
4. Beat the eggs into the creamed mixture, a little at a time.
5. Fold in the flour mixture together with the walnuts, adding a little milk to give a soft, but not runny, consistency. Spoon the mixture into the tin and level the top.
6. Bake for about 1 hour, or until the loaf is risen, firm to the touch and just beginning to shrink from the sides of the tin. Leave to firm up in the tin for 5 minutes then turn out onto a wire tray, peel off the lining paper and allow to cool.

Store in an airtight tin for 3–4 days, or freeze for up to 1 month.

DATE TEA BREAD

Start the night before.

Makes 2 × 450-g/1-lb loaves

450 g/1 lb packet dates, stoned and finely chopped
225 g/8 oz granulated sugar
450 ml/¾ pint strained warm tea
1 large egg, beaten
2 rounded tablespoons thick cut marmalade
450 g/1 lb self-raising white flour, sifted

1. Put the chopped dates into a large mixing bowl. Add the sugar and 300 ml/½ pint of the warm tea. Stir well and leave overnight.
2. Next day, stir the remaining cold tea into the date mixture. Add the egg and the marmalade, and beat the mixture really well. Lastly, mix in the flour until well blended.
3. Grease and line the base and sides of two 450-g/1-lb loaf tins. Preheat the oven to moderate, Gas 3, 325°F, 160°C.
4. Spoon the mixture into the tins, and weigh them to ensure the mixture is evenly divided. Level the tops carefully.
5. Bake for about 1¾ hours, or until the loaves are well risen and springy. Leave to firm up in the tins for about 10 minutes, then turn out onto wire trays, peel off the lining papers and allow to cool.

Store in an airtight tin for up to 2 weeks, or freeze for up to 3 months.

COLD TEA BREAD

I use a smoked tea such as Earl Grey for this loaf. You could also use an ordinary tea with a small teaspoon of Lapsang Souchong added to give flavour. Start the night before.

Makes 1 × 900-g/2-lb loaf

275 g/10 oz mixed sultanas and raisins
200 g/7 oz light soft brown sugar
300 ml/½ pint cold smoked tea, strained
275 g/10 oz self-raising wholewheat flour, sifted
1 large egg, beaten

1. Put the fruit and sugar into a large mixing bowl, pour over the tea and leave overnight.
2. Next day, stir well and fold in the flour, together with any residue of bran left in the sieve, and the egg until the mixture is smooth.
3. Lightly grease and line the base and sides of a 900-g/2-lb loaf tin. Preheat the oven to moderate, Gas 4, 350°F, 180°C.
4. Pour the mixture into the tin and level the surface carefully. Bake for about 1½ hours. Allow to firm up in the tin for 5 minutes then lift the loaf out with the help of the lining paper onto a wire tray. Peel off lining paper and leave to cool.

Store in an airtight tin for 6–7 days, or freeze for up to 1 month.

ORANGE TEA LOAF

Makes 1 × 900-g/2-lb loaf

125 g/4 oz butter, softened
175 g/6 oz caster sugar
Grated rind and juice of 1 large orange
2 medium eggs, beaten
175 g/6 oz self-raising white flour, sifted
A little milk
75 g/3 oz granulated sugar for topping
2 teaspoons concentrated orange juice

1. Grease and line the base and sides of a 900-g/2-lb loaf tin. Preheat the oven to moderate, Gas 4, 350°F, 180°C.
2. In a large mixing bowl, cream together the butter and caster sugar until fluffy. Beat in the grated orange rind.
3. Gradually beat in the eggs, a little at a time, then fold in the flour together with about 3–4 tablespoons of milk to give a soft consistency.
4. Spoon the mixture into the tin and level the surface carefully.
5. Bake for about 50 minutes, or until the loaf is beginning to shrink from the sides of the tin. Leave the loaf in the tin for about 10 minutes until it has cooled down a little, then make the topping.
6. Put the concentrated orange juice into a small bowl and add enough of the fresh orange juice to make 2 tablespoons altogether. Stir in the granulated sugar and immediately pour this over the surface of the loaf. The juice will sink into the loaf leaving an orange-flavoured crusty topping.

Store in an airtight tin for 3–4 days, or freeze for up to 3 months.

APPLE AND CHEESE TEA BREAD

Grate the apples at the last minute as they go brown very quickly.

Makes 1 × 900-g/2-lb loaf

125 g/4 oz butter, very soft
125 g/4 oz caster sugar
2 large eggs, beaten
275 g/10 oz plain white flour
1 teaspoon baking powder
1 teaspoon salt
75 g/3 oz strong Cheddar cheese, grated
75 g/3 oz walnuts, chopped
450 g/1 lb cooking apples, peeled and grated

1. Grease and line the base and sides of a 900-g/2-lb loaf tin. Preheat the oven to moderate, Gas 3, 325°F, 160°C.
2. In a large mixing bowl, cream the butter and sugar until pale and fluffy.
3. Beat in the eggs, a little at a time, then sift in the flour, baking powder and salt. Fold in carefully then add the cheese, nuts and apples. Mix well.
4. Pour the mixture into the tin and level the surface.
5. Bake for about 1 hour, or until the loaf is well risen and firm. Allow to firm up in the tin for 5 minutes before turning out onto a wire tray. Peel off the lining paper and allow to cool.

Best eaten fresh. Store in an airtight tin for 2 days, or freeze for up to 1 month.

WALNUT AND APPLE TEA BREAD

This tea bread is made with oil instead of margarine or butter (*see page 10*).

Makes 1 × 900-g/2-lb loaf

275 g/10 oz self-raising wholemeal flour
1 teaspoon baking powder
1 pinch salt
225 g/8 oz cooking apple (peeled weight), finely chopped
75 g/3 oz walnuts, finely chopped
120 ml/4 fl oz vegetable oil
2 medium eggs, beaten
3 tablespoons milk
150 g/5 oz caster sugar
2 teaspoons grated lemon rind

1. Grease and line the base and sides of a 900-g/2-lb loaf tin. Preheat the oven to moderate, Gas 4, 350°F, 180°C.
2. Sift the flour, baking powder and salt into a large mixing bowl, adding any residue of bran left in the sieve, and stir in the chopped apples and walnuts.
3. In another bowl, whisk together the oil, eggs, milk and sugar, then fold in the flour mixture and the lemon rind.
4. Spoon the mixture into the tin and level the surface.
5. Bake for about 1 hour, or until the loaf is risen, firm to the touch and just beginning to shrink from the sides of the tin. Allow to firm up in the tin for 8–10 minutes then lift out with the help of the lining paper. Peel off lining paper and cool on a wire tray.

Store in an airtight tin for 4–5 days, or freeze for up to 3 months.

SLICING LOAVES

BANANA NUT LOAF

I thought everybody in the world knew this recipe but I was recently asked for it by a viewer. It is very simple and foolproof – great if you want something in a hurry. Make sure the bananas are very ripe (black spotted). You can make it in one big loaf tin, but it also makes two nice small loaves and they freeze well in a polythene bag or foil.

Makes 1 × 900-g/2-lb loaf, or 2 × 450-g/1-lb loaves

2 medium, ripe bananas, peeled
50 g/2 oz tub margarine
150 g/5 oz caster sugar
2 medium eggs
225 g/8 oz mixed white and brown self-raising flour, sifted and residue of bran from sieve added
40 g/1½ oz walnuts, chopped

1. Grease and base line a 900-g/2-lb loaf tin or two 450-g/1-lb tins. Preheat the oven to moderately hot, Gas 5, 375°F, 190°C.
2. Mash the bananas until they are thick and smooth.
3. In a large mixing bowl, cream the margarine and sugar until white and fluffy and beat in the eggs, a little at a time.
4. Add the flour, bananas and nuts and mix well. Pour the mixture into the tin(s) and bake for about 1 hour for the large loaf and about 45 minutes for the smaller ones. They should be risen and springy to the touch and beginning to shrink away from the sides of the tin. Leave to firm up in the tin for 10–15 minutes, then turn out onto a wire tray, peel off the lining paper and allow to cool.

Store in an airtight tin for 4–5 days, or freeze for up to 1 month.

SUNFLOWER BANANA LOAF

As well as bananas, this recipe uses sunflower seeds and sunflower margarine. Toasting the sunflower seeds really brings out their flavour. No sugar is used, but the bananas, which should be very ripe, add their own sweetness.

Makes 1 × 900-g/2-lb loaf

325 g/12 oz bananas, peeled
3 medium eggs, beaten
1 teaspoon vanilla essence
225 g/8 oz sunflower margarine
275 g/10 oz plain wholewheat flour
2 teaspoons baking powder
2 teaspoons ground ginger
50 g/2 oz desiccated coconut
50 g/2 oz sunflower seeds

1. Grease and line the base and sides of a 900-g/2-lb loaf tin. Preheat the oven to moderate, Gas 4, 350°F, 180°C.
2. Mash the bananas to a pulp in a large bowl and beat in the eggs and vanilla essence.
3. Sift the flour, baking powder and ginger into another bowl, adding any residue of bran left in the sieve, and rub in the margarine. Stir in the coconut and 25 g/1 oz of the sunflower seeds.
4. Fold the dry ingredients into the banana mixture and pour it into the tin. Level off the surface.
5. Put the remaining sunflower seeds under the grill until lightly browned, then sprinkle them over the top of the uncooked loaf.
6. Bake for about 1 hour 10 minutes, or until the loaf is shrinking from the sides of the tin. Leave to firm up in the tin for 5 minutes, then turn out onto a wire tray, peel off the lining paper and allow to cool.

Store in an airtight tin for 4–5 days, or freeze for up to 3 months.

BARM BRACK

The word barm is an old one meaning yeast and this used to be an easily-made fruity loaf using risen white bread dough. However, nowadays the name often refers to a fruit loaf or buttering cake as this is. The finished cake feels quite hard and dry but leave it wrapped in foil or in an airtight tin for a few days and you will find that the texture changes and becomes moist. This applies to most fruity loaves, cakes and gingerbreads, and especially those with little or no fat. Start the day before.

Makes 1 × 18-cm/7-inch square loaf

125 g/4 oz currants, washed and dried
125 g/4 oz raisins, washed and dried
125 g/4 oz sultanas, washed and dried
300 ml/½ pint strong black hot tea
1 medium egg, beaten
2 tablespoons chunky marmalade
1 teaspoon mixed spice
200 g/7 oz caster sugar
400 g/14 oz self-raising white flour, sifted

1. Put the dried fruit into a large mixing bowl and pour over the hot tea. Leave overnight.
2. Next day, stir in all the remaining ingredients. Mix very well to disperse the fruit and spice.
3. Grease and base line an 18-cm/7-inch square cake tin. Preheat the oven to moderately hot, Gas 5, 375°F, 190°C.
4. Spoon the mixture into the tin and level off the surface carefully. Bake for about 1½ hours, or until the loaf is risen, firm and just beginning to shrink from the sides of the tin.
5. Allow to firm up in the tin, then turn out onto a wire tray, peel off the lining paper and allow to cool.

Store in an airtight tin for 2 weeks, or freeze for up to 3 months.

CURRANT LOAF

I like the very small Vostizza currants, which don't have seeds. I buy mine loose from a health food shop.

Makes 1 × 450-g/1-lb loaf

175 g/6 oz butter, softened
75 g/3 oz caster sugar
3 tablespoons runny honey
3 medium eggs, beaten
225 g/8 oz self-raising white flour, sifted
125 g/4 oz currants, washed and dried
50 g/2 oz nibbed almonds
3 tablespoons milk

1. Grease and line the base and sides of a 900-g/2-lb loaf tin. Preheat the oven to moderate, Gas 4, 350°F, 180°C.
2. In a large mixing bowl, cream the butter and sugar until light and fluffy. Beat in the honey.
3. Beat the eggs into the mixture, a little at a time. Add a little of the measured flour if the mixture starts to separate.
4. Fold in the flour, currants and almonds, and add enough milk to get a soft but not wet consistency.
5. Spoon the mixture into the tin and bake for about 1 hour, or until the loaf is risen, firm to the touch and beginning to shrink from the sides of the tin. Leave to cool slightly in the tin then use the lining paper to lift it out and onto a wire tray. Peel off lining paper and leave to cool.

Store in an airtight tin for up to 10 days, or freeze for up to 3 months.

RUM AND RAISIN LOAF

The combination of rum and raisins is unusual, but rather attractive, in this easily made loaf. Use orange juice instead of rum, if you prefer, for another pleasant blend of flavours. Be certain that the margarine is really soft.

Makes 1 × 900-g/2-lb loaf

125 g/4 oz block margarine, softened
225 g/8 oz self-raising white flour, sifted
150 g/5 oz caster sugar
2 large eggs, beaten
4 tablespoons milk
2 tablespoons dark rum, or orange juice
125 g/4 oz dark seedless raisins, washed and dried

1. Grease and line the base and sides of a 900-g/2-lb loaf tin. Preheat the oven to moderate, Gas 4, 350°F, 180°C.
2. Put all the ingredients into a large mixing bowl. Beat well and mix thoroughly so that all the flavours are dispersed.
3. Spoon the mixture into the tin and level the top. Bake for approximately 1 hour 35 minutes, or until the loaf is shrinking from the sides of the tin. Cool in the tin, then lift the loaf out with the help of the lining paper. Peel off paper and allow to cool.

Store in an airtight tin for up to 10 days, or freeze for up to 4 months.

BRAN FRUIT LOAF

This loaf was popular long before high fibre diets were talked about. Start the day before.

Makes 1 × 450-g/1-lb loaf

125 g/4 oz bran cereal
75 g/3 oz dark soft brown sugar
50 g/2 oz currants, washed and dried
50 g/2 oz raisins, washed and dried
175 ml/6 fl oz milk
125 g/4 oz self-raising wholewheat flour, sifted
15 g/½ oz sesame seeds

1. Put the bran, sugar and fruit into a mixing bowl and add the milk. Stir well to encourage the sugar to dissolve, and leave overnight.
2. Next day, stir in the flour and mix well.
3. Grease and line the base and sides of a 450-g/1-lb loaf tin. Preheat the oven to moderately hot, Gas 5, 375°F, 190°C.
4. Spoon the mixture into the tin, level the surface and sprinkle the sesame seeds all over.
5. Bake for about 25 minutes, then reduce the heat slightly to cool, Gas 2, 300°F, 150°C, and bake for a further 30 minutes. Cool slightly in the tin then turn out onto a wire tray and strip off the lining paper.

Store in an airtight tin for 1 week, or freeze for up to 3 months.

SALLY LUNNS

This is a slicing loaf which used to be glazed with just sugar and milk. Nowadays, however, it is often topped with thick white icing.

Makes 2 × 15-cm/6-inch round slicing buns

25 g/1 oz fresh yeast, crumbled, or 15 g/½ oz dried yeast
50 g/2 oz caster sugar
150 ml/¼ pint warm milk and water, mixed
450 g/1 lb strong white flour, sifted
½ teaspoon salt
50 g/2 oz butter, cut into pieces
2 medium eggs, beaten
50 g/2 oz currants, washed and dried
40 g/1½ oz mixed peel, finely snipped
225 g/8 oz icing sugar, sifted
A little hot water

1. In a small round bowl, mix the crumbled fresh yeast with 1 teaspoon of the measured sugar and stir this into the warm milk and water. (If using dried yeast, sprinkle it over the warm milk and water mixture and stir it in with 1 teaspoon of sugar. Allow to go frothy before using.)
2. Put the flour into a warm bowl and stir in the salt. Rub in the butter with the tips of the fingers and then stir in the sugar.
3. Whisk the eggs and add to the yeasted liquid, then pour it into the flour mixture. Use a wooden spoon to draw the mixture together, then set the spoon aside and use your hand to knead the dough in the bowl until it is really soft and elastic. You may need to add a little extra warm water.
4. Work the currants and peel into the kneaded dough. (This prevents the fruit from being broken up.)
5. Set aside the bowl of dough, lightly covered, in a warm place to rise for about 1 hour.
6. Well grease two 15-cm/6-inch cake tins, at least 7.5 cm/3 inches deep.
7. Knock back the risen dough and knead gently in the bowl. Divide the dough into two pieces and knead each again on a lightly floured surface to achieve a very smooth finish. Put each ball of dough into the tins with the smooth surface uppermost. Lightly cover the tins and set aside in a warm place to prove until almost doubled in size – about 30 minutes.
8. Bake in a moderately hot oven, Gas 5, 375°F, 190°C, for about 45 minutes. Leave to firm up in the tin for 10 minutes, then turn out onto a wire tray and allow to go cold.
9. Put the icing sugar into a bowl and mix with a tiny amount of hot water to give a thick but spreadable icing. (Add the water very carefully – it is easy to overdo it.) Spread a cap of white icing over the top of each round loaf and allow to set.

Best eaten very fresh but will store in an airtight tin for 2 days. Best frozen without the icing for up to 2 months.

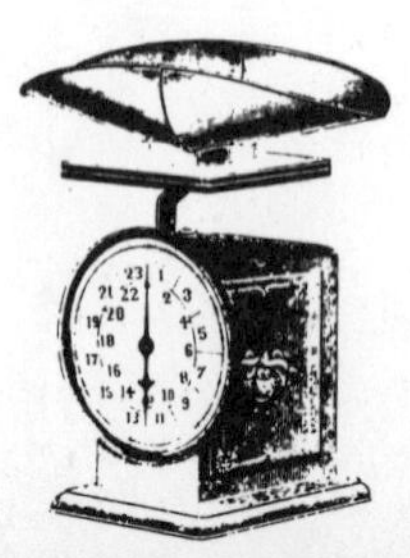

MRS AYKROYD'S FRUIT LOAVES

If you live in a village, as I do, you will be asked to contribute to all sorts of money-raising events for charities, church repairs and the like. This batch baking recipe for three large fruit loaves is always very popular. You will need a good big old-fashioned mixing bowl or a very clean washing-up bowl. It can also be made into six 450-g/1-lb loaves but cut the cooking time by 20–30 minutes.

Serve it sliced, plain or buttered, and it is also very nice with cheese, in the Yorkshire manner. Wensleydale is excellent or any other mild hard cheese.

Start the day before.

Makes 3 × 900-g/2-lb loaves

450 g/1 lb small currants
450 g/1 lb sultanas
800 g/1¾ lb self-raising white flour
225 g/8 oz block margarine
125 g/4 oz solid vegetable fat
450 g/1 lb dark soft brown sugar
3 medium eggs, beaten
600 ml/1 pint milk
125 g/4 oz peel, finely chopped
50 g/2 oz glacé cherries, washed, dried and finely chopped
1 tablespoon golden syrup
Grated rind of 1 lemon
½ teaspoon bicarbonate of soda

1. Put the currants and sultanas into a large bowl and cover with hot water. Leave to steep until the water is cold. Squeeze out the water and spread the fruit in the bottom of a large roasting tin. Leave to dry overnight in a warm place, stirring the fruit from time to time.
2. Grease and line the base and sides of three 900-g/2-lb loaf tins. Preheat the oven to cool, Gas 2, 300°F, 150°C.
3. Sift the flour into a very large mixing bowl, or clean washing-up bowl. Rub in the fats with the tips of your fingers and then stir in the sugar.
4. Mix in the eggs, fruit and enough milk to give a soft dropping consistency.
5. Stir in the peel, cherries, syrup and lemon rind.
6. Dissolve the bicarbonate of soda in a little of the milk and stir this into the mixture. Add enough of the remaining milk to achieve a soft but not sloppy consistency – you may not need all of it.
7. Pour the mixture into the tins and weigh them to ensure it is evenly divided.
8. Bake for about 2 hours, or until the loaves are firm to the touch and beginning to shrink from the sides of the tins. Turn out and cool on wire trays. Peel off the lining papers and wrap each loaf tightly in foil or clingfilm.

Store for up to 1 week in an airtight tin, or freeze for up to 3 months.

APRICOT AND ALMOND LOAF

Start the night before.

Makes 1 × 900-g/2-lb loaf

175 g/6 oz dried apricots, finely chopped
200 ml/7 fl oz unsweetened fruit juice (e.g. apple)
125 g/4 oz sunflower margarine
450 g/1 lb self-raising wholemeal flour, sifted and residue of bran from sieve added
2 tablespoons golden syrup, warmed
300 ml/½ pint skimmed milk
2–3 drops almond essence
40 g/1½ oz nibbed almonds

1. Soak the chopped apricots in the fruit juice overnight. Next day, drain the apricots.
2. Grease and line the base and sides of a 900-g/2-lb loaf tin. Preheat the oven to moderate, Gas 4, 350°F, 180°C.
3. In a large mixing bowl, rub the margarine into the flour. Stir in all the remaining ingredients, except 1 teaspoon of nibbed almonds. Mix very thoroughly.
4. Spoon the mixture into the tin and level the surface. Sprinkle over the nuts.
5. Bake for about 55 minutes. Leave to firm up in the tin for 5 minutes, then turn out onto a wire tray, peel off the lining paper and allow to cool.

Store in an airtight tin for up to 5 days, or freeze for up to 3 months.

DATE AND WALNUT LOAVES

Always a good combination; these loaves freeze well if closely wrapped in clingfilm or foil.

Makes 2 × 450-g/1-lb loaves

175 g/6 oz block margarine, softened
175 g/6 oz dark soft brown sugar
3 large eggs, beaten
400 g/14 oz self-raising white flour, sifted
325 g/12 oz packet dates, finely chopped
125 g/4 oz walnuts, finely chopped
Demerara sugar for sprinkling

1. Well grease and line the base and sides of two 450-g/1-lb loaf tins. Preheat the oven to moderate, Gas 3, 325°F, 160°C.
2. In a large mixing bowl, cream the margarine and sugar until pale and fluffy, then beat in the eggs, a little at a time.
3. Fold in the flour, dates and walnuts and mix well. Spoon into the tins, level the surface of each and sprinkle with some demerara sugar.
4. Bake for 30 minutes and then reduce the heat slightly to cool, Gas 2, 300°F, 150°C, and bake for a further 40–50 minutes. Leave to firm up in the tin for 5 minutes then turn out onto a wire tray, peel off the lining papers and allow to cool.

Store in an airtight tin for 4–5 days, or freeze for up to 2 months.

ST CLEMENT'S SLICE

Makes 1 × 900-g/2-lb loaf

125 g/4 oz block margarine, softened
225 g/8 oz self-raising white flour, sifted
125 g/4 oz caster sugar
3 medium eggs, beaten
4 tablespoons milk
Grated rind and juice of 1 large orange
Grated rind and juice of 1 lemon
225 g/8 oz icing sugar, sifted

1. Grease and line the base and sides of a 900-g/2-lb loaf tin. Preheat the oven to moderate, Gas 4, 350°F, 180°C.
2. Warm a large mixing bowl and put in the margarine and sugar. Beat until very soft. Add the flour, eggs and milk and beat together until smooth.
3. Add half the orange and lemon rinds and juice and beat well.
4. Spoon the mixture into the tin and level the surface.
5. Bake for about 1¼–1½ hours, or until the loaf is risen and firm to the touch. Leave in the tin for about 1½ hours to cool, then turn out of the tin but leave the lining paper on to hold the icing until it sets.
6. Blend the icing sugar with 2 tablespoons of the mixed juice to get a very thick glacé icing. Spread it thickly over the loaf. Sprinkle with the remaining mixed orange and lemon rind and allow to set.

Store in an airtight tin for 3 days, or freeze for up to 3 months.

CINNAMON AND PEAR LOAF

I like to use fairly firm pears for this recipe. They combine well with the cinnamon.

Makes 1 × 900-g/2-lb loaf

175 g/6 oz light soft brown sugar
50 g/2 oz butter
1 medium egg, beaten
150 ml/¼ pint milk
225 g/8 oz plain white flour
1 teaspoon bicarbonate of soda
2 teaspoons ground cinnamon
1 large pear or 2 small pears, peeled, cored and finely chopped
40 g/1½ oz chopped walnuts

1. Grease and line the base and sides of a 900-g/2-lb loaf tin. Preheat the oven to moderate, Gas 4, 350°F, 180°C.
2. In a small pan, melt the sugar and butter over a low heat. Set aside to cool.
3. Pour the melted butter and sugar into a large mixing bowl and stir in the beaten egg and milk.
4. Sift the flour, bicarbonate of soda and cinnamon into the mixture, and stir in, then beat well. Lastly, add the chopped pears and walnuts.
5. Pour the mixture into the tin and bake for about 1½ hours, or until the loaf starts to shrink from the sides of the tin. Allow to firm up in the tin, then remove, using the lining paper to lift it out, peel off paper and cool on a wire tray.

Store in an airtight tin for 2–3 days, or freeze for up to 2 months.

MINCEMEAT RING

I make this loaf mixture in a ring mould. It is easy to slice and, because it is in a ring, does not take long to cook even though it is quite a large quantity.

Will cut into about 24 slices

125 g/4 oz butter, softened
125 g/4 oz light soft brown sugar
3 large eggs, beaten
275 g/10 oz mincemeat
50 g/2 oz currants, washed and dried
1 teaspoon ground cinnamon
200 g/7 oz self-raising wholewheat flour, sifted and any residue of bran in the sieve added
Milk to mix

1. Grease a 1.2-litre/2-pint metal ring mould. Cut a circle of greaseproof paper the size of the ring, then cut out the centre of the paper so that you are left with an outer ring about 5 mm/¾ inch wide. Lay this in the bottom of the ring. Preheat the oven to moderate, Gas 3, 325°F, 160°C.
2. In a large mixing bowl, cream the butter and sugar, then beat in the eggs, a little at a time.
3. Fold in all the remaining ingredients, with enough milk to give a soft consistency. Spoon the mixture into the tin and level off carefully.
4. Bake for 10 minutes, then reduce the heat to cool, Gas 2, 300°F, 150°C, and bake for another hour, or until the mixture has risen, is firm to the touch and beginning to shrink from the sides of the ring. Cool for 10–15 minutes in the tin, then run a knife round the loaf and ease it out onto a wire tray to cool.

Store in an airtight tin for 10 days, or freeze for up to 3 months.

NO-FAT CARROT LOAF

You will be surprised to find grated carrots and parsnips in this recipe. These give the loaf a good moist texture.

Makes 1 × 900-g/2-lb loaf

225 g/8 oz skimmed milk cottage cheese
150 g/5 oz light soft brown sugar
3 medium eggs, beaten
125 g/4 oz fresh, hard carrots, scraped and grated
50 g/2 oz parsnips, scraped and grated
225 g/8 oz self-raising wholemeal flour
1 teaspoon baking powder
50 g/2 oz rolled oats (porridge)
1 teaspoon finely snipped rosemary needles, or 2 fat pinches dried rosemary

1. Grease and line the base and sides of a 900-g/2-lb loaf tin. Preheat the oven to moderate, Gas 4, 350°F, 180°C.
2. Reduce the cottage cheese to a finer texture by either passing it through a food processor for 1–2 minutes, or pressing it through a sieve. Use a metal spoon to push it back and forwards. Put the smooth cheese into a large mixing bowl, add the sugar and beat well.
3. Beat in the eggs, a little at a time.
4. If you have grated your carrots and parsnips into long strands, take a pair of scissors and chop them up and add them to the mixture.
5. Sift the flour and baking powder into the mixture, adding any residue of bran left in the sieve, and stir in the rolled oats and rosemary. Mix all the ingredients thoroughly.
6. Spoon the mixture into the tin and level the surface. Bake for about 1 hour, or until the loaf is firm and starting to shrink from the sides of the tin. Leave to firm up in the tin for 5 minutes, then turn out onto a wire tray, peel off the lining paper and allow to cool.

Store in an airtight tin for up to 3 days, or freeze for up to 3 months.

PINEAPPLE LOAF

Makes 2 × 450-g/1-lb loaves

1 × 350-g/13-oz can crushed pineapple
200 g/7 oz caster sugar
225 g/8 oz sultanas, washed and dried
125 g/4 oz block margarine
125 g/4 oz plain white flour, sifted
125 g/4 oz self-raising white flour, sifted
1 teaspoon bicarbonate of soda
2 medium eggs, beaten

1. Drain the pineapple and reserve the juice. Put the pineapple into a large pan and add the sugar, sultanas and margarine. Stir over a low heat until the sugar and margarine have melted. Set aside to cool.
2. Grease and line the base and sides of two 450-g/1-lb loaf tins. Preheat the oven to cool, Gas 2, 300°F, 150°C.
3. When the fruit mixture is cold, fold in both flours, bicarbonate of soda and the eggs. Mix very thoroughly to a soft consistency, using a little of the reserved pineapple juice if necessary.
4. Spoon the mixture into the tins and weigh them to ensure the mixture is evenly divided. Level the tops.
5. Bake for about 1½ hours, or until the loaves have risen and are firm to the touch. Leave to firm up in the tin for 10 minutes, then turn out onto a wire tray, peel off the lining papers and cool.

Store in an airtight tin for 1 week, or freeze for up to 3 months.

RICE CAKE LOAF

A traditional English cake with a lovely crumbly texture.

Makes 1 × 900-g/2-lb loaf

125 g/4 oz butter, cut into pieces
225 g/8 oz caster sugar
Grated rind of ½ lemon
4 medium eggs, separated
1 tablespoon milk
125 g/4 oz ground rice
125 g/4 oz plain white flour, sifted

1. Grease and line the base and sides of a 900-g/2-lb loaf tin. Preheat the oven to moderate, Gas 4, 350°F, 180°C.

2. In a large mixing bowl, cream the butter and sugar until pale and fluffy. Beat in the lemon rind.
3. Beat the egg yolks, one at a time, into the creamed mixture, then beat in the milk.
4. In a clean, grease-free bowl, whisk the egg whites until very stiff. Fold about half into the mixture, followed by the ground rice and flour. Lastly, fold in the remaining egg whites.
5. Spoon the mixture into the tin, and level the surface. Bake for about 1 hour. Leave to firm up in the tin for 10 minutes, then turn out onto a wire tray, remove the lining paper and allow to cool.

Store in an airtight tin for 5–6 days, or freeze for up to 3 months.

GINGERBREAD

Traditionally, gingerbread used to be baked in a roasting tin and the pieces were cut into generous squares. I now make the same recipe in two bread tins and they slice much more neatly. Eat it at tea-time when the hot tea will bring out the flavour even more. The loaves freeze well, closely wrapped in clingfilm.

Makes 2 × 900-g/2-lb loaves

125 g/4 oz golden syrup
125 g/4 oz black treacle
125 g/4 oz butter
125 g/4 oz granulated sugar
275 g/10 oz plain white flour
2 pinches salt
2 teaspoons ground ginger
1 teaspoon ground cinnamon
1 teaspoon bicarbonate of soda
1 large egg, beaten
225 ml/8 fl oz milk
50–75 g/2–3 oz preserved ginger, chopped (optional)

1. Put a small pan on the scales, weigh it and then weigh the syrup and treacle into it. Add the butter and sugar and set over a low heat. When all traces of sugar grittiness have gone, lift the pan off the heat and set it aside to cool.
2. Lightly grease and line the base and sides of two 900-g/2-lb bread tins. Preheat the oven to moderate, Gas 3, 325°F, 160°C.
3. Sift the flour, salt, ginger, cinnamon and bicarbonate of soda into a mixing bowl. Pour in the melted mixture and stir well. Beat in the egg and enough milk to give a thick, heavy mixture.
4. Pour evenly into the tins and bake for 1–1¼ hours, or until risen and firm to the touch. Allow to firm up for a few minutes in the tin then slide a flat-bladed knife down each short end to release and use the lining papers to lift the loaves onto wire trays. Peel off papers and allow to cool.

Store in an airtight tin for 4–5 days. I do not care for gingerbread from the freezer as it goes very sticky, but I do know many people who like this texture. Freeze for no more than 2 months.

BUNS AND MUFFINS

RASPBERRY BUNS

These old favourites are even better when made with really good quality or home-made raspberry jam.

Makes about 10

75 g/3 oz block margarine, cut into pieces
225 g/8 oz plain white flour, sifted
75 g/3 oz caster sugar
1 teaspoon baking powder
1 medium egg, beaten
A little milk, if necessary
3 tablespoons good raspberry jam

1. Grease a baking tray. Preheat the oven to fairly hot, Gas 6, 400°F, 200°C.
2. In a large mixing bowl, rub the margarine into the flour.
3. Stir in the sugar and baking powder and mix to a softish dough with the beaten egg and a little milk, if necessary.
4. Dampen your hands slightly and roll the mixture into balls about the size of a golf ball. Set the balls well apart on the baking tray, flatten each bun slightly with your hand, and make a dent in each one with your thumb. Spoon a little raspberry jam into each hole.
5. Bake for about 15 minutes. Cool on a wire tray.

Best eaten fresh. Store in an airtight tin for 2–3 days, or freeze for up to 3 months.

LONDON BUNS

Makes 8

225 g/8 oz self-raising white flour
1 pinch salt
50 g/2 oz block margarine, cut into pieces
50 g/2 oz caster sugar
25 g/1 oz peel, finely cut
1 medium egg, beaten
2–3 drops essence of lemon *(see page 16)*, **or lemon juice**
2 tablespoons milk
6 sugar cubes, crushed in a plastic bag with a rolling pin

1. Grease one or two baking trays. Preheat the oven to fairly hot, Gas 6, 400°F, 200°C.
2. Sift the flour and salt into a large mixing bowl.
3. Rub in the margarine until the mixture resembles breadcrumbs. Stir in the sugar and the peel.
4. Add the beaten egg, reserving a little to brush over the buns. Mix the lemon essence with the milk, add this to the mixture and mix to a softish dough.
5. Divide the dough evenly into eight pieces. Flour your hand and shape each piece into a round. Place the rounds on the baking trays, brush the top of each bun with the reserved egg and sprinkle with the coarse sugar.
6. Bake for about 20 minutes. Cool on a wire tray.

Store in an airtight tin for 2–3 days, or freeze for up to 3 months.

CHELSEA BUNS

Made with a rich dough, these buns were said to have been made originally for the pensioners at the Royal Hospital, Chelsea, London. Best eaten warm and fresh from the oven.

Makes 6

325 g/12 oz strong white flour
50 g/2 oz butter, cut into small pieces
15 g/½ oz fresh yeast, or 7 g/¼ oz dried yeast
1 teaspoon caster sugar
200 ml/7 fl oz warm milk and water, mixed
25 g/1 oz melted butter
40 g/1½ oz caster sugar
40 g/1½ oz currants, washed and dried
Extra caster sugar for sprinkling

FOR THE GLAZE
1 tablespoon caster sugar
2 tablespoons milk

1. Sift the flour into a large, warm mixing bowl and rub in the 50 g/2 oz butter.
2. In a small bowl, mix the fresh yeast with 1 teaspoon caster sugar and stir this into the warm milk and water (or sprinkle the dried yeast onto the milk and water, stir in 1 teaspoon of sugar and leave until frothy).
3. Stir the yeasted liquid into the flour with a wooden spoon. When the mixture comes together in the bowl, use your hand to knead in the bowl until the dough is smooth and elastic.
4. Cover the bowl lightly and set aside in a warm place until the dough has doubled in size – about 45 minutes.
5. Knock back the risen dough and knead again. Turn out the dough onto a lightly floured board and shape into a rectangle measuring about 30 × 23 cm/12 × 9 inches. Use your hands or, if you prefer, a rolling pin.
6. Brush the surface of the dough all over with the melted butter. Sprinkle on the 40 g/1½ oz sugar and finally the currants on top of that. Roll the dough up tightly like a Swiss roll, starting from the long end. Take a sharp knife and cut six slices, about 4 cm/1½ inches thick. Set these slices, cut sides up, well apart on a greased cake tin or small roasting tin. Cover lightly and leave to prove for a further 20 minutes until puffy.
7. Bake in a hot oven, Gas 7, 425°F, 220°C, for 20 minutes. Allow to firm up in the tin for 5 minutes then turn out onto a wire tray while you make the glaze.

8. Boil together the sugar and milk in a pan and brush this over the surface of the buns while they are still hot. Sprinkle lightly with sugar and leave to cool. Pull the buns apart when cold.

Store in an airtight tin for 2–3 days, or freeze for up to 3 months.

HOT CROSS BUNS

Good hot cross buns are hard to find. Most of the shop-bought ones have little taste except for the last minute glaze on the outside of the bun. I suggest you make the crosses with a flour and water paste instead of pastry strips which always fall off.

Makes about 12

25 g/1 oz candied orange peel
450 g/1 lb strong white flour
1 sachet easy blend dried yeast
1 teaspoon salt
1 teaspoon mixed spice
50 g/2 oz caster sugar
125 g/4 oz currants, washed and dried
50 g/2 oz butter, melted
1 medium egg, beaten
250 ml/8 fl oz milk and water, mixed, plus a little extra

FOR THE CROSSES
40 g/1½ oz plain white flour
2 tablespoons water
1 teaspoon oil

FOR THE GLAZE
2 tablespoons milk
2 tablespoons caster sugar

1. Wash the sugar off the candied peel and soak the peel for 15 minutes in water. Dry the peel and, using scissors, snip it into small pieces.
2. Sift the strong flour into a large mixing bowl, and sprinkle over the yeast. Stir in the salt, spice, sugar, currants, peel, butter, egg and, lastly, the milk and water mixture. Mix in an electric machine with a dough hook for about 15 minutes, or mix by hand first with a wooden spoon and then by hand. Knead for about 10 minutes until you have a smooth soft dough – you may need to add a little extra liquid as some flours absorb more liquid than others.
3. When you have a smooth, very soft, elastic dough, divide it into twelve equal pieces – weigh each piece to ensure the dough is evenly divided. Shape each piece into a neat ball and place them, well spaced out, on a lightly greased baking tray or roasting tin. Cover lightly with an oiled sheet of plastic and set aside in a very warm place to rise until doubled in size – about 20 minutes.
4. To make the crosses, beat together the flour, water and oil. Spoon this into a small paper icing bag, snip off the end of the paper bag and decorate each risen bun with a cross of paste.
5. Bake in a hot oven, Gas 7, 425°F, 220°C, for about 15 minutes until brown all over. Set the buns on a wire tray to cool a little.
6. Make up the glaze by simmering the milk and sugar for 2 minutes in a small pan. Brush this mixture over the hot buns and leave to set.

Store in an airtight tin when cold for 2–3 days, or freeze for up to 2–3 months.

SEED BUNS

Caraway seeds are often hard and I like to bruise them with a pestle and mortar, or use the end of your rolling pin in a strong bowl.

Makes about 10

225 g/8 oz plain white flour
75 g/3 oz butter or block margarine, cut into small pieces
1 medium egg, beaten
A little milk
125 g/4 oz caster sugar
1 teaspoon baking powder
1 teaspoon caraway seeds, crushed

TO DECORATE
A few extra caraway seeds

1. Grease a baking tray. Preheat the oven to fairly hot, Gas 6, 400°F, 200°C.
2. Sift the flour into a large mixing bowl and rub in the butter or margarine.
3. In another bowl, beat the egg into 1 tablespoon of milk and stir into the mixture.
4. Add all the remaining ingredients and mix to a fairly firm dough, using extra milk if necessary.
5. Dampen your hands slightly and roll the dough into small balls about the size of a golf ball. Set the balls well apart on the baking tray. Flatten each one slightly, brush lightly with milk and sprinkle two or three caraway seeds on each one.
6. Bake for about 15 minutes. Cool on a wire tray.

Best eaten fresh. Store in an airtight tin for 2–3 days, or freeze for up to 1 month.

PLAIN ROCK BUNS

Makes about 12

225 g/8 oz self-raising white flour
75 g/3 oz caster sugar
75 g/3 oz block margarine, cut into pieces
75 g/3 oz currants, washed and dried
25 g/1 oz peel, very finely cut
1 medium egg, beaten
A little milk

1. Grease a baking tray. Preheat the oven to hot, Gas 7, 425°F, 220°C.
2. Sift the flour into a mixing bowl and stir in the sugar.
3. Rub in the margarine until the mixture resembles breadcrumbs, then stir in the currants and peel.
4. Mix to a firm dough with the egg and just a little milk.
5. Place about twelve rough heaps of the mixture on the baking tray and bake for about 20 minutes. Cool on a wire tray.

Store in an airtight tin for 2–3 days, or freeze for up to 3 months.

SPICED ROCK BUNS

Makes about 20

125 g/4 oz self-raising white flour
125 g/4 oz Granary flour (sometimes called malt flour)
¼ teaspoon ground nutmeg
1 teaspoon mixed spice
125 g/4 oz margarine, cut into pieces
125 g/4 oz demerara sugar
125 g/4 oz raisins, washed and dried
Milk to mix

1. Grease two baking trays. Preheat the oven to moderately hot, Gas 5, 375°F, 190°C.
2. Sift the two flours into a large mixing bowl, adding the malted grains in the sieve to the bowl. Stir in the nutmeg and spice.
3. Rub the margarine into the flour, then stir in the sugar and raisins.
4. Mix to a stiff dough with the milk.
5. Drop large teaspoons of the mixture well apart onto the trays and bake for 15–20 minutes. Cool on a wire tray.

Store for 2–3 days in an airtight tin, or freeze for up to 3 months.

CORN MUFFINS

These muffins are made with oil (*see page 10*). This is a sweet and savoury mixture which may sound rather odd but I think you will be surprised at just how nice and unusual they are. The recipe came originally from America where I imagine that cooked fresh corn kernels would be used.

Makes about 12

125 g/4 oz rice flour
175 g/6 oz plain wholewheat flour
½ teaspoon salt
3 teaspoons baking powder
50 g/2 oz caster sugar
300 ml/½ pint milk and water, mixed
1 medium egg, beaten
2 tablespoons vegetable oil
½ × 190 g/7 oz can sweetcorn with peppers
75 g/3 oz grated Cheddar cheese

1. Grease a tray of deep bun tins. Preheat the oven to hot, Gas 7, 425°F, 220°C.
2. Sift the two flours, salt and baking powder into a large mixing bowl, adding any residue of bran left in the sieve. Stir in the sugar.
3. In another bowl, whisk together the milk and water mixture, egg and vegetable oil until creamy, then fold in the dry ingredients and mix well. Stir in the drained sweetcorn and cheese.
4. Spoon the mixture into the tins, filling them just over half full.
5. Bake for 10–12 minutes, or until the muffins are risen and brown. Cool on a wire tray.

Best eaten warm and fresh, or freeze for up to 1 month.

LEMON MUFFINS

These muffins are more like cakes. Made with lemon curd and bran, they are full of flavour. Use a deep bun tray to bake them or paper bun cases set in a bun tray.

Makes 9

50 g/2 oz bran cereal
150 ml/¼ pint milk
50 g/2 oz butter, softened
50 g/2 oz light soft brown sugar
3 tablespoons lemon curd
25 g/1 oz walnuts, finely chopped
1 medium egg, beaten
125 g/4 oz plain white flour
2 heaped teaspoons baking powder

1. Grease a 9-hole, deep bun tray, or set paper bun cases in a bun tray. Preheat the oven to fairly hot, Gas 6, 400°F, 200°C.
2. Put the bran cereal into a strong plastic bag and crush it with a rolling pin. Put the crushed cereal into a bowl and pour over the milk.
3. In another larger mixing bowl, cream the butter and sugar until fluffy, then beat in the lemon curd.
4. Stir the nuts and egg into the creamed mixture followed by the milk and bran.
5. Sift in the flour and baking powder, mixing it thoroughly but gently.
6. Divide the mixture between the bun spaces or paper bun cases, and bake for about 15–20 minutes, or until the buns are risen and firm. Turn out and cool on a wire tray.

Best eaten fresh. Store in an airtight tin for 2–3 days, or freeze for up to 3 months.

SCONES

The raising agent for scones can be either plain flour and baking powder or plain flour with bicarbonate of soda and cream of tartar. The other alternative is to use self-raising flour which has its raising agent already mixed into it. While people argue about the different merits of self-raising flour as opposed to plain flour with bicarbonate of soda and cream of tartar, I think it is far more important to mix your scones to as soft a dough as possible, put them straight onto a heated baking tray and then straight into a preheated hot oven. It is also important to cut the scones not less than 2 cm/¾ inch thick.

PLAIN WHITE SCONES

Plain scones used to be scones without sugar and, split in two, they make a pleasant alternative to bread for an open sandwich.

Makes 10

225 g/8 oz plain white flour
1 teaspoon bicarbonate of soda
2 teaspoons cream of tartar
40 g/1½ oz block margarine, cut into pieces
25 g/1 oz caster sugar (optional)
1 pinch salt
150 ml/¼ pint milk and water mixed
Extra milk, if necessary

1. Set the oven to hot, Gas 8, 450°F, 230°C, and put a greased baking tray in to heat up.
2. Sift the flour with the bicarbonate of soda and cream of tartar into a large mixing bowl.
3. Rub the margarine into the flour until the mixture resembles breadcrumbs, then stir in the sugar, salt and milk and water mixture.
4. Using a long-bladed knife, work together all the ingredients until you have a soft but not sticky dough. You may need just a little more milk for the mixing.
5. Once the dough has come together in the bowl, sprinkle a little flour over the dough and use your hand to lightly knead it in the bowl until smooth.

6. Turn out onto a lightly floured surface and quickly roll the dough to a thickness of about 2 cm/¾ inch. Using a 5-cm/2-inch metal cutter, cut out rounds, gather up the trimmings, reroll and cut again. Brush the tops of the scones with milk and transfer them to the heated baking tray.
7. Bake for 7–10 minutes. Cool on a wire tray.

Store in an airtight tin for 3–4 days, or freeze for up to 3 months.

VARIATION

To get an even softer scone – that is, one which has had little handling – pat (do not roll) the mixed dough out to a rough circle and cut into wedges. Brush the tops with milk, transfer the triangular scones to the heated baking tray, and reassemble the circle, leaving a little space in between each wedge. Bake for 7–10 minutes.

WHEATMEAL SCONES

A plain brown scone warm from the oven and buttered with good unsalted butter takes a lot of beating. Wheatmeal flour gives a much lighter scone than wholemeal flour.

Makes 8–10

225 g/8 oz plain wheatmeal flour
3 teaspoons baking powder
1 pinch salt
25 g/1 oz caster sugar
40 g/1½ oz block margarine, cut into pieces
150 ml/¼ pint milk and water mixed
A little extra milk

1. Set the oven to hot, Gas 8, 450°F, 230°C, and put a greased baking tray in to heat up.
2. Sift the flour, baking powder and salt into a large mixing bowl, adding the residue of bran from the sieve. Stir in the sugar.
3. Rub in the margarine until the mixture resembles dry breadcrumbs.
4. Using the milk and water mixture, quickly bind the ingredients together. (I like to use a long-bladed knife for this job.) Once the dough has come together, sprinkle a little flour over it and use your hand to knead the dough in the bowl until it is fairly smooth.
5. Turn out onto a lightly floured surface and roll the dough to a thickness not less than 2 cm/¾ inch thick. Cut out rounds with a small metal cutter. Gather up the trimmings, reroll and cut again. Quickly brush the top of each scone with milk and set them on the hot baking tray in the oven.
6. Bake for about 8–10 minutes until nicely brown. Cool on a wire tray.

Store in an airtight tin for 2–3 days, or freeze for up to 3 months.

CHEESY SCONES

Use a good, strongly flavoured cheese. I also like to grate the cheese onto a piece of kitchen paper and leave it to dry off slightly before using – an hour should be long enough.

Makes 8–10

225 g/8 oz plain white flour
1 teaspoon bicarbonate of soda
2 teaspoons cream of tartar
1 pinch salt
1 pinch pepper
1 pinch cayenne pepper
½ teaspoon mustard powder
40 g/1½ oz block margarine
150 ml/¼ pint milk and water mixed
125 g/4 oz strong cheese, finely grated
Extra milk

1. Set the oven to hot, Gas 8, 450°F, 230°C, and put a greased baking tray in to heat up.
2. Sift the flour, bicarbonate of soda, cream of tartar, salt, the two peppers and mustard powder into a large mixing bowl.
3. Rub in the margarine until the mixture resembles breadcrumbs.
4. Using a long-bladed knife, stir the milk and water mixture into the dry ingredients. Reserve about 1 teaspoon of the cheese and stir the rest in. Use extra milk if needed to get a soft dough.
5. Once the dough has come together, sprinkle a little flour over it and knead it gently by hand in the bowl until fairly smooth.
6. Turn out onto a floured surface and, using a rolling pin, very lightly roll the dough out to a thickness of about 2 cm/¾ inch. Cut into rounds with a 6-cm/2½-inch cutter. Gather up the trimmings, reroll and cut again.
7. Brush the top of each scone with milk and sprinkle on the reserved grated cheese. Set the scones quickly on the hot baking tray in the oven.
8. Bake for 8–10 minutes until risen and brown. Remove to a wire tray to cool.

Store in an airtight tin for 2–3 days, or freeze for up to 3 months.

HERBED SCONES

This is an unsweetened scone with the flavour of freshly chopped herbs – lovely with a bowl of soup.

Makes 8–10

40 g/1½ oz butter, cut into small pieces
225 g/8 oz self-raising white flour, sifted
1 pinch salt
1 pinch cayenne pepper
1 teaspoon mustard powder
1 tablespoon fresh chopped herbs (parsley, chives, thyme, marjoram or any other mixture)
150 ml/¼ pint milk
Extra milk, if necessary

1. Set the oven to hot, Gas, 7, 425°F, 220°C, and put a greased baking tray in to heat up.
2. Rub the butter into the flour with your fingertips. When the mixture resembles breadcrumbs, stir in the salt, cayenne pepper, mustard and herbs. Mix well.
3. Using a long-bladed knife, work the dry ingredients to a soft dough with the milk. Add extra milk if necessary so that the dough is really soft. Sprinkle a little flour over the dough and knead it gently by hand in the bowl.
4. Turn out onto a floured surface and, using a rolling pin, very lightly roll the dough out to a thickness of about 2 cm/¾ inch. Using a 5-cm/2-inch cutter, cut into rounds. Gather up the trimmings, reroll and cut again.
5. Put the scones on the hot baking tray and bake for about 12 minutes until risen and brown.

Store in an airtight tin for 2 days, or freeze for up to 2 months.

APPLE AND ONION FARLS

These savoury scones are a perfect accompaniment for cheese and pickles. I also like just a scraping of garlic in the mixture.

Will cut into 8 wedges

15 g/½ oz butter
1 teaspoon vegetable oil
175 g/6 oz onion, peeled and very finely chopped
¼ clove garlic, peeled and crushed
225 g/8 oz self-raising wholemeal flour
1 heaped teaspoon baking powder
1 teaspoon mustard powder
½ teaspoon salt
50 g/2 oz block margarine, cut into pieces
175 g/6 oz cooking apples (peeled weight), finely chopped
150 ml/¼ pint milk and water, mixed
A little extra milk

1. Melt the butter and oil in a frying pan, add the onion and garlic and cook gently, covered, until soft. Drain and set aside to go cold.
2. Set the oven to fairly hot, Gas 6, 400°F, 200°C, and put a greased baking tray in to heat up.
3. Sift the flour, baking powder, mustard and salt into a large mixing bowl, adding the residue of bran left in the sieve.
4. Rub in the margarine until the mixture resembles dry breadcrumbs. Stir in the apples and the cooked onion and garlic.
5. Stir the milk and water mixture into the dry ingredients and mix to a soft but not sticky dough. You may need a little extra liquid. Knead this dough lightly and then roll it out on a floured board to a circle about 20 cm/8 inches across. Use the metal base of a quiche tin or two fish slices to scoop up the circle and transfer it to the hot baking tray.
6. Quickly mark the circle into eight wedges, brush the tops with milk and bake for 20–25 minutes until the scones are well risen and brown. Cool on a wire tray.

Store in an airtight tin for 3–4 days, or freeze for up to 3 months.

APPLE SCONES

Scones need a light hand and the dough should be mixed as soft as possible but should not be wet and sticky. They must go into a hot oven so that they start to rise immediately. Bake them in a ring for a soft result.

Will cut into 8 wedges

225 g/8 oz self-raising white flour
1 teaspoon baking powder
50 g/2 oz block margarine, cut into small pieces
40 g/1½ oz caster sugar
1 Bramley cooking apple, peeled, cored and finely chopped
150 ml/¼ pint milk and water mixed
Extra milk
25 g/1 oz demerara sugar

1. Set the oven to fairly hot, Gas 6, 400°F, 200°C, and put a greased baking tray in to heat up.
2. Sift the flour and baking powder into a large mixing bowl.
3. Rub in the margarine and add the sugar. Stir in the chopped apples.
4. Using a knife or a fork, add sufficient milk and water mixture to make a soft dough.
5. Turn out onto a lightly floured surface, dust the dough with flour to prevent sticking, and knead it gently by hand.
6. Pat or roll the dough out to a circle about 20 cm/8 inches across, and cut it into eight wedges.
7. Take the hot baking tray out of the oven, sprinkle it lightly with flour and reassemble the ring shape, leaving just a little space between each wedge. Brush the top of each scone with milk and sprinkle with the demerara sugar.
8. Bake for about 20–25 minutes. If the scones show signs of scorching reduce the heat slightly. Cool on a wire tray and eat fresh.

Store in an airtight tin for 3–4 days, or freeze for up to 1 month.

FRUIT SCONES

Lard was, of course, the fat used for all plain baking in the past. It gives quite a distinctive flavour so margarine can be used if you prefer.

Makes 8–10

225 g/8 oz self-raising white flour
1 pinch salt
25 g/1 oz caster sugar
50 g/2 oz lard or block margarine, cut into pieces
50 g/2 oz mixed currants and raisins, washed and dried
1 tablespoon lemon juice
175 ml/6 fl oz milk

1. Set the oven to hot, Gas 7, 425°F, 220°C, and put a greased baking tray in to heat up.
2. Sift the flour and salt into a large mixing bowl and stir in the sugar.
3. Rub in the lard or margarine with your finger-tips, and then stir in the dried fruit.
4. Stir the lemon juice into the milk to sour it and use this liquid to mix the dry ingredients to a very soft dough. You may not need all of it. Using a long-bladed knife, draw the dough together then use your hand to knead it gently in the bowl.
5. Turn out onto a lightly floured surface and roll the dough out to not less than 2 cm/¾ inch thick. Using a 5-cm/2-inch metal cutter, cut out as many circles as possible, then gather up the trimmings, reroll and cut again.
6. Brush the top of each scone with the remaining sour milk and set them on the hot baking tray. Bake for about 10 minutes, or until the scones are brown. Cool on a wire tray.

Store in an airtight tin for 2–3 days, or freeze for up to 3 months.

WALNUT SCONES

Makes 10

225 g/8 oz self-raising white flour
1 teaspoon baking powder
50 g/2 oz butter, cut into pieces
1 tablespoon caster sugar
50 g/2 oz walnuts, chopped
1 medium egg, beaten
65 ml/2½ fl oz milk and water, mixed

1. Set the oven to hot, Gas 8, 450°F, 230°C, and put a greased baking tray in to heat up.
2. Sift the flour and baking powder into a large mixing bowl.
3. Rub the butter into the flour with your fingertips, then stir in the sugar and walnuts.
4. Bind the dry ingredients together with the beaten egg and milk and water mixture to form a soft dough. You may need a little extra liquid.
5. Using a long-bladed knife, draw the dough together in the bowl, then sprinkle a little flour over the top and knead the dough by hand in the bowl until smooth.
6. Turn out onto a lightly floured surface, and roll the dough out to a thickness not less than 2 cm/¾ inch. Cut out rounds using a 6-cm/2½-inch metal cutter. Gather up the trimmings, reroll and cut again.
7. Brush the top of each scone with milk and transfer the scones to the hot baking tray. Bake for 10–12 minutes, then cool on a wire tray.

Store in an airtight tin for 2–3 days, or freeze for up to 2 months.

YOGHURT SCONES

The use of yoghurt gives these scones a very pleasant flavour. It is particularly good with the wholemeal flour.

Will cut into 8–10 wedges

225 g/8 oz self-raising wholemeal flour
1 teaspoon baking powder
25 g/1 oz caster sugar
1 pinch salt
25 g/1 oz butter, cut into small pieces
150 ml/¼ pint natural yoghurt
Extra milk if needed

1. Set the oven to fairly hot, Gas 6, 400°F, 200°C, and put a greased baking tray in to heat up.
2. Sift the flour, baking powder, sugar and salt into a large mixing bowl, adding the residue of bran left in the sieve.
3. Rub the butter into the flour with the tips of your fingers.
4. Pour in the yoghurt and, using a long-bladed knife, mix to a soft but not sticky dough. You may need a little extra milk.
5. Turn out the dough onto a floured surface and shape into a circle about 2 cm/¾ inch thick. Cut the circle into eight or ten wedges. Take the hot baking tray out of the oven and reassemble the wedges on it into a ring shape, leaving a little space between each wedge.
6. Bake for about 10–12 minutes until risen and brown. Cool on a wire tray.

Store in an airtight tin for up to 2 days, or freeze for up to 3 months.

WELSH CAKES

These delicious Welsh currant delicacies are traditionally baked on a bakestone or its Scottish equivalent, a girdle. A heavy based frying pan will also give very good results. I find they all work much better when they are heated up slowly. Judging the correct temperature of the bakestone, girdle or frying pan is a matter for experience. The easiest way is to cook one cake on its own. If it starts to burn before the centre is cooked then you know the temperature is too high. If it takes so long to cook that the texture of the cake is leathery then you know to increase the temperature a little. I can only describe the heat needed as moderately hot.

A Welsh viewer tells me these cakes are not supposed to be buttered since they are really quite rich enough. They are thinner than oven scones.

Makes about 24

225 g/8 oz self-raising white flour, sifted
1 pinch salt
50 g/2 oz lard
50 g/2 oz block margarine
75 g/3 oz caster sugar
40 g/1½ oz currants, washed and dried
1 small egg, beaten
A little extra milk
Knob of suet, the size of a walnut

1. Put the bakestone, girdle or frying pan over a very low heat until moderately hot.
2. Sift the flour and salt into a large mixing bowl.
3. Chop the lard and margarine together roughly, then rub into the flour as you would for pastry. Stir in the sugar, currants and egg with enough milk to mix to a fairly firm dough.
4. Roll out the dough on a lightly floured surface to approximately 7 mm/¼ inch thick. Using a scone or biscuit cutter, either fluted or plain, cut out 6-cm/2½-inch rounds. Gather up the trimmings, reroll and cut again.
5. Tie up the suet in a circle of muslin and grease the surface of the pan by running the suet knob lightly over it (*see page 10*).
6. Bake the scones on both sides, a few at a time, depending on the size of the bakestone. Skim the surface of the bakestone with the suet knob between each batch. Cool the cakes on a wire tray.

Store in layers interleaved in greaseproof paper in an airtight tin for up to 4 days, or freeze for up to 3 months.

SCOTCH PANCAKES

Although they are not strictly baked, I am including pancakes just because they are so good and economical. If you do not have a girdle (or bakestone, as the Welsh call it) a heavy frying pan will do. You can also use a nonstick pan but take care that it does not get too hot.

Makes about 30 small pancakes

225 g/8 oz plain white flour, sifted
½ teaspoon bicarbonate of soda
1 teaspoon cream of tartar
1 pinch salt
2 tablespoons caster sugar
1 medium egg, beaten
Just under 300 ml/½ pint milk
1 heaped teaspoon golden syrup
Knob of suet, the size of a walnut

1. Put the girdle, bakestone or frying pan over a very low heat until moderately hot.
2. Sift the flour, bicarbonate of soda, cream of tartar and salt into a large mixing bowl. Stir in the sugar.
3. Beat the egg, milk and syrup into the dry ingredients until you have a thick but pouring batter.
4. Tie up the suet in a circle of muslin and grease the surface of the pan by running the suet knob lightly over it (*see page 10*).
5. Experiment with one pancake so that you can regulate the temperature. Pour on about 1 dessertspoon of batter from the end of the spoon. When bubbles appear all over the surface, flip the pancake over to cook the other side. If the pan is too hot the underside of the pancake will burn before the bubbles burst. If too cold, the bubbles will burst and the underside of the pancake will still be pale. Cool on a clean teacloth set on a wire tray, then cover with a clean teacloth to keep moist.

Eat on the day the pancakes are made, or freeze for up to 3 months.

BAKING WITH YEAST

Bread making is very simple, but as it is done in stages it has the image of being a long and complicated business. However, once you have mastered the art, there is no going back – it is definitely addictive. Every sense is stimulated. The feel of raw bread dough is very special – warm, soft and silkily pliable. The rhythm of kneading is satisfying and easy to learn. Lastly, the blissful smell of baking bread is one of the great joys for a home baker and his or her family. The supermarket bakeries use this wonderful smell to draw you through the whole length of the store to be tempted all the way there and back again.

I get a lot of letters from viewers with suggestions and ideas and only this week I had one from an 88-year-old man from Somerset who said that he did not cook much now 'but I couldn't do without my home-made bread which I make every Friday'. Good for you, Dan Oates.

Apart from a large bowl, there is little else you need. Even bread tins are not absolutely necessary as you can just shape your loaves into fat round cobs or long fat bloomers. However, tins do give you a loaf which is easier to slice. Grease them before use and they will soon develop a dark skin which is much more reliable than any nonstick tin. Keep your tins for bread only. If you start using unlined tins for fruit bread or sweet loaves, when you use them again for bread making you will find unsightly black marks on the corners of your loaves. Do not wash your bread tins after use, just wipe them with a damp cloth.

I do recommend that you freeze your bread to keep it in good condition (see page 171)*. Use good strong freezer bags and note on them the date so that you can use your bread in rotation.*

EQUIPMENT

Special equipment is not really necessary for yeast cookery. (*See general notes on equipment on page 18.*) A large mixing bowl, or a very clean washing-up bowl, is important to hold dough when it is rising. A measuring jug is also useful.

To speed up the kneading process, a dough hook fitted to an electric mixer is very effective, but remember to check the limit of the machine's capacity.

Bread loaves can be baked on heavy baking trays or in special loaf tins. These are available in 450-g/1-lb and 900-g/2-lb sizes. Bread buns, sticks and rolls etc. can be baked on ordinary baking trays. Clay pots were fashionable at one time and the clay flowerpot loaf gives a good result and shape (*see page 178*).

INGREDIENTS

FLOUR

We grow soft wheat in this country which gives us soft flour, excellent for making cakes and pastry. However, while soft flour will also make a perfectly good loaf, much better results are obtained using a strong flour made from hard wheat. These hard wheats are grown mostly in Canada and in Russia, and it is their high gluten content which allows the dough to stretch and expand, and thus make better bread.

Store your flour in a dry place away from damp. Use white flour within 3 months and wholemeal flour within 6 weeks. After these times the flour will be perfectly safe to use but will not be in peak condition and your baking could be affected.

Notes on all the various flours available are on page 10.

YEAST

Yeast is a traditional raising agent which was universally used until about 100 years ago when chemical raising agents became common. Yeast cookery has many advantages. It opens up a whole new range of recipes not just for bread, but for cakes, puddings, batters, pizzas etc. Baking with yeast is economical because smaller quantities of fat and sugar are used and it gives a big yield. Yeast for home baking can be bought in four forms:

Fresh yeast

This is quick and easy to use but it is difficult to obtain in some areas. Health food shops and some bakers keep it. Fresh yeast should be cool and firm to the touch. It is creamy in colour and looks like putty.

Fresh yeast will keep for 1 month in a fridge if tightly wrapped, or it will freeze for up to 6 months. Freeze it in tightly wrapped pieces of about 25 g/1 oz. Frozen yeast may be blended straight into the warm mixing liquid, or allowed to thaw for 20 minutes before using.

Dried yeast

Dried yeast is granular in appearance and is available in 25-g/1-oz sachets or in tins. Dried yeast will keep for up to 6 months if kept in an airtight container, but deteriorates quickly once opened. As dried yeast is concentrated, only half the quantity is needed compared to that of fresh yeast. Generally speaking, 25 g/1 oz fresh yeast or 15 g/½ oz dried yeast should be used with 1.5 kg/3 lb bag white flour. Extra yeast will be needed for wholemeal flour and mixtures high in fat and sugar.

When using dried yeast, it is important to remember that it should be frothing strongly in the warm mixing liquid before being added to the flour.

Easy bake dried yeast

This is a dried baking yeast in a fine powdered form which you simply stir into the dry flour before adding the warm liquid. This yeast has vitamin C (ascorbic acid, *see page 169*) incorporated with it, which enables the bread dough to be made very quickly. One sachet will rise 675 g/1½ lb flour.

Easy blend dried yeast

This dried yeast is also in powder form and is sold in sachets. It is stirred into the dry flour at the beginning of the recipe. It must not be mixed with water or it will not work. One sachet will rise 675 g/1½ lb flour.

ALTERNATIVE METHODS OF ADDING YEAST

Sponge batter

This is another method of introducing yeast to the flour in a recipe. It is used for rich yeast mixtures, e.g. Stollen (*see page 192*). The fresh or dried yeast is added to the warm liquid with a little sugar and about one-third of the flour in the recipe. This forms a batter which must be left in a warm place until it froths up like a sponge.

Rubbing in fresh yeast

This method is not often used these days. The yeast is rubbed in like fat, then the warm liquid is added. The mixture needs to be very well beaten to distribute the yeast.

VITAMIN C (ASCORBIC ACID)

Available from chemists, vitamin C tablets are used to reduce the kneading and proving time when making bread. The tablet is crushed between two teaspoons and added to the warm liquid with the yeast. By using one 25-mg tablet with 675 g/ 1½ lb strong flour, the first rising period is reduced to 5 minutes and the second proving to about 45 minutes. Dough made with vitamin C added is usually known as short-time bread.

EGG WASH

1 medium egg
1 tablespoon water
2 fat pinches sugar

Stir all the ingredients together until the sugar is dissolved and use a brush to apply.

SUGAR

A little sugar is usually added to most yeast mixtures to give the yeast a good start. Any type of sugar may be used, including golden syrup, honey, malt or treacle. They sometimes need to be warmed slightly so that they will be easier to mix in. Malt and black treacle are used only in brown mixtures because of their colour.

SALT

I don't think bread is bread without a touch of salt. The proportion used to be 1 or 2 teaspoons for every 450 g/1 lb of flour. However, nowadays I use much less.

FAT

Fat enriches dough and improves the softness and colour. It also helps to keep the bread mixture from going stale. Any type of fat can be used (*see page 10*) although butter and lard give the best flavour and texture.

LIQUID

This may be water or milk or a mixture of both. Water is normally used in basic breads. Milk improves the nutritional value of bread and gives a softer, browner crust.

The usual temperature of the mixing liquid is 100°F/38°C. An easy way to achieve this is to mix one-third boiling liquid with two-thirds cold liquid.

The usual ratio of liquid to flour is 300 ml/ ½ pint to 450 g/1 lb flour. Wholewheat and wholemeal flour need rather more liquid.

EGGS

Eggs often go into enriched and sweeter yeast mixtures. They improve the nutritional value, keeping qualities and colour.

THE DIFFERENT STAGES IN YEAST COOKERY

All mixtures made with yeast are prepared in several different stages. Mixing the wet and dry ingredients together to form a dough, kneading or beating, rising, knocking back, shaping, proving and, lastly, baking.

MIXING AND KNEADING

It is not absolutely necessary to have all your utensils and flour warm before starting to bake with yeast but it does speed things up.

When mixing by hand, add all the yeasted liquid to the flour at once and stir with a wooden fork or spoon until the dough starts to form. I like to knead by hand at this stage and continue kneading in the bowl until the dough is beginning to come together. Turn it out onto a lightly floured surface and fold the dough over towards yourself, then push it down and away from you with the heel of your hand. Give the dough a quarter turn and carry on with this folding and pushing action for about 10 minutes. The dough starts off by being soft and sticky but will end up smooth, elastic, silky, and no longer sticking to your hands. This will take only about 4 minutes for a wholemeal or brown dough.

RISING

After kneading, the dough must be left for a length of time to enable the yeast to produce the carbon dioxide gas which makes the dough rise. While this is happening, the dough should be covered with a very lightly greased polythene bag, or even put into a polythene bag, to prevent a thick skin forming or the dough drying out.

Traditional bread doughs are risen twice, although quick methods of bread making have been developed, using vitamin C (ascorbic acid, *see page 169*), which involve only one rising. However, keen breadmakers insist that better results are obtained with two risings.

It is impossible to give exact rising times for yeast baking. Dough will rise in 45–60 minutes in a warm place, but will take 1½–2 hours at normal room temperature. In a cold room or larder you can expect to wait 8–12 hours, and in a fridge the dough will take 24 hours to rise. This does mean that the dough can be held back overnight then returned to room temperature the next day. Dough should never be allowed to get too hot while rising, e.g. near a radiator or fire, as this will kill the yeast and prevent rising.

KNOCKING BACK

The risen dough has to be literally 'knocked back' before shaping, i.e. the air kneaded out of it. Punch the dough to deflate it, then knead it until it becomes firm. The dough is then shaped and placed in tins or on baking trays.

PROVING

Some doughs are baked without proving (second rising) e.g. pizzas, but most yeasted breads need this step. Cover the dough in the tins or on the trays with lightly oiled polythene, or just muslin, and leave to prove for 20–40 minutes, when it will have become light and puffy and almost doubled in size.

BAKING

A very hot oven is needed to kill off the yeast. Basic bread doughs are normally baked at Gas 8, 450°F, 230°C, and richer doughs at Gas 6, 400°F, 200°C. When fully cooked, loaves shrink away from the sides of the tin. If the sides of the loaves are pale when removed from the tins, just put the loaves, without the tins, back in the oven for a further 5–10 minutes to brown the sides.

FINISHING

Bread finishes have become an important part of breadmaking nowadays. An old tip is to put a small bowl of water in the bottom of the oven while baking to make the crust crisper. Bread and rolls can be brushed with water and sprinkled with poppy seeds, cracked wheat, rye flakes or sesame seeds before baking to give a crunchy finish.

GLAZES FOR BREAD

Although not absolutely necessary, a glaze is often a pleasant alternative if you have not used one of the finishes described above and can look very attractive. These glazes can go on before baking or immediately after when the bread or rolls are still hot.

For a soft crust glaze

Brush with oil or dust with flour. For a really brown soft crust – brush with a mixture of milk and sugar.

For a shiny brown crust

Brush with beaten egg. For a shiny finish only – brush with egg white.

For a crisp crust

Brush with a salt water glaze – dissolve 1 teaspoon salt in 2 tablespoons water.

For a sweet glaze

Stir 1 tablespoon water and a little sugar into a beaten egg and brush over the dough.

Dissolve 1 tablespoon sugar in 1 tablespoon water and brush over the dough.

For a honey glaze

Stir 1 tablespoon runny honey into 2 tablespoons water and brush over the dough.

LOAF AND ROLL SHAPES

Most of the roll shapes can be made into loaves using larger quantities of dough.

FREEZING DOUGH AND BREAD

Raw bread dough freezes well. After kneading, form the dough into a ball and place in a large, lightly greased polythene bag. Seal very tightly to keep air out, label and freeze immediately. Use within 1 month if the dough is for plain white or brown bread, or 3 months if the dough is enriched with fat, milk or egg.

To freeze baked breads, do ensure that the loaves are completely cold before freezing – a loaf from the oven will take 3–4 hours to cool completely. It is often a good idea to slice the loaf before freezing so that individual slices can be used without having to defrost the whole loaf. Wrap the cold loaf well and label before freezing.

A tip about freezing pizza bases. I worked this one out after a query from a viewer. Roll out each pizza dough base to the size you need and freeze it on a paper plate. Once frozen, the dough slips easily off the pliable plate and your pizzas will not stick when you put them together in a plastic bag.

BREADS AND ROLLS

PLAIN WHITE BREAD

Makes 2 × 900-g/2-lb loaves or 4 × 450-g/1-lb loaves or 36 small rolls

1.3 kg/3 lb strong white flour
2 teaspoons salt
25 g/1 oz lard or solid vegetable fat
25 g/1 oz fresh yeast, or 15 g/½ oz dried yeast
1 teaspoon caster sugar
900 ml/1½ pints warm water

1. Sift the flour into a large mixing bowl, add the salt and rub in the lard or solid vegetable fat.
2. Crumble the fresh yeast into the sugar and stir into the warm water (or sprinkle the dried yeast onto the water with the sugar, whisk and leave until frothy).
3. Stir the yeasted liquid into the flour with a wooden fork or spoon until it starts to come together, then knead with your hand in the bowl. Turn out the dough onto a lightly floured board and knead for 10 minutes (or for 2–3 minutes with a dough hook in an electric mixer). The dough should now be elastic but not at all sticky. Shape into a large ball, place in a lightly greased bowl, cover and set aside in a warm place to rise for about 1 hour.
4. When the dough has risen to almost double its size, turn it out and knead it for 1–2 minutes. Divide into two if you are using 900-g/2-lb loaf tins or into four if you are using 450-g/1-lb tins.
5. Grease the tins and press the dough in to fit. Cover them lightly and set aside to prove – about 1 hour for the small loaves, but longer for the large ones. For small rolls, divide the dough into 50-g/2-oz pieces and shape into small balls. Put them on greased baking trays and leave to prove for about 20 minutes.
6. Bake in a hot oven, Gas 8, 450°F, 230°C. Bake the 900-g/2-lb loaves for about 1 hour and the 450-g/1-lb loaves for 30 minutes. Bake the small rolls for 12–15 minutes. Turn out and cool on a wire tray.

Keeps fresh for about 1 week, or freeze for up to 3 months.

WHITE BREAD MADE WITH EASY BLEND DRIED YEAST

Makes 2 × 450-g/1-lb loaves

675 g/1½ lb strong white flour
1 teaspoon salt
25 g/1 oz lard
1 sachet easy blend dried yeast
450 ml/¾ pint warm water

1. Sift the flour and salt into a warm mixing bowl and rub in the lard. Add the yeast and mix well, then stir in the warm water.
2. Stir and mix until the dough starts to form. Knead first in the bowl and then on a lightly floured surface until you have a soft elastic dough. Put the dough into a clean, lightly greased bowl, cover and set aside in a warm place to rise until almost doubled in size – about 30–40 minutes.
3. Grease two 450-g/1-lb loaf tins. Knock back the risen dough, divide it into two pieces and shape to fit the loaf tins. Press the dough into the tins, cover and leave to prove for a further 10–15 minutes, or until the dough is just above the top of the tins.
4. Bake in a hot oven, Gas 8, 450°F, 230°C, for about 30–40 minutes until brown. Turn out and cool on a wire tray.

Keeps fresh for 3–4 days, or freeze for up to 1 month.

VARIATION

ROLLS

Makes 12–18 depending on size

1. Follow steps 1 and 2 above. Knock back the risen dough and divide it into pieces. Weigh them to ensure each piece is a similar size.
2. Knead each piece to make round rolls or fancy shapes (*see pages 177 and 184*) and place them well apart on greased baking trays, leaving room for them to rise. Brush with one of the non-sweet glazes (*see page 170*) and set aside to prove for about 15 minutes.
3. Bake in a hot oven, Gas 8, 450°F, 230°C, for 10–15 minutes. Turn out and cool on a wire tray.

Eat within 3–4 days, or freeze for up to 1 month.

SHORT-TIME WHITE BREAD

By adding vitamin C (ascorbic acid) to a bread dough it is possible to cut down one of the rising periods to just five minutes. It is easier to use fresh yeast for this method.

Makes 2 × 450-g/1-lb loaves or 2 round cobs

675 g/1½ lb strong white flour, sifted
1 teaspoon salt
½ teaspoon caster sugar
40 g/1½ oz lard
7 g/¼ oz fresh yeast
425 ml/14 fl oz warm water
1 × 25-mg tablet vitamin C (ascorbic acid) *(see page 169)*

1. Mix the flour, salt and sugar into a large mixing bowl and rub in the lard.
2. Blend the yeast with a little warm water then pour the mixture into the remaining water and stir. Crush the vitamin C tablet between two teaspoons, add to the mixture and stir again.
3. Pour the yeasted liquid into the flour and mix with a wooden fork or spoon, then use your hand to knead it briefly in the bowl.
4. Turn out the dough onto a lightly floured surface and knead for 10 minutes (or for 2–3 minutes with a dough hook in an electric mixer). Shape the dough into a ball, cover and leave for 5 minutes.
5. Divide the dough into two. Shape the pieces either to fit into two greased 450-g/1-lb tins, or as two round cobs and laid on a greased baking tray. Cover and leave in a warm place to prove for about 45 minutes.
6. Bake in a hot oven, Gas 8, 450°F, 230°C, for 35 minutes. Turn out and cool on a wire tray.

Eat within 1 week, or freeze for up to 3 months.

MILK BREAD

This is an enriched dough which makes a very light loaf. Because it has fat in it as well as milk, it stays fresh for longer than plain bread and it also freezes well.

Makes 2 × 450-g/1-lb loaves

450 g/1 lb strong white flour
1 teaspoon salt
50 g/2 oz lard or butter
1 sachet easy blend dried yeast
300 ml/½ pint warm milk
1 large egg, beaten

1. Sift the flour and salt into a warm mixing bowl and rub in the fat. Stir in the yeast and mix well.
2. Mix the milk with the egg, stir into the dry ingredients and mix and knead to a soft dough. This will take 5–6 minutes.
3. Put the dough into a clean, lightly greased mixing bowl, cover and leave in a warm place to rise. It should have almost doubled in size in 30 minutes.
4. Grease two 450-g/1-lb loaf tins. Knock back the risen dough and divide into two pieces. Shape the pieces to fit the tins and press the dough into them. Cover and leave in a warm place to prove for 15 minutes.
5. Bake in a hot oven, Gas 8, 450°F, 230°C, for about 30 minutes. Turn out and cool on wire trays.

Keeps fresh for about 1 week, or freeze for up to 2 months.

VARIATIONS

BRIDGE ROLLS

These rolls join together during baking, making soft sides.

Makes 12–16 rolls depending on size

1. Make as above to step 3. Knock back the risen dough and divide it into equal pieces. Roll each piece into a fat cigar shape.
2. Place the rolls fairly close together on a greased baking tray and brush with a beaten egg. Cover lightly and leave in a warm place to prove for 15 minutes.
3. Bake in a hot oven, Gas 8, 450°F, 230°C, for about 30 minutes. Turn out and cool on a wire tray.

Eat within 4 days, or freeze for up to 2 months.

MILK PLAIT

Makes 1 × 900-g/2-lb plait

1. Reserve 1 teaspoon beaten egg and 1 teaspoon milk for the glaze. Make as above to step 3. Knock back the risen dough and roll into an oblong measuring about 10 × 20 cm/4 × 8 inches. Cut this oblong lengthways into three strips but leave them attached at one end (*see diagram below*).
2. Plait the strips together loosely and squeeze the three end pieces together securely. Lay the plait on a greased baking tray.

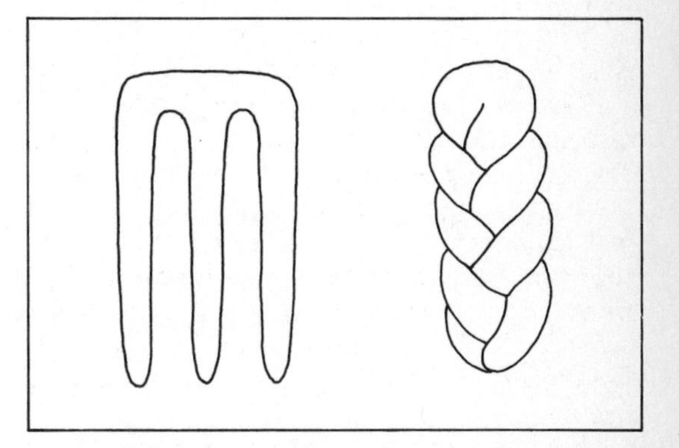

3. Combine the reserved egg and milk for the glaze and brush over the top of the plait. Sprinkle with one of the finishes suggested on page 170, e.g. sesame seeds or poppy seeds.
4. Bake in a hot oven, Gas 8, 450°F, 230°C, for about 30 minutes. Turn out and cool on a wire tray.

Keeps well for 4–5 days, or freeze for up to 2 months.

PLAIN WHOLEMEAL BREAD

Because wholemeal flour makes a dense loaf, it is never a good idea for the home baker to try and make a 900-g/2-lb loaf. It ends up with a very heavy crust.

Makes 4 × 450-g/1-lb loaves

1.3 kg/3 lb strong wholemeal flour
2 teaspoons salt
25 g/1 oz dark soft brown sugar
25 g/1 oz lard or solid vegetable fat
50 g/2 oz fresh yeast, or 25 g/1 oz dried yeast
900 ml/1½ pints warm water

1. Sift the flour and salt into a large mixing bowl, adding any residue of bran left in the sieve. Add all but 1 teaspoon of the sugar and rub in the lard or solid vegetable fat.
2. Crumble the fresh yeast into a small bowl with the reserved sugar. Pour over half the warm water and stir to dissolve the sugar and yeast. (If using dried yeast, sprinkle it with the sugar onto the warm water, whisk and leave until frothy.)
3. Work all the liquid into the flour with a wooden fork or spoon until it starts to come together, then use your hand to knead the dough briefly in the bowl. Turn out the dough onto a lightly floured surface and knead for about 10 minutes (or for 3 minutes with a dough hook in an electric mixer). Shape the dough into a ball, place in a lightly greased bowl, cover and set aside in a warm place to rise for about 1 hour. It should then have risen but not quite doubled in size.
4. Turn out the risen dough and knock it back, then knead for 2 minutes. Grease four 450-g/1-lb loaf tins lightly with lard or solid vegetable fat. Divide the dough into four pieces, shape to fit the tins and press the dough into each one. Cover and leave in a warm place to prove for about 1 hour or until the dough reaches the top of the tins.
5. Bake in a hot oven, Gas 8, 450°F, 230°C, for 40 minutes. Turn out and cool on a wire tray.

Store in a bread bin for 1 week, or freeze for up to 3 months.

WHOLEMEAL BREAD MADE WITH EASY BLEND DRIED YEAST

Makes 2 × 450-g/1-lb loaves

675 g/1½ lb strong wholemeal flour
1 tablespoon salt
25 g/1 oz lard
1 sachet easy blend dried yeast
1 tablespoon dark soft brown sugar
450 ml/¾ pint warm water

1. Sift the flour and salt into a warm mixing bowl, adding any residue of bran left in the sieve. Rub in the lard, then add the yeast and mix well.
2. Stir the sugar into the warm water and pour into the dry ingredients. Stir and mix to a soft elastic dough. Turn out the dough onto a lightly floured surface and knead briefly until smooth. Put the dough back into a clean, lightly greased bowl, cover and set aside in a warm place to rise until doubled in size – about 30 minutes.
3. Grease two 450-g/1-lb loaf tins. Knock back the risen dough, divide it into two pieces and shape to fit the loaf tins. Press the dough into the tins, cover and leave to prove for about 30 minutes when the dough should have risen just above the tins.
4. Bake in a hot oven, Gas 8, 450°F, 230°C, for 10 minutes. Reduce the heat to fairly hot, Gas 6, 400°F, 200°C, and bake for a further 10 minutes. Turn out and cool on a wire tray.

Keeps fresh for 2–3 days, or freeze for up to 1 month.

SHORT-TIME WHOLEWHEAT BREAD

This bread recipe uses an easy bake dried yeast which has incorporated into it some vitamin C and so cuts down the proving time. The yeast is added directly to the ingredients and not mixed with liquid first. The wholewheat flour produces a slightly lighter dough than normal.

Makes 2 × 450-g/1-lb loaves

450 g/1 lb strong wholewheat flour
1 sachet easy bake dried yeast
1 dessertspoon salt
1 dessertspoon caster sugar
15 g/½ oz vegetable fat or lard
450 ml/¾ pint warm water

1. Grease two 450-g/1-lb loaf tins.
2. Sift the flour into a large mixing bowl, adding any residue of bran left in the sieve, and stir in the yeast, salt and sugar. Rub in the fat.
3. Pour in the water and stir with a wooden fork or spoon until the dough comes together then knead by hand in the bowl. Turn out the dough on a lightly floured surface and knead for about 10 minutes (or for 2–3 minutes with a dough hook in an electric mixer).
4. Shape the dough into a ball, cover lightly and leave for 5 minutes.
5. Divide the dough into two and shape each piece to fit the tins. Press the dough into the tins, cover with a polythene bag and leave in a warm place to prove for about 30 minutes when it should have risen above the tins and almost doubled in size.
6. Bake in a hot oven, Gas 8, 450°F, 230°C, for 30–35 minutes. Turn out and cool on a wire tray.

Eat within 1 week, or freeze for up to 3 months.

VARIATION

BUN RINGS

Makes 1 × 7-bun bread ring and 1 × 450-g/1-lb loaf, or 2 × 7-bun bread rings

1 quantity short-time wholewheat dough *(left)*

FOR THE TOPPINGS
A little milk
1 dessertspoon sesame seeds
1 dessertspoon poppy seeds
1 dessertspoon rye flakes
1 teaspoon kibbled wheat

1. Make the dough as above, following steps 1–3.
2. Divide the dough into two and shape one half to fit a greased 450-g/1-lb loaf tin. Take the other half and divide the dough into seven equal pieces. Or divide all the dough into fourteen equal pieces if making two bread rings.
3. Grease one or two 20-cm/8-inch cake tins. Place the topping ingredients in individual saucers. Knead each piece of dough into a neat round ball and brush the top of each with milk. Dip the top of two rolls into the sesame seeds, two into the poppy seeds and two into the rye flakes. Dip the remaining roll into the kibbled wheat. If making two bread rings, repeat with the other rolls.
4. Set each roll in the cake tin, dressed side up. Place six rolls around the edge and put the final roll in the centre. Lightly cover the loaf and the ring and set aside in a warm place to prove. The loaf will take about 45 minutes, and the bun ring about 25 minutes.
5. Bake in a hot oven, Gas 8, 450°F, 230°C, for about 35 minutes for the loaf and about 30 minutes for the ring. Turn out and cool on a wire tray.

Eat within 1 week, or freeze for up to 3 months.

BROWN BREAD WITH SUNFLOWER SEEDS

Sunflower seeds are very nice to eat raw but by toasting them briefly their flavour is even more developed.

Makes 2 × 450-g/1-lb loaves

50 g/2 oz sunflower seeds*
450 g/1 lb plain wholewheat flour
125 g/4 oz strong white flour
2 teaspoons salt
15 g/½ oz lard
25 g/1 oz fresh yeast
300 ml/½ pint warm water plus 3–4 tablespoons warm water
1 dessertspoon black treacle

* *If your teeth can't cope with whole sunflower seeds, they can be chopped in a food processor very easily.*

1. Spread the sunflower seeds on a metal tray and briefly toast them under a grill.
2. Sift the flours and salt into a large mixing bowl, adding any residue of bran left in the sieve. Rub in the lard.
3. Whisk the crumbled yeast into the warm water.
4. Stir the yeasted water, treacle and sunflower seeds into the dry ingredients and mix until the dough comes together. If the mixture is dry, add a little more warm water. Turn out the dough onto a floured board and knead for about 5 minutes until the dough is smooth and elastic. Put back into a clean lightly greased bowl, cover and leave in a warm place to rise for about 30 minutes.
5. Generously grease two 450-g/1-lb loaf tins. Knock back the risen dough and knead briefly, then divide it into two and shape to fit the tins. Press the dough into the tins, cover them lightly and set aside in a warm place to prove for about 30–45 minutes.
6. Bake in a hot oven, Gas 7, 425°F, 220°C, for about 25 minutes. Turn out and cool on a wire tray.

Store in an airtight tin and eat within 3–4 days, or freeze for up to 3 months.

WHITE IRISH SODA BREAD

Makes 1 cake, 18 cm/7 inches across

450 g/1 lb strong white flour
1 teaspoon salt
1 teaspoon bicarbonate of soda
2 teaspoons cream of tartar
300 ml/½ pint milk plus 1–2 extra tablespoons

1. Preheat the oven to fairly hot, Gas 6, 400°F, 200°C.
2. Sift the flour into a mixing bowl and stir in the dry ingredients.
3. Pour in the milk and stir together quickly into a soft dough, adding more milk if necessary.
4. Knead the dough very lightly and turn out onto a floured surface. Knead carefully until you get a nice smooth top. Put this cake onto a floured baking tray and press out until the cake is about 18 cm/7 inches across and 5 cm/2 inches deep. Score a deep cross on top of the dough.
5. Bake for about 40 minutes. Turn out, wrap in a clean tea towel to soften the crust and cool on a wire tray.

Eat fairly fresh. Will keep for 4 days in an airtight tin, or freeze for up to 2 months.

GRANARY SODA BREAD

This is my own favourite soda bread. I bake it regularly.

Makes 1 round cake, 23 cm/9 inches across

450 g/1 lb Granary flour
225 g/8 oz strong white flour
2 teaspoons caster sugar
1 teaspoon bicarbonate of soda
1 teaspoon cream of tartar
1 teaspoon salt
600 ml/1 pint milk, or milk and water mixed

1. Preheat the oven to moderately hot, Gas 5, 375°F, 190°C.
2. Put the Granary flour into a large mixing bowl. Sift in the white flour, sugar, bicarbonate of soda, cream of tartar and salt.
3. Pour in almost half the liquid and stir once or twice, then add the remaining liquid and mix to a soft dough. Add a little extra liquid if the mixture looks too dry. Work it together in the bowl then

turn it out onto a floured surface. Dust the dough with flour and shape it into a large cake with a smooth top.

4. Put this cake, smooth side up, onto a floured baking tray and press out until the cake is 23 cm/9 inches across and 5 cm/2 inches deep. Score a deep cross on top of the dough.

5. Bake for about 50 minutes. Turn out and cool on a wire tray.

Eat as fresh as possible but will keep in an airtight tin for up to 4 days. Freeze for up to 2 months.

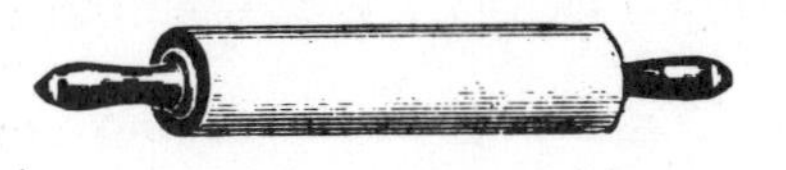

FRUITED IRISH SODA BREAD

This is a simple bread without yeast. If you do not like it very crusty, put a large cake tin over the top of the round of bread while it is cooking. Mix the dough to a fairly soft consistency and lose no time in getting it into the oven.

Makes 1 round cake, 20 cm/8 inches across

275 g/10 oz plain brown flour
175 g/6 oz strong white flour
1 teaspoon salt
1 teaspoon bicarbonate of soda
1 teaspoon cream of tartar
2 teaspoons caster sugar (optional)
125 g/4 oz sultanas, washed and dried
About 300 ml/½ pint milk

1. Preheat the oven to moderately hot, Gas 5, 375°F, 190°C.

2. Put the brown flour into a large mixing bowl and sift in the white flour, salt, bicarbonate of soda and cream of tartar. Stir in the sugar, if using, and sultanas.

3. Add the milk and mix to a soft dough. If the mixture looks dry, add a little more milk – the dough should be slack but not wet. Work it together in the bowl then turn it out onto a floured surface. Dust the dough with flour and knead carefully and briefly into a soft round.

4. Lift onto a floured baking tray and press out to a cake about 4 cm/1½ inches thick. Score a deep cross on top of the dough.

5. Bake for about 40 minutes. Turn out and cool on a wire tray.

Best eaten fresh but will keep in an airtight tin for 3–4 days. Freezes well for up to 2 months.

COTTAGE LOAF

Everybody recognizes this shape of a fat round bottom and a top which is also fat but much smaller. Miniature rolls made on the same principle are very attractive but time consuming.

Makes 1 cottage loaf

675 g/1½ lb strong white or brown flour
2 teaspoons salt
25 g/1 oz lard
1 sachet easy blend dried yeast
450 ml/¾ pint warm water (a little extra if using brown flour)

1. Sift the flour and salt into a warm mixing bowl and rub in the lard. Add the yeast and mix well, then stir in the warm water.

2. Using a wooden fork or spoon, mix and stir until the dough starts to come together, then use your hand to knead it in the bowl. Turn out the dough onto a floured surface and knead again until the dough is soft and elastic.

3. Put the dough into a clean greased bowl, cover and set aside in a warm place to rise until doubled in size – about 30 minutes.

4. Knock back the risen dough, cut off about one-third and shape and knead this to a ball. Shape and knead the other piece of dough and set it on a greased baking tray. Moisten the bottom of the smaller round of dough and set it on top of the larger round. Flour the handle of a clean wooden spoon and push it down through the centre of both pieces of dough (*see below*). Dust the top of the loaf with flour, cover and leave in a warm place to prove for about 40–45 minutes.

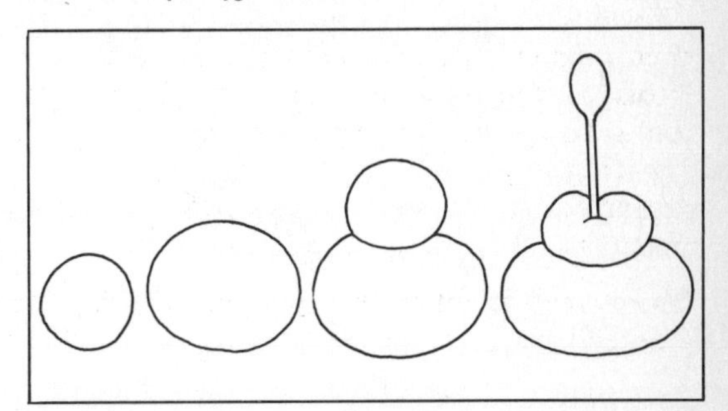

5. Bake in a hot oven, Gas 7, 425°F, 220°C, for 15 minutes, then reduce the heat to moderate, Gas 3, 325°F, 160°C, and bake for a further 25 minutes. Turn out and cool on a wire tray.

Store in an airtight tin and eat within 1 week, or freeze for up to 3 months.

CLAY FLOWERPOT LOAVES

This is a light brown loaf mixture and the novelty of baking in a flowerpot never fails to interest. It is also one way of achieving round, rather than square, slices of bread.

First, the flowerpots have to be prepared. Use new pots, made of clay and measuring 12.5 cm/5 inches across the top. Wash and dry them, then brush the inside of each pot with oil or melted fat. Put the greased empty pots into a hot oven for about 1–2 hours. Cool and grease again before use. After baking, wash the flowerpots, dry and reserve for future use.

Makes 2 small flowerpot-shaped loaves

175 g/6 oz strong white flour
225 g/8 oz plain wholemeal flour
1 teaspoon salt
25 g/1 oz lard
15 g/½ oz fresh yeast, or 7 g/¼ oz dried yeast
1 teaspoon caster sugar
300 ml/½ pint warm water

1. Sift the flours and salt into a large mixing bowl, adding any residue of bran left in the sieve, and rub in the lard.
2. Crumble the fresh yeast into the sugar and stir into the warm water (or sprinkle the dried yeast onto the water with the sugar, whisk and leave until frothy).
3. Pour the yeasted liquid into the flour and mix with a wooden fork or spoon to a soft dough. Using your hand, knead in the bowl, then turn out the dough on a lightly floured surface and knead until smooth. Put the dough into a clean lightly greased bowl, cover and leave in a warm place to rise for about 1 hour.
4. Knock back the risen dough and divide into two pieces. Shape into two smooth balls and put into the well greased clay flowerpots. Stand the pots on a baking tray. Leave to prove for about 20 minutes.
5. Preheat the oven to hot, Gas 8, 450°F, 230°C.
6. Bake for 35 minutes. Turn out and cool on a wire tray.

Eat within 3–4 days, or freeze for up to 1 month.

NAAN BREAD

Unlike most breads, this version of an Indian speciality is cooked under a very hot grill after it has had 3–4 minutes in a hot oven. I have tried the recipes in which the naan is cooked only under the grill and I find the result just a bit leathery. Authentic naan bread is baked in a special type of clay oven.

Freshly made, as an accompaniment to Indian food, it is excellent.

Makes 6 pieces

150 ml/¼ pint warm milk and water, mixed
2 teaspoons caster sugar
15 g/½ oz dried yeast
450 g/1 lb plain white flour, sifted
½ teaspoon salt
1 teaspoon baking powder
2 tablespoons sunflower oil
150 ml/¼ pint natural yoghurt
1 large egg, beaten
A little extra oil

1. Put the milk and water mixture into a jug and whisk in 1 teaspoon sugar and the yeast. Cover and set aside in a warm place for 20 minutes until frothy.
2. Sift the flour, salt and baking powder into a warm mixing bowl. Add the remaining sugar, yeasted liquid, oil, yoghurt and the egg.
3. Mix with a wooden fork or spoon then, when the dough starts to come together, use your hand to knead it in the bowl. Turn out the dough on a lightly floured surface and knead for about 10 minutes. The dough should be very smooth and pleasant to touch. Return the dough to a lightly greased bowl, cover and leave in a warm place to rise until doubled in size – about 1 hour.
4. Find a baking tray which will fit under your grill. Set the oven to its highest temperature and put the tray in the oven to heat up.
5. Set the grill to high temperature. Knock back the risen dough and knead it briefly then divide into six equal pieces. Roll two pieces of dough out into an oval shape, each measuring about 23 × 15 cm/9 × 6 inches.
6. Take the hot baking tray out of the oven and brush it quickly with a little oil. Lay the two ovals of dough on it and put them in the oven for 3–4 minutes until well risen.
7. Take them out of the oven and immediately put them under the hot grill. Leave them there just long enough to brown each side – they are often

very slightly scorched and this adds to their flavour. Although the naan puffs up in the oven, it becomes quite flat when grilled, and should be soft inside. Keep the cooked naans warm in a clean tea towel while the others are rolled out and cooked.

Eat freshly made. Do not freeze.

PITTA BREAD

This way of making pitta bread was quite new to me but it is very easy to do and the flavour is very good. The shapes, however, are not so easy to control.

Makes 6 pieces

2 teaspoons caster sugar
375 ml/13 fl oz warm water
15 g/½ oz dried yeast
2 teaspoons salt
450 g/1 lb plain wholewheat flour, sifted and residue of bran in sieve added

1. Dissolve the sugar in the warm water in a large jug. Stir in the yeast. Cover and set aside in a warm place for 10 minutes until frothy.
2. In a large mixing bowl, stir the salt into the flour, and pour in the yeasted liquid. Mix and stir with a wooden fork or spoon to get a smooth dough then turn out the dough onto a floured board and knead for about 3 minutes.
3. Return the dough to a clean lightly greased bowl, cover lightly and leave in a warm place to rise until doubled in size – about 25 minutes.
4. Knock back the risen dough and divide into six pieces, each weighing about 60 g/2½ oz. Shape into balls and leave, uncovered, for 20 minutes on the floured board to prove.
5. Preheat the oven to hot, Gas 8, 450°F, 230°C.
6. Using the heel of your hand, ease and flatten the risen dough into rounds about 10 × 12.5 cm/4 × 5 inches. Leave, uncovered, on the board for another 15 minutes to puff up, then put onto greased baking trays.
7. Bake for 8 minutes until well risen and crisp.
8. Take the breads out of the oven and split open along one side. Wrap them in a clean tea towel, to keep them soft, and set aside to cool.

Best eaten very fresh, but will freeze in plastic bags for up to 3 months.

HARVEST BREADS

In autumn it is the custom to celebrate the gathering in of the harvest. Churches in town and country are decorated with the fruits of the earth, and pride of place is usually given to the wheat crop symbolized by the harvest bread. I remember years ago helping to make the traditional wheatsheaf and searching dozens of recipe books for help. I finally got it from the Flour Advisory Bureau. Here are my recipes based on their instructions.

The breads are never eaten but are usually sprayed with varnish and used as decorations. The dough used is high in salt to slow down the rising so that half the design does not puff up before the other half is made. It is a lovely family occupation, but I warn you it is a slow one. Find a baking tray big enough to accommodate the design – it will be about 46 cm/18 inches high and 4 cm/1½ inches thick. Some ovens have solid shelves as well as wire ones – this is ideal. It is also a good idea to turn the oven shelf upside down so that the 'work of art' can be slid off easily. Perhaps two large baking trays clipped together in some way would also work – again turn them upside down.

WHEATSHEAF

BASIC DOUGH
1.3 kg/3 lb strong white flour
50 g/2 oz salt
2 sachets easy blend dried yeast
900 ml/1½ pints warm water
2 currants

TO GLAZE
1 beaten egg

1. Sift the flour and salt into a very large mixing bowl and stir in the yeast. Mix really well, then stir in the warm water.
2. Stir with a wooden fork or spoon until the dough comes together, then use your hand to knead it in the bowl. Turn out the dough on a lightly floured surface and knead until the dough is soft and elastic.
3. When the dough is really silky, put it back into a large lightly greased bowl, cover and leave in a warm place to rise until it has almost doubled in size – 2–3 hours.
4. Knock back the risen dough and cut off two pieces, one weighing 225 g/8 oz and the other weighing 325 g/12 oz. These will form the base of

the design. Cover the remaining dough with a clean tea towel.

5. Take the 225-g/8-oz piece and roll and shape it into an oblong measuring about 30 cm/12 inches long and 18 cm/7 inches wide (*a*). Take the other piece of dough and roll, cut and shape it into a crescent (*b*), which will form the base of the 'ears of the corn'. Lay the crescent on one short edge of the oblong, using a little water to join them together, and press out the dough so that it is the same thickness all over. You should now have a shape like a giant mushroom. Grease a large baking tray and carefully lay the dough on it. Prick the dough all over with a fork.

6. Cut the remaining dough in two. Set aside one half, well covered. From the other half, cut, shape and roll about twenty-four strips of dough to the thickness of a thin pencil and about 30 cm/12 inches long.

7. Brush the stem part of the 'mushroom' with water and lay the strips of dough closely together onto it to simulate the stems of corn. Take three of the strips, plait them neatly and lay this plait across the top half of the 'stems' to look like string. Tuck the ends underneath.

8. There is nearly always a mouse on the harvest wheatsheaf. Take a small piece of dough – about 50 g/2 oz – and shape a small mouse. Give him a long thin tail and use currants for his eyes. Stick him at the base of the stalks using a little water.

9. Cut the remaining piece of dough into 25-g/1-oz pieces. Roll each one into a thick pencil shape and cut these into small sausage shapes measuring about 3 cm/1¼ inches long. Using scissors, snip the 'ears of corn' three or four times to give a spikey appearance. Brush the 'mushroom' cap with water and lay all these ears fanwise starting at the top and working down. Overlap the top of the stems.

10. Brush the whole wheatsheaf with beaten egg.

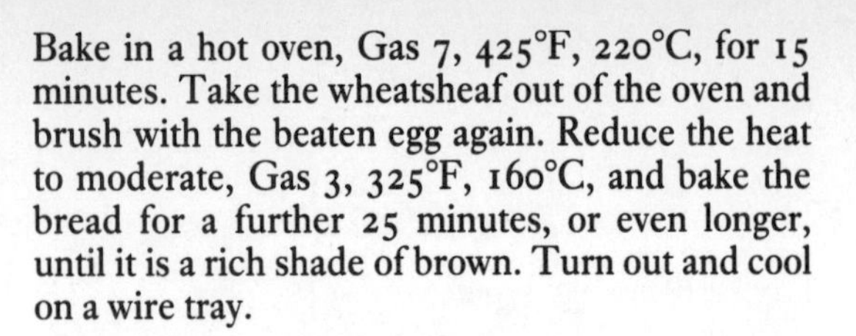

Bake in a hot oven, Gas 7, 425°F, 220°C, for 15 minutes. Take the wheatsheaf out of the oven and brush with the beaten egg again. Reduce the heat to moderate, Gas 3, 325°F, 160°C, and bake the bread for a further 25 minutes, or even longer, until it is a rich shade of brown. Turn out and cool on a wire tray.

When cold, the wheatsheaf can be sprayed back and front with artist's picture varnish and it should keep for years.

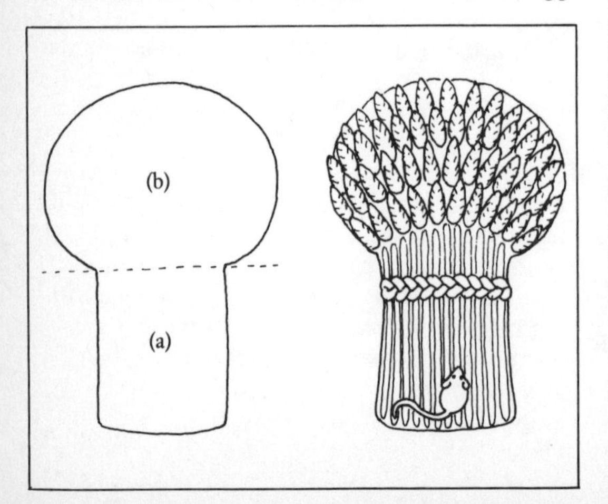

LOAVES AND FISHES

The other famous design for harvest bread is the Miracle of the Loaves and Fishes. However, I think a little more artistry is needed for this one.

1 quantity basic dough *(see page 179)*

1. Make the dough and leave to rise as for the Wheatsheaf Loaf.

2. Prepare and grease a large baking tray or use two large baking trays upside down and close together.

3. To make the plate or platter, cut off a piece of dough weighing about 450 g/1 lb and roll this out to an oval measuring 23 × 30 cm/9 × 12 inches – use an oval plate to get a good shape. Or just make a rectangle.

4. To make the loaves, cut off five 50-g/2-oz pieces of dough and divide each piece into two – a tiny ball of dough weighing 15 g/½ oz and the other weighing 40 g/1½ oz. Using a little water, stick the small ball of dough on top of the larger one. Flour the handle of a clean wooden spoon and push it down through the top of both pieces to help them to stick together. Repeat this procedure until you have five cottage loaves.

5. To make the fishes, cut off two 50-g/2-oz pieces of dough. Shape each piece into an oval tapering to a point at one end. Cut a mouth out of the widest end and pinch the other end into a tail shape. Use a currant for the eye and mark the gill and tail by scoring with the blunt side of a knife. Use scissors to snip a scaled effect to the body.

6. Put the oval or rectangle piece of dough on the baking tray, brush it with water and stick on the five loaves and two fishes (*see diagram on page 181*).

7. To finish off the outer edge of the platter, divide the remaining dough into three pieces. Roll each piece into a strand and plait into a rope long enough to go round the edge of the platter. Brush the edge of the oval or rectangle and fix the plait in position. Brush the whole platter with beaten egg.

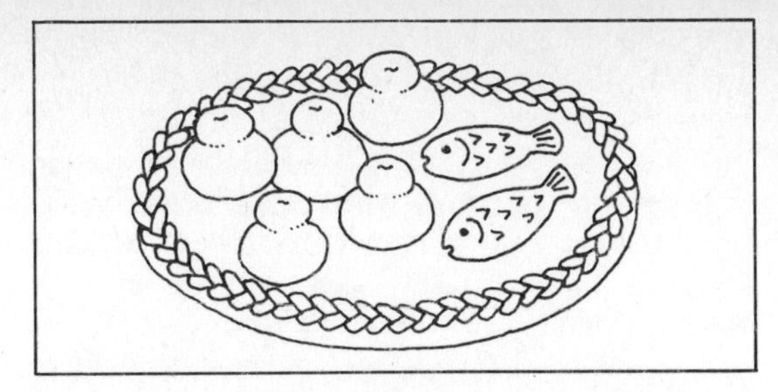

8. Bake in a hot oven, Gas 7, 425°F, 220°C, for 15 minutes. Remove from the oven and brush with the beaten egg again. Reduce the heat to moderate, Gas 3, 325°F, 160°C, and bake for a further 25 minutes. Turn out and cool on a wire tray.

When cold, spray the platter back and front with artist's varnish and it should last for years.

RYE BREAD

Popular in Scandinavia, rye bread is made using the lengthy 'sour-dough' process. Natural yoghurt adds the authentic flavour. Use the bread for open sandwiches as the Scandinavians do.

Makes 2 small loaves

25 g/1 oz fresh yeast, or 15 g/½ oz dried yeast
1 teaspoon caster sugar
175 ml/6 fl oz warm water
125 g/4 oz strong white flour
325 g/12 oz rye flour
1 teaspoon salt
15 g/½ oz lard
150 g/5 oz natural yoghurt
Rye flakes for sprinkling

1. Crumble the fresh yeast into the sugar and stir into the warm water (or sprinkle the dried yeast onto the warm water with the sugar, whisk and set aside to become frothy).
2. Sift the flours and salt into a large mixing bowl, adding any residue of bran left in the sieve and rub in the lard. Stir in the yeasted liquid and the yoghurt to form a soft dough. Using a wooden fork or spoon, stir and mix until the dough begins to form, then use your hand to knead it in the bowl. Turn out the dough onto a well-floured surface and knead for 5 minutes. Put the dough into a clean, greased bowl, cover it lightly and leave to rise in a warm place for 1¼ hours.
3. Knock back the risen dough, divide into two pieces and shape each piece into a fat sausage. Put them on greased baking trays. Make 5-mm/¼-inch deep cuts across the bread, brush with water and sprinkle the rye flakes generously on top. Cover and set aside in a warm place to prove for about 15 minutes.
4. Bake in a hot oven, Gas 7, 425°F, 220°C, for about 35 minutes. Turn out and cool on a wire tray.

Keeps well for about 3–4 days. Freeze for up to 2 months.

GARLIC AND CHEESE LOAF

This savoury combination is at its tastiest when made with a good wholemeal flour. It makes a dense loaf which is easy to cut into thin slices.

Makes 2 × 450-g/1-lb loaves

450 g/1 lb plain wholemeal flour
2 teaspoons salt
175 g/6 oz strong cheese, grated
1 clove of garlic, peeled and crushed (either in a garlic press or under the flat blade of a knife)
50 g/2 oz lard or butter
1 sachet easy blend dried yeast
300 ml/½ pint warm milk (a little more if you want a soft dough)
1 medium egg, beaten
Extra 25 g/1 oz grated cheese

1. Sift the flour and salt into a warm mixing bowl, adding any residue of bran left in the sieve. Mix in the 175 g/6 oz cheese and the garlic and rub in the fat. Mix in the dried yeast.
2. Pour the milk and egg into the dry ingredients and mix with a wooden fork or spoon to an elastic dough. Add a little extra milk if the dough is stiff. Using your hand, knead in the bowl, and then turn the dough out onto a floured board and knead again until smooth. Put the dough in a clean lightly greased bowl, cover and leave to rise in a warm place for 1½ hours until doubled in size.
3. Generously grease two 450-g/1-lb loaf tins. Knock back the risen dough, and cut and shape to fit the loaf tins. Sprinkle the inside of the tins with the 25 g/1 oz grated cheese and tip out any excess. Put the dough into the tins and sprinkle the tops with any remaining cheese. Cover and set aside in a warm place to prove for about 20 minutes.
4. Bake in a hot oven, Gas 7, 425°F, 220°C, for 35 minutes. Turn out and cool on a wire tray.

Store in an airtight tin and eat within 3 days, or freeze for up to 2 months.

HERB BREAD OR ROLLS

Do use fresh herbs if you can.

Makes 2 × 450-g/1-lb loaves or 12 rolls

225 g/8 oz strong white flour
225 g/8 oz plain wholemeal flour
1 teaspoon salt
2 tablespoons fresh parsley plus 2 tablespoons any other fresh herbs, finely chopped, or 2 teaspoons mixed dried herbs
1 sachet easy blend dried yeast
350 ml/12 fl oz warm milk
1 tablespoon oil
1 large egg, beaten
1 large clove of garlic, peeled and very finely chopped
1 tablespoon kibbled wheat
25 g/1 oz butter, melted

1. Sift the flours and salt into a warm mixing bowl, adding any residue of bran left in the sieve, and add the dried herbs, if using them. Stir in the yeast and mix well.
2. Pour in the milk, oil and beaten egg and mix with a wooden fork or spoon until the dough forms, then use your hand and knead the dough briefly in the bowl. Turn out the dough on a lightly floured surface and knead until the dough has a smooth elastic consistency. Put it back into a clean lightly greased bowl, cover and set aside in a warm place to rise for 1½ hours until it has doubled in size.
3. Knock back the risen dough and knead briefly. Work in the garlic and fresh herbs, if you are using them, and knead to distribute them evenly.
4. Grease two 450-g/1-lb loaf tins or a baking tray. If you are making loaves, divide the dough into two pieces. Shake a little kibbled wheat into each loaf tin and shape the dough to fit. Cover lightly and set aside in a warm place to prove for about 15 minutes. If you are making rolls, cut up the dough into twelve even pieces. Shape them into neat balls and lay them on the baking tray, fairly close together so that they will join up on proving. Cover lightly and set aside in a warm place to prove for about 25 minutes, or until risen and puffy.
5. Brush the tops of the loaves or the rolls with melted butter and sprinkle with the remaining kibbled wheat. Bake in a moderately hot oven, Gas 5, 375°F, 190°C, for 40 minutes for the loaves and 25–30 minutes for the rolls. Turn out and cool on a wire tray.

Eat within 3 days, or freeze for up to 2 months.

CARAWAY SEED BREAD

My first taste of caraway seed in bread was in Tübingen in Germany when our son was at the university there. I was astonished at the huge range of breads for sale in the bakery shops – far more varieties than I have ever seen before or since. The loaf we tried had grated cheese added on top. Here is my recipe.

Makes 1 bloomer-shaped loaf

450 g/1 lb strong white or brown flour
½ teaspoon salt
2 teaspoons caraway seeds, crushed (use a pestle and mortar, or the end of a rolling pin in a strong bowl)
25 g/1 oz lard
15 g/½ oz fresh yeast, or 7 g/¼ oz dried yeast
1 teaspoon light soft brown sugar
300 ml/½ pint warm water
75 g/3 oz strong Cheddar cheese, grated

1. Sift the flour and salt into a large mixing bowl. Stir in the crushed caraway seeds and then rub in the lard.
2. Crumble the fresh yeast into the sugar and stir into the warm water (or sprinkle the dried yeast onto the warm water with the sugar, whisk and leave until frothy).
3. Stir the yeasted liquid into the flour and mix to a dough. Turn out the dough onto a floured surface and knead well. Return it to a clean greased bowl, cover and set aside in a warm place to rise for about 1 hour.
4. Knock back the risen dough and shape into a long fat sausage. Using a sharp knife, make four or five cuts diagonally across the top of the loaf and set it on a greased baking tray. Cover and set aside in a warm place to prove for about 45 minutes.
5. Bake in a fairly hot oven, Gas 6, 400°F, 200°C, for about 30 minutes. Remove from the oven and brush the top of the loaf with water, then quickly pile the grated cheese on top. Put the loaf back into the oven and bake for a further 10 minutes.

This loaf will store in an airtight tin for 3–4 days but is really better eaten fresh. However, it does freeze well for up to 3 months.

MUFFINS

Traditionally, muffins were cooked on a girdle (*see page 166*), but I have also included the method for baking them in an oven.

Makes 10

275 g/10 oz strong white flour
1 teaspoon salt
½ sachet easy blend dried yeast
225–300 ml/8–10 fl oz warm water
1 tablespoon oil

1. Sift the flour and salt into a warm mixing bowl and stir in the yeast.
2. Pour in the warm water and oil and mix and knead to a soft dough, adding more warm water if necessary. Put the dough into a clean lightly greased bowl, cover and leave to rise in a warm place for 1½ hours until doubled in size.
3. Knock back the risen dough and roll it out to a thickness of 1 cm/½ inch. Using a biscuit cutter 7.5 cm/3 inches across, cut out rounds of dough. Gather up the trimmings, reroll and cut.
4. Lightly dust a baking tray with flour. Set the muffins on it, cover and leave to prove for 30–40 minutes.
5. Bake in a hot oven, Gas 8, 450°F, 230°C, for 5 minutes, turn the muffins over and bake for a further 5 minutes. Cool on a wire tray.

TO COOK ON A GIRDLE

Lightly grease a girdle or heavy frying pan, and heat to a moderate temperature. Set four or five risen muffins on at a time. Cook for 5–6 minutes. Turn them over and cook for a further 6–7 minutes. Cool on a wire tray.

Best eaten fresh or toasted. Will freeze well for up to 3 months.

OAT CAKES

These are not at all crisp like Scottish oat cakes (*see page 104*), but are more like thick pancakes. They are lovely fried with bacon and egg for breakfast or grilled and buttered at tea time.

Makes 12

225 g/8 oz plain white flour, sifted
225 g/8 oz fine oatmeal (not rolled oats)
1 teaspoon salt
15 g/½ oz fresh yeast, or 7 g/¼ oz dried yeast
1 teaspoon sugar
1 litre/1½ pints warm milk and water, mixed

1. Stir the flour, oatmeal and salt together in a large jug.
2. Crumble the yeast into the sugar and stir into the milk and water mixture. Whisk lightly.
3. Stir the yeasted liquid into the dry ingredients in the jug and whisk until smooth. Cover and set aside in a warm place for about 1 hour.
4. Bake on a well greased griddle or in a heavy based frying pan. Whisk the batter well between each oat cake. Pour out just enough batter to cover the base of the pan thinly. Keep the temperature moderately hot and cook for 2–3 minutes. If the top of the oat cake looks dry and the underside is golden brown, turn the oat cake over and bake for 2–3 minutes more.

The oat cakes will keep well for 4–5 days in a polythene bag in the fridge. They also freeze well for up to 3 months.

BREAD STICKS

You can make bread sticks from almost any plain bread recipe. They are excellent for eating with a savoury dip or with soup.

Makes about 20

325 g/12 oz plain white or wholewheat flour
1 teaspoon salt
1 teaspoon caster sugar
300 ml/½ pint milk and water mixed (half boiling water and half cold milk)
2 teaspoons dried yeast
25 g/1 oz sesame seeds or poppy seeds
A little extra milk

1. Sift the flour into a large mixing bowl, adding any residue of bran left in the sieve if using wholewheat flour, and add the salt.
2. In a large jug, dissolve the sugar in the warm milk and water mixture. Sprinkle the yeast on top and whisk with a fork. Set aside for 10 minutes or until there is a good froth.
3. Pour the yeasted liquid into the flour and knead for 2–3 minutes to form a soft dough. Put the dough in a greased bowl, cover lightly and set aside in a warm place to rise for about 30 minutes, or until doubled in size.
4. Knock back the risen dough and divide into pieces weighing about 25 g/1 oz each. On a floured surface, roll each piece first into a ball and then into a pencil shape. Place on a greased baking tray, cover and leave in a warm place to prove for about 20–30 minutes.
5. Bake in a fairly hot oven, Gas 6, 400°F, 200°C, for about 15 minutes. Take the tray out of the oven, turn the sticks over, lightly brush the surface of each with milk and sprinkle sesame seeds or poppy seeds over. Return the sticks to the oven for a further 5 minutes.

If really crisp, these sticks will keep in an airtight tin for 1 month. They will also freeze for up to 3 months.

POPPY SEED KNOTS

This enriched dough makes a very pleasant dinner roll. Tying the dough in knots and liberally covering them with poppy seeds makes them very attractive indeed.

Makes about 16

450 g/1 lb strong white flour or wholemeal flour
2 teaspoons salt
50 g/2 oz butter
1 sachet easy blend dried yeast
1 large egg, beaten
300 ml/½ pint warm milk (a little extra if using wholemeal flour)
A little extra milk
2 tablespoons poppy seeds

1. Sift the flour and salt into a warm mixing bowl, adding any residue of bran left in the sieve, and rub in the butter. Stir in the yeast and mix well.
2. Reserve 1 teaspoon of beaten egg for the glaze. Combine the remaining beaten egg with the warm milk and pour this mixture into the dry ingredients.
3. Using a wooden fork or spoon, stir and mix to a soft elastic dough, then use your hand to knead the dough briefly in the bowl. Turn out the dough onto a lightly floured surface and knead until smooth – about 5–6 minutes. Put the ball of dough into a clean, lightly greased bowl, cover and leave in a warm place to rise for about 30 minutes.
4. Grease two baking trays. Knock back the risen dough and knead briefly, then pat it out on a lightly floured surface to an oblong shape. Cut sixteen narrow strips and roll out each strip with the flat of your hand until it measures about 18 cm/7 inches long. Tie each long strip of dough in a knot and set it on the baking tray. When all the knots have been

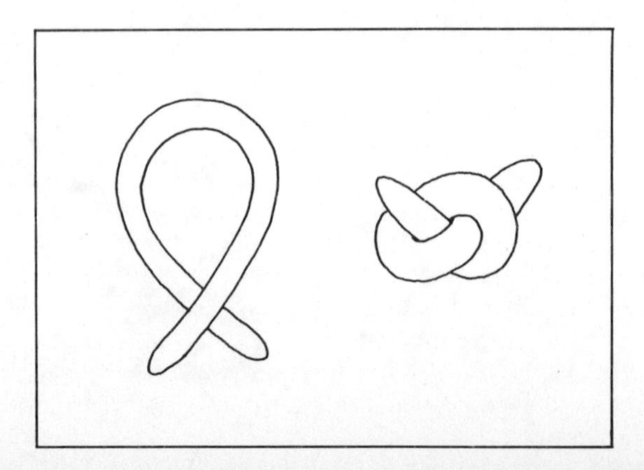

tied, combine the reserved egg with a little milk, and brush over the top of each one. Scatter the poppy seeds very liberally on the rolls, cover the trays and set aside in a warm place to prove for about 30 minutes.
5. Bake in a moderately hot oven, Gas 5, 375°F, 190°C, for about 20 minutes until the rolls are nicely browned. Turn out and cool on a wire tray.

Store in an airtight tin for up to 4 days, or freeze for up to 3 months.

FRENCH CROISSANTS

These are the classic crisp flaky rolls which are served for breakfast in France. They are a bit of a toil to do but it does make you appreciate why real croissants are so expensive to buy. They should always be made with good butter.

Makes 12

175 g/6 oz good quality butter, unsalted or lightly salted
450 g/1 lb strong white flour
1 teaspoon salt
25 g/1 oz butter
25 g/1 oz fresh yeast, or 15 g/½ oz dried yeast
1 teaspoon caster sugar
225 ml/8 fl oz warm water
1 medium egg, beaten

FOR THE EGG WASH
1 medium egg, beaten
1 pinch sugar
1 tablespoon water

1. Chill the 175 g/6 oz butter and cut it into thin slices. Cut these slices into flat 1-cm/½-inch squares. Lay them out on a large flat plate, divide roughly into three and allow them to soften to room temperature, but they should not be too soft.
2. Sift the flour and salt into a large mixing bowl and rub in the 25 g/1 oz butter.
3. Crumble the fresh yeast into the sugar and stir into the warm water (or sprinkle the dried yeast onto the water with the sugar, whisk and leave until frothy).
4. Pour the yeasted liquid and the beaten egg into the flour and mix with a wooden fork or spoon. Once the dough is formed, use your hand to knead it in the bowl until the dough is smooth.
5. Turn out the dough on a lightly floured surface and roll it out to a rectangle measuring 20 × 50 cm/8 × 20 inches. Mark the rectangle roughly into three by lightly scoring two horizontal lines.
6. Take one-third of the butter pieces and dot them over the top two-thirds of the dough. Fold up the unbuttered bottom third to cover the middle third, then fold the buttered top third down to make a parcel. Give the dough parcel a quarter turn so that the fold is on the right. Seal the top, bottom and open end of the parcel firmly with the rolling pin and reroll the dough out to a rectangle again. Wrap the dough in foil and rest it in the fridge for 10 minutes. Repeat the rolling, turning and resting process twice. After the last rolling, leave the dough in the fridge for 30 minutes.
7. Lightly dust a worktop with flour and roll out the dough to a 30 × 45-cm/12 × 18-inch rectangle. Cover with a sheet of polythene or tissue paper and leave in a warm place to rise for 10 minutes.
8. Trim the edges and cut the dough into six squares, then cut each square into two triangles.
9. In a small bowl, thoroughly mix the ingredients for the egg wash. Brush each triangle with the egg wash then roll each piece up towards the point, ending with the tip underneath. Bend each roll into a crescent shape.

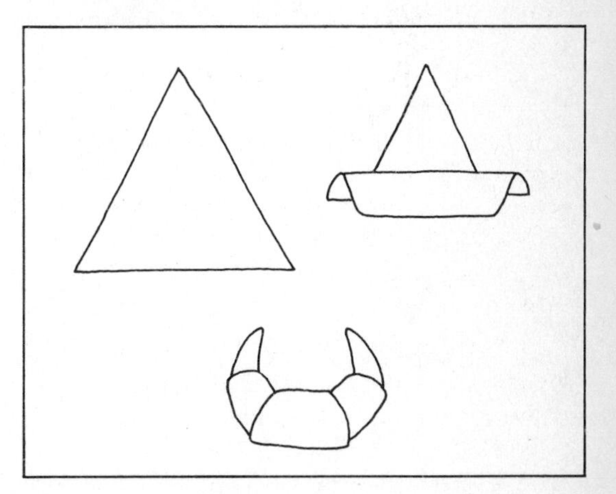

10. Grease a baking tray and lay the croissants on it. Brush them again with the egg wash, cover lightly and leave in a warm place to prove for 30 minutes.
11. Bake in a hot oven, Gas 7, 425°F, 220°C, for about 20 minutes. Cool on a wire tray.

Eat within 4 days, or freeze for up to 3 months.

PIZZAS

BASIC PIZZA DOUGH

Makes 1 oblong pizza base, 30 × 20 cm/12 × 8 inches, or 2 round pizza bases 20 cm/8 inches across

225 g/8 oz strong white flour
½ teaspoon salt
25 g/1 oz lard
½ sachet easy blend dried yeast
150 ml/¼ pint warm water

1. Sift the flour and salt into a warm mixing bowl and rub in the lard. Stir in the yeast.
2. Pour the warm water into the dry ingredients and mix and knead in the bowl to a soft elastic dough, adding a little more water if necessary. Return the dough to a clean greased bowl, cover and leave in a warm place to rise until doubled in size – about 30 minutes.
3. Generously grease one 30 × 20-cm/12 × 8-inch tin, or two 20-cm/8-inch pie plates or tins.
4. Knock back the risen dough and turn out onto a lightly floured surface. Roll out very thinly to fit the tins, or as the dough will be very springy, it is sometimes easier to put the half-rolled dough onto the tin and push it out to the edges and up the sides with your fingers.
5. Fill with one of the following toppings and cook as described.

TOPPINGS

CHEESE, ONION AND TOMATO

(for 30 × 20-cm/12 × 8-inch pizza base – serves 6)

2 tablespoons oil
450 g/1 lb onions, peeled and chopped
2 × 400-g/14-oz cans Italian tomatoes, drained and chopped
1 teaspoon dried oregano
Salt and pepper
125 g/4 oz Bel Paese, Mozzarella or Cheddar cheese, diced
1 × 50-g/2-oz can anchovies, drained

1. Heat the oil in a frying pan and gently fry the onions. Cool, then spread them on the raw pizza dough. Cover with the tomatoes.
2. Sprinkle the tomatoes with the dried oregano, season with salt and pepper to taste and scatter the diced cheese over. Cut the anchovies in two lengthways and lay them on top of the cheese in a lattice pattern. Lightly cover the pizza and set aside for 15 minutes to prove.
3. Bake in a hot oven, Gas 8, 450°F, 230°C, for 20 minutes. Reduce the heat to fairly hot, Gas 6, 400°F, 200°C, and bake for a further 15 minutes, or until the dough is well cooked underneath. (Use a fish slice to lift up the base and have a look.)

Best eaten very fresh, or freeze uncooked for up to 1 month.

CHEESE, HAM AND TOMATO

(for 1 × 20-cm/8-inch pizza base – serves 4)

1 × 200-g/7-oz can Italian tomatoes, drained and chopped
1 teaspoon dried oregano or marjoram
Salt and pepper
50 g/2 oz cold spiced cooked ham, cut in strips
50 g/2 oz Mozzarella cheese, grated
1 teaspoon olive oil

1. Chop the tomatoes and spread them on the raw pizza dough.
2. Sprinkle the tomatoes with the oregano or marjoram and season with salt and pepper to taste. Lay the cooked ham strips across the top of the tomatoes, and scatter the grated cheese over. Dribble the olive oil over the top and leave, lightly covered, for 15 minutes to prove.
3. Bake in a hot oven, Gas 8, 450°F, 230°C, for 20–25 minutes, or until the dough is well cooked underneath.

Eat fresh, or freeze uncooked for up to 1 month.

PEARS AND CHESHIRE CHEESE

(for 1 × 20-cm/8-inch pizza base – serves 4)

3 juicy pears, peeled, cored and sliced
Grated rind and juice of ½ lemon
50 g/2 oz Cheshire cheese, grated
25 g/1 oz plain chocolate, grated
25 g/1 oz walnuts, chopped
25 g/1 oz butter

1. Lay the pears on the raw pizza dough and sprinkle with the lemon rind and juice.

2. Cover the pears with the grated cheese, sprinkle on the chocolate and walnuts and dot with butter. Cover lightly and set aside in a warm place to prove for 15 minutes.
3. Bake in a hot oven, Gas 8, 450°F, 230°C, for 5 minutes, then reduce the heat to Gas 7, 425°F, 220°C, and bake for about 15 minutes more. Serve hot or cold.

Eat fresh. Do not freeze.

TOMATO AND OREGANO PIZZA

This recipe uses a short-time bread dough (*see page 172*) and the quantities given are enough for two pizza bases. Divide the uncooked dough into two equal portions and freeze one half for future use.

Will cut into 6 large slices

FOR THE PIZZA DOUGH (ENOUGH FOR 2 BASES)

1 × 25-mg tablet vitamin C (ascorbic acid) (*see page 169*)
15 g/½ oz fresh yeast, or 7 g/¼ oz dried yeast and ½ teaspoon caster sugar
150 ml/¼ pint warm water
15 g/½ oz block margarine or butter
225 g/8 oz strong white flour, sifted
½ teaspoon salt

FOR THE TOPPING (ENOUGH FOR 1 BASE)

25 g/1 oz block margarine
450 g/1 lb onions, peeled and finely chopped
1 clove of garlic, peeled and crushed
2 × 400-g/14-oz cans tomatoes, well drained and chopped
1 small teaspoon dried oregano
Salt and pepper
1 teaspoon sugar
75 g/3 oz Cheddar cheese, grated
3 raw mushrooms, wiped and very finely sliced

1. Crush the vitamin C tablet between two spoons. Blend this powder with the fresh yeast and half the water. (If using dried yeast, sprinkle it onto half the water with the sugar and vitamin C tablet, whisk and leave until frothy.)
2. Rub the margarine or butter into the flour in a mixing bowl and add the salt. Pour the yeasted liquid into the dry ingredients. Mix well and add enough of the remaining warm water to make a soft dough.
3. Knead well in the bowl then turn out onto a lightly floured surface and knead until the dough is smooth and elastic. Cover lightly and set aside for 5 minutes. The dough is now ready to use. Cut into two equal pieces and wrap and freeze one half.
4. Grease a large Swiss roll tin measuring 33 × 23 cm/13 × 9 inches. Take the remaining piece of dough and roll it out to fit the base and sides of the tin. Trim the edges. Prick it all over with a fork, cover lightly and leave in a warm place to rise and go puffy – 10–15 minutes.
5. To make the topping, melt the margarine in a pan and fry the onion and garlic until softening. Add the tomatoes, oregano, salt, pepper and sugar and cook gently until very thick – about 15 minutes.
6. Meanwhile, preheat the oven to hot, Gas 7, 425°F, 220°C. Bake the risen pizza base for just 5 minutes. Take it from the oven and, using a slotted spoon, cover with the tomato topping, leaving the juice in the pan. Sprinkle on the grated cheese and top with the mushrooms.
7. Reduce the heat to moderate, Gas 4, 350°F, 180°C, return the pizza to the oven and cook for about 20 minutes.

Best eaten freshly cooked. To freeze, cool the pizza after adding the topping, but before the final baking, and freeze for up to 2 months. The uncooked dough will freeze for 1 month.

ANCHOVY AND ONION SLICE

Will cut into 6 large pieces

½ quantity bread dough pizza base *(see page 186)*
25 g/1 oz block margarine
450 g/1 lb onions, peeled and finely chopped
1 clove of garlic, peeled and chopped
1 × 400-g/14-oz can tomatoes, drained and chopped
1 × 50-g/2-oz can anchovies, drained, rinsed in water, dried and finely chopped
1 teaspoon caster sugar
Salt and pepper
75 g/3 oz Cheddar cheese, grated

1. Grease a large Swiss roll tin measuring 33 × 23 cm/13 × 9 inches. Preheat the oven to hot, Gas 7, 425°F, 220°C.
2. Roll out the dough on a lightly floured work surface and line the base and sides of the tin. Trim the edges. Prick the dough all over with a fork, cover lightly and leave to go puffy.
3. To make the topping, heat the margarine in a pan and cook the onions and garlic until soft. Add the tomatoes, anchovies and sugar and cook gently until thick, then season with salt and pepper.
4. Bake the dough base briefly for 5 minutes. Take out of the oven and cover the dough with the topping mixture. Use a draining spoon to do this and leave as much juice behind as possible. Spread carefully then scatter on the grated cheese.
5. Reduce the heat to moderate, Gas 4, 350°F, 180°C, and return the slice to the oven to bake for about 20 minutes.

Best eaten freshly cooked. To freeze, cool the pizza after adding the topping, but before the final baking, and freeze for up to 2 months.

SWEET LOAVES

BRIOCHE

Brioche is halfway between a bread and a cake and originated in France. It is easily recognized by its distinctive shape. The whole loaf is baked in a deeply fluted tin and the top has a knob on it. Small brioches are made in exactly the same way.

Makes 1 large loaf or 12 small loaves

225 g/8 oz strong white flour
1 pinch salt
½ sachet easy blend dried yeast
1 tablespoon caster sugar
1½–2 tablespoons warm water
2 medium eggs, beaten
50 g/2 oz butter, melted

FOR THE EGG WASH
1 medium egg
1 pinch sugar
1 tablespoon water

1. Sift the flour and salt into a warm mixing bowl and stir in the yeast and sugar.
2. Add the water, eggs and melted butter and mix to a soft dough. Knead in the bowl for about 5 minutes until the dough is smooth and silky. Place the dough in a clean, greased bowl, cover and set aside to rise in a warm place for 1–1½ hours when it should have doubled in size.
3. To make the large brioche, grease a 1.2-litre/2-pint fluted mould. Knock back the risen dough and use three-quarters of it to make a round ball. Put it in the bottom of the mould. Shape a second ball with the remaining quarter. Using the floured handle of a wooden spoon, make a hole down through the top of the larger ball of dough. Enlarge the hole a little and sit the smaller ball of dough in it.
4. Beat together the ingredients for the egg wash. Brush the dough with it, cover and set aside in a warm place to prove for 30–40 minutes.

To make the small individual brioches, grease twelve tins (castle pudding tins or deep patty tins). Divide the risen dough into twelve equal pieces. Shape three-quarters of each piece into a ball and put into a tin. Shape a second ball with the remaining quarter. Press a hole in the larger ball of dough with the floured handle of a wooden spoon. Enlarge the hole a little and sit the smaller ball of dough in it. Repeat this with each piece of dough.
5. Brush each brioche with the egg wash, cover

lightly and set aside in a warm place to prove for 40 minutes. Place the small tins on a baking tray.
6. Bake in a hot oven, Gas 8, 450°F, 230°C. The large brioche will take about 20 minutes and the individual ones will take 10 minutes. Turn out and cool on a wire tray.

Best eaten fresh but will keep in an airtight tin for 2–3 days. Freeze for up to 3 months.

WALNUT BREAD

By making this bread with walnuts as the only flavouring, the real taste of good walnuts comes through very well. It is particularly nice toasted.

Makes 2 × 450-g/1-lb loaves

175 g/6 oz plain wholemeal flour
225 g/8 oz strong white flour
½ teaspoon salt
75 g/3 oz butter
75 g/3 oz dark soft brown sugar
125 g/4 oz light-skinned walnuts, chopped (but not too small)
25 g/1 oz fresh yeast, or 15 g/½ oz dried yeast
300 ml/½ pint warm milk
1 medium egg, beaten

1. Sift the two flours and salt into a large mixing bowl, adding any residue of bran left in the sieve, and rub in the butter.
2. Reserve 1 teaspoon of sugar and stir in the remainder.
3. Crumble the fresh yeast into the reserved sugar and stir into the warm milk (or sprinkle the dried yeast onto the warm milk with the sugar, whisk and leave until frothy.)
4. Stir the yeasted liquid and the egg into the dry ingredients and mix with a wooden fork or spoon to a soft dough, then use your hand to knead it briefly in the bowl. Turn out the dough onto a lightly floured surface and knead until smooth. Return the dough to a lightly greased bowl, cover and leave in a warm place to rise for 30 minutes.
5. Grease two 450-g/1-lb loaf tins. Knock back the risen dough and work in the chopped walnuts. Divide the dough and shape to fit the tins. Press the dough into the tins, cover and set aside in a warm place to prove for about 15 minutes, or until well risen and puffy.
6. Bake in a hot oven, Gas 7, 425°F, 220°C, for about 30 minutes. Turn out and cool on a wire tray.

Store in an airtight tin and eat within 4 days, or freeze for up to 2 months.

BUN LOAF

This is another way of putting the dough in the tin and it is said to give a better rise.

Makes 1 × 450-g/1-lb loaf

325 g/12 oz risen milk bread dough *(see page 173)*
125 g/4 oz raisins, washed and dried
25 g/1 oz glacé cherries, washed, dried and finely chopped
15 g/½ oz caster sugar
Sugar and water glaze *(see page 171)*

1. Generously grease a 450-g/1-lb loaf tin.
2. Knock back the risen dough, knead briefly and work in the fruit, cherries and, lastly, the sugar.
3. Cut the dough into three even pieces and roll and knead each one into a ball. Set the three balls together in the tin. Cover lightly and set aside in a warm place to prove for about 50 minutes, or until the dough is risen well above the tin.
4. Preheat the oven to fairly hot, Gas 6, 400°F, 200°C.
5. Brush the surface carefully with the sugar and water glaze and bake for about 40 minutes. Turn out and cool on a wire tray.

Best eaten fresh but will keep fairly well for 2–3 days in an airtight tin. Freeze for up to 3 months.

VARIATION

ICED BUN LOAF

FOR THE LEMON GLACÉ ICING
125 g/4 oz icing sugar, sifted
Lemon juice
Toasted almonds

Mix enough lemon juice into the icing sugar to give a thick icing. Coat the top of the cooled bun loaf with the icing and scatter on some toasted almonds. Leave to set.

SAFFRON BREAD

Saffron bread or cake is a local speciality in Cornwall. Saffron, which flavours the cake and also gives the cake crumb its light marigold colour, is the dried stigma of a variety of crocus and is, therefore, expensive. Powdered saffron is also available but real devotees are scornful of this as it can be adulterated.

Makes 1 × 20-cm/8-inch round cake or 1 large plait

225 g/8 oz plain white or brown flour
1 pinch salt
50 g/2 oz butter
2 teaspoons easy blend dried yeast
50 g/2 oz caster sugar
125 g/4 oz raisins, washed and dried
25 g/1 oz peel, chopped
½ packet saffron strands, crushed, or 2 fat pinches of saffron powder
3 tablespoons boiling water
150 ml/¼ pint warm milk

TO GLAZE
5–6 sugar cubes
A little milk

1. Sift the flour and salt into a warm mixing bowl and rub in the butter. Stir in the yeast, sugar, raisins and peel.
2. Steep the crushed saffron strands, or powder, in the boiling water and stir to release the colour. When the saffron liquid is really well coloured, stir again and strain into the milk.
3. Pour the saffron milk into the dry ingredients and, using a wooden fork or spoon, mix and stir to a soft dough. Knead the dough briefly by hand in the bowl then turn out the dough onto a lightly floured surface and knead until smooth and silky. Put the dough back into a clean greased bowl, cover and leave to rise in a warm place for 1½ hours until it has doubled in size.
4. Knock back the risen dough and knead briefly. If making the round cake, grease a 20-cm/8-inch round cake tin and shape the dough to fit. If making the plait, grease a baking tray. Roll the dough into an oblong and cut lengthways into three strips, leaving them attached at one end (*see page 173*). Plait the three strips loosely and squeeze the three end pieces together securely. Lay the plait on the baking tray.
5. To make the topping, put the sugar cubes into a plastic bag and crush them with a rolling pin into small crunchy pieces. Paint the top of the cake or the plait with milk and scatter the sugar pieces all over. Cover lightly and set aside in a warm place to prove for about 30 minutes.
6. Bake in a fairly hot oven, Gas 6, 400°F, 200°C, for about 30 minutes, or until nicely browned. Turn out and cool on a wire tray.

Store in an airtight tin and eat within 3 days, or freeze for up to 3 months.

MALT LOAF

This delicious loaf is best made with plain flour and not strong flour which is used in most bread making. The malt flavour is very pleasant combined with the sultanas and black treacle.

Makes 2 × 450-g/1-lb loaves

25 g/1 oz fresh yeast, or 15 g/½ oz dried yeast and 2 teaspoons caster sugar
300 ml/½ pint warm water
450 g/1 lb plain white or brown flour
1 teaspoon salt
75 g/3 oz malt extract
50 g/2 oz black treacle
25 g/1 oz block margarine
225 g/8 oz sultanas, washed and dried
A little melted butter

1. Crumble the fresh yeast into the warm water and stir (or stir the dried yeast and sugar into the water, whisk and leave until frothy).
2. Sift the flour and salt into a large mixing bowl. Put an empty pan on the scales, weigh it and then measure the malt and treacle into it. Add the margarine and place over a gentle heat until just melted (do not get this mixture too hot).
3. Stir both the yeasted liquid and malt mixture into the flour and, using a wooden spoon, beat this mixture well for 3 minutes. Stir in the sultanas.
4. Grease two 450-g/1-lb loaf tins. Spoon the mixture into the tins, cover lightly and leave in a warm place to rise for about 1 hour, or until the mixture rises almost to the rim of the tins.
5. Bake in a fairly hot oven, Gas 6, 400°F, 200°C, for about 45 minutes, or until a skewer inserted in the middle of the loaf comes out clean. Reduce the heat slightly after 25 minutes if the top browns too quickly. Remove from the oven and brush the top of the loaf with melted butter. Cool on a wire tray.

Keeps well in an airtight tin for 1 week, or freeze for up to 3 months.

SPICY FRUIT LOAF

Makes 1 × 450-g/1-lb loaf

225 g/8 oz plain brown flour
1 teaspoon mixed spices – cinnamon, nutmeg and cloves
½ teaspoon salt
25 g/1 oz dark soft brown sugar
125 ml/4 fl oz warm water
15 g/½ oz dried yeast
75 g/3 oz malt extract
25 g/1 oz butter
75 g/3 oz raisins, washed and dried

1. Sift the flour, spices and salt into a warm mixing bowl.
2. Dissolve 1 teaspoon of the sugar in the warm water. Whisk in the yeast and set aside in a warm place for about 10 minutes until frothy.
3. Put a small pan on the scales, weigh it and weigh the malt extract into it. Take the pan off the scales and set it over a low heat. Add the butter, remaining sugar and the raisins and stir until the butter melts. Set aside until cool.
4. Pour the yeasted liquid and the cooled malt mixture into the dry ingredients. Mix well with a wooden spoon, then use your hand to knead the dough in the bowl. Turn out the dough onto a lightly floured surface and knead for about 3–4 minutes to get a nice smooth dough. Cover and set aside in a warm place to rise for 1–1½ hours.
5. Grease and base line a 450-g/1-lb loaf tin. Knock back the risen dough and shape it to fit the tin. Press the dough into the tin, pushing it well into the corners. Cover and set aside in a warm place to prove for 25 minutes.
6. Bake in a moderately hot oven, Gas 6, 400°F, 200°C, for 45 minutes. Reduce the heat slightly after 20 minutes if the loaf is getting too brown to moderate, Gas 4, 350°F, 180°C. Turn out and cool on a wire tray.

Eat fresh and store for up to 3 days in an airtight tin, or freeze for up to 2 months.

BARA BRITH

This is the Speckled Bread of Wales. I like both names. Although some recipes are made without yeast, I think it is much nicer with the real thing. This time I am using the old batter method.

Makes 1 × 900-g/2-lb loaf

25 g/1 oz fresh yeast, or 15 g/½ oz dried yeast
2 teaspoons sugar
225 ml/8 fl oz warm milk
450 g/1 lb strong white flour
1 teaspoon salt
1 teaspoon mixed spice
75 g/3 oz margarine
75 g/3 oz light soft brown sugar
1 medium egg, beaten
450 g/1 lb mixed currants, raisins, sultanas, washed and dried

1. To make the yeast batter, stir the crumbled fresh yeast and the granulated sugar into the milk and stir (or sprinkle the dried yeast onto the warm milk with the sugar, whisk and leave for 5 minutes until frothy).
2. Whisk in 50 g/2 oz flour and set aside in a warm place until frothy – about 20 minutes.
3. Sift the remaining flour, salt and spice into a large mixing bowl. Rub in the margarine and stir in the sugar. Pour the yeast batter and the beaten egg into the dry ingredients, and mix to a soft dough. Stir first with a wooden fork or spoon, then use your hand to knead the dough in the bowl. Lightly dust the worktop with flour, turn out the dough and knead it until it is no longer sticky. Cover the dough and leave in a warm place to rise until doubled in size – about 1½ hours.
4. Grease a 900-g/2-lb loaf tin. Work the fruit into the risen dough until evenly distributed. Knead briefly and shape to fit the loaf tin. Press the dough into the tin, cover and set aside in a warm place to prove for about 1¼ hours.
5. Bake in a hot oven, Gas 7, 425°F, 220°C, for 15 minutes, then reduce the heat to moderate, Gas 4, 350°F, 180°C, and bake for a further 40–45 minutes. Keep an eye on the top crust. If it gets too brown, cover with a lid of foil – squeeze up the corners of a square of foil to make a 'cap'. Turn out and cool on a wire tray.

Store in an airtight tin and eat within 1 week, or freeze for up to 3 months.

CURRANT BREAD

There is a very good reason for not putting the currants into this mixture until after the main part of the kneading has been done – currants are very soft and would be torn and broken in the mixing.

Makes 2 × 450-g/1-lb loaves

450 g/1 lb strong white flour (or half white and half wholemeal flour)
1 teaspoon salt
25 g/1 oz caster sugar
25 g/1 oz butter
25 g/1 oz fresh yeast, or 15 g/½ oz dried yeast
300 ml/½ pint warmed milk and water mixed
125 g/4 oz currants, washed and dried
Extra milk
Extra caster sugar for sprinkling

1. Sift the flour and salt into a mixing bowl, adding any residue of bran left in the sieve if using wholemeal flour. Reserve 1 teaspoon sugar, stir in the remainder and rub in the butter.
2. Crumble the fresh yeast into the reserved sugar and stir into the warm milk and water mixture (or sprinkle the dried yeast onto the liquid with the reserved sugar, whisk and leave until frothy).
3. Stir the yeasted liquid into the flour mixture and, using a wooden fork or spoon, work to a firm dough. Then knead with your hand, either in the bowl or on a lightly floured surface, until smooth. Cover and leave to rise for about 45 minutes.
4. Grease two 450-g/1-lb loaf tins. Knock back the risen dough and work the currants into it as evenly as possible. Divide it into two pieces and shape to fit the tins. Press the dough into the tins, cover and leave in a warm place to prove for about 30 minutes.
5. Bake in a hot oven, Gas 7, 425°F, 220°C, for about 40 minutes.
6. While the loaves are hot, brush the tops with milk and sprinkle with a little sugar. Cool on a wire tray.

Store in an airtight tin and eat within 1 week, or freeze for up to 3 months.

STOLLEN – A CONTINENTAL RICH BREAD

This rich dough is made by the sponge batter method (*see page 169*). It gives a very light texture.

Makes 1 long flattish loaf

FOR THE BATTER
75 ml/3 fl oz warm milk
15 g/½ oz fresh yeast, or 7 g/¼ oz dried yeast
½ teaspoon caster sugar
50 g/2 oz strong white flour, sifted

FOR THE DOUGH
175 g/6 oz strong white flour, sifted
½ teaspoon salt
25 g/1 oz caster sugar
25 g/1 oz margarine
1 medium egg, beaten

FOR THE FILLING
25 g/1 oz walnuts, chopped
Grated rind of 1 lemon
50 g/2 oz currants, washed and dried
50 g/2 oz sultanas, washed and dried
15 g/½ oz mixed chopped peel
50 g/2 oz glacé cherries, cut in two, washed and dried

TO FINISH
15 g/½ oz butter, melted
Icing sugar for dredging

1. First, make the batter. Pour the milk into a large mixing bowl. Crumble the fresh yeast into the sugar and stir into the milk (or sprinkle the dried yeast onto the milk with the sugar and leave to stand for 5 minutes).
2. Whisk the 50 g/2 oz flour into the yeasted liquid and set aside until the mixture becomes frothy – about 20 minutes.
3. To make the dough, mix together the flour, salt and sugar and rub in the margarine. Stir the beaten egg and the flour mixture into the yeast batter and mix to a soft dough. Knead briefly in the bowl then turn out onto a lightly floured board and knead until the dough is elastic and no longer sticky. Put the dough into a lightly greased bowl, cover and leave to rise in a warm place until doubled in size – about 1 hour.
4. Knock back the risen dough and work all the filling ingredients into it except the glacé cherries. Knead briefly then roll out the dough on a lightly floured surface to a rough oblong.

5. Brush the oblong all over with the melted butter and lay the cherries in a row across the middle. Folding lengthways, bring the bottom half up and over to cover the cherries and bring the top half down and over the bottom half. Squeeze the open ends together slightly. Using a fish slice, turn the parcel over so that the join is underneath and lay it on a greased baking tray. Brush again with the remains of the butter, cover lightly and leave to prove until light and puffy – about 30 minutes.
6. Bake in a fairly hot oven, Gas 6, 400°F, 200°C, for 35–40 minutes. Turn out and cool on a wire tray. When cold, dredge with icing sugar.

Eat within 4 days, or freeze without the icing sugar for up to 2 months.

SULTANA LOAF

The sugar and water glaze gives this loaf a brilliant shine.

Makes 1 × 450-g/1-lb loaf

325 g/12 oz risen milk bread dough *(see page 173)*
125 g/4 oz sultanas, washed and dried
1 tablespoon chopped peel
15 g/½ oz caster sugar
Egg glaze *(see page 170)*
Sugar and water glaze *(see page 171)*

1. Generously grease a 450-g/1-lb loaf tin.
2. Knock back the risen dough and work into it the sultanas, peel and sugar. Knead and shape the dough and fit into the tin. Brush the top with the egg glaze, cover and set aside in a warm place to prove for about 1½ hours until the dough rises above the tin.
3. Preheat the oven to fairly hot, Gas 6, 400°F, 200°C. Bake the loaf for about 40 minutes. Remove the loaf from the tin, place it on a wire tray and, while it is still hot, brush it all over with the sugar and water glaze.

Best eaten fresh but will keep in good condition for 3–4 days in an airtight tin. Freeze for up to 3 months.

YULE BREAD

Yule bread is always said to be the forerunner of our traditional Christmas cake. The high butter content ensures it has a rich flavour and keeps well.

Makes 1 × 900-g/2-lb loaf or 2 × 450-g/1-lb loaves

450 g/1 lb strong white flour
1 pinch salt
225 g/8 oz butter
15 g/½ oz fresh yeast, or 7 g/¼ oz dried yeast
300 ml/½ pint warm water
175 g/6 oz caster sugar
2 medium eggs, beaten
275 g/10 oz currants, washed and dried
50 g/2 oz raisins, washed and dried
125 g/4 oz mixed chopped peel
½ teaspoon grated nutmeg
½ teaspoon ground cinnamon

1. Grease one 900-g/2-lb loaf tin or two 450-g/1-lb loaf tins.
2. Sift the flour and salt into a large mixing bowl and rub in the butter.
3. Crumble the fresh yeast into the warm water and stir (or sprinkle the dried yeast and 1 teaspoon of the caster sugar onto the warm water, whisk and leave until frothy).
4. Stir the yeasted liquid and the beaten eggs into the flour mixture and work to a soft dough. Knead the dough lightly in the bowl until smooth, then cover, and leave in a warm place to rise for about 1 hour when it should have almost doubled in size.
5. Knock back the risen dough in the bowl and work into it the remaining sugar, currants, raisins, peel and spices.
6. Turn out the dough onto a floured surface and knead and shape to fit the tin(s). Push the dough into the tin(s), cover with a polythene bag and leave to prove in a warm place. The large tin could take about 1½–2 hours and the smaller tins only 45 minutes.
7. Bake in a moderate oven, Gas 4, 350°F, 180°C, for about 2 hours for the large loaf and 1 hour for the small loaves. Turn out and cool on a wire tray.

These loaves will store well for up to 3 weeks in an airtight tin or freeze for up to 3 months.

LARDY CAKE

Many people have happy memories of lardy cake. It really is only at its best when eaten freshly made. I have used an enriched milk bread dough to make the finished cake lighter.

Makes 1 × 20-cm/8-inch square cake

450 g/1 lb milk bread dough *(see page 173)*
225 g/8 oz lard
225 g/8 oz light soft brown sugar
125 g/4 oz mixed dried fruit, washed and dried
Caster sugar for sprinkling

1. Make the dough as described on page 173, cover and leave in a warm place to rise.
2. Knock back the risen dough and roll out thinly on a floured surface to an oblong about 4 cm/1½ inches thick.
3. Divide the lard and sugar into five portions of each. Spread one-fifth of the lard over the whole of the oblong of dough and sprinkle one-fifth of the sugar and a little of the dried fruit on top. Bring the bottom third of dough up and fold the top third of dough over it. Seal the open ends with the side of your hand, give the parcel a quarter turn and roll again into an oblong. Repeat the process four times, using up all the lard, sugar and dried fruit.
4. Fold the oblong again in three and roll out to a 20-cm/8-inch square. Score the top lightly and sprinkle with caster sugar. Cover and leave in a warm place to prove until puffy – about 30 minutes.
5. Bake in a hot oven, Gas 7, 425°F, 220°C, for at least 1 hour. Make sure the underneath is cooked – use a fish slice to lift it up and have a look. Traditionally, the lardy cake is turned upside down to let the fat soak back into the dough as it cools.

Best eaten very fresh but will keep for up to 3 days in an airtight tin. Freeze for up to 3 months.

MARZIPAN TEA RING

Makes 1 ring, serves 16 pieces

225 g/8 oz plain white flour
¼ teaspoon salt
50 g/2 oz butter
40 g/1½ oz light soft brown sugar
15 g/½ oz fresh yeast, or 7 g/¼ oz dried yeast
125 ml/4 fl oz warm milk
1 small egg, beaten

FOR THE MARZIPAN FILLING
50 g/2 oz ground almonds
50 g/2 oz caster sugar
2 drops almond essence
A very little beaten egg

TO DECORATE
Glacé icing, made with 125 g/4 oz sifted icing sugar and a little lemon juice to give a thick icing *(see page 244)*
25 g/1 oz walnuts, chopped
4 glacé cherries, sliced
Angelica strips, finely sliced

1. Sift the flour and salt into a large mixing bowl and rub in the butter. Add all but 1 teaspoon of the sugar.
2. Crumble the fresh yeast into the reserved sugar and stir into the warm milk (or sprinkle the dried yeast onto the milk with the sugar, whisk and leave for 10 minutes until frothy).
3. Stir the yeasted liquid and the egg into the dry ingredients and mix to a soft dough. Knead in the bowl until you have a soft elastic dough. Put the dough back into a clean, lightly greased bowl, cover and leave to rise in a warm place for about 1 hour.
4. Knock back the risen dough and knead briefly. Roll out the dough on a floured surface to a rectangle 30 × 10 cm/12 × 4 inches.
5. Place all the ingredients for the marzipan filling into a mixing bowl and work together to a thick paste. You will only need a minute amount of beaten egg. Sprinkle the worktop with caster sugar and roll out the paste into a thick sausage about 30 cm/12 inches long.
6. Lay the strip of marzipan down the length of the dough. Wet one long edge of the dough and roll it over to enclose the almond paste. Bend the filled dough into a ring, moisten the ends with a little water and press together to seal. Grease a baking tray, lay the ring on it, cover lightly and set aside in a warm place to prove for about 50 minutes.

7. Bake in a hot oven, Gas 7, 425°F, 220°C, for 20–25 minutes.
8. Cool on a wire tray then dribble the thick glacé icing in a random way over the top and scatter with the chopped walnuts. Set pieces of glacé cherry here and there with a sliver of green angelica on each side.

Eat very fresh or store in an airtight tin for 2–3 days. Freeze for up to 3 months.

CINNAMON AND GINGER RING

Ground cinnamon loses its flavour very quickly so buy it in very small quantities.

Makes 1 ring, serves 15 pieces

225 g/8 oz strong white flour
1 pinch salt
75 g/3 oz caster sugar
15 g/½ oz fresh yeast, or 7 g/¼ oz dried yeast
4 tablespoons warm milk
25 g/1 oz butter, melted
1 medium egg, beaten

FOR THE FILLING
25 g/1 oz butter, melted
25 g/1 oz caster sugar
1 heaped teaspoon ground cinnamon
50 g/2 oz preserved ginger (either in syrup or crystallized), very finely chopped
Extra caster sugar for sprinkling

1. Sift the flour and salt into a mixing bowl and stir in all but 1 teaspoon of the sugar.
2. Crumble the fresh yeast into the reserved sugar and stir into the warm milk (or sprinkle the dried yeast onto the warm milk with the sugar, whisk and leave for about 10 minutes until frothy.)
3. Stir the yeasted liquid, 25 g/1 oz melted butter and egg into the flour. Mix and stir with a wooden fork or spoon and then knead in the bowl to a soft dough. Add a little extra milk if necessary. Put the dough into a clean, lightly greased bowl, cover and set aside in a warm place to rise for about 1 hour.
4. Knock back the risen dough and roll out thinly on a lightly floured surface to a rectangle 30 × 10 cm/12 × 4 inches. Brush the upper surface of the dough with the 25 g/1 oz melted butter and sprinkle with the sugar, cinnamon and half the chopped ginger.
5. Roll up the dough from the long end, like a Swiss roll, and twist it into a ring. Moisten the ends with a little water and squeeze together to seal. Set the ring on a greased baking tray, and pull it into a good shape. Using a pair of scissors, snip the top of the ring at 2.5-cm/1-inch intervals. These cuts will open up while baking. Brush the top of the ring with milk and sprinkle on the reserved ginger plus a little caster sugar. Cover and leave to prove for about 45 minutes.
6. Bake in a fairly hot oven, Gas 6, 400°F, 200°C, for about 25 minutes. Cool on a wire tray.

Best eaten fresh but will keep in an airtight tin for 2–3 days. Freeze either raw, before the final proving, or cooked. Use within 3 months.

CAKES AND PASTRIES

CREAM SPLITS

The dough for the splits must be really soft so that the baked bun is light and feathery.

Makes 8

15 g/½ oz fresh yeast, or 7 g/¼ oz dried yeast and 1 teaspoon caster sugar
150 ml/¼ pint warm milk
225 g/8 oz strong white flour
½ teaspoon salt
2 teaspoons sugar
25 g/1 oz butter or margarine

FOR THE FILLING
Whipped cream
Strawberry or raspberry jam
A little icing sugar (optional)

1. Crumble the fresh yeast into the warm milk (or stir the dried yeast and sugar into the milk, whisk and leave until frothy).
2. Sift the flour and salt into a large mixing bowl. Stir in the sugar and rub in the butter or margarine.
3. Pour the yeasted liquid into the flour mixture and mix with a wooden fork or spoon to a soft dough. Turn out the dough on a well floured surfacc and kncad with your hand until the dough loses its stickiness. Cover and leave to rise in a warm place for about 1 hour when the dough should have doubled in size.
4. Knock back the risen dough and divide it into eight pieces. Shape each piece into a round bun with a smooth top. Place the buns well apart on a greased baking tray, cover again and leave to prove in a warm place for about 20 minutes or until the buns are light and puffy.
5. Bake in a hot oven, Gas 7, 425°F, 220°C, for about 15 minutes, or until golden brown in colour. Cool on a wire tray.
6. When the buns are cold, split and fill each with whipped cream and home-made strawberry or raspberry jam. A dusting of icing sugar also looks nice, but not if you sneeze easily!

Eat on the day they are made. Unfilled buns freeze well for up to 2 months.

INDIVIDUAL RUM BABAS

Rum babas used to be baked in little moulds like miniature plant pots. I like them the way they are baked now – in individual small flan tins.

Makes about 8

225 g/8 oz plain white flour, sifted
1 sachet easy blend dried yeast
25 g/1 oz caster sugar
1 pinch salt
150 ml/¼ pint warm milk
4 medium eggs, beaten
125 g/4 oz butter, melted

FOR THE SYRUP
125 g/4 oz granulated sugar
225 ml/8 fl oz water
4–5 tablespoons rum

TO SERVE
A little whipped cream

1. Mix the flour, yeast, sugar and salt in a large mixing bowl.
2. In a jug, mix the milk and eggs and pour this into the flour and yeast mixture. Beat well with a wooden spoon. Add the melted butter and continue beating for 3 minutes.
3. Well grease eight miniature flan tins, 7.5 cm/3 inches across, and half fill with the baba mixture. Put the tins on a baking tray, cover lightly and leave to rise in a warm place for 20–30 minutes, or until the mixture rises almost to the top of the tins.
4. Bake in a fairly hot oven, Gas 6, 400°F, 200°C, for 10–15 minutes. Cool in the tins then turn out onto a wire tray.
5. In a heavy based pan, boil together the sugar and water until syrupy. Remove from the heat and, when the bubbles die down, add the rum.
6. The syrup should not be poured on the babas until just before serving. Warm the babas slightly, warm the syrup and pour over. Serve with a little whipped cream.

Must be eaten fresh, or freeze the dry babas for up to 2 months.

DANISH PASTRIES

Making Danish pastries is a bit of an endurance test for the home baker, but when well done they are superb. Made with yeast, this flaky pastry can be fashioned into many traditional shapes, and the fillings are just as varied. Choose from those below. Another popular filling is mincemeat.

Makes about 16 depending on size

FOR THE PASTRY

225 g/8 oz plain white flour
1 pinch salt
25 g/1 oz butter
2 teaspoons easy blend dried yeast
1 tablespoon caster sugar
5 tablespoons warm water
1 egg, beaten
150 g/5 oz butter, softened

FOR THE FILLINGS

Almond Paste
15 g/½ oz butter
75 g/3 oz caster sugar
75 g/3 oz ground almonds
½ beaten small egg

Cinnamon Butter
50 g/2 oz butter
50 g/2 oz icing sugar
2 teaspoons ground cinnamon

Apple Purée
1 large apple, peeled, cored and sliced
2 tablespoons water
1 dessertspoon light soft brown sugar

Custard Cream
150 ml/¼ pint milk
1 tablespoon plain flour
1 tablespoon caster sugar
1 large egg yolk
Vanilla essence

TO GLAZE

1 medium egg
2 teaspoons water
½ teaspoon granulated sugar

FOR THE TOPPING

½ quantity thin glacé icing *(see page 244)* **using only 1 tablespoon water to mix, or apricot jam, warmed and sieved**
Toasted flaked almonds or chopped glacé cherries

1. Sift the flour and salt into a warm mixing bowl and rub in the 25 g/1 oz butter. Stir in the yeast and sugar.
2. Stir the water and egg into the dry ingredients and mix with a wooden fork or spoon until the dough comes together, then knead it briefly with your hand in the bowl. Turn out the dough onto a lightly floured surface and knead until it is soft and elastic. Cover and chill the dough for 10 minutes.
3. Dust the work surface with a little flour and roll out the dough to a 25-cm/10-inch square. Spread the softened butter in a strip down the middle of the square.
4. Fold over the unbuttered sides of the dough so that they just overlap and cover the butter. Seal the top and bottom of the parcel by pressing with the side of your hand. Roll this parcel into a long rectangle – three times longer than its width. Fold this into three by bringing the bottom third up to cover the middle third and the top third down to cover the other two layers. Seal the two open ends with the side of your hand.
5. Cover and leave the pastry in a cool place to rest for 10 minutes. Repeat the turning, folding, rolling and resting twice more. The pastry can be frozen at this point if wished.
6. Make the fillings.

To make the almond paste, put all the ingredients into a mixing bowl and beat to form a paste.

Make the cinnamon butter in the same way.

To make the apple purée, place the apple slices with the water in a saucepan, cover and cook gently until soft and pulpy. Drain off excess liquid, add the sugar and mash to a thick sauce.

To make the custard cream, pour the milk into a small pan and whisk in the flour. Stir in the sugar and egg yolk and cook gently, stirring, until the sauce is thick. Stir in a few drops of vanilla essence.

7. Roll and shape the pastry as required – see Shapes on page 198.
8. Place the filled pastries onto greased baking trays. Beat together the ingredients for the glaze and brush it over the pastries. Cover lightly and set aside to prove for about 15 minutes.
9. Bake in a hot oven, Gas 7, 425°F, 220°C, for 15 minutes. Remove the pastries from the oven, cool a little and then, while they are still warm, add the toppings. Using a pastry brush, coat each pastry with a little glacé icing or apricot jam and scatter on a few toasted flaked almonds or one or two pieces of glacé cherry.

Best eaten fresh, but can be stored in an airtight tin for 2–3 days. Freeze for up to 1 month.

SHAPES

STARS

Roll out the dough very thinly and cut into 7.5-cm/3-inch squares. Make diagonal cuts from each corner to within 1 cm/½ inch of the centre. Place 1 large teaspoon of chosen filling in the centre and fold one corner of each cut section down to the centre (*see page 198*). (This is just like an old-fashioned paper windmill.)

PINWHEELS

Roll out the dough into an oblong measuring about 20 × 30 cm/8 × 12 inches. Spread with the chosen filling and roll up like a Swiss roll. Cut into 2.5-cm/1-inch slices and lay, cut side up, on baking trays.

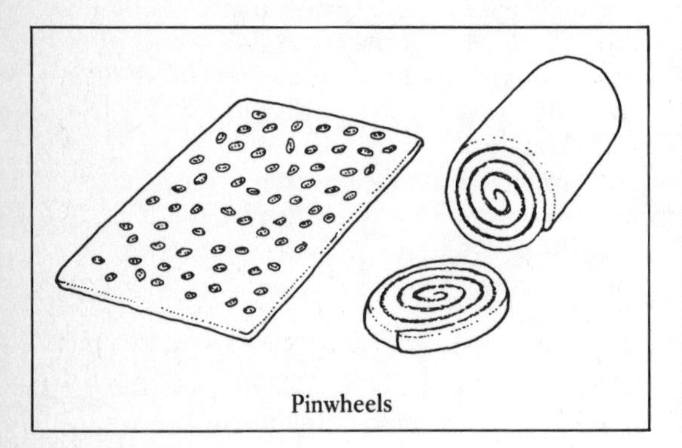

Pinwheels

CUSHIONS OR ENVELOPES

Roll out the dough very thinly and cut into 7.5-cm/3-inch squares. Place 1 large teaspoon of chosen filling in the centre and fold each corner into the centre.

DIAMONDS

Roll out the dough very thinly and cut into 7.5-cm/3-inch squares. Place 1 large teaspoon of chosen filling in the centre and fold two opposite corners into the centre.

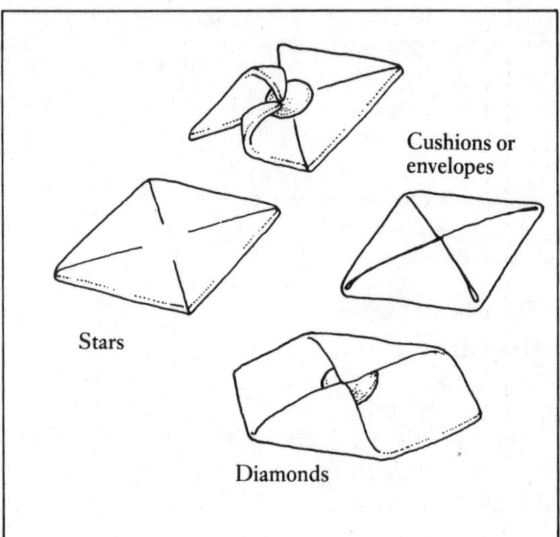

BATCH BAKING AND TRAY BAKES

Being a Scot, I associate the words 'batch baking' with the peculiarly Scottish way of baking, what in Scotland is called, Plain Bread. It is a method whereby a huge number of loaves are baked side by side in very large tins. When the bread is baked all the loaves fuse together at the sides, then when cool they are pulled apart. The sides are without a crust and the rounded tops and flat bottoms have thick dark crusts. Sadly, it is no longer possible to buy this type of bread unwrapped, and the wrapped variety seems to me to have lost its distinctive flavour.

The batch baking recipes are mostly baked in Swiss roll-type tins, the idea being to make a lot at once and freeze most of it for future use. Making one large quantity is always easier than doing several individual recipes.

The phrase 'tray bake' sounds American to me but I have been unable to trace its origin. The recipe mixtures are spread out in shallow tins and baked whole. They are then cut up when cool or cold. It is better to avoid using nonstick tins for tray bakes since many of them are cut up in the tin and the nonstick surface would scratch. Tray bakes are very useful, especially for families. You can cut the pieces as large or as small as you wish depending on the children's ages.

SAVOURY TRAY BAKES

LEEK AND BACON OPEN SLICE

This tasty open flan is full of the good flavours of leeks, bacon and cheese. Be particularly careful when preparing leeks. Top and tail them and remove any very coarse outer layers. Slice each leek in two lengthways and hold it together in your hands under a running tap to make sure each layer is free from grit. Shake off all the water and chop the leek into small pieces. (If there is a hard white core in the leek be sure to remove it.)

Will cut into 24 pieces

325 g/12 oz shortcrust pastry *(see page 28)*
4–5 large leeks, washed and chopped
25 g/1 oz butter
1 tablespoon vegetable oil
Salt and pepper
150 g/5 oz smoked streaky bacon, de-rinded, grilled and chopped
4 medium eggs, beaten
300 ml/½ pint single cream
125 g/4 oz Cheddar cheese, grated

1. Well grease a large Swiss roll tin measuring 33 × 23 cm/13 × 9 inches. Preheat the oven to moderate, Gas 4, 350°F, 180°C.
2. Roll out the pastry on a floured surface and line the base and sides of the tin. Trim the edges.
3. Cook the leeks in a pan with the butter and vegetable oil until almost done. Do not let them get too soft. Allow to cool.
4. Drain the leeks and arrange in the pastry case. Season well with salt and pepper and sprinkle the cooked bacon on top.
5. Beat the eggs into the cream, season with pepper and pour into the pastry case. Sprinkle the grated cheese on top.
6. Bake for about 35 minutes, or until the pastry is cooked and the custard set. Eat as soon as possible.

Will keep fairly well in a fridge for 2 days but the pastry does go soft. I do not think these mixtures freeze well.

SAVOURY SLICE PIE

This is an excellent pie for a picnic. I use an oblong flan frame measuring 35.5 × 11 cm/14 × 4½ inches, and the pie cuts into very neat slices. A small Swiss roll tin will do just as well. The pie could be cut in two lengthways and then in narrow slices. Good hot or cold.

Will cut into 12 large pieces

325 g/12 oz shortcrust pastry *(see page 28)*
450 g/1 lb good quality pork sausagemeat
125 g/4 oz streaky smoked bacon, de-rinded and finely chopped
1 small dessert apple, peeled, cored and grated
1 tablespoon chopped fresh parsley
½ teaspoon dried marjoram
Salt and pepper
2 medium eggs, beaten
A little milk

1. Well grease a small Swiss roll tin measuring 28 × 18 cm/11 × 7 inches. Preheat the oven to moderately hot, Gas 5, 375°F, 190°C.
2. Roll out three-quarters of the pastry on a lightly floured surface and line the base and sides of the tin. Trim the edges.
3. Put all the remaining ingredients into a large mixing bowl, retaining just a little beaten egg and the milk. Work the mixture very thoroughly and season well.
4. Spread the mixture evenly in the pastry, pressing it down with a spatula or wide-bladed knife.
5. Roll out the remaining pastry to form a lid, moisten the edges of the bottom half of the pie and cover with the pastry lid. Trim off the excess pastry and seal the edges together with the back of a fork.
6. Pierce the pie top in several places – this can be quite decorative. Make leaves out of the pastry trimmings, if liked, and place on top of the pie.
7. Mix 1 tablespoon of milk with the reserved beaten egg and brush this over the top of the pie.
8. Bake for about 30 minutes, then reduce the heat to moderate, Gas 4, 350°F, 180°C, and bake for a further 15 minutes. Allow to go cold in the tin.

Will store for 2–3 days in an airtight tin in the fridge, or freezes well for up to 1 month.

SKINNY STEAK SLICE

This is just like a flat skinny steak pie. I like it cold with some good English mustard so it is ideal for a picnic in cold weather when something substantial is needed. The ingredients for the filling must be cut wafer thin so that they are all cooked at the same time. I am using suet pastry for this recipe so remember that, because self-raising flour is needed for the heavier fat, the pastry should be used soon after it is made up.

Will cut into 18 generous pieces

325 g/12 oz suet or shortcrust pastry *(see pages 28 and 29)*
675 g/1½ lb braising steak in a piece
25 g/1 oz lard
1 large onion (about 225 g/8 oz), peeled and finely chopped
¼ teaspoon mustard powder
1 tablespoon fresh parsley, chopped
Salt and pepper
175–225 g/6–8 oz potato, peeled and very finely sliced
175–225 g/6–8 oz yellow turnip, peeled and very finely sliced
1 small egg, beaten

1. Lightly grease a large Swiss roll tin measuring 33 × 23 cm/13 × 9 inches. Preheat the oven to fairly hot, Gas 6, 400°F, 200°C.
2. Roll out the pastry on a lightly floured surface. Use about three-quarters of the pastry to line the base and sides of the tin. Trim the edges.
3. Prepare the meat. Cut away as much fat as possible and slice the meat into wafer thin slices about 5 cm/2 inches long. (It makes the slicing easier if the meat is chilled in the freezer to stiffen it up slightly.) Dry the strips of meat on kitchen paper and fry them briskly in the lard. Just aim to brown the meat, not to cook it. Lift the meat out with a draining spoon, then briefly fry the chopped onions.
4. Spoon the meat and onions into the pastry case, spreading them evenly over the base. Sprinkle with the mustard and parsley and season well with salt and pepper. Spread the potato and turnip over the meat and season again. Take about 1 tablespoon of the juices left in the frying pan and pour that over the vegetables.
5. Knead together the pastry trimmings and the remaining pastry and roll out a lid to fit the pie. Moisten the pastry edges, place the lid on the pie and seal carefully. Trim off the excess pastry. Using the back of a fork, make a pattern around the edge. Brush the lid with beaten egg and snip a series of steam holes down the centre of the pie. Place the pie on a metal baking tray.
6. Bake for 15 minutes then reduce the heat to moderate, Gas 4, 350°F, 180°C, and continue baking for a further 1½ hours.

Best eaten fresh or will keep for up to 2 days, covered with foil, in the fridge. Freezes well for up to 1 month.

SAUSAGE LATTICE

This is very like the Savoury Slice Pie *(see page 200)* but it uses new flaky pastry and is not made in a tin.

Will cut into 12 large slices

325 g/12 oz new flaky pastry *(see page 31)*
225 g/8 oz good quality pork sausagemeat
1 small onion, peeled and very finely chopped
3 tablespoons frozen mixed chopped vegetables, thawed
125 g/4 oz Cheddar cheese, grated
Pepper
1 small egg, beaten

1. On a lightly floured board, roll out the pastry until you have a square measuring about 30 cm/12 inches all round. Cut this square in two to give you the bottom and top of the lattice. Put half the pastry on a wetted baking tray.
2. Mix together the sausagemeat, onion, vegetables and cheese. Season with pepper and spread on the pastry base, leaving uncovered a 2.5-cm/1-inch border all round. Moisten this border slightly.
3. Dredge the other piece of pastry with flour and fold it over lengthways. Using scissors, cut a series of slits along the folded edge, stopping about 1 cm/½ inch from the cut edge. Open the pastry out. Brush away the spare flour and carefully place the pastry over the filling to cover. Press the edges to seal, using the back of a fork.
4. Brush all over the top of the pastry with the beaten egg and chill for 20 minutes.
5. Preheat the oven to hot, Gas 7, 425°F, 220°C. Bake the pie for about 30 minutes. If the pastry gets very brown, reduce the heat a little.

Best eaten fresh. Cool and store in the fridge for up to 2 days, or freeze for up to 4 weeks.

EGG, ONION AND MUSHROOM SLICE

In this recipe I partially cook the pastry before adding the wet filling to help it to stay crisp. Use field mushrooms – the large, flat, dark ones – to get a lovely rich flavour. Be sure to cook the mushrooms long enough to evaporate most of the juice and so concentrate the flavour. Double cream makes this a real luxury dish.

Will cut into 8 large pieces

175 g/6 oz shortcrust pastry *(see page 28)*
2 large eggs, beaten
25 g/1 oz butter
2 teaspoons vegetable oil
1 medium onion, peeled and very finely chopped
225 g/8 oz field mushrooms (if possible), wiped and finely chopped
300 ml/½ pint double cream
Salt and pepper
Grated nutmeg

1. Lightly grease a small Swiss roll tin measuring 28 × 18 cm/11 × 7 inches. Preheat the oven to moderate, Gas 4, 350°F, 180°C.
2. Roll out the pastry on a lightly floured surface and line the base and sides of the tin. Trim the edges. Prick the pastry all over with a fork and bake for 15 minutes. Keep an eye on the pastry in case it bubbles up, which means that air is trapped underneath. Prick the bubble with a skewer and pat the pastry down with a wooden spoon.
3. After 15 minutes, take out the pastry and brush a little beaten egg all over the base of the pastry. Return the tin to the oven and cook for a further 5 minutes to dry off the egg.
4. In a saucepan, heat the butter and oil and gently cook the onion for 4–5 minutes. Stir in the chopped mushrooms and cook uncovered for about 20–30 minutes, stirring often, or until most of the juice has evaporated.
5. Using a slotted spoon, transfer the mixture into the pastry base and spread evenly.
6. Whisk the eggs into the cream, season well with salt and pepper and pour on top of the mushrooms. Grate nutmeg over the surface.
7. Bake at the same temperature as for the pastry for a further 35–40 minutes. Serve hot.

Will keep fairly well for 2–3 days in the fridge, but the texture of the pastry gets very soft. Can be frozen but may go soggy.

DANISH BLUE FLAN

If you are fond of strong flavours then you will enjoy this mixture. I prefer to eat it hot.

Will cut into 9 squares

225 g/8 oz shortcrust pastry *(see page 28)*
75 g/3 oz butter
275 g/10 oz onions, peeled and finely chopped
40 g/1½ oz plain flour
300 ml/½ pint milk
150 g/5 oz Danish Blue cheese, crumbled
2 pinches mustard powder
Pepper

1. Grease a small Swiss roll tin measuring 28 × 18 cm/11 × 7 inches. Preheat the oven to hot, Gas 7, 425°F, 220°C.
2. Set aside about 50 g/2 oz pastry. Roll out the rest on a lightly floured surface to line the base and sides of the tin. Trim the edges.
3. Put the butter in a pan and melt it. Add the onions and cook gently until they are soft – about 5 minutes.
4. Sprinkle the flour over the onions. Stir and allow the flour to sizzle in the hot mixture. Gradually add the milk, stirring continuously, and cook over a low heat until thick and creamy, then mix in the cheese, mustard and pepper. Take off the heat and stir until the cheese melts. Pour the cheesy mixture into the pastry case and level it off.
5. Roll out the remaining pastry and cut narrow strips about 5 mm/¼ inch wide. Twist the strips into spirals and lay them across the flan in a decorative way. Fix at each end with a spot of water.
6. Bake for about 15 minutes, then reduce the heat to moderate, Gas 4, 350°F, 180°C, and bake for a further 25 minutes. Serve immediately.

Will keep fairly well in the fridge for up to 2 days but the pastry does tend to go soft. Freezes fairly well for up to 2 months.

PAN BAKE CHEESY PIZZA

This pizza base is not made with bread dough (*see page 186*), but is cooked in a frying pan so is really quick and easy to do. The pizza is finished under a grill.

Will cut into 8 slices

FOR THE BASE

125 g/4 oz self-raising white flour
¼ teaspoon salt
3 tablespoons vegetable oil
2 rashers of streaky bacon, de-rinded

FOR THE TOPPING

25 g/1 oz butter
1 small onion, peeled and finely chopped
225 g/8 oz canned tomatoes, well drained and chopped
½ teaspoon caster sugar
2 pinches dried basil
75 g/3 oz Cheddar cheese, grated

1. To make the base, sift the flour and salt into a mixing bowl. Stir in 1 tablespoon of oil and enough water to make a pliable dough. On a floured board, roll out the dough to fit a frying pan about 20–23 cm/8–9 inches across.
2. Heat 1 tablespoon of oil in the pan and swirl it to coat the base and sides. Put the dough in the pan and cook over a moderate to low heat for 5–6 minutes. When one side is done put the remaining oil in the pan, flip over the dough and cook the other side for a further 4–5 minutes.
3. While the dough is cooking, grill the bacon rashers until crisp, chop in small pieces and set aside to keep warm.
4. To make the topping, melt the butter in a small pan. Cook the onion until it is soft then add the tomatoes, sugar and basil. Cook for a further 2–3 minutes then drain off as much liquid as possible.
5. Spread the tomato mixture on top of the dough in the pan. Sprinkle with the chopped bacon and cover with the grated cheese. Slip under a moderate grill until the cheese melts. Eat immediately.

LATTICE PIZZA

Baked in a large Swiss roll tin, this savoury tart is easy to cut up either into generous squares or just fingers for informal eating.

Shortcrust pastry is used for the base, although strictly speaking a pizza should have a bread base (*see page 186*).

Serves 8–10

400 g/14 oz shortcrust pastry *(see page 28)*
2 tablespoons vegetable oil
900 g/2 lb onions, peeled and thinly sliced
1 × 400-g/14-oz can tomatoes, very well drained and finely chopped
125 g/4 oz Cheddar cheese, grated
½ teaspoon dried basil
2 × 50-g/2-oz cans anchovies, drained and halved lengthways (use scissors)
A few black olives, stoned and cut into pieces

1. Grease a large shallow Swiss roll tin measuring 30 × 20 cm/12 × 8 inches. Preheat the oven to hot, Gas 7, 425°F, 220°C.
2. Roll out the pastry on a lightly floured surface and line the base and sides of the tin. Trim the edges. Prick the pastry all over with a fork.
3. Heat the oil in a large pan and cook the onions gently until almost done, stirring frequently. Allow to cool.
4. Chop out any green cores in the tomatoes. Stir the tomatoes into the onions. Drain this mixture thoroughly in a large sieve and spread it evenly over the pastry base.
5. Sprinkle the cheese and basil evenly over the tomatoes.
6. Make a lattice design with the halved anchovy strips on top of the cheese and put a piece of black olive in each space.
7. Bake for 25–30 minutes until the pastry is crisp and brown. Leave in the tin to go cold.

Will keep for up to 2 days in a fridge. Do not freeze.

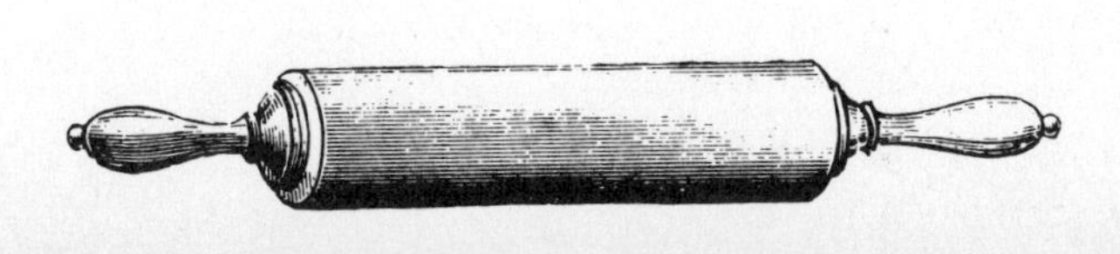

COURGETTE AND PARMESAN TART

This delicious open tart is flavoured with Parmesan cheese and sour cream. It is good hot or cold.

Will cut into 16 thin slices

400 g/14 oz shortcrust pastry *(see page 28)*
325 g/12 oz firm courgettes, wiped, topped and tailed
2 tablespoons vegetable oil
1 medium onion, peeled and finely chopped
1 heaped teaspoon fresh chopped tarragon, or ½ teaspoon dried tarragon
150 ml/¼ pint sour cream
2 large eggs, beaten
75 g/3 oz grated Parmesan cheese
Salt and pepper

1. Grease a large Swiss roll tin measuring 20 × 30 cm/8 × 12 inches. Preheat the oven to fairly hot, Gas 6, 400°F, 200°C.
2. Roll out the pastry on a lightly floured surface to fit the tin. Lift it carefully by draping it over a rolling pin then lower it into the tin, to line the base and sides. Trim the edges and set the tin aside to chill for 10 minutes.
3. Bake the pastry blind (*see page 26*) for about 25–30 minutes altogether but 10 minutes before the end of the cooking time remove the paper and beans. Leave the pastry shell in the tin to go cold.
4. Do not peel the courgettes but chop them into small cubes (smaller than a sugar lump).
5. Heat the vegetable oil in a large pan. Add the onion and cook for 1–2 minutes over a gentle heat. Add the courgettes and tarragon. Shake and stir until the courgettes are just beginning to cook. Remove the pan from the heat and set aside to cool.
6. In a mixing bowl, beat together the cream and the eggs. Stir in the Parmesan cheese. Fold this mixture into the courgettes and season generously with salt and pepper. Pour into the cooked pastry case and level it off carefully.
7. Reduce the heat to moderate, Gas 4, 350°F, 180°C, and bake the tart for about 30 minutes, or until the custard is set.

Best eaten fresh but will keep, covered with foil, for 2–3 days in a fridge. Do not freeze.

BROCCOLI TRAY BAKE

This delicious open tart has a strong flavour and looks very appetizing. Only the florets of the broccoli are used – cook the stems as a vegetable.

Serves 6

225 g/8 oz cheese pastry *(see page 30)*
225 g/8 oz carrot, very finely sliced into rings
225 g/8 oz small broccoli florets
125 g/4 oz Danish Blue cheese, finely crumbled
75 g/3 oz salted peanuts, finely chopped
Salt and pepper
2 medium eggs, beaten
150 ml/¼ pint milk

1. Grease and line a small Swiss roll tin measuring about 28 × 18 cm/11 × 7 inches. Preheat the oven to fairly hot, Gas 6, 400°F, 200°C.
2. Roll out the pastry on a lightly floured surface and line the base and sides of the tin. Trim the edges. Prick the pastry base several times.
3. Bake the pastry blind (*see page 26*) for about 20 minutes altogether but 5 minutes before the end of the cooking time remove the paper and beans. Allow the pastry to cool.
4. Cook the carrots in boiling salted water for 5 minutes, drain in a sieve and run cold water over them to stop the cooking. Do the same with the broccoli florets but cook them for just 2 minutes before refreshing them in cold water. Drain well.
5. Layer all the ingredients, except the eggs and milk, into the cooked pastry base – cheese, nuts, carrots, nuts, broccoli, cheese and, finally, a layer of nuts. Season each layer to taste.
6. Beat together the eggs and milk and pour into the pastry case.
7. Bake at the same temperature as the pastry case for about 50 minutes, or until the custard has set.

Best eaten on the day it is made, but will store for 2 days in a fridge. Do not freeze.

KIPPER AND EGG TRAY BAKE

In this recipe the pastry is partially cooked before the filling is added to ensure the pastry base remains as crisp as possible. To get really moist kipper flakes I prefer to poach the fish in hot water rather than grill it.

Will cut into 8 large pieces

325 g/12 oz kippers
175 g/6 oz shortcrust pastry *(see page 28)*
2 large eggs, beaten
½ teaspoon mustard powder
1 hard-boiled egg, shelled and chopped
300 ml/½ pint milk (or a mixture of milk and single cream)
Salt and pepper
1 tablespoon grated Parmesan cheese

1. Cut the head and tail off the kipper and place it in the bottom of a grill pan. Cover with hot water and slip the pan under a hot grill for about 10 minutes or more depending on the thickness of the fish, until the flesh is no longer 'glassy' near the bone. Take out of the water, cool a little then remove all the meat from the skin, discarding any bones, and flake it.
2. Lightly grease a small Swiss roll tin measuring 28 × 18 cm/11 × 7 inches. Preheat the oven to moderate, Gas 4, 350°F, 180°C.
3. Roll out the pastry on a lightly floured surface and line the base and sides of the tin. Trim the edges. Prick the pastry all over with a fork and bake for 15 minutes. Keep an eye on the pastry in case it bubbles up, which means that air is trapped underneath. Prick the bubble with a skewer and pat the pastry down with a wooden spoon.
4. After 15 minutes, take out the pastry and brush a little beaten egg all over the base of the flan.
5. Return the tin to the oven and bake for a further 5 minutes, then remove and lay the flaked kipper all over the base. Sprinkle over the mustard powder and then the chopped egg.
6. To mix the savoury custard, whisk the beaten eggs into the milk, or milk and cream, season with salt and pepper and pour over the kipper and egg mixture. You may not need all the mixture if the Swiss roll tin is very shallow. Sprinkle the cheese over and bake for a further 30 minutes, or until the filling is set and puffy. A gentle shake will soon tell you if the filling has set and is no longer liquid. Eat hot or cold.

Best eaten fresh.

VEGETABLE AND CHEESE TRAY BAKE

This tasty vegetable slice is best eaten hot, I think. You can, of course, vary the vegetables according to the season.

Serves 8

225 g/8 oz shortcrust pastry *(see page 28)*
50 g/2 oz butter
125 g/4 oz carrots, scraped and finely sliced in rings
125 g/4 oz French beans, topped, tailed and very finely sliced diagonally
1 small onion, peeled and finely chopped
1 small green pepper, stem and white seeds removed, cut into fine strips
2 small tomatoes, skinned and flesh chopped
125 g/4 oz smoked streaky bacon, de-rinded and chopped
175 g/6 oz low fat cheese (e.g. Gouda), grated

1. Grease a small Swiss roll tin measuring about 28 × 18 cm/11 × 7 inches. Roll out the pastry on a lightly floured surface and line the base and sides of the tin. Trim the edges. Chill for 10 minutes.
2. Melt the butter in a large pan and cook all the vegetables and the bacon for 8–10 minutes. Pour the mixture into a large sieve suspended over a bowl and leave to go cold.
3. Preheat the oven to fairly hot, Gas 6, 400°F, 200°C. Pour the vegetable mixture into the pastry case and cover the vegetable filling with a rectangle of foil to protect it. Bake for about 40–45 minutes in all. About 10 minutes before the end of the cooking time remove the foil, sprinkle over the grated cheese and continue baking uncovered until the cheese has melted.

Eat as soon as possible as the wet vegetables make the pastry go soggy eventually.

SWEET TRAY BAKES

PARKIN CRUNCH

Will cut into 12 bars

125 g/4 oz block margarine
50 g/2 oz light soft brown sugar
2 tablespoons black treacle
2 tablespoons golden syrup
225 g/8 oz rolled porridge oats
50 g/2 oz walnuts, chopped

1. Grease a shallow 18-cm/7-inch square tin. Preheat the oven to moderate, Gas 4, 350°F, 180°C.
2. In a roomy pan, melt the margarine, sugar, treacle and syrup. Check that the sugar has dissolved. Stir in the porridge oats and the walnuts.
3. Press this mixture evenly into the tin and bake for about 30 minutes or until shrinking from the sides of the tin. Mark into twelve bars in the tin while warm. Cool on a wire tray.

Store in an airtight tin for up to 4 days. Freeze for up to 2 weeks but it is rather soft on thawing. Crisp up, if liked, in the oven before eating.

HAZELNUT BAKE

This is a quick way to make a shortbread-type biscuit without all the rolling and cutting. If you want the real taste of shortbread use butter. You can make these biscuits with ground hazelnuts, which you can buy in a wholefood shop, but for a really superior flavour and texture roast your own hazelnuts (*see page 252*).

Will cut into 24 fingers

225 g/8 oz butter, softened
50 g/2 oz light soft brown sugar
175 g/6 oz plain white flour, sifted
25 g/1 oz ground rice or semolina
125 g/4 oz hazelnuts, roasted and chopped

1. Lightly grease a small Swiss roll tin measuring 23 × 18 cm/9 × 7 inches. Preheat the oven to moderate, Gas 3, 325°F, 160°C.
2. If you have a large mixer with a beater you can put all the ingredients into the warmed (not hot) bowl and beat at medium speed until you have a firm dough. Knead it together in the bowl.

If you do not have a mixer, cream the butter and sugar in a warmed mixing bowl and stir in the remaining ingredients. Knead with your hand until you have a firm dough.

3. Press this dough evenly into the tin. Use a large palette knife to level and smooth it down.
4. Bake for about 35–40 minutes, or until evenly golden in colour. Remove from the oven and, while still soft, mark lightly into twenty-four fingers. Leave to cool in the tin. When firm lift out of the tin onto a wire tray. Break into pieces when cold.

Store in an airtight container for 5–6 days. You could freeze these biscuits if you wish – 2–3 weeks only – but they need to be crisped up again when thawed.

DATE AND ROLLED OAT BAKE

Will cut into 15 bars

125 g/4 oz packet dates, stoned and finely chopped
125 g/4 oz self-raising wholemeal flour
125 g/4 oz butter or block margarine
125 g/4 oz caster sugar
125 g/4 oz rolled oats

1. Well grease a small Swiss roll tin measuring 20 × 30 cm/12 × 8 inches. Preheat the oven to moderate, Gas 4, 350°F, 180°C.
2. Put the dates into a small pan and barely cover with cold water. Cook gently, stirring often, until the mixture is like thick jam. Set aside to cool.
3. Sift the flour into a mixing bowl and rub in the butter or margarine until the mixture resembles breadcrumbs. Stir in the sugar and the oats.
4. Press half the crumbly mixture into the tin and level it off. Spread the date mixture carefully on top of this and top with the remaining mixture. Press down well.
5. Bake for about 20 minutes, or until the surface is nicely browned. Remove from the oven and mark out the bars while the mixture is warm. Allow to cool a little but remove from the tin before the bars get really cold.

Store in an airtight tin for up to 3–4 days, or freeze for up to 3 months.

PARKIN BAKE

This is a traditional Guy Fawkes' night treat. It is baked in a roasting tin and is usually cut into squares and kept in a tin for a couple of days. This allows the parkin to 'give' and become rather damp and sticky. It is made by the melting method (*see page 57*) and is therefore very easy to put together.

Will cut into 24 squares

200 g/7 oz plain wholemeal flour
150 g/5 oz medium oatmeal
1 teaspoon ground cinnamon
2 teaspoons ground ginger
2 pinches ground nutmeg
125 g/4 oz black treacle, warmed
175 g/6 oz golden syrup, warmed
125 g/4 oz block margarine
75 g/3 oz light soft brown sugar
1 large egg, beaten
1 teaspoon bicarbonate of soda
150 ml/¼ pint milk

1. Lightly grease and line the base and sides of a roasting tin measuring about 20 × 30 cm/8 × 12 inches and grease the lining paper. Preheat the oven to cool, Gas 2, 300°F, 150°C.
2. Place the flour, oatmeal, cinnamon, ginger and nutmeg in a large mixing bowl and stir well.
3. Stand the containers of treacle and syrup in hot water to warm them. Put a small pan on the scales, weigh it and then weigh the treacle and syrup into it. Put the pan on a low heat and stir in the margarine and sugar.
4. When the margarine and sugar have dissolved, pour the contents of the pan into the dry ingredients with the egg. Mix the bicarbonate of soda with a little of the milk and stir that into the mixture. Mix well, adding enough of the remaining milk to give the consistency of a thick batter.
5. Pour into the prepared tin, spreading well into the corners. Bake for about 1 hour, or until the cake is shrinking away from the sides of the tin. Leave in the tin to go cold then turn out and peel off the lining papers. Use a sharp knife to cut into squares.

Store in an airtight tin for about 1 week. Not suitable for freezing as it goes too sticky.

WILFRA APPLE CAKE

The cathedral at Ripon is dedicated to St Wilfred and he is remembered during Wilfra Week. There is a procession of decorated floats and bands and a custom arose that householders offered jam tarts and lemon tarts to passers-by. How the apple recipe became associated with the Saint's day, I do not know. However, the Yorkshire custom of cheese with apple is delicious.

Will cut into 24 squares

325 g/12 oz shortcrust pastry (*see page 28*)
675 g/1½ lb Bramley cooking apples, peeled, cored and finely sliced
75 g/3 oz demerara sugar
125 g/4 oz Wensleydale cheese, grated
A little milk
Caster sugar to glaze

1. Well grease a Swiss roll tin measuring 20 × 30 cm/8 × 12 inches. Preheat the oven to moderate, Gas 4, 350°F, 180°C.
2. Roll out the pastry on a lightly floured surface and use two-thirds of it to line the base and sides of the tin. Trim the edges.
3. Lay the apple over the pastry base, sprinkle with the sugar and then cover with the grated cheese.
4. Roll out the remaining pastry to make a lid. Moisten the edges of the pastry, place on top of the filling and seal carefully. Brush over the lid with a little milk and scatter on a little caster sugar. Snip a row of steam holes down the centre.
5. Bake for about 40 minutes. When cold, cut into squares. Eat hot or cold.

Best eaten fresh but will keep fairly well for 2–3 days. Best frozen unbaked for up to 1 month.

APPLE TRAY BAKE

Any variety of apple can be used but cooking apples have a good sharp flavour which contrasts well with the cake mixture.

Will cut into 18 pieces

125 g/4 oz butter or block margarine, softened
125 g/4 oz caster sugar
1 large egg, beaten
225 g/8 oz self-raising white flour
4 tablespoons milk
225 g/8 oz apples, peeled, cored and finely chopped
½ teaspoon ground cinnamon
Extra caster sugar for dredging

1. Lightly grease a Swiss roll tin measuring 25 × 20 cm/10 × 8 inches. Preheat the oven to moderately hot, Gas 5, 375°F, 190°C.
2. Cream the butter or margarine and the sugar in a mixing bowl until pale and fluffy. Add the egg a little at a time, beating well between each addition.
3. Sift the flour into the mixture and stir in the milk and the apples. Mix well.
4. Turn this mixture into the tin and level it off carefully.
5. Bake for 25–30 minutes, or until the cake is risen, firm to the touch and just beginning to shrink from the sides of the tin. Remove the tray from the oven. Use a sieve to sprinkle the cinnamon all over the surface and then dredge with caster sugar. Cool then cut into pieces.

Store in an airtight tin for up to 4 days, or freeze for up to 3 months.

ALMOND TRAY BAKE

Ground almonds are expensive so in this recipe I extend them by using a little ground rice. The finished block can be cut into generous portions or very dainty fingers. Allow to cool in the tin before turning it out to slice.

Will cut into 20 bars

175 g/6 oz shortcrust pastry *(see page 28)*
2 tablespoons raspberry jam (or any red jam)
125 g/4 oz ground almonds
50 g/2 oz ground rice
2 medium eggs, beaten
175 g/6 oz caster sugar
1–2 drops almond essence
15 g/½ oz flaked almonds

1. Grease a shallow Swiss roll tin measuring about 18 × 28 cm/7 × 11 inches. Preheat the oven to moderate, Gas 4, 350°F, 180°C.
2. Roll out the pastry thinly on a lightly floured board and line the base and sides of the tin. Trim the edges.
3. If the jam is very stiff warm it slightly, then spread it on the pastry.
4. Mix the ground almonds, ground rice, eggs, sugar and almond essence in a bowl. Pour this mixture on top of the jam and level it off, taking care to seal in all the jam. Sprinkle with the flaked almonds.
5. Bake for about 40 minutes until the pastry and almond filling are brown and crisp. Allow to cool in the tin then cut into bars.

Will store in an airtight tin for 4–5 days, or freezes well for up to 3 months.

PLUM AND ALMOND FINGERS

Apart from in fruit tarts, we rarely use plums for cakes. Their sharp flavour is an excellent contrast in this substantial tray bake. Cut into generous pieces, it makes a good pudding with custard or single cream.

Will cut into about 20 pieces

225 g/8 oz shortcrust pastry *(see page 28)*
675 g/1½ lb ripe red plums, stoned and thinly sliced
225 g/8 oz tub margarine
175 g/6 oz caster sugar
3 large eggs, beaten
1 teaspoon baking powder
3–4 drops almond essence
2–3 tablespoons milk
25 g/1 oz flaked almonds

1. Grease a deep tin measuring 33 × 23 cm/13 × 9 inches. (A roasting tin is a good depth.) Preheat the oven to moderately hot, Gas 5, 375°F, 190°C.
2. Roll out the pastry on a lightly floured surface and line the bottom of the tin, taking the pastry up the sides a little. Cover the pastry with the plums.
3. In a large, warm mixing bowl, beat all the remaining ingredients together, with the exception of the milk and flaked almonds. Beat in enough of the milk to give a soft consistency.
4. Spread this mixture over the plums and smooth it down. Sprinkle with the flaked almonds.
5. Bake for about 30 minutes until golden and brown. Allow to cool in the tin then slice.

Store in an airtight tin for 3–4 days, or freeze for up to 3 months.

FRUIT AND ALMOND BARS

This is another useful tray bake. It looks very pretty when cut into bars. Watch out that it does not get too brown towards the end of cooking time – both ground rice and ground almonds scorch easily. You can either reduce the heat or cover the top of the tray bake with a sheet of greaseproof paper. Try to buy the very small currants without seeds.

Will cut into 20 bars

175 g/6 oz shortcrust pastry *(see page 28)*
75 g/3 oz block margarine
75 g/3 oz caster sugar
1 large egg, beaten
75 g/3 oz currants, washed and dried
50 g/2 oz red glacé cherries, finely chopped
60 g/2½ oz ground rice
50 g/2 oz ground almonds
1–2 drops almond essence

1. Lightly grease a Swiss roll tin measuring 28 × 18 cm/11 × 7 inches. Preheat the oven to moderate, Gas 4, 350°F, 180°C.
2. Roll out the pastry on a lightly floured surface and line the base and sides of the tin. Trim the edges.
3. Cream the margarine and sugar in a mixing bowl until light and fluffy. Beat in the egg, a little at a time, then fold in the remaining ingredients.
4. Spread the filling over the pastry base and smooth it down.
5. Bake for about 40 minutes. Allow to cool in the tin and then cut into neat bars with a sharp knife.

Store in an airtight tin for 4–5 days, or freeze for up to 3 months.

LEMON AND CHERRY FINGERS

The combination of lemon curd and glacé cherries makes a nice change.

Will cut into 20 fingers

175 g/6 oz plain white flour
1 tablespoon icing sugar
1 pinch salt
75 g/3 oz mixed margarine and solid vegetable fat
5 tablespoons good lemon curd
125 g/4 oz tub margarine
125 g/4 oz caster sugar
2 medium eggs, beaten
125 g/4 oz self-raising flour, sifted
75 g/3 oz glacé cherries, finely chopped
2 teaspoons grated lemon rind

1. Grease and line a shallow Swiss roll tin measuring 30 × 20 cm/12 × 8 inches.
2. Sift the plain flour, salt and icing sugar into a medium sized mixing bowl. Rub in the fats until the mixture resembles breadcrumbs, then add 2–3 tablespoons cold water to make a firm dough. Set the pastry aside for 20 minutes to rest.
3. Preheat the oven to fairly hot, Gas 6, 400°F, 200°C. Roll out the pastry on a lightly floured surface and line the base and sides of the tin. Trim the edges and spread the lemon curd in the bottom.
4. Cream the margarine and sugar together until light and fluffy. Beat in the eggs, a little at a time. Fold in the self-raising flour, cherries and lemon rind. Spread this mixture over the lemon curd.
5. Bake for 10 minutes, then reduce the heat to moderate, Gas 4, 350°F, 180°C, and bake for about 20 minutes more, or until the mixture is risen, golden and firm. Leave in the tin to cool for about 15 minutes, then turn out onto a wire tray. Peel off the lining paper and cut into fingers when cold.

Store in an airtight tin for about 4 days, or freeze for up to 3 months.

LEMON CAKE BARS

Will cut into 15 pieces

FOR THE BASE
175 g/6 oz butter or block margarine, softened
175 g/6 oz caster sugar
175 g/6 oz self-raising white flour
2 large eggs
2–3 drops vanilla essence

FOR THE TOPPING
Juice of 1 lemon (about 2 tablespoons)
125 g/4 oz granulated sugar

1. Lightly grease a small Swiss roll tin measuring about 20 × 30 cm/8 × 12 inches, and line the base and sides with greaseproof paper. Preheat the oven to moderate, Gas 4, 350°F, 180°C.
2. Put all the ingredients for the base into a warm mixing bowl and beat together until smooth. Pour this mixture into the prepared tin and level it off.
3. Bake for about 30–40 minutes, or until the cake is risen, firm and just beginning to shrink from the sides of the tin. Remove from the oven and allow to cool for 10 minutes.
4. Mix together the lemon juice and the sugar and swiftly, before the sugar starts to melt, pour this over the baked cake. Smooth the sugar evenly over the surface. The lemon juice will sink into the cake and the crunchy lemon sugar will be left on top. Allow to go cold in the tin then turn out, remove the lining papers and cut into fifteen pieces.

Store in an airtight tin for 3–4 days, or freeze for up to 2 months.

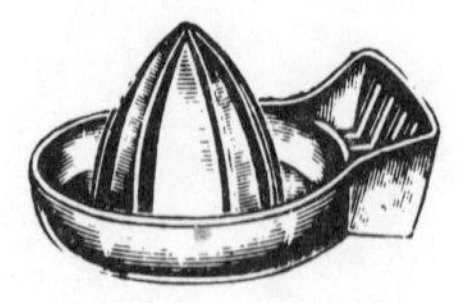

COFFEE BARS

Will cut into 32 small bars

FOR THE BASE
175 g/6 oz block margarine
175 g/6 oz light soft brown sugar
175 g/6 oz self-raising white flour
2 large eggs, beaten

FOR THE TOPPING
1 tablespoon instant coffee powder
1 tablespoon water
125 g/4 oz granulated sugar

1. Grease and base line a large Swiss roll tin measuring 32 × 23 cm/13 × 9 inches. Preheat the oven to moderate, Gas 4, 350°F, 180°C.
2. Melt the margarine in a roomy pan and remove from the heat. Stir in the sugar, flour and eggs. Mix well.
3. Pour the mixture into the tin and level off.
4. Bake for about 30 minutes, or until shrinking from the sides of the tin. Remove from the oven and allow to cool a little before adding the topping.
5. Dissolve the instant coffee in the water and stir in the sugar. Before the sugar has time to melt, pour this syrup all over the surface of the slab. Smooth the sugar evenly over the surface. The liquid coffee will sink in and the crunchy coffee sugar will be left on top.
6. Allow to go cold in the tin, then turn out, remove the lining paper and cut into thirty-two small bars with a sharp knife.

Store in an airtight tin for up to 5 days, or freeze for up to 1 month.

CHOCOLATE AND BANANA BARS

Use a cake tin for this and not a Swiss roll tin, which would be too shallow.

Will cut into 15 bars

FOR THE BASE
125 g/4 oz tub margarine
225 g/8 oz self-raising white flour
125 g/4 oz caster sugar
2 medium eggs, beaten
4 tablespoons milk
1 ripe fat banana, peeled and well mashed
50 g/2 oz plain chocolate, grated

FOR THE TOPPING
125 g/4 oz plain chocolate, grated
25 g/1 oz margarine
2 tablespoons water
50 g/2 oz icing sugar, sifted

1. Grease and base line an oblong tin measuring 28 × 18 cm/11 × 7 inches and 4 cm/1½ inches deep. Preheat the oven to moderate, Gas 4, 350°F, 180°C.
2. In a large mixing bowl, beat together all the ingredients for the base. Spoon into the tin and level it off carefully.
3. Bake for about 40 minutes, or until risen and just beginning to shrink from the sides of the tin.
4. Remove from the tin and cool on a wire tray before adding the topping.
5. Put the chocolate, margarine and water into a heatproof bowl set over a pan of simmering water and stir until melted. Pour this over the icing sugar and beat until smooth. Spread over the slab then, when set, cut into fifteen bars.

Will keep in an airtight tin for 3–4 days, or freeze for 1 week only.

APRICOT BARS

This tray bake is made in two parts. The base is baked in the tin and allowed to cool, then the topping ingredients are mixed and spread on the base and the whole cooked again.

Will cut into 14–16 bars

125 g/4 oz dried apricots
190 g/6½ oz plain white flour
50 g/2 oz caster sugar
75 g/3 oz butter or block margarine, cut into small pieces
1 teaspoon baking powder
1 pinch salt
175 g/6 oz light soft brown sugar
2 medium eggs, beaten
3–4 drops vanilla essence
50 g/2 oz walnuts, chopped
1 teaspoon grated lemon rind

1. Grease and base line a 20-cm/8-inch square tin. Preheat the oven to moderate, Gas 3, 325°F, 160°C.
2. Put the dried apricots into a small pan, cover with cold water and bring to a gentle boil for about 8 minutes. Drain, cool and chop quite small using scissors.
3. Set aside 40 g/1½ oz of the flour. Mix the remaining flour with the caster sugar and rub in the butter or margarine until the mixture resembles damp breadcrumbs.
4. Press the buttered crumbs into the bottom of the tin, level off and bake for about 20–25 minutes. Leave in the tin and allow to go cold.
5. In a mixing bowl, sift together the reserved 40 g/1½ oz flour, the baking powder and salt.
6. In another bowl, beat the soft brown sugar with the eggs and vanilla essence and stir in the dry ingredients. Stir in the chopped walnuts, apricots and lemon rind. Spread over the cooked base and bake again in a moderate oven, Gas 3, 325°F, 160°C, for 30 minutes.
7. Allow to go cold in the tin then turn out, peel off the lining paper and cut into neat bars.

Keeps well in an airtight tin for 1 week, or freeze for up to 3 months.

PARADISE BARS

This base is easy to make – it is rather like the texture of shortbread. The topping could be altered by substituting raisins for the cherries and chopped peanuts for the walnuts.

Will cut into about 24 bars

225 g/8 oz plain white flour
50 g/2 oz icing sugar
125 g/4 oz block margarine, cut into pieces
2 medium eggs, beaten
175 g/6 oz caster sugar
75 g/3 oz mixed red and green glacé cherries, finely chopped
75 g/3 oz walnuts, chopped
75 g/3 oz coarse desiccated coconut

1. Grease a large Swiss roll tin measuring 33 × 25 cm/13 × 10 inches. Preheat the oven to cool, Gas 2, 300°F, 150°C.
2. Sift the flour and icing sugar into a large mixing bowl. Rub in the margarine until the mixture resembles damp breadcrumbs. Press this mixture evenly into the tin.
3. In a clean mixing bowl, whisk the eggs and the sugar until they are thick and creamy, then fold in the cherries, nuts and coconut. Spread this evenly over the base.
4. Bake for about 40 minutes. Allow to cool in the tin for about 25 minutes then cut into bars before the mixture is completely cold.

Store in an airtight tin for up to 7 days, or freeze for up to 3 months.

FRESH FRUIT CASKET

This oblong shape is often called a *tranche* in French recipes and the pastry used is usually flaky or puff. No matter how crisp the pastry, I never manage to cut this up neatly, so I suggest that you use rich sweet shortcrust pastry instead. Fresh fruit always looks at its best if glazed and shiny so do take care when doing this. Fill the pastry case as near to the serving time as possible so that the pastry remains crisp.

Will cut into 18 slices

225 g/8 oz rich sweet shortcrust pastry *(see page 28)*
3 tablespoons apricot jam glaze *(see page 248)*
150 ml/¼ pint double cream, whipped firmly
275 g/10 oz fresh strawberries, halved
2 tablespoons redcurrant jelly

1. Thoroughly grease a large Swiss roll tin measuring 33 × 23 cm/13 × 9 inches.
2. Roll out the pastry on a lightly floured surface to a thickness of 5–10 mm/¼–½ inch, and line the base and sides of the tin. Trim the edges, prick the pastry all over with a fork and set it aside for 20 minutes.
3. Preheat the oven to fairly hot, Gas 6, 400°F, 200°C. Bake the pastry case blind (*see page 26*) for about 10 minutes and then remove the paper and the beans. Reduce the heat to moderate, Gas 4, 350°F, 180°C, and bake for a further 15 minutes, or until the pastry is well browned and crisp. Leave in the tin to go cold.
4. Heat the apricot jam glaze by putting it in a cup and standing it in a pan of hot water. Brush a layer of glaze onto the base of the cold pastry. Allow to go cold.
5. Just before serving, slide the pastry case onto a flat board from which to serve it. Cover the apricot glaze with a thin layer of whipped cream and level this off.
6. Dry the strawberry halves on kitchen paper and lay them in neat rows on top of the cream. The casket will be easier to serve if the fruit is in straight rows.
7. For the glaze, put the redcurrant jelly into a small heatproof bowl in a pan of hot water in order to soften it. Remove from the pan when it is liquid and allow to go syrupy and cold again. Brush carefully over the fruits and the filling.

Eat on the day the casket is assembled.

ALTERNATIVE FRUIT

Green and black grapes, pips removed, and halved
Mandarin oranges
Fresh firm raspberries
A mixture of the above

ALTERNATIVE TOPPING GLAZE

Redcurrant jelly is fine for red fruits like strawberries, cherries, dark grapes, raspberries etc., but if you are using light coloured fruits, such as apricot pieces, green grapes, mandarins, try this alternative glaze:

50 g/2 oz caster sugar
150 ml/¼ pint water
2 squares from a jelly tablet (light coloured – lemon, lime or pineapple)

1. In a very small pan, dissolve the sugar in the water and boil hard for 2–3 minutes.
2. Stir in the jelly until dissolved. Allow to go cold but not set. Brush this over the fruits in the pastry case.

FIG SQUARES

A viewer sent me this recipe when I remarked on a programme that I hardly ever use dried figs in baking. These squares have a crisp bottom and a sponge top. I hope you like them.

Will cut into 20 squares

FOR THE FILLING
200 g/7 oz dried figs, finely chopped
300 ml/½ pint water
2 tablespoons lemon juice
2 teaspoons grated lemon rind

FOR THE BASE
200 g/7 oz butter or block margarine, cut into small pieces
300 g/11 oz plain white flour, sifted
75 g/3 oz caster sugar

FOR THE TOPPING
2 medium eggs, beaten
2 teaspoons baking powder
50 g/2 oz caster sugar

1. Cook the filling mixture well in advance to allow it to cool. Put all the ingredients for the filling into a pan, cover and cook very gently until a jam-like consistency is achieved. Set aside to cool.
2. Well grease a Swiss roll tin measuring 28 × 18 cm/11 × 7 inches and line the base and sides with nonstick paper or foil. Preheat the oven to moderate, Gas 4, 350°F, 180°C.
3. Rub the butter or margarine into the flour, or mix it in a food processor. Stir in the sugar, and then divide the mixture in two.
4. Take one half of the rubbed-in mixture and press firmly into the tin. Level the mixture off carefully.
5. Spread the cooled fig mixture on top of the base.
6. Make the topping by beating the eggs, baking powder and sugar into the remaining rubbed-in mixture to make a soft dropping consistency. Spread this on top of the fig mixture.
7. Bake for about 40–45 minutes, or until the sponge is firm to the touch. Leave in the tin to firm up then lift the block out and cool on a wire tray. Peel off the lining paper and cut into squares when cold.

Will store in an airtight tin for 3–4 days. Freeze for up to 1 month but the base does become less crisp.

MINT AND CHOCOLATE SHORTCAKE SQUARES

Will cut into 20 squares

125 g/4 oz butter, softened
50 g/2 oz light soft brown sugar
125 g/4 oz self-raising white flour, sifted
125 g/4 oz icing sugar, sifted
2–3 drops peppermint oil or flavouring essence
125 g/4 oz plain chocolate, broken into pieces

1. Lightly grease a small Swiss roll tin measuring 28 × 18 cm/11 × 7 inches. Preheat the oven to moderately hot, Gas 5, 375°F, 190°C.
2. In a warm mixing bowl, cream the butter and soft brown sugar then stir in the flour. Press this mixture firmly and evenly into the tin, and level it.
3. Bake for about 20 minutes, or until the shortcake is brown all over. Set aside in the tin to go cold.
4. Put the icing sugar into a small bowl and add the peppermint flavouring with great care. Stir in water, 1 teaspoon at a time, until you have a thick icing. Spread this icing over the top of the shortbread and allow to cool.
5. Put the chocolate into a heatproof bowl set over a pan of simmering water, and stir gently until melted. Pour the chocolate over the peppermint icing and allow to set, then cut into squares.

Store for 3–4 days in an airtight tin, or freeze for up to 1 month.

PRUNE AND APRICOT SQUARES

Use the soft, ready-to-eat prunes and apricots.

Will cut into 15 squares

125 g/4 oz block margarine
2 tablespoons golden syrup
50 g/2 oz light soft brown sugar
175 g/6 oz rolled oats (porridge oats)
50 g/2 oz soft prunes, finely chopped
50 g/2 oz soft apricots, finely chopped

1. Grease a Swiss roll tin measuring 28 × 18 cm/11 × 7 inches and line the base and sides with nonstick paper. Preheat the oven to moderate, Gas 4, 350°F, 180°C.

2. Melt the margarine with the syrup and sugar in a roomy pan.
3. Remove from the heat and stir in the oats, prunes and apricots. Mix well.
4. Spoon the mixture into the tin and level off but do not compress.
5. Bake for about 40 minutes. Mark into squares while still warm, peel off the lining paper and cool on a wire tray.

Store in an airtight tin for 3–4 days. It will freeze for up to 1 month but tends to be very soft on thawing.

APPLE AND DATE SLICE

The combination of sharp apples and sweet dates makes a particularly delicious filling, and the crunchy wholewheat topping is very pleasant.

Will cut into about 15 slices

225 g/8 oz wholemeal pastry *(see page 30)*
325 g/12 oz Bramley cooking apples, finely chopped
125 g/4 oz packet dates, stoned and finely chopped
50 g/2 oz cashew nuts, finely chopped

FOR THE TOPPING
125 g/4 oz butter
175 g/6 oz wholemeal flour
50 g/2 oz plain white flour
½ teaspoon ground ginger
½ teaspoon ground cinnamon
25 g/1 oz light soft brown sugar

1. Grease a shallow baking tin or Swiss roll tin measuring 18 × 28 cm/7 × 11 inches. Preheat the oven to fairly hot, Gas 6, 400°F, 200°C.
2. Roll out the pastry on a lightly floured surface and line the base and sides of the tin. Trim the edges.
3. Mix the apples, dates and nuts and spread them evenly in the tin, pressing down gently.
4. In a mixing bowl, rub the butter into the wholemeal flour (or mix in a food processor). Sift the plain flour with the ginger and cinnamon and stir this and the sugar into the rubbed-in crumbs. Sprinkle this mixture evenly over the fruit and level as much as possible.
5. Bake for about 40 minutes. Take out of the oven, allow to cool a little, then mark into fifteen slices while still warm. Allow to go cold in the tin.

Keep in an airtight tin for 2–3 days. (It soon goes soft.) Freeze for up to 1 month but, again, it goes soft.

VARIATION

The fruit in the filling can easily be varied, but the mixture should be fairly dry and not too juicy. Try one of the following:

325 g/12 oz fresh pears, peeled, cored, chopped and drained

125 g/4 oz packet dates, stoned (if necessary) and finely chopped

50 g/2 oz walnuts, chopped

COCONUT SLICE

Some loose coconut is sweetened, but this usually applies to the stranded kind and not desiccated. If your coconut is sweetened, just deduct 25 g/1 oz sugar from the recipe. Raspberry jam is the best to use as there are no large pieces of fruit in it.

Will cut into 12 slices

225 g/8 oz shortcrust pastry *(see page 28)*
3 tablespoons red jam
2 large egg whites
125 g/4 oz caster sugar
25 g/1 oz plain white flour, sifted
125 g/4 oz desiccated coconut

1. Grease a Swiss roll tin measuring 18 × 28 cm/7 × 11 inches. Preheat the oven to moderate, Gas 4, 350°F, 180°C.
2. Roll out the pastry on a lightly floured surface and line the base and sides of the tin. Trim the edges.
3. If the jam is stiff, warm it slightly by standing the jar in a pan of hot water. Spread the jam in a thin layer on top of the raw pastry.
4. In a clean grease-free bowl, whisk the egg whites until they are very stiff and peak easily. Using a spatula, fold in the sugar, flour and coconut and spread this evenly over the jam-covered pastry.
5. Bake for about 30 minutes, or until the top is evenly brown and the pastry crisp. Cool for a short time in the tin, then cut into slices.

Store in an airtight tin for up to 1 week, or freeze for up to 4 weeks.

CARAMEL SLICE

Will cut into 18 small slices

125 g/4 oz block margarine
50 g/2 oz caster sugar
150 g/5 oz self-raising white flour, sifted

FOR THE TOFFEE FILLING
125 g/4 oz block margarine, softened
125 g/4 oz caster sugar
2 tablespoons golden syrup
1 × 200-g/7-oz can Nestlés condensed milk

FOR THE TOPPING
125 g/4 oz plain chocolate, broken into small pieces

1. Grease a small Swiss roll tin measuring 28 × 18 cm/11 × 7 inches. Preheat the oven to moderate, Gas 4, 350°F, 180°C.
2. Cream the margarine and sugar until pale and fluffy. Stir in the flour.
3. Spread this paste-like mixture into the tin with a palette knife, making sure that the corners are evenly covered.
4. Bake for about 20 minutes, when the shortbread should be golden all over and risen slightly up the sides of the tin. Allow to cool in the tin.
5. Put all the ingredients for the toffee filling into a heavy-based pan and cook gently until the mixture is a rich toffee colour and beginning to leave the sides of the pan (about 20 minutes). (This is called the soft ball stage – when a few drops of the mixture dribbled into a jug of cold water sets to toffee and you can pick it up and roll it into a soft ball in your fingers.)
6. Pour this over the shortbread and level it carefully – a sharp tap on the table with the tray will do a good levelling job.
7. Lastly, put the chocolate into a heatproof bowl set over a pan of simmering water and stir until melted. Pour over the toffee and spread quickly before it starts to set. Draw wavy lines with the prongs of a fork down the length of the tray. Leave to set. When cold, turn the slice out and cut into small bars.

Store in an airtight tin for 3–4 days. Freezes fairly well for 1 month but the shortbread loses its crispness.

DATE AND GINGER SLICE

Will cut into 15 slices

125 g/4 oz block margarine
125 g/4 oz light soft brown sugar
125 g/4 oz black treacle
175 g/6 oz packet dates, finely chopped
150 ml/¼ pint water
225 g/8 oz plain white flour, sifted
1 teaspoon bicarbonate of soda
1 medium egg, beaten
1 heaped teaspoon finely chopped preserved ginger
½ teaspoon ground ginger

1. Grease and line the base and sides of a Swiss roll tin measuring 28 × 18 cm/11 × 7 inches, or a small roasting tin. Preheat the oven to moderately hot, Gas 5, 375°F, 190°C.
2. In a roomy pan, melt the margarine, sugar, treacle, dates and water. Stir in the flour, bicarbonate of soda, egg, preserved ginger and ground ginger. Mix well and spoon into the tin. Level off.
3. Bake for about 35 minutes, or until risen and firm to the touch. Cool in the tin for about 15 minutes then remove to a wire tray and peel off the lining papers. Cut into slices when cold.

Store in an airtight tin for 4–5 days, or freeze for up to 2 weeks.

SHORTIE GINGER SLICE

This slice has a shortbread base with a fudge-like ginger topping added afterwards.

Will cut into 16 bars

325 g/12 oz plain white flour
125 g/4 oz caster sugar
175 g/6 oz butter or block margarine

FOR THE TOPPING
75 g/3 oz butter
175 g/6 oz light soft brown sugar
1 teaspoon ground ginger

1. Lightly grease a small Swiss roll tin measuring 29 × 19 cm/11½ × 7½ inches. Preheat the oven to moderate, Gas 4, 350°F, 180°C.
2. Sift the flour into a mixing bowl and stir in the caster sugar.
3. In a small pan, melt the butter or margarine and pour into the dry ingredients. Mix well and press in an even layer into the tin.
4. Bake for 20–25 minutes, or until brown all over. Leave to cool in the tin.
5. Put the butter, sugar and ground ginger into a small, heavy-based pan over a low heat. Stir with a wooden spoon until the sugar is no longer gritty under the spoon. Bring to a gentle boil without stirring, but shaking the pan occasionally, until you can see the mixture just beginning to change into a caramel coloured fudge-like sauce.
6. Take off the heat and beat with a wooden spoon until the icing begins to thicken and go dull. Pour over the cooling shortbread and spread evenly. Allow to cool in the tin and cut into sixteen bars.

Store in an airtight tin for about 5–6 days. Not suitable for freezing.

TREACLE TART

Treacle tart is an old-fashioned favourite. Be generous with the lemon juice or you will find the filling sickly sweet. The wholewheat pastry goes well with it.

Will cut into 15 slices

225 g/8 oz wholemeal pastry *(see page 30)*
3 heaped tablespoons golden syrup
2 tablespoons fresh lemon juice
175 g/6 oz fresh breadcrumbs

1. Grease and line the base and sides of a small Swiss roll tin measuring 28 × 18 cm/11 × 7 inches. Preheat the oven to fairly hot, Gas 6, 400°F, 200°C.
2. Roll out all but 50 g/2 oz of the pastry on a lightly floured surface and line the base and sides of the tin. Trim the edges.
3. Soften the golden syrup by standing the jar in a pan of simmering water, then measure it into a mixing bowl, add the lemon juice and breadcrumbs and stir well.
4. Pour this mixture into the tin and level it off.
5. Roll out the remaining pastry to a thickness of about 5 mm/¼ inch, and use picot edging scissors, or plain scissors, to cut strips of pastry about 1 cm/½ inch wide. Lay these in a lattice design over the treacle filling.
6. Bake for about 30 minutes, or until the pastry is cooked. Allow the treacle tart to go cold, peel off the lining paper and cut into fifteen slices. Eat as soon as possible.

It stores fairly well in an airtight tin for 2–3 days but tends to go very soft. Will freeze for 2 months but again it is soft on thawing.

SPICY FLAPJACK

Will cut into 15 pieces

125 g/4 oz block margarine
2 tablespoons golden syrup
50 g/2 oz dark soft brown sugar
175 g/6 oz rolled oats (porridge oats)
25 g/1 oz coarse desiccated coconut
1 teaspoon ground cinnamon
1 heaped teaspoon sesame seeds

1. Lightly grease a shallow Swiss roll tin measuring 28 × 18 cm/11 × 7 inches. Preheat the oven to moderate, Gas 4, 350°F, 180°C.
2. Put the margarine, syrup and sugar into a roomy pan and melt over a low heat.
3. When the sugar is no longer gritty under your spoon, remove the pan from the heat and stir in the oats, coconut and cinnamon. Mix well.
4. Press this mixture into the tin, making it as level as possible but do not press down too much. Sprinkle on the sesame seeds.
5. Bake for about 20 minutes. Leave to cool for about 5 minutes, then mark out the pieces while still warm.

Store in an airtight tin for 1 week, but you will find the crispness goes. Freeze for up to 3 weeks.

TRAY BAKE SPONGE WITH COCONUT TOPPING

This is an ideal cake to bake and freeze in slices as the pieces thaw very quickly. The topping is delicious.

Will cut into 15 small pieces

175 g/6 oz plain white flour
175 g/6 oz caster sugar
1½ teaspoons baking powder
175 g/6 oz tub margarine
3 medium eggs, beaten
2 tablespoons milk

FOR THE TOPPING
50 g/2 oz tub margarine
75 g/3 oz light soft brown sugar
125 g/4 oz coarse desiccated coconut
3–4 drops vanilla essence
2 tablespoons milk

1. Grease and line the base and sides of an oblong tin like a Swiss roll tin but slightly deeper, measuring 28 × 18 cm/11 × 7 inches and 3 cm/1¼ inches deep. Preheat the oven to moderate, Gas 4, 350°F, 180°C.
2. Sift the flour into a large mixing bowl and add the sugar, baking powder, margarine, eggs and milk. Beat well until smooth.
3. Turn this mixture into the tin and bake for about 20–25 minutes, or until the cake is firm to the touch and beginning to shrink from the sides of the tin. Leave aside while you make the topping.
4. Put all the topping ingredients into a small pan over a low heat and stir until the sugar is dissolved. Spread this topping carefully over the sponge.
5. Put the sponge back in the oven for a further 10 minutes. Allow to cool in the tin then remove from the tin with the help of the lining paper. Peel off the paper and cut the sponge into small pieces.

Store in an airtight tin for 3–4 days, or freeze for up to 3 months.

FUDGE AND DATE SPONGE

This is a good recipe for a crowd. I use a roasting tin lined with nonstick or greaseproof paper. The paper is also a help when lifting the slab of cake out of the tin.

Prepare the dates well in advance to allow them to go cold.

Will cut into 24 squares or 30 bars

225 ml/8 fl oz boiling water
225 g/8 oz packet dates, stoned and finely chopped
1 teaspoon bicarbonate of soda
75 g/3 oz butter, softened
225 g/8 oz caster sugar
1 large egg, beaten
4–5 drops vanilla essence
275 g/10 oz plain white flour
1 teaspoon baking powder
1 pinch salt
125 g/4 oz walnuts, finely chopped

FOR THE TOPPING
125 g/4 oz light soft brown sugar
75 g/3 oz butter
2 tablespoons double cream or milk

1. Pour the boiling water over the dates in a large mixing bowl. Stir in the bicarbonate of soda and leave to become cold.
2. In a clean mixing bowl, cream the butter and sugar until very soft. Beat in the egg, a little at a time, and add the vanilla essence.
3. Sift the flour, baking powder and salt into the creamed mixture and fold in together with the dates and 50 g/2 oz of the walnuts.
4. Grease and line the base and sides of a large roasting tin measuring 20 × 30 cm/8 × 12 inches. Preheat the oven to moderate, Gas 3, 325°F, 160°C.
5. Pour the cake mixture into the tin and level it off.
6. Bake for 25–30 minutes, or until the cake is firm to the touch and springy. Leave in the tin to go cold.
7. Now make the fudge topping. In a small heavy-based pan, gently melt the sugar, butter and cream or milk. Bring to a gentle boil for about 2–3 minutes or until the mixture looks thick and toffee coloured. To test if the topping is at the right stage, allow the mixture to cool down when it should be the consistency of thick spreadable icing. If it is too thin, just warm it up again and boil for a further 30 seconds.
8. Allow the mixture to cool, then spread it quickly over the top of the cake in the tin. It does not need to be very smooth. Press in the remaining walnuts and allow the icing to set. Lift out of the roasting tin, using the lining paper to help, and peel off the paper. Use a very sharp knife to cut the cake into squares or bars.

Store in an airtight tin for 4–5 days, or freeze for up to 3 months.

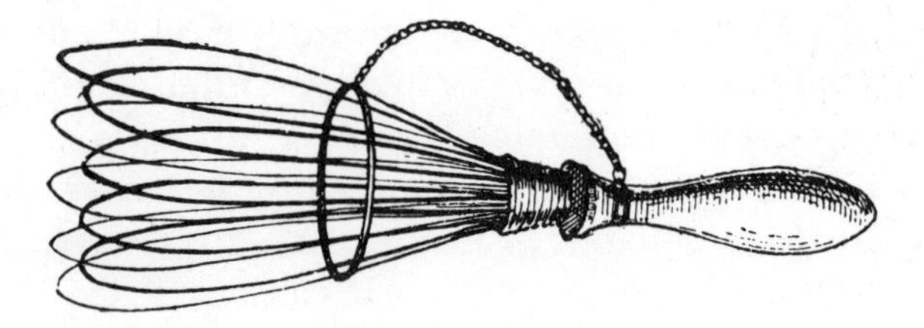

WEDDING AND CELEBRATION CAKES

Celebration cakes can be as simple or as elaborate as you wish to make them, and whereas in the past rich fruit cake was usually the base, nowadays it is just as likely to be a sponge or rice cake mixture.

Careful preparation of ingredients for expensive celebration cakes makes good sense. Anybody can put together a cake but it is the care taken in preparing high quality ingredients which will show in the finished result.

I have tried to give very simple instructions for icing the large cakes. Allow yourself plenty of time and try to do so much every day instead of rushing everything at the last minute. Take enormous care when adding liquid to icing sugar. It is extremely easy to add too much and end up with double the amount of icing you intended because you have had to add more and more icing sugar.

When it comes to adding food colourings for decoration – be a miser. Add just one drop of colour at a time. An old fashioned eye dropper is good for this, or a skewer.

All the cakes in this section can be adapted or personalized for various occasions – just use your imagination and select appropriate trimmings and decorations.

ROUND THREE-TIER WEDDING CAKE

Deciding to make a wedding cake, especially a tiered one, is an ambitious and expensive project. By making it yourself, however, you can save almost half the cost of a shop-bought one, although, if you want an elaborately iced cake, I strongly recommend that you seek out a skilled amateur or professional icer. Be sure to have a good look at his/her work before you give an order. I have seen a tiered cake topple at a wedding.

It should not be necessary to buy tins; many kitchenware shops will hire these for a small charge. Otherwise a quick visit to all your baking friends, with a tape measure in your hand, might very well produce all the tins you need. Check that your oven will take the largest cake tin easily.

The cake I have designed for you needs the minimum of icing skills. Of course these can always be enhanced by the careful use of silk flowers, heather sprays, silver shoes, bells and horseshoes. You can also buy sugar roses in many colours.

The weight-bearing tops of the tiers of a wedding cake are usually iced with three layers of very hard royal icing – that is, made without glycerine. This supports the cake well but makes it difficult when it comes to the cutting of the cake by the bride and groom, or later when the cake is being cut up for the guests. I have suggested a way round this by the use of thin silver cake cards on top of the two weight-bearing tiers, i.e. the bottom and middle, on which the pillars are placed. By doing this the weight is more evenly distributed. This method was suggested to me by a very skilled cake maker in my village, Thora Aykroyd, and I think it is a sensible idea for an amateur.

You can make your own marzipan or you can buy it ready-made. There is not much difference in the price. Take care if you buy it that the marzipan is still soft and pliable and not old stock. Look for natural coloured marzipan and not the very canary yellow kind.

Do try out the cake mixture first by baking the smallest cake. Note how it bakes in your oven and, by tasting it, decide whether or not to alter the recipe slightly.

ROUND THREE-TIER WEDDING CAKE

Tin size	***Bottom cake*** **Makes 1 round cake 30 cm/12 inches across and 7.5 cm/3 inches deep**	***Middle cake*** **Makes 1 round cake 23 cm/9 inches across and approx. 6 cm/2½ inches deep**	***Top cake*** **Makes 1 round cake 18 cm/7 inches across and approx. 6 cm/2½ inches deep**
Ingredients			
Vostizza currants	1 kg/2¼ lb	400 g/14 oz	225 g/8 oz
Seedless raisins	800 g/1¾ lb	325 g/12 oz	200 g/7 oz
Glacé cherries	275 g/10 oz	140 g/4½ oz	50 g/2 oz
Whole almonds	200 g/7 oz	50 g/2 oz	25 g/1 oz
Plain flour	675 g/1½ lb	300 g/11 oz	175 g/6 oz
Butter	600 g/1 lb 5 oz	250 g/9 oz	150 g/5 oz
Caster or soft brown sugar	600 g/1 lb 5 oz	250 g/9 oz	150 g/5 oz
Large eggs	11	4	2½
Lemon rind	4 teaspoons	3 teaspoons	2 teaspoons
Crystallized orange peel (*see page 253*)	200 g/7 oz	75 g/3 oz	25 g/1 oz
Mixed spice	2 teaspoons	½ teaspoon	¼ teaspoon
Cinnamon	2 teaspoons	½ teaspoon	¼ teaspoon
Brandy	3 tablespoons	2 tablespoons	1 tablespoon
Gravy browning	2–3 drops	2–3 drops	2 drops
A little extra brandy			
Approx. baking time	6½–7 hours	3–3½ hours	2½–3 hours
Servings	90–100	40–50	25–30
Bought marzipan	1.1 kg/2½ lb	800 g/1¾ lb	450 g/1 lb
OR			
Home-made marzipan			
Ground almonds	575 g/1¼ lb	450 g/1 lb	225 g/8 oz
Icing sugar, sifted	325 g/12 oz	225 g/8 oz	125 g/4 oz
Caster sugar	325 g/12 oz	225 g/8 oz	125 g/4 oz
Lemon juice	3 teaspoons	2 teaspoons	1 teaspoon
Almond essence	4–5 drops	3–4 drops	2–3 drops
Ratafia essence	4–5 drops	3–4 drops	2–3 drops
Beaten egg	1 large egg plus 1 small egg	1 large egg	1 small egg

To apply marzipan to the cakes
1 egg white or sieved apricot jam or glaze (*see page 248*)
Greaseproof paper
Nonstick paper
A little cornflour, for dusting

Royal Icing			
Egg whites	6	3	2
Icing sugar	1.3 kg/3 lb	675 g/1½ lb	450 g/1 lb
Glycerine	3 teaspoons	1½ teaspoons	1 teaspoon
Lemon juice	3 teaspoons	1½ teaspoons	1 teaspoon

ALSO NEEDED			
	1 round silver drum board 37.5 cm/15 inches across	1 round silver drum board 28 cm/11 inches across	1 round silver drum board 18 cm/7 inches across
	1 round silver cake card 23 cm/9 inches across	1 round silver cake card 18 cm/7 inches across	
	4 × 9-cm/3½-inch tall plaster or plastic pillars	4 × 7.5-cm/3-inch tall plaster or plastic pillars	
	1 small spray of flowers	1 small spray of flowers	Silver vase and spray of flowers

PLUS

3 metres/3⅓ yards of 1-cm/½-inch wide fancy silver banding
7 metres/7⅔ yards of fine white baby ribbon cut in 25-cm/10-inch lengths
Roll of greaseproof paper
Greaseproof paper icing bags
Plain icing nozzles sizes small, medium, large
Metal or plastic ruler
Long palette knife
Plastic scraper

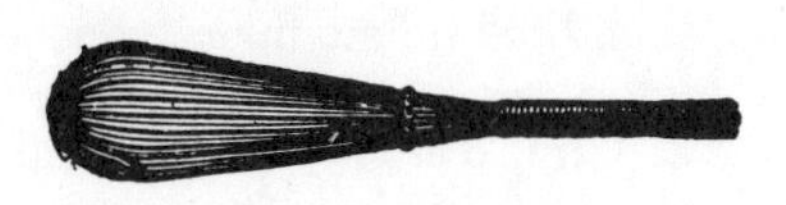

TIMETABLE

1. Make the cakes about 2–3 months before the wedding.
2. Coat the cakes with a layer of marzipan 3–4 weeks before the wedding. Bear in mind that the marzipaned cakes have to dry out for 7–10 days before you start the royal icing, so that the oils in the marzipan do not seep into the icing.
3. Aim to ice the cakes about 2 weeks before the actual day.
4. Assemble the cake on the morning of the wedding.

MAKING THE CAKES

Use the same method for all three cakes, but bake just one cake at a time, unless you have a fan oven and are absolutely certain it will bake evenly with more than one cake in the oven without moving them around.

PREPARATION

TINS

1. Wash the cake tins, being particularly careful to use a brush in the corners, then dry them. Melt a little solid vegetable oil and brush a thin film over the inside of each tin. Fully line the tins with greaseproof paper (*see page 21*).
2. Prepare a thick collar of folded brown paper to go round the outside of each tin.
3. Set aside a thick sheet of cardboard to go between the cake tin and the baking tray. All these precautions are to protect the cake during baking.

INGREDIENTS

Start the day before.

1. Prepare the Vostizza currants. They come in two sizes: pinhead and small – either will do. Larger currants are often very seedy so avoid them. I also like to wash currants – they seem to need it. Just pour boiling water over them, give them a stir and leave them until they are cool enough to handle. Give them one more stir and squeeze out the water by taking them up in handfuls. Spread them in a deep roasting tin to dry, blot off some more moisture with kitchen paper and leave in a warm place overnight.
2. I do not wash the raisins but I do like them chopped to the size of currants. Chop about 225/8 oz at a time in a food processor. Watch carefully, it only takes seconds. Otherwise, put them in a narrow straight-sided container like a jug and chop them roughly with scissors.
3. Cut the cherries in two and rinse them in warm water, then drain them and dry well on kitchen paper. Chop small.
4. Pour boiling water over the almonds, leave for 3–4 minutes then slip off their skins. Dry the nuts and chop small.

TO BAKE EACH CAKE (USING THE INGREDIENTS SHOWN IN THE CHART OPPOSITE)

1. Preheat the oven to cool, Gas 2, 300°F, 150°C.
2. Sift the flour into a mixing bowl.
3. In a large mixing bowl, cream the butter until soft then add the sugar and beat until light and fluffy.
4. Beat the eggs, a little at a time, into the creamed mixture, adding a spoonful of the measured flour if the mixture shows signs of separating.
5. Fold in the rest of the flour, followed by the fruit, nuts, lemon rind, orange peel, spices and brandy. Add 2–3 drops of gravy browning to ensure you get a good dark colour. Mix thoroughly.
6. Spoon the mixture into the prepared tin and press down carefully. Make a slight hollow in the centre of the mixture to help ensure an even rise.
7. Line a baking tray with a thick piece of cardboard and set the tin on the cardboard. Surround the tin with the collar of folded brown paper and staple this in position, or use a paperclip.
8. Bake the cake on the lowest shelf of the oven for about half the cooking time (*see chart*). Reduce the heat to Gas 1, 275°F, 130°C, for the remainder of the time. If the top of the cake is getting very brown, cover it with a sheet of greaseproof paper. When

the cake has finished cooking, it will be firm on top with no wobble underneath, and be starting to shrink away from the sides of the tin.

9. Leave the cake to firm up in the tin for at least 1 hour, then turn out carefully onto a wire tray. Peel off the papers when cold. Introduce the extra brandy if you wish by pricking the cake with a fine skewer all over and dribbling in the brandy. You can do this again during the storage period prior to the wedding. Wrap the cake well in greaseproof paper then in foil. Store away from heat.

MAKING THE MARZIPAN

Make up the marzipan for each cake separately, using the quantities shown in the chart on page 222.

1. Place the dry ingredients in a mixing bowl and mix well.

2. Add the essences and just enough beaten egg to give a firm consistency. Be extremely careful to add only a minute quantity of egg at a time or you may have to add more ground almonds to ensure the right consistency – it should be fairly stiff. Knead in the bowl until smooth. Wrap in clingfilm until needed. It will keep in good condition for 4–5 days.

COVERING THE CAKES

1. If the top of the cake is not level, take a sharp knife and slice off the risen piece. Turn the cake over and use the bottom as the top. Using the baking tin as a guide, draw a circle the size of the cake top on greaseproof paper. Cut just inside the line you draw. Again using the tin as a guide, wrap a piece of paper halfway round it to use as a pattern. Make it 7.5 cm/3 inches deep for the top cake and 6 cm/2½ inches deep for the other two cakes.

2. Dust your working surface with cornflour. Take about two-thirds of the marzipan and roll it out in a long strip to a thickness of between 3–5 mm/⅛–¼ inch. Using the paper pattern for the side of the cake, and a ruler to get a really straight line, cut out one strip. Gather up the trimmings, reroll and cut a second strip. Using a pastry brush, paint the surface of the two strips with egg white or sieved apricot jam.

3. There are two ways to apply the two strips of marzipan to the cake. You can either hold the cake like a wheel and roll it onto the marzipan, or you can take each strip of marzipan up in the palm of your hand and wrap it around the cake. Either way, press the marzipan firmly to the cake and make very clean joins then smooth it over with a flat knife. The marzipan should completely cover the side of the cake and the top edge should be straight. Use a straight sided jam jar or rolling pin and roll it round the marzipan to get a smooth result.

4. Take the trimmings from the strips and reroll them into the remaining marzipan. Dust a piece of nonstick paper with cornflour. Using the circle of greaseproof paper as a guide, roll out the marzipan to fit the top of the cake.

5. Paint the surface of the cake with egg white or sieved apricot jam and lay the marzipan on it. The paper is particularly helpful with a large cake as you can lift the marzipan on it easily and slide it into place. (Another way of getting the marzipan onto the top of the cake is to invert the cake and press it down on the circle of marzipan. You cannot, of course, do this with a large cake.)

6. Take the rolling pin and lightly smooth over the top of the cake. Trim neatly, cover the cake lightly with tissue paper, and leave in a cool place to dry off. Repeat the process with the other cakes.

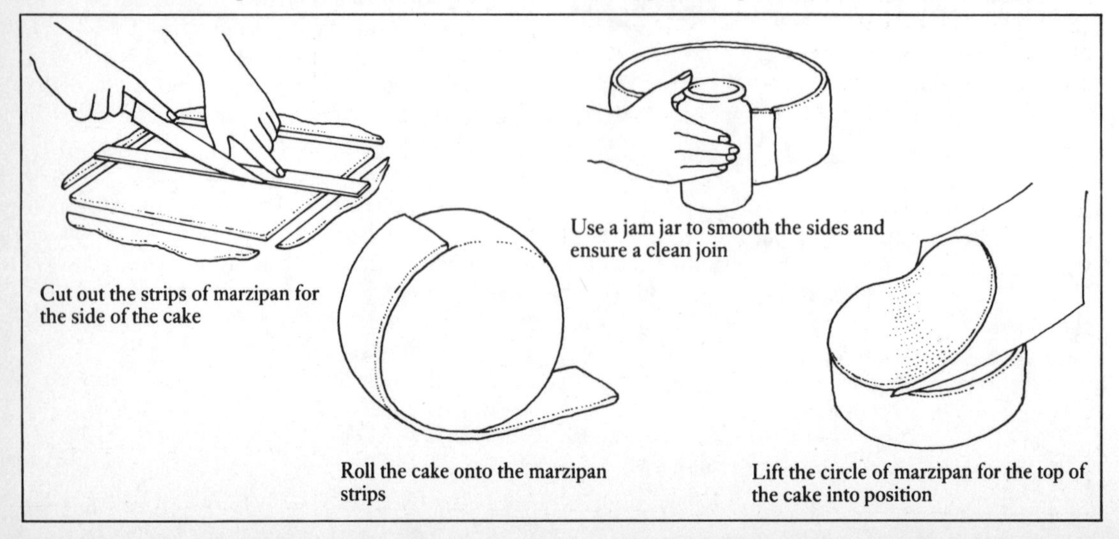

Cut out the strips of marzipan for the side of the cake

Use a jam jar to smooth the sides and ensure a clean join

Roll the cake onto the marzipan strips

Lift the circle of marzipan for the top of the cake into position

ICING THE CAKES

It is better to ice the top and sides on different days, or ice all the tops one day and the sides the next. An icing turntable is very useful when doing the sides of the cakes, but an upturned plate is a fair substitute. A palette knife or ruler, slightly longer than the cake, and a plastic scraper are also useful.

Keep the icing covered with a clean, damp cloth while you are working with it (*see page 243*).

MAKING THE ROYAL ICING

1. Put the egg whites into a large mixing bowl and break them up lightly with a fork. Add the icing sugar 1 tablespoon at a time and beat with a wooden spoon. Continue beating and adding more icing sugar. A spatula is handy to push the icing back down into the bowl.
2. With the last tablespoon of icing sugar, add the glycerine and the lemon juice. The texture is about right when you can pull the wooden spoon up sharply and the icing forms soft peaks. Cover and set aside for 3–4 hours, or overnight if possible, to allow the bubbles to rise and disperse.

TO ICE THE TOP OF THE CAKE

1. Place the cake on a flat, non-slip surface (not the turntable or plate). Take up about half the total amount of icing you need for the cake and spread it on the top, taking it right to the edge. It is easier to achieve a smooth result by putting on too much and skimming it off again, using the palette knife or ruler.
2. Hold the ruler with both hands at an angle and draw it smoothly from the back of the cake to the front. Scrape the surplus icing back into the bowl and cover. You may have to do this several times until you get a fairly smooth thin layer of icing. Take a knife and, holding it parallel to the side of the cake, skim off any icing which has crept over the edge.

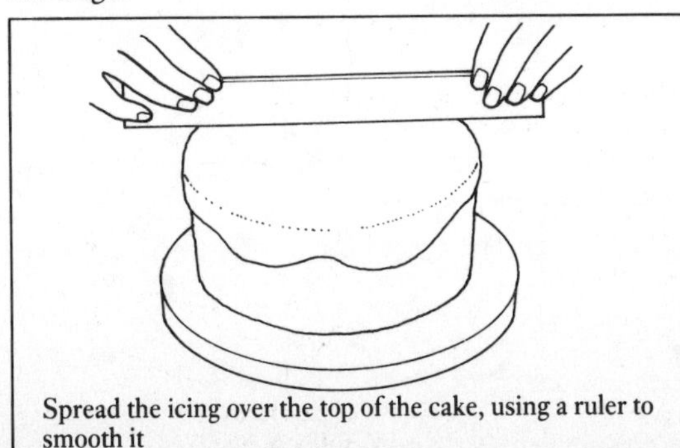

Spread the icing over the top of the cake, using a ruler to smooth it

TO ICE THE SIDES OF THE CAKE

1. Next day, put a spoonful of icing onto the appropriate drum board and settle the cake onto it. This will help to keep the cake in position. Put the board with the cake on it onto the icing turntable. Spread a layer of icing all round the side of the cake. Take the plastic scraper and hold the straight edge at an angle of 45° to the cake. Starting at the back of the cake, rotate the cake with your left hand and smooth the icing all round with the scraper. You may have to do this once or twice. Scrape away any icing left on the drum board.
2. The following day, take a sharp knife and cut away any bumps or rough edges. You can also use clean fine sandpaper for a smooth finish, brushing the surface clean with a pastry brush.
3. For the second and final coat, repeat the whole process but, since the first coat is now quite hard, you can apply more pressure to get a smooth result. Set aside to dry off. When the icing is set, cover lightly with tissue paper. Repeat the process with the other two cakes.

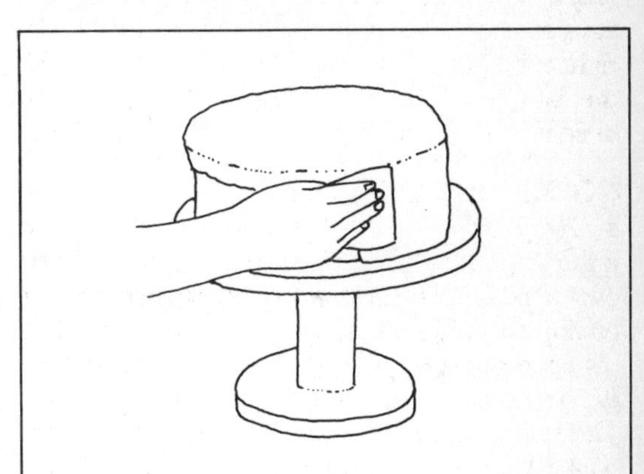

Smooth the icing round the sides of the cake using a plastic scraper

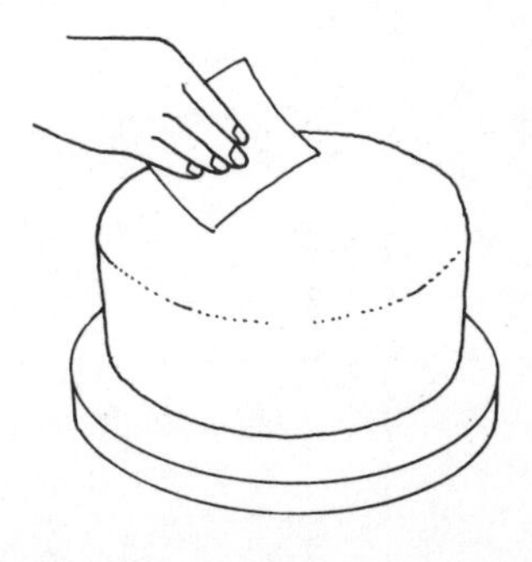

Use fine sandpaper to smooth away any bumps on the icing

DECORATING THE CAKES

When decorating with royal icing, only small quantities are used at a time. It is not easy working with large piping bags of icing. You should wash out the nozzle and fill a fresh bag for each batch of icing.

1. Measure the depth of each cake. They should be:

Bottom cake – 9 cm/3½ inches
Middle cake – 7.5 cm/3 inches
Top cake – 7.5 cm/3 inches

Cut three strips of greaseproof paper long enough to go round each cake, the depths as above. Fold each strip for the bottom and middle cakes into eight sections. Fold the strip for the top cake into six sections.

2. Fasten the paper strips round the cakes, securing with sellotape, and, using a pin or a needle, pierce rows of holes through each crease line to divide the sides into six for the top cake and eight for the middle and bottom cakes. Ensure the holes are clearly visible on the icing then remove the paper strips.

3. Using the pin or needle and a ruler, measure and mark the dots and triangles as shown in the diagram. Drop a medium writing tube with plain nozzle into a greaseproof paper cone, and snip off the tip of the cone to allow the metal tube to come through. Half fill the paper cone with icing and fold the open end up very tightly. Tilt the cake and wedge at an angle to help with the icing.

4. To pipe the straight lines, use two hands on the bag. Place the point of the nozzle where the straight line is to begin, hold the bag at an angle of 45° and apply slight pressure to the icing bag. As the icing starts to flow, lift the bag up about 2.5 cm/1 inch above the cake and allow the line of icing to be suspended. About 1 cm/½ inch before the line is to finish, stop squeezing and gently lower the tip of the nozzle to the cake. A little practice is required to get some speed up. Basically you touch down where you want to start, allow the icing to sag a little then touch down at the end. Just remember to stop the pressure on the bag before the last descent.

5. Using the same medium writing tube with a plain nozzle, pipe in the dots as shown below. To pipe these, hold the point of the nozzle upright on the surface of the cake. Squeeze the icing bag slightly and, at the same time, lift the nozzle to form a nice round dot. (Different sizes of dots can be made by varying the pressure on the icing bag.)

6. The next step is to pipe the icing scribbles inside the triangles. This is an easy way to cover up

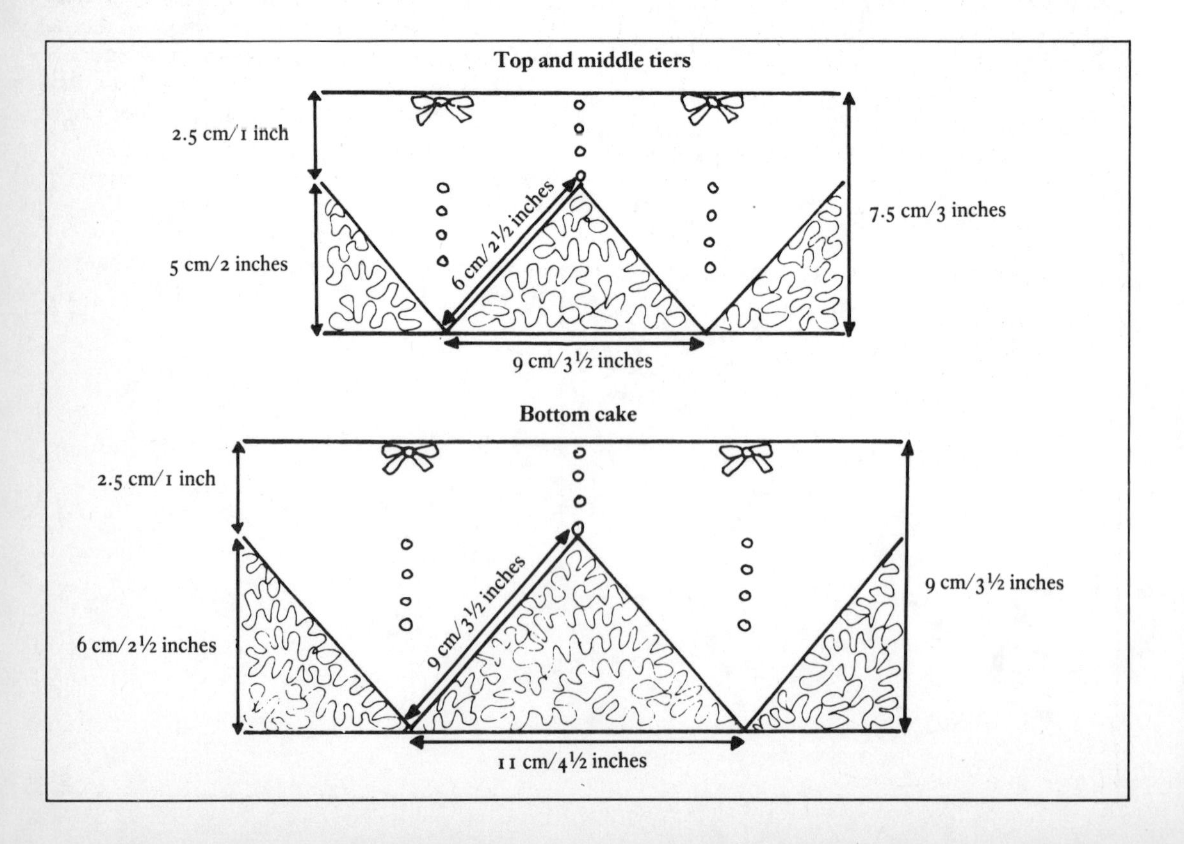

less than perfect icing and they look very pretty and lacy. Using the medium writing tube with a plain nozzle, pipe a continuous wiggle by holding the nozzle quite close to the cake and squeezing gently all the time. Fill in the triangles as shown on page 226. Repeat for each cake.

7. To decorate the bottom edge of the bottom cake, use a slightly larger writing tube with a plain nozzle. Pipe quite strong large decorative dots close to the bottom of the cake and overlapping the silver drum board.

8. Still working on the bottom cake, put the larger thin silver cake card in position on top of the cake – paint some icing over the base so that it will stick in position. Press it down, using a weight if necessary. Using the same larger writing tube, pipe strong even dots round the edge of the silver card. Repeat this edging on the outside edge of the cake.

9. Now move on to the middle cake and, using the medium writing tube, again pipe large decorative dots close to the bottom of the cake and overlapping the silver drum board. Stick the smaller thin silver cake card in position on top of the cake, as before, and press it down. Using the same larger writing tube, again pipe strong even dots onto the cake round the edge of the silver card and around the outside edge.

10. For the top tier, use the medium writing tube to pipe decorative dots close to the bottom of the cake and overlapping the silver drum board. Using the same writing tube, pipe one row of dots only onto the top of the cake around the outside edge.

11. Make the ribbon bows, using the white baby ribbon, and fix them in position on the cakes as shown on page 226, using a spot of icing.

12. Now that the cakes are finished, cover them lightly with tissue paper and set them aside for two weeks to dry out thoroughly. After two weeks, have a practice run and assemble the cake. Line up the decorative design on each cake with the one below and, using the pillars, assemble the tiers. Mark the position of the pillars on the cake cards so that it will be easy to do on the morning of the wedding. Take the cake apart and store carefully.

13. On the morning of the wedding, set the bottom cake on the cake stand and centre it carefully. Assemble the other two tiers and position a small spray of flowers between the pillars on both the bottom and middle cakes. Place the silver vase and matching flowers in the centre of the top tier. Attach the decorative silver banding to the edges of the drum boards with a little glue or sellotape.

STORING THE TOP TIER

According to custom, the top tier of the wedding cake is kept for the first christening. For long-term storage, the best thing to do is to remove all the icing and marzipan and store only the fruit cake. Wrap it well, first in greaseproof paper and then in foil. Or, it can go into a rigid box in the freezer.

To store part of a cake with the icing and marzipan intact, wrap well in greaseproof paper and foil but eat within 8–9 weeks.

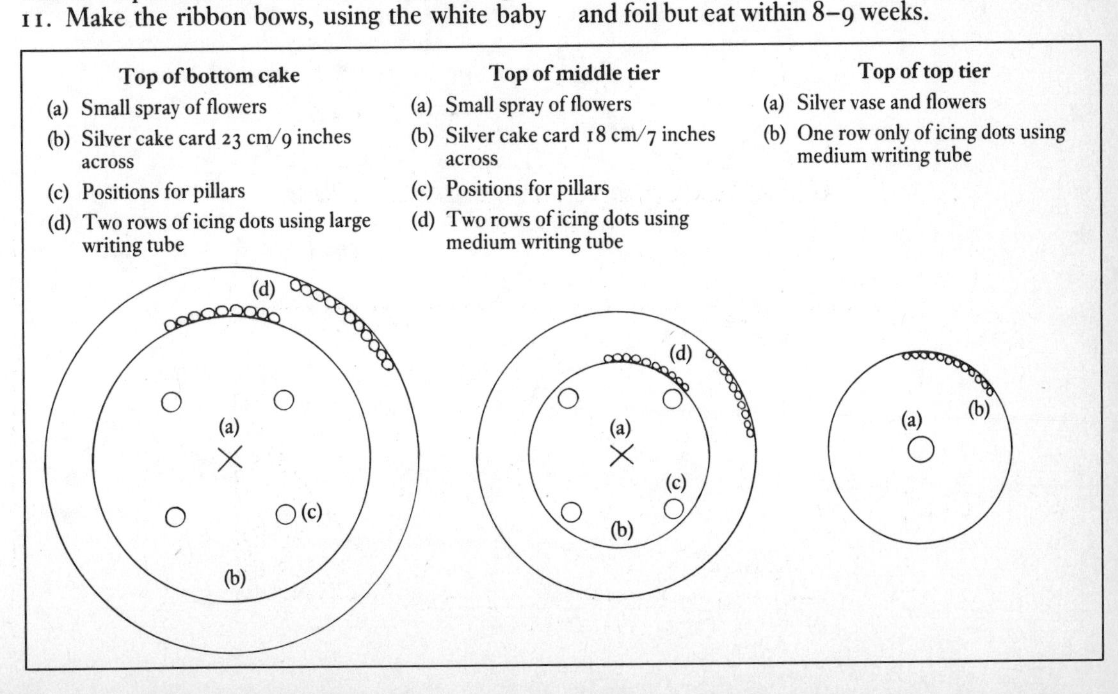

SQUARE WEDDING CAKE – ONE TIER

This single-tier wedding cake uses the same recipe as the bottom cake of the three-tier cake on page 222. However, the cake is baked in a 28-cm/11-inch square tin and the decoration for the top of the cake is more elaborate. Refer to the timetable on page 223 for applying the marzipan and icing.

Makes 1 × 28-cm/11-inch square cake (approximately 90 servings)

Ingredients and preparation for cake, marzipan and royal icing as for 30-cm/12-inch bottom cake *(see chart on page 222)*

ALSO NEEDED:

1 × 28-cm/11-inch square tin, lined *(see page 21)*
1 medium-sized star icing nozzle
1 × 35-cm/14-inch square silver drum board
68 silk flowers – very dainty ones, no bigger than 1 cm/½ inch across*
3 metres/3⅓ yds fine white baby ribbon, cut into 25-cm/10-inch lengths
3¼ metres/3⅔ yds of 1-cm/½-inch silver fancy banding
Silver vase and matching silk flowers for top

* *These are usually sold in sprays at florist shops and you have to cut them up yourself.*

1. Make the cake, following the instructions on page 223, and bake in the square tin.
2. Make up the marzipan (*see page 224*), cover it and set aside.
3. Cut out a square of greaseproof paper to fit the top of the cake – it should measure about 28 cm/11 inches square. Make a paper pattern of one of the sides of the cake – it should measure about 28 cm/11 inches long and 5 cm/2 inches deep.
4. Take about two-thirds of the marzipan and roll it out in a long strip to a thickness of about 3–5 mm/⅛–¼ inch. Using the pattern for the side of the cake, cut out four pieces. Using a pastry brush, paint the sides of the cake with a little egg white or apricot glaze and stick the marzipan strips in position. Check that the corners are neat and, using a straight-sided jar or rolling pin, smooth down the marzipan.
5. Roll out the remaining marzipan and, using the paper pattern for the top of the cake, cut out the square. Using a pastry brush, paint the top of the cake with egg white or apricot glaze. Lift the marzipan onto the rolling pin and lay it on the top of the cake. Check that all the edges of the marzipan meet and squeeze them gently together. Give the top of the marzipan a final light rolling using the jar or rolling pin.
6. Leave the cake uncovered, or very lightly covered, to dry out for about two weeks.
7. About two weeks before the wedding, give the cake two coats of royal icing, following the instructions on page 225. By the time the cake is baked, and covered with marzipan and two layers of royal icing it will probably measure about 30 cm/12 inches square.

DECORATING THE SIDES

Measure and mark out the design (*see below*), using a series of pin dots to make the outline. The black lines are piped with a medium size icing nozzle and the scribble icing is done with the same icing nozzle. See page 227 for detailed suggestions for doing this icing. The series of dots can also now be done. Leave the ribbon bows to the end.

DECORATING THE TOP

The design for the top of the square cake echoes the design for the sides. The whole thing can be measured out and marked with a ruler (*see page 229*). Use a pin to mark out the lines. Mark out the

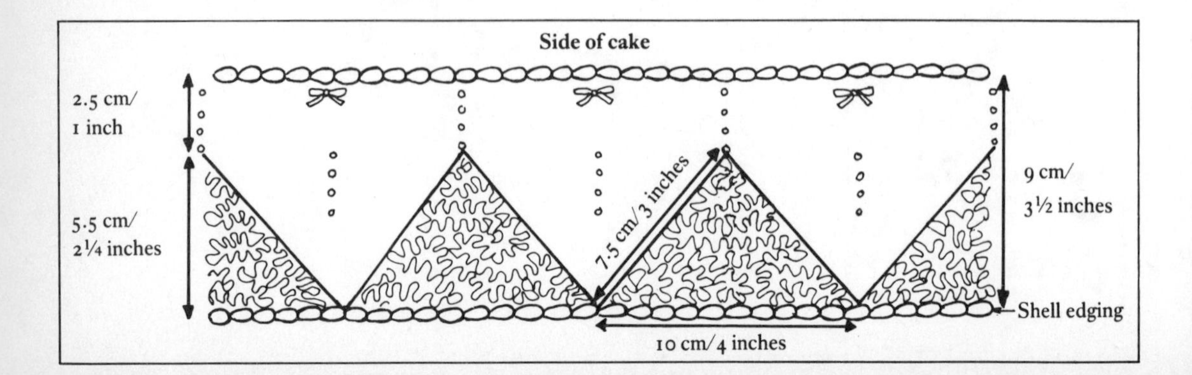

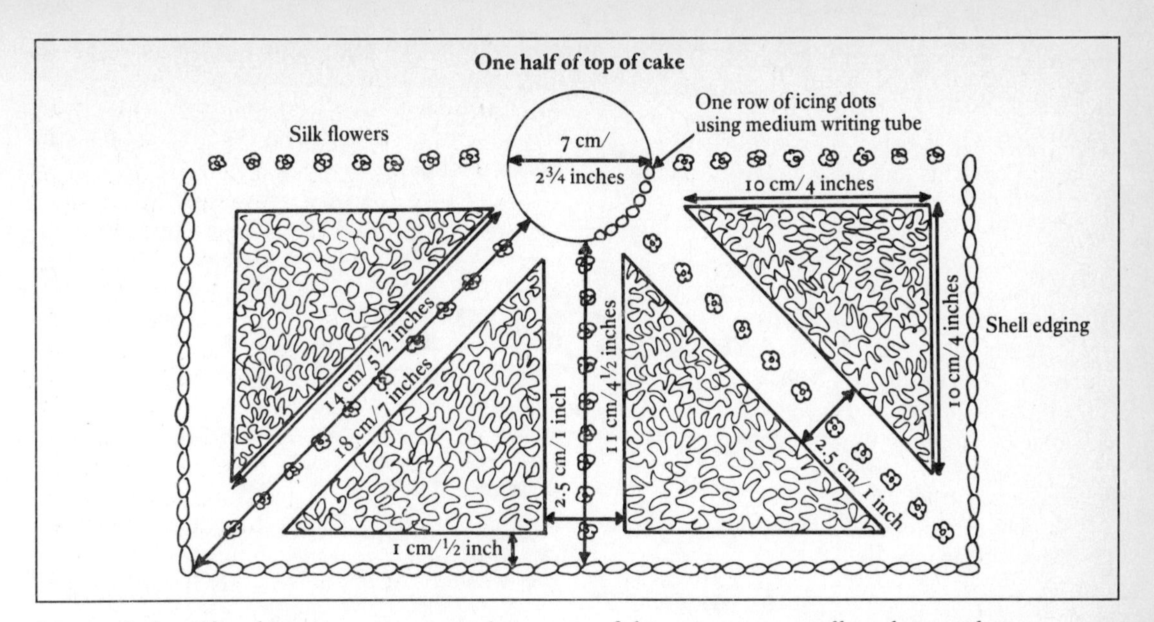

centre circle with a biscuit cutter measuring 7.5 cm/3 inches across. Pipe the straight lines marked in black using the medium size plain icing nozzle. Use the same icing nozzle to do the scribble icing inside the black lines. Now fix the silk flowers in rows as shown above. A small spot of icing on the back of each one will be enough. Then, once attached, another small dot of icing in the centre of each flower will finish it off nicely. Finish off the bottom edge of the cake and the outer top edge with a strong shell edging. Use a medium size star nozzle for this. See that the icing when piped holds the design and does not sink into a blob. Beat more icing sugar into the royal icing to stiffen it up a bit so that when a wooden spoon is pulled away sharply the peak it forms stays up.

PIPING THE SHELL BORDERS

1. Pipe the shells around the base of the cake first. Put the star nozzle in an icing bag and cut off the tip of the paper cone to allow the metal star to come through. Half fill the icing bag with royal icing and fold the open end securely.
2. Holding the nozzle at a slight angle to the surface of the cake and just above it, squeeze the icing out until a blob of icing is formed at the bottom of the cake, slightly overlapping the silver drum board. Gradually release the pressure and pull away to leave a well formed shell. A border is achieved by piping a series of shells which very slightly overlap each other.
3. Pipe the same edging on the top outer edge of the cake.
4. Cover the cake lightly and set it aside to dry in a cool place.
5. Lastly, make up the tiny bows, using the baby ribbon, and fix them in position on the sides of the cake with a blob of icing. Glue the silver fancy banding to the outer edge of the cake board. Place the silver vase and flowers in the centre circle on top of the cake.

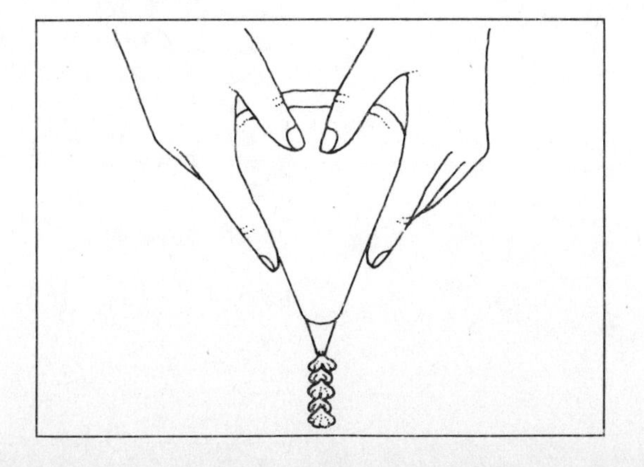

CHRISTENING CAKE

This moist cake is based on cherries and ginger instead of currants and raisins, and is decorated with butterflies and flowers. If you prefer the traditional fruit cake, use the recipe for the middle tier of the wedding cake on page 222.

I am using fondant icing without marzipan for this cake but there is no reason why you should not add this extra layer if you choose. Again, the recipe and instructions for making both are on pages 224 and 245. Fondant can also be bought ready-made.

If you are using a loose-bottomed tin, grease in the usual way but line only the base of the tin with a circle of greaseproof paper.

The flowers can be made from fondant icing as described, or use tiny silk flowers.

Makes 1 × 23-cm/9-inch round cake (approximately 24 servings)

125 g/4 oz crystallized ginger
275 g/10 oz self-raising white flour
125 g/4 oz ground almonds
50 g/2 oz whole almonds, skinned and chopped
325 g/12 oz glacé cherries – red, yellow and green, halved, washed, dried and finely chopped
275 g/10 oz butter, softened
275 g/10 oz caster sugar
4 large eggs, beaten
1 teaspoon glacé icing, made with 1 teaspoon icing sugar and 2–3 drops of water
A little cornflour
1.1 kg/2½ lb fondant icing *(see page 245)*, **for the cake, plus 225 g/8 oz fondant icing for the butterflies and flowers**
Pink or blue food colouring
3 tablespoons apricot jam, sieved
Green food colouring

TO DECORATE
Greaseproof paper, for tracing
1 piece thick card
1 × 28-cm/11-inch round silver drum board
Foam sponge
1-cm/½-inch wide plunger cutter for fondant flowers, or 84 tiny silk flowers about 1 cm/½ inch across*
450 g/1 lb icing sugar, sifted
A little egg white
Green food colouring
No. 1 writing tube, for lettering, grass and flower centres
Greaseproof paper icing bags *(see page 243)*
1 metre/1⅛ yds of 1-cm/½-inch silver fancy banding

* *If you are using silk flowers, take care to look for really tiny ones. They are usually sold in sprays at florist shops and you have to cut them up yourself.*

TO MAKE THE CAKE

1. Grease and line the base and sides of a 23-cm/9-inch round tin, or the base only if using a loose-bottomed tin. Preheat the oven to moderate, Gas 4, 350°F, 180°C.
2. Prepare the ginger by washing off the sugar and drying the ginger really well, then chop it into small pieces.
3. Sift the flour into a large mixing bowl and stir in the ground almonds, chopped almonds, ginger and cherries. Mix well.
4. In another large mixing bowl, cream the butter using a wooden spoon, then add the sugar and beat until the mixture is light and fluffy. Add the eggs a little at a time, beating well between each addition. Using a strong spatula, mix and fold in the flour mixture.
5. Spoon the mixture into the tin and level the surface. Bake for 1 hour then reduce the heat to Gas 3, 325°F, 160°C, and bake for a further 30 minutes or until the cake is firm and beginning to shrink from the sides of the tin.
6. Leave to firm up in the tin for about 15 minutes then turn out onto a wire tray. Leave the paper on until the cake is almost cold, then remove. The undecorated cake will store, well wrapped in greaseproof paper and then in foil, in an airtight tin for about 1 week. It freezes well but use after 1 month.

If you are going to use a covering of marzipan, this is the stage at which you should apply it (*see page 224*).

TO COVER THE CAKE WITH FONDANT ICING

1. If the cake has a domed surface, take a sharp knife and trim to level the surface. Put a spoonful of very wet glacé icing in the middle of the silver drum board, turn the cake over and set it in position on the board.
2. To colour the 1.1 kg/2½ lb fondant either very pale pink or very pale blue, work 2–3 drops of the appropriate food colouring into the soft icing. Pull, roll and fold until the colour is evenly spread. Be very miserly in adding the colouring – it is extremely easy to get the icing too vivid.
3. Warm the apricot jam by standing the jar in a pan of hot water. Brush the jam lightly over the whole cake.
4. Dust the working surface with cornflour, and roll out the icing to a circle about 32.5 cm/13 inches across. Quickly drape the icing over your rolling pin and position it on the cake. Dust your hands with cornflour and gently smooth and ease the icing into the sides of the cake. Trim off any excess icing with a sharp knife, put it into a plastic bag and keep tightly wrapped. Use to make the flower decorations, if necessary.

If by chance the icing tears, you can usually patch up the tear by working the torn edges together with a little water. If it tears badly it means the icing is just too hot and fragile. Carefully lift it off the cake – try to avoid lifting the jam, too. Roll up the icing and leave in the fridge to cool, then start all over again.

TO DECORATE THE CAKE

1. Refer to the diagrams on page 232. Trace the shape of the butterfly onto a piece of greaseproof paper. Turn the paper over and trace again onto a piece of thickish card. Cut out the shape carefully.
2. Roll out the remaining 225 g/8 oz fondant until it is about 3 mm/⅛ inch thick, or a little thicker. Place the butterfly shape on the icing and cut out seven butterflies.
3. To put the butterflies evenly onto the side of the cake, cut a strip of greaseproof paper 69 cm/27 inches long and 5 cm/2 inches wide. Fold the strip into six even sections and crease the folds. Open this out and place it round the cake, securing with sellotape. Using a skewer or a pin, pierce rows of holes through each crease line. Ensure the holes are clearly visible on the icing then remove the paper. Fix one butterfly on each crease line, keeping them about 5 mm/¼ inch from the bottom of the cake. A little brush of water should be enough to secure the butterflies. Put the one remaining butterfly on the top of the cake on the left hand side.
4. If you are making fondant flowers, cut them out now so that they can dry off a bit and be easy to handle. Gather up the white fondant trimmings of the butterflies and colour one half either pink or blue, the opposite colour to that of the cake covering. Unwrap the reserved fondant trimmings from the cake. Roll out these three pieces of fondant – white, pink and blue – so that they are about 3 mm/⅛ inch thick.

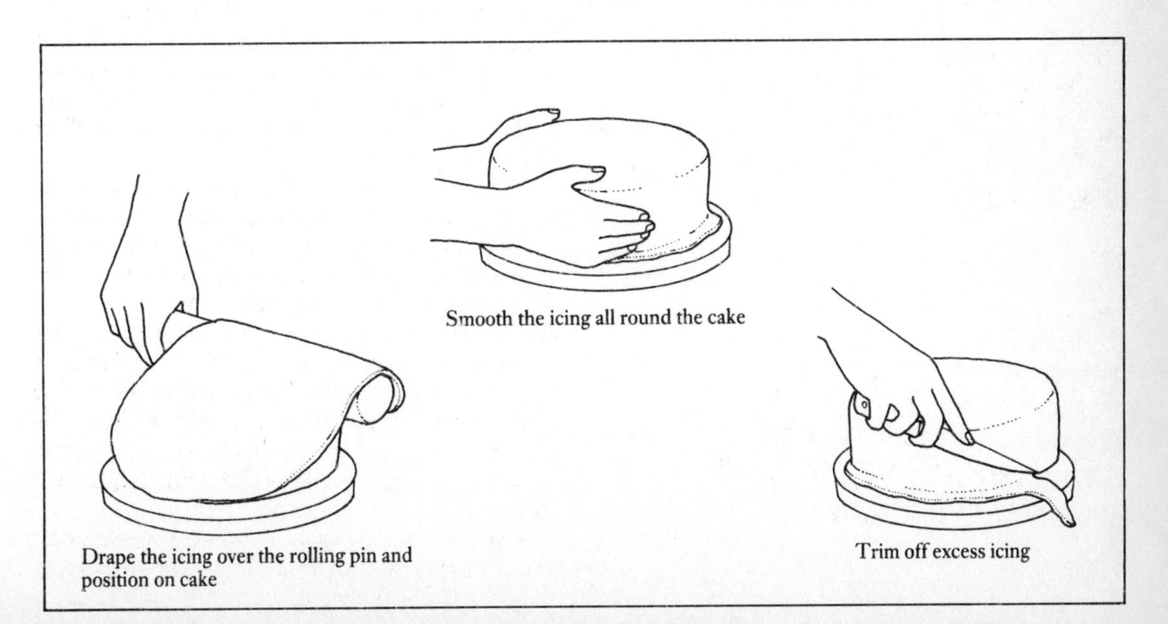

Smooth the icing all round the cake

Drape the icing over the rolling pin and position on cake

Trim off excess icing

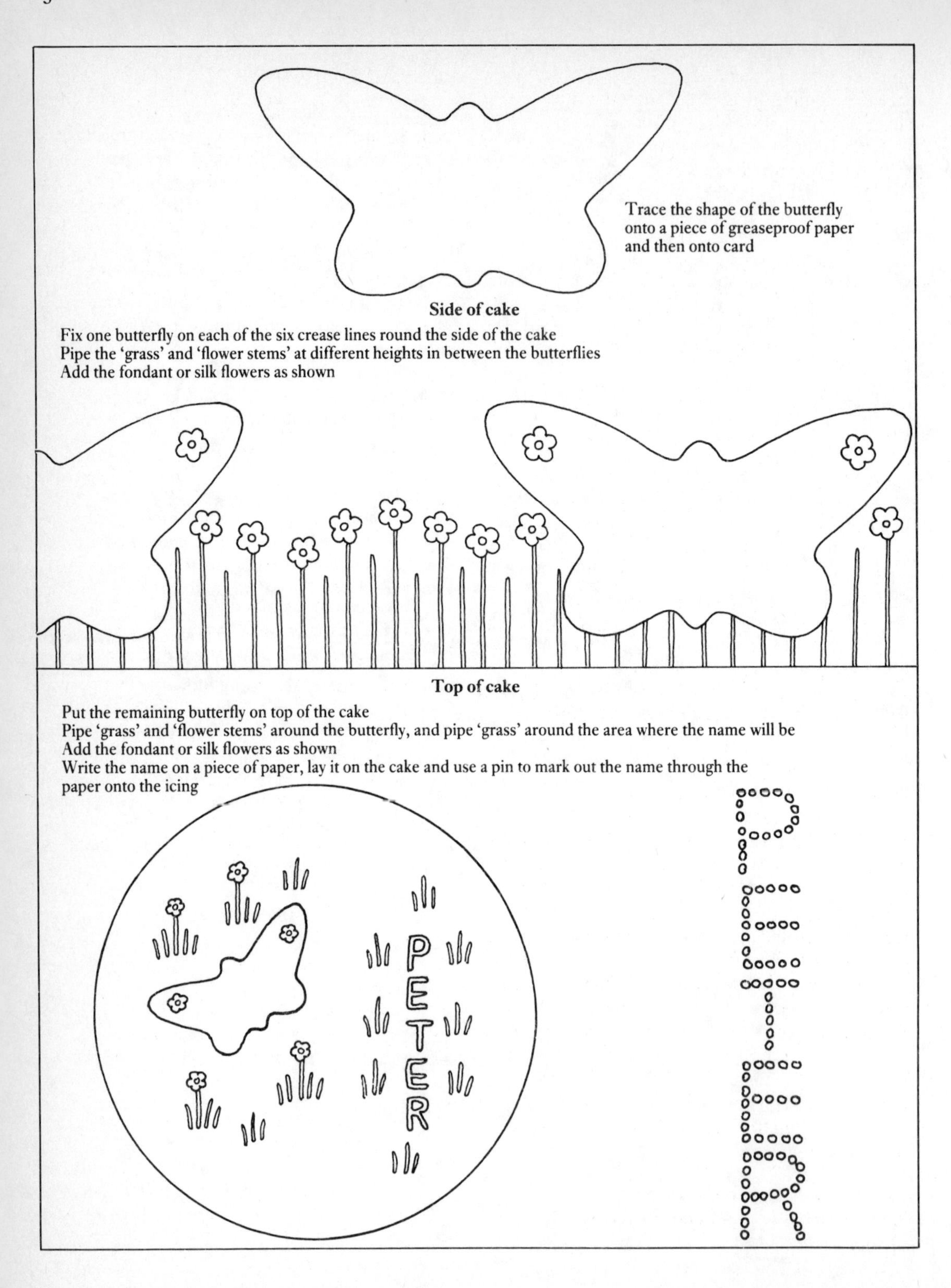
Trace the shape of the butterfly onto a piece of greaseproof paper and then onto card
Side of cake
Fix one butterfly on each of the six crease lines round the side of the cake
Pipe the 'grass' and 'flower stems' at different heights in between the butterflies
Add the fondant or silk flowers as shown
Top of cake
Put the remaining butterfly on top of the cake
Pipe 'grass' and 'flower stems' around the butterfly, and pipe 'grass' around the area where the name will be
Add the fondant or silk flowers as shown
Write the name on a piece of paper, lay it on the cake and use a pin to mark out the name through the paper onto the icing
PETER
PETER

5. Using the plunger cutter, cut out one flower and eject it into a soft piece of foam sponge, pushing it into the sponge to give an attractive flower cup shape. (You can do this into the palm of your hand.) Cut out about six dozen flowers altogether in white, pink and blue. Set them aside to dry.
6. The next step is to simulate flower stems and grass around the bottom edge of the cake. Using 225 g/8 oz icing sugar and a minute quantity of egg white, make some royal icing to a piping consistency. Colour the icing pale green. Put the no. 1 writing tube into the paper icing bag and half fill with the green icing. Fold the bag up tightly and pipe grass and flower stems in a haphazard way around the sides of the cake (*see left*). They do not have to be straight, and also it looks better with stems of different heights. Pipe some grass round the butterfly on top of the cake and also round the area where the name is to be piped.
7. Wash the tube from the green icing bag and put it into a clean greaseproof paper bag. Using the remaining icing sugar and a little egg white, make another batch of royal icing but do not colour it. Half fill the bag with some of this icing and, as carefully as possible, pipe out the name of the child to be christened on top of the cake. If you have not done this before, one very easy way is to write out the name on a piece of paper, lay the paper on the cake and use a pin to mark out the name through the paper onto the icing. When the paper is lifted off, you have an outline of the name. Mark out the name in a series of very close tiny dots of icing.
8. The next step is to fix all the fondant or silk flowers. Colour the remaining royal icing the same colour as the cake – either blue or pink. Wash the piping tube again and slip it into a clean greaseproof paper bag. Half fill the bag with the royal icing and fold the open end securely. Pipe one tiny dot of icing at the back of each flower petal and fix eight flowers at different heights in the grass on the side of the cake, as shown in the diagram. Put one flower in the middle of each butterfly wing. Fix a few flowers on top of the cake near the grass tufts and around the name. Put one tiny dot of icing in the centre of each flower. Lastly, fix the silver fancy banding around the edge of the drum board with a piece of sellotape.

This cake will keep fresh for about 1 week. Cover it lightly with tissue paper and store in an airtight tin. Do not freeze.

TRADITIONAL CHRISTMAS CAKE

Some people love to make their Christmas cake several months before the great day. I normally aim to have my cake made by December 1st. I leave it wrapped up for a week and then cover it with marzipan and set it aside uncovered for two weeks, to allow the marzipan to dry out, before icing and decorating it.

Makes 1 × 20-cm/8-inch round cake or 1 × 18-cm/7-inch square cake

175 g/6 oz plain white flour
125 g/4 oz self-raising white flour
¼ teaspoon salt
¼ teaspoon ground cinnamon
¼ teaspoon ground nutmeg
½ teaspoon mixed spice
225 g/8 oz butter, softened
225 g/8 oz light soft brown sugar
4 large eggs, beaten
1 tablespoon black treacle
¼ teaspoon almond essence
¼ teaspoon vanilla flavouring
450 g/1 lb currants, washed and dried
175 g/6 oz raisins, washed, dried and finely chopped
175 g/6 oz sultanas, washed, dried and finely chopped
50 g/2 oz red glacé cherries, cut in two, washed, dried and finely chopped
50 g/2 oz mixed whole peel, washed, dried and finely chopped
50 g/2 oz ground almonds
50 g/2 oz whole almonds, skinned and chopped
Grated rind of 1 orange and 1 lemon
4 tablespoons sherry
A little brandy
450 g/1 lb marzipan *(see page 222)*
450 g/1 lb royal icing *(see page 222)*

TO DECORATE
Miniature sprigs of holly or a miniature Christmas tree

1. Grease the cake tin and line the base and sides with greaseproof paper. Preheat the oven to cool, Gas 2, 300°F, 150°C.

2. Sift the flours, salt and spices into a mixing bowl.
3. In another bowl, cream the butter until soft, then beat in the sugar until the mixture is light and fluffy.
4. Add the eggs a little at a time, adding some of the flour between each addition. Beat in the treacle, almond essence and vanilla.
5. Fold in the remaining flour, the fruit, peel, ground and chopped almonds and orange and lemon rind. Add the sherry and mix well.
6. Spoon the cake mixture into the tin and smooth over the top. Line a baking tray with a thick piece of cardboard and set the tin on the cardboard. Secure a thick collar of brown paper round the outside of the tin with paperclips so that it stands up above the rim of the cake.
7. Bake for 2 hours then reduce the heat to Gas 1, 275°F, 140°C, and bake for a further 1½ hours or until the cake is firm to the touch and shrinking from the sides of the tin. Look at the cake after 1½ hours and if it is getting too brown, crumple up a piece of greaseproof paper and cover the top.
8. Leave the cake in the tin until it is cold then turn out and strip off the base lining paper. Turn the cake over and prick the base with long skewers, then dribble some brandy into the holes. Allow the cake to dry out for about 2 hours, then wrap it in greaseproof paper and overwrap in foil. Repeat the addition of brandy twice more, leaving two or three days in between.
9. Two or three weeks before Christmas, cover the cake with marzipan (*see page 224*) and set it aside, uncovered, for two weeks to dry out.
10. Apply the royal icing (*see page 225*) and decorate the top with sprigs of holly or a miniature Christmas tree.

SUNNY CHRISTMAS CAKE

Bright golden sultanas taste just the same as the darker ones but they are the basic fruit in this light-coloured Christmas cake.

The preserved pineapple is not the sweet shop kind but the real fruit preserved in sugar.

Decorate as you would a traditional Christmas cake, or decorate without icing, with fruit and nuts on top.

Makes 1 × 20-cm/8-inch round cake

125 g/4 oz crystallized pineapple
175 g/6 oz butter or block margarine
175 g/6 oz caster sugar
4 medium eggs, beaten
250 g/9 oz self-raising white flour
325 g/12 oz golden sultanas, washed, dried and chopped
125 g/4 oz yellow glacé cherries (or a mixture of yellow and green), halved, washed, dried and finely chopped
3 tablespoons light-coloured sherry, sweet or dry
125 g/4 oz light-coloured walnuts or pecans, chopped

TO DECORATE
3 tablespoons sieved apricot jam or glaze *(see page 248)*
50 g/2 oz golden sultanas, washed and dried
50 g/2 oz mixed green and yellow glacé cherries
25 g/1 oz small whole walnuts
25 g/1 oz pecan nuts
1 cube crystallized pineapple

1. Grease and line a 20-cm/8-inch round cake tin. Preheat the oven to moderate, Gas 3, 325°F, 160°C.
2. Wash the sugar off the 125 g/4 oz pineapple and chop small.
3. In a large mixing bowl, cream the butter or margarine with the sugar until pale and fluffy. Beat in the eggs a little at a time, adding a spoonful of flour if the mixture starts to separate.
4. Fold in the remaining flour with the fruit, sherry and nuts. Mix well but do not beat.
5. Spoon the cake mixture into the tin and level the surface. Line a metal baking tray with a piece of thick cardboard and set the tin onto the cardboard. Place a collar of folded brown paper round the outside of the tin to rise above the rim of the tin. This will protect the cake during the slow baking.
6. Bake for about 1 hour, then reduce the heat slightly to cool, Gas 2, 300°F, 150°C, and bake for a further 1½ hours or until the cake is firm to the touch and shrinking slightly from the sides of the tin. Leave in the tin to cool for 15 minutes and turn out onto a wire tray to go cold.
7. Before decorating, if the cake is not flat on the top take a sharp knife and slice off the raised piece. Turn the cake upside down and use the bottom as the top. Brush the apricot jam or glaze over the top fairly thickly, then decorate by laying the fruit and nuts in lines or circles. You may like to cut the cherries in two and the pineapple in strips to get a nice pattern. Press the fruit and nuts well into the jam.

This cake keeps well in a tin for about 2 weeks. It also freezes well for up to 2 months.

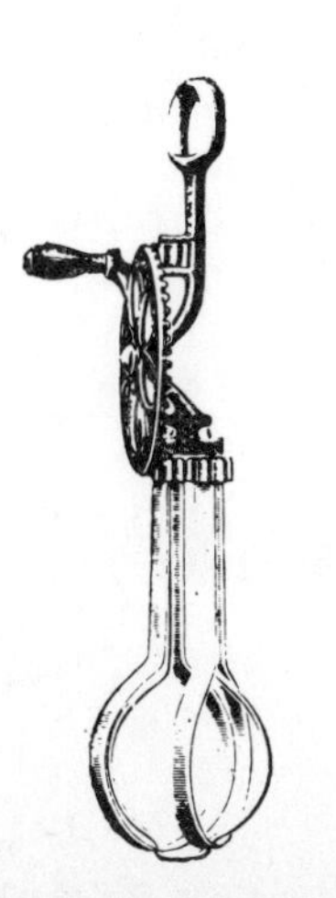

CHRISTMAS RING CAKE

This simple cake is easy to make and easy on the pocket, but is not for long keeping.

Makes about 14 slices

125 g/4 oz butter or block margarine, softened
125 g/4 oz light soft brown sugar
3 large eggs
325 g/12 oz mincemeat
75 g/3 oz currants, washed and dried
50 g/2 oz walnuts, finely chopped
200 g/7 oz self-raising wholewheat flour, sifted and residue of bran in sieve added
Milk to mix

FOR THE ICING
225 g/8 oz icing sugar, sifted
A little boiling water

TO DECORATE
3 glacé cherries, halved
Angelica strips

1. Grease a 1.2-litre/2-pint ring tin. Cut a circle of greaseproof paper the same size as the ring, then cut out the middle, leaving a 2.5-cm/1-inch wide circle. Lay this in the tin. Preheat the oven to moderate, Gas 3, 325°F, 160°C.
2. In a large mixing bowl, cream the butter or margarine with the sugar until light and fluffy, then beat in the eggs, one at a time.
3. Stir in the mincemeat, the currants and walnuts alternately with the flour and mix well. If the mixture is stiff add a little milk.
4. Spoon the moist mixture carefully into the ring tin and level off the surface.
5. Bake for 10 minutes, then reduce the heat to cool, Gas 2, 300°F, 150°C, and bake for about another hour or until the cake is risen, firm to touch and shrinking from the sides of the tin. This cake always has a crack on top but this will not show once the cake is inverted onto the serving plate.
6. Leave the cake to firm up in the tin for about 15 minutes, then turn it out onto a wire tray to cool.
7. Sift the icing sugar into a bowl and add just enough boiling water to give a thickish icing. Set the ring cake on a serving plate and spoon the icing on in a haphazard way so that it trickles down the sides of the cake but does not completely cover it. Decorate with halved cherries and little leaves made of angelica.

The cake will store for 2–3 weeks in a tin, or freeze for up to 2 months.

CHRISTMAS YULE LOG

This is quite a large chocolate log with a delicious icing.

Serves 12

3 large eggs
75 g/3 oz caster sugar
1 tablespoon boiling water
1 teaspoon instant coffee powder or granules
1 tablespoon cocoa powder (not drinking chocolate), sifted
75 g/3 oz self-raising white or wholewheat flour
Extra caster sugar

FOR THE BUTTER CREAM ICING
175 g/6 oz plain chocolate, melted (or chocolate flavour cake covering)
125 g/4 oz butter, softened
125 g/4 oz icing sugar, sifted
175 g/6 oz cream cheese
3–4 tablespoons rum (optional)

1. Grease and base line a 28 × 23-cm/11 × 9-inch Swiss roll tin. Preheat the oven to fairly hot, Gas 6, 400°F, 200°C.
2. Use a mixing machine with a whisk. Put the eggs and sugar into the bowl and whisk at high speed until the mixture is very thick, almost like marshmallow. A definite trail left across the surface with the whisk should not sink immediately.
3. While the eggs and sugar are being mixed, put the boiling water, coffee powder or granules and cocoa powder into a small bowl and blend well.
4. When you are satisfied that the eggs and sugar are really thick, stop the machine, add the cocoa mixture and whisk again until well blended.
5. Take the mixing bowl off the stand and sift about one-third of the flour over the surface of the mixture, adding any residue of bran left in the sieve if you are using wholewheat flour. Using a rubber spatula or the edge only of a large spoon, fold the flour into the mixture with a figure of eight movement and incorporate all the flour as lightly as possible. Repeat twice with the remaining flour.
6. Pour into the Swiss roll tin and level quickly, paying particular care that the level of mixture in the corners is even. Tapping the tin gently on the work surface helps.
7. Bake for about 20 minutes, or until the sponge is firm to touch and slightly shrinking from the sides of the tin.
8. Have ready a sheet of nonstick paper the same size as the tin and liberally dredged with caster sugar. Invert the hot cake onto the sugared paper and peel off the lining paper. With a sharp knife, trim off a narrow strip from each long side. Make a light cut across the sponge about 2.5 cm/1 inch in from the short side nearest you. This helps to start the roll off. Using the paper to help you, roll up the sponge with the paper inside. Lift the sponge with the join underneath onto a wire tray and leave to cool. Don't worry if the sponge cracks a little as it will be covered later with butter cream.

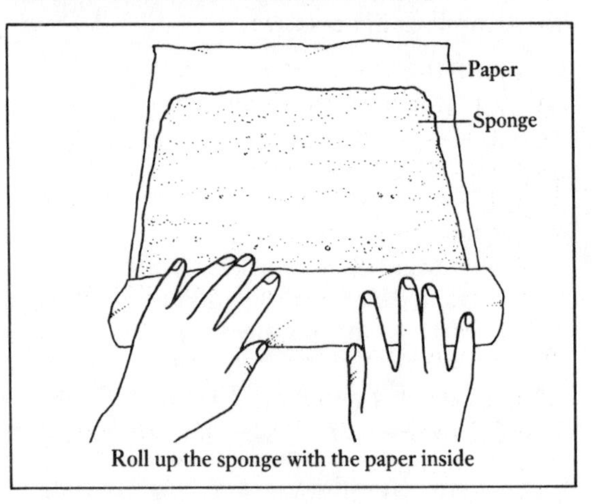

Roll up the sponge with the paper inside

9. In a small bowl, mix all the icing ingredients together, except the rum, to a spreadable cream.
10. Unroll the sponge, remove the paper and sprinkle over the rum, if using. Spread approximately half the butter icing on the sponge, leaving a narrow edge uncovered all round. Roll up the sponge again and set it on an oblong plate or board.
11. Spread the remaining butter icing over the surface and ends of the roll. Use the flat of a knife blade to pull the icing out in spikes. At each end smooth the surface and, using a skewer, mark rings in the icing to resemble those of a real log. Allow the icing to set slightly, then sprinkle over a very little icing sugar to simulate snow, and decorate with a sprig of holly or a little Christmas tree.

Can be stored in an airtight box in the fridge for 4–5 days. This log freezes well. When the icing is solid, put in a rigid plastic container and eat the log within 2 months.

VALENTINE'S DAY HEART

You need a heart-shaped tin for this cake. Or you can use a 20-cm/8-inch round tin and, using a paper heart shape as a template, trim the round cake into a heart shape using a very sharp knife. The topping is a thin layer of marzipan.

Will cut into 18 pieces

175 g/6 oz self-raising white flour
1 teaspoon baking powder
3 large eggs, beaten
175 g/6 oz tub margarine
175 g/6 oz caster sugar
1–2 drops vanilla essence

FOR THE MARZIPAN TOPPING
125 g/4 oz ground almonds
75 g/3 oz caster sugar
75 g/3 oz icing sugar, sifted
½ teaspoon lemon juice
2 drops almond essence
½ small egg, beaten
1 tablespoon sieved apricot jam or glaze *(see page 248)*
A little extra caster sugar

TO DECORATE (OPTIONAL)
A small spray of silk flowers or a ribbon bow with streamers

1. Using the cake tin as a pattern, make two paper hearts. Grease the tin thoroughly and lay one paper heart in the bottom. Preheat the oven to moderate, Gas 3, 325°F, 160°C.
2. Sift the flour and baking powder into a large mixing bowl. Add the eggs, margarine, sugar and vanilla essence and mix thoroughly. Pour the mixture into the tin and level the surface.
3. Bake for 25–30 minutes or until the cake is risen, firm to the touch and beginning to shrink from the sides of the tin.
4. Allow the cake to firm up in the tin for 5 minutes then run a knife carefully round the edge to make sure the cake is free. Turn it out onto your hand, peel off the lining paper and set the cake on a wire tray to cool.
5. Make the marzipan topping by mixing the almonds, sugars, lemon juice and almond essence with a tiny amount of beaten egg to get a stiffish paste. Be extremely careful to add only a small amount of egg at first. If the paste is too soft to roll, add more ground almonds.
6. Put the cake on a flat plate or board and brush the top with the apricot jam or glaze. Sprinkle a pastry board with caster sugar and roll out the almond paste evenly. Sprinkle more caster sugar to keep it from sticking to the rolling pin.
7. Using the other paper heart as a pattern, place it on the icing and cut round it carefully. Remove all the trimmings and set aside. Mark the marzipan heart all round the edge with the back of a fork. Lift the heart with the help of two fish slices or the base of a quiche tin and lay it carefully on top of the cake. Press down gently.
8. Work some red food colouring into the trimmings of almond paste, roll out and cut two miniature hearts. Decorate the cake with the hearts, and with a small spray of silk flowers or a bow of ribbon with two long streamers set at the top angle of the heart.

This cake will store in a tin for 2 weeks. It freezes well but should be eaten within 2 months.

MIMOSA CAKE FOR SPRING

This is a light fruit cake with a distinctive flavour. Green cherries and pale green icing carry the spring theme through, and the cake is decorated with fondant mimosa flowers.

Makes 1 × 20-cm/8-inch cake

175 g/6 oz tub margarine
125 g/4 oz light soft brown sugar
½ teaspoon almond essence
200 g/7 oz plain white flour
1 teaspoon baking powder
175 g/6 oz sultanas, washed, dried and chopped
175 g/6 oz currants, washed and dried
50 g/2 oz green glacé cherries, finely chopped
25 g/1 oz ground almonds
3 large eggs, beaten
2 tablespoons apricot jam, sieved, or apricot glaze *(see page 248)*
450 g/1 lb fondant icing (commercial or home-made, *see page 245***)**
Green food colouring
Cornflour
Yellow food colouring
Angelica leaves
A strip of pale green ribbon about 69 cm/27 inches long and 2.5 cm/1 inch wide

1. Grease and base line a 20-cm/8-inch round tin. Preheat the oven to moderate, Gas 3, 325°F, 160°C.
2. In a mixing bowl, cream together the margarine, sugar and almond essence.
3. Sift the flour and baking powder into another bowl, and stir in the fruit and almonds. Fold into the creamed mixture and add the eggs a little at a time, mixing well between each addition. Spoon the mixture into the tin and level the surface.
4. Line a metal baking tray with a piece of thick cardboard and set the tin on the cardboard. Fix a double thickness of brown paper like a collar round the outside of the tin so that it stands up above the rim of the cake.
5. Bake for about 20 minutes then reduce the heat to cool, Gas 2, 300°F, 150°C, and bake for another hour or until the cake is firm and beginning to shrink from the sides of the tin. Leave to firm up in the tin for 15 minutes then turn out onto a wire tray to cool.
6. If the top of the cake is domed, take a sharp knife and slice off the risen piece. Turn the cake over and set it on a flat plate or a silver board, about 28 cm/11 inches across.

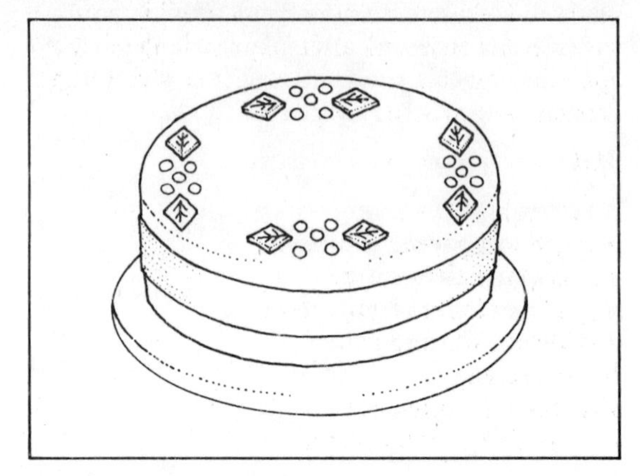

7. Warm the apricot jam or glaze in a bowl over a pan of hot water. Brush the jam or glaze all over the surface of the cake.
8. Break off a piece of fondant icing the size of a marble, put it into a plastic bag and reserve. Colour the remaining fondant a very pale green – 4 drops of green colouring should be enough. (Be very careful when adding colour to food – a skewer or an eye dropper is ideal to measure a small quantity.)
9. Dust the working surface with cornflour and quickly roll out the icing to 5 cm/2 inches larger than the top of the cake. Drape the icing over the rolling pin and lift into position on the cake. Dust your hands with cornflour and ease the icing round the sides of the cake, pressing gently to smooth and shape it *(see page 231)*. Trim the icing at the bottom and put the trimmings in a plastic bag and use for making decorations.
10. Colour the reserved marble of white fondant a pale yellow by adding 1–2 drops yellow food colouring and working it through – kneading and folding until the colour is even all over. With the fondant trimmings from the cake, roll dozens of minute mimosa balls. Flick just a little water onto the green icing on top of the cake and quickly set the mimosa balls into it in groups of five or six *(see diagram)*. Add the angelica leaves either side of each group. Finish the cake off by tying the ribbon around the cake and securing it with sellotape.

This cake will keep in a tin for 2 weeks. To freeze, put it into a rigid plastic box; eat within 2 months.

SIMNEL CAKE FOR EASTER

This semi-rich cake is made by the melting method. Decorate it either in the traditional way, with eleven marzipan balls to represent the faithful apostles, or with a pond and chicks for a children's version (*see variation on page 240*).

Makes 1 × 18-cm/7-inch round cake

FOR THE MARZIPAN

225 g/8 oz ground almonds
125 g/4 oz caster sugar
125 g/4 oz icing sugar, sifted
2–3 drops almond essence
½ beaten egg
1 tablespoon apricot jam, sieved
A little extra caster sugar

FOR THE CAKE

75 g/3 oz butter
75 g/3 oz light soft brown sugar
60 ml/2½ fl oz water
75 g/3 oz sultanas, washed and dried
50 g/2 oz raisins, washed and dried
125 g/4 oz currants, washed and dried
25 g/1 oz mixed peel, finely chopped
140 g/4½ oz plain wholemeal flour
½ teaspoon bicarbonate of soda
½ teaspoon mixed spice
1 teaspoon ground cinnamon
1 teaspoon ground ginger
1 large egg, beaten

1. Make up the marzipan by mixing together the almonds, sugars and almond essence with just enough beaten egg to get a firm texture. Knead lightly.
2. Dust a board with caster sugar. Divide the marzipan in three. Roll out one piece and cut a circle measuring 18 cm/7 inches across. Cover the other two pieces tightly with clingfilm and set aside.
3. Grease and line the base and sides of an 18-cm/7-inch round cake tin. Preheat the oven to moderate, Gas 3, 325°F, 160°C.
4. Melt the butter in a roomy pan. Add the sugar and water and bring to the boil.
5. Stir in the dried fruit and peel and simmer for 1 minute. Remove the pan from the heat and allow to cool until just warm.
6. Sift the flour, bicarbonate of soda, mixed spice, cinnamon and ginger into the fruit, adding any residue of bran left in the sieve, and stir in the beaten egg. Mix well but do not beat.
7. Put half the cake mixture into the tin. Level the surface and position the circle of marzipan on top of the cake mixture. Press down gently and spoon in the rest of the cake mixture. Level the surface again.
8. Line a baking tray with a piece of thick cardboard and set the cake tin on the cardboard. Surround the tin with a thick collar of folded brown paper to rise about 5 cm/2 inches above the rim of the tin. This will protect the cake and keep the fruit from being scorched while it is cooking.
9. Bake for about 1½ hours or until the cake is risen, firm and shrinking from the sides of the tin. Leave in the tin for about 20 minutes then carefully lift it out and cool on a wire tray.
10. When the cake is cold, use a sharp knife to level the top.
11. Roll out one of the remaining pieces of marzipan and cut an 18-cm/7-inch circle. Gather up the trimmings, add to the third piece of marzipan and roll this into eleven even-sized balls about the size of a large marble. Cover and set these aside until needed.
12. Turn the cake over and use the bottom as the top. Paint this with a thin film of warmed apricot jam.
13. Position the circle of marzipan on top and press it down gently. Score the surface lightly in a criss-cross pattern and put the cake under a hot grill to toast the top. Watch it carefully as it burns easily.
14. Put the eleven balls of marzipan on a baking tray and put them under the grill to toast very slightly. Finish the cake by placing the marzipan balls evenly round the edge of the cake. If the balls won't stick, a spot of beaten egg should do the trick.

VARIATION

TO DECORATE THE CAKE FOR CHILDREN

175 g/6 oz ground almonds
75 g/3 oz caster sugar
75 g/3 oz icing sugar, sifted
2–3 drops almond essence
½ beaten egg
1 tablespoon apricot jam, sieved
3–4 teaspoons icing sugar, sifted
2–3 drops water
1 tiny spot of blue food colouring
2 small fluffy chicks
Yellow ribbon (optional)

1. Make up the marzipan by mixing together the almonds, caster sugar, 75 g/3 oz icing sugar and almond essence with just enough beaten egg to get a firm texture. Knead lightly.
2. Dust a board with caster sugar. Divide the marzipan in two pieces. Roll out two circles of marzipan, each measuring 18 cm/7 inches across. (Use a pan lid or a plate to get a good shape.) One circle of marzipan goes inside the cake at step 7 above. Cover the other circle until you are ready to use it.
3. Make the cake, following the instructions on page 239, to step 12. Before putting the remaining circle of marzipan on the top of the cake, cut a hole out of it, either in the centre or at one side using a 5 cm/2-inch biscuit cutter. Use the cut out piece of marzipan to mould four or five tiny eggs. Lay the large circle of marzipan on the cake and press down gently. Make sure that the edges of the marzipan round the hole are pressed closely down to the cake.
4. To simulate a pond, fill this hole with icing made with the icing sugar, water and a tiny spot of blue food colouring. The icing should be fairly thick. Position the two chicks and the eggs on the edge of the pond. Finish the cake off with a circle of yellow ribbon, if wished.

These cakes store well in an airtight tin for about 2 weeks. They also freeze well but eat within 2 months.

BLACK BUN FOR HOGMANAY

Makes 1 × 20-cm/8-inch round bun, or 1 × 900-g/2-lb loaf

225 g/8 oz shortcrust pastry *(see page 28)*
50 g/2 oz whole almonds, peeled and finely chopped
325 g/12 oz currants, washed and dried
125 g/4 oz raisins, washed, dried and finely chopped
50 g/2 oz orange peel, finely chopped
25 g/1 oz dark soft brown sugar
Grated rind of 1 medium lemon
1 teaspoon ground ginger
1 teaspoon ground cinnamon
½ teaspoon ground allspice
½ teaspoon bicarbonate of soda
125 g/4 oz butter, melted
2 medium eggs, beaten
2 tablespoons whisky

1. Well grease a 20-cm/8-inch round tin, or a 900-g/2-lb loaf tin. Preheat the oven to moderate, Gas 3, 325°F, 160°C.
2. Roll out two-thirds of the pastry to a large circle about 35 cm/14 inches across and line the base and sides of the round tin. Do not trim the edges. Try not to stretch the pastry and avoid folds if possible. Press it firmly into the angle at the bottom of the tin. If using a loaf tin, roll out two-thirds of the pastry in a large oblong 35 × 41 cm/14 × 16 inches, and press it firmly into the tin.
3. In a large mixing bowl, stir together the almonds, currants, raisins, peel, sugar, lemon rind, spices and bicarbonate of soda.
4. Stir in the melted butter. Reserve 1 teaspoon of beaten egg, and stir the remainder into the mixture. Finally, stir in the whisky and mix well.
5. Pack this mixture into the pastry lined tin and level the surface.
6. Fold over the top of the lining pastry onto the fruit mixture and trim it to leave a 2.5-cm/1-inch border.
7. Roll out the remaining pastry to make a lid. To measure this, put the bun or loaf tin on top of the pastry and, using a knife, cut just outside it to allow

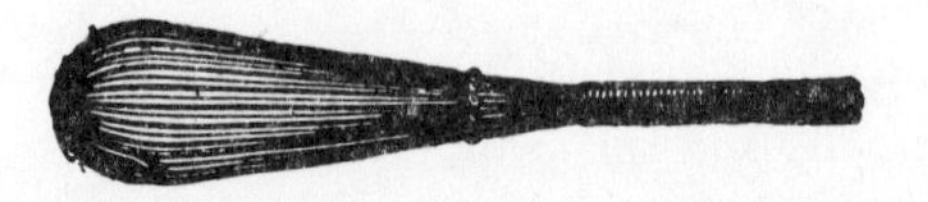

for the join. Wet the top edges of the pastry with water, position the lid on top of the fruit and seal the edges firmly. Trim away any excess pastry and use to make a decoration – a thistle, if you can, or just leaves. Use the reserved beaten egg plus a little milk to brush over the bun lid. Set the decorations in place and brush over again to give a nice glaze. Using a sharp fork, prick the pastry lid here and there in a decorative pattern.

8. Line a baking tray with a sheet of cardboard and set the tin on the cardboard. Surround the tin with a thick collar of brown paper, to rise above the rim of the tin. This will protect the bun while it is cooking.

9. Bake for 2 hours. If the top of the bun starts to get too brown, crumple up a piece of greaseproof paper and cover the top with it. Cool on a wire tray.

This bun will keep well in an airtight tin for 4–5 weeks. It also freezes well. Eat within 3 months.

FILLINGS, TOPPINGS AND ICINGS

For the recipes in this chapter, the best advice I can give is when you are using icing sugar be sure it is lump-free. A freshly opened packet should be in perfect condition but icing sugar can get damp if it is standing in a damp cupboard. Pass it through a sieve to be on the safe side. Indeed, to make royal icing for very fine piping and decorative work it is advisable to sift the icing sugar twice before adding the egg white.

Butter gives the best flavour for butter cream. See that it is very soft before adding the icing sugar.

Flavourings like vanilla or rum essence do make a difference, but use sparingly. Sherry and brandy are also good for adding a delicate flavour, but again use judiciously!

PIPING

Many people are put off by the thought of piping but, with practice, it really can be a simple procedure.

PIPING BAGS AND NOZZLES

Piping bags are nearly always made of strong, closely woven nylon and are washable and re-usable. The large ones can be quite expensive and I have made my own in the past. These bags are for use with creamed potatoes, whipped double cream, meringues and large quantities of butter cream.

Small icing bags made of greaseproof paper are easy to make (*see below*) and are particularly useful for very decorative icing. They can be used with both butter cream and royal icing.

For small piping tasks, such as dribbling lines of chocolate over biscuits or where it is not important to be accurate, a small clean paper bag can be filled, without an icing nozzle inserted, and one corner of the bag snipped off and the filling squeezed out through the hole.

There is a huge range of piping nozzles on the market – from very fine ones for writing with icing, to quite large ones for piping out whirls of potato. They are available in many different shapes – stars, leaves etc. The very fine nozzles tend to be made of metal but there are now plastic nozzles of many sizes available.

OTHER USEFUL EQUIPMENT FOR PIPING AND ICING

Turntable
This is particularly handy when icing or decorating a cake. For a home-made substitute, place two large shallow plates, bottoms together, on a flat surface and place the cake on top.

Spatulas
I like a rubber spatula for mixing icing as well as scraping down the sides of the bowl.

Damp cloth
All icing should be covered closely once it is made and while you are working with it. A damp tea towel should be kept handy to throw over the bowl. Both glacé and royal icing soon develop a 'skin' which can be difficult to beat down to a smooth icing again.

Ruler and compass
Both these items used carefully can save hours of your time when mapping out a cake design or decorations.

Plastic scraper
Used to smooth the icing on the sides of a cake. Can have a straight or serrated edge. The serrated edge gives a pleasant ridged effect – a quick and simple way to decorate.

To make a paper icing bag

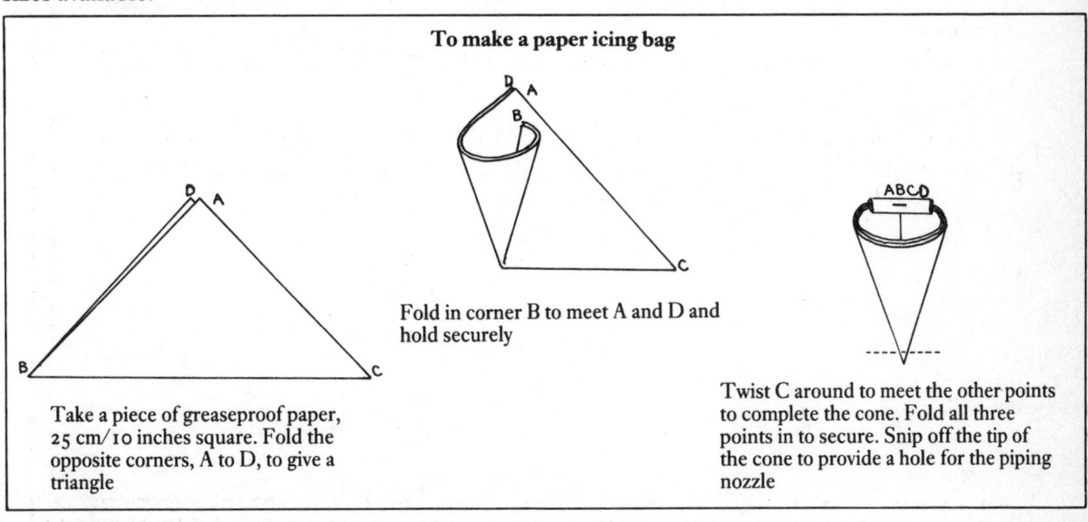

Take a piece of greaseproof paper, 25 cm/10 inches square. Fold the opposite corners, A to D, to give a triangle

Fold in corner B to meet A and D and hold securely

Twist C around to meet the other points to complete the cone. Fold all three points in to secure. Snip off the tip of the cone to provide a hole for the piping nozzle

ICINGS

SIMPLE GLACÉ ICING

This simple decoration for the top of a sponge is swiftly made. Use it also on the top of a square or oblong tray bake sponge.

To cover and feather ice 1 × 18-cm/7-inch sponge

225 g/8 oz icing sugar
3–4 tablespoons hot water or stock syrup *(see page 246)*
Food colouring (optional)

1. Sift the icing sugar into a mixing bowl.
2. Make a well in the centre and gradually beat in the hot water. Beat the icing well with a wooden spoon adding more icing sugar or liquid to achieve a consistency which will just find its own level in the mixing bowl. Colour it at this point if you wish.

Use immediately.

VARIATION

To make a small amount of strongly contrasting icing, spoon out 2 tablespoons of the mixed icing into a small bowl and add 1 teaspoon of cocoa mixed with a tiny amount of hot water to colour it. Adjust the consistency as necessary.

TO ICE A SPONGE USING TWO ICINGS

1. Make a small paper icing cone (*see page 243*).
2. Pour enough pale icing onto the sponge so that you can work it back and forth with a palette knife.
3. When it is fairly smooth, take up the paper icing cone and put the chocolate icing into it. Close the opening carefully, and snip off the point of the cone so that a narrow stream of icing can be pushed out.
4. Create one of the following patterns. Pipe two or three fine circles of icing round the top of the sponge. Before it dries, use a skewer or a wooden cocktail stick to pull lines radiating from the centre in a spider's web design. Or, draw decorative circles to give a flower or snowflake design. On a square or oblong cake, use parallel lines on their own, or to create a feathered design.

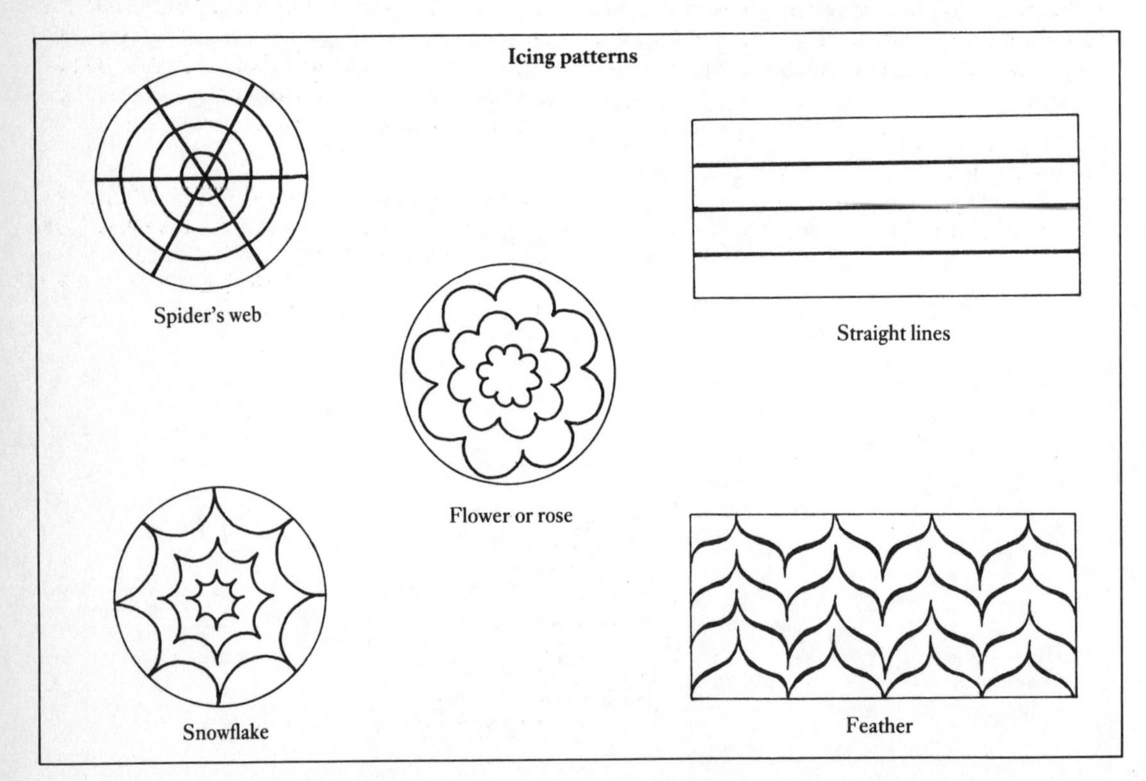

Icing patterns

FONDANT ICING

This is really a mock fondant icing. Proper fondant is a skilled job and entails boiling sugar and then beating and working the cooling syrup. This mock home-made fondant is useful for covering cakes quickly, making sweets, and decorating celebration cakes.

Any leftover fondant icing can be flavoured and used to make mint sweets. Just add 3–4 drops peppermint oil to the fondant and cut into shapes.

To cover the top and sides of 1 × 20-cm/8-inch round cake (see page 231)

1 small egg white
1 heaped tablespoon liquid glucose (buy at a chemist)
450 g/1 lb icing sugar, sifted

1. Place the egg white in a large mixing bowl with the liquid glucose and stir. Add about half the icing sugar and mix thoroughly. Continue adding the icing sugar, a little at a time, until the fondant is stiff.
2. Turn out the fondant onto a working surface dusted with cornflour, and knead in the remaining icing sugar until you have a smooth, pliable ball of fondant.

Use at once, or store in a very tightly sealed plastic bag for about 1 week. May be frozen, but a little sifted icing sugar may have to be kneaded into it to bring the fondant back to its original texture.

ROYAL ICING

This is the traditional crisp icing for wedding cakes. It covers well, and for decorative fine work there is nothing to beat it. It sets rock hard and therefore glycerine is often added, especially to coatings, to make it softer so that the cake cuts easily. The lemon juice keeps the icing white.

Always keep the icing covered when you are working with it – a damp cloth is ideal to slip over the bowl – otherwise the icing forms a skin which is not easy to disperse.

To cover the top and sides of 1 × 18-cm/7-inch round cake (see page 225)

2 small egg whites
450 g/1 lb icing sugar, sifted
1 teaspoon glycerine
1 teaspoon lemon juice

1. Put the egg whites into a large grease-free mixing bowl and whisk until they are just beginning to froth. Add the icing sugar, 1 tablespoon at a time. Use a wooden spoon and beat hard.
2. Add the glycerine and lemon juice. The consistency should be thickish. Cover the icing with a thick, clean, damp towel to keep it from drying out. Professional cake decorators leave the icing to stand overnight to get rid of the bubbles before using.

Do not keep in the fridge as it 'weeps'. Will keep in good condition in a cool room for 1 week only in a bowl with a damp cloth actually laid on the wet icing and another damp cloth placed over the top of the bowl. Royal icing will not freeze.

STOCK SYRUP

If you are keen on the art of icing and cake decoration, you will know that you can make a perfectly good glacé icing with water. It is very much better, however, to use stock syrup as this gives a really lovely sheen to the finished icing.

You could also dilute it and use it as the basic juice in a fruit salad.

450 g/1 lb sugar
300 ml/½ pint cold water

1. Stir the sugar into the water in a heavy-based pan and heat gently until the sugar dissolves.
2. Bring to the boil and allow to boil steadily without stirring until it reaches a temperature of 220°F/109°C on a sugar thermometer.
3. Strain into a heatproof jug and transfer to the fridge when cold.

This syrup will keep for 2 weeks in the fridge.

EXTRA SPECIAL CHOCOLATE ICING

To cover the top and sides of 1 × 18-cm/7-inch cake.

100 ml/3½ fl oz double cream
2 teaspoons brandy
125 g/4 oz plain chocolate, broken into small pieces
Chocolate rose leaves (*see page 251*), to decorate

1. Pour the double cream and the brandy into a small pan and bring almost to boiling point. Stir in the chocolate pieces.
2. Take the pan off the heat and stir well. If the chocolate is slow to melt, you can give it a little more heat.
3. Beat the icing well. Set the cake on a wire tray so that any icing which runs off can be rescued and used for something else.
4. Pour the icing evenly over the cake. Smooth with a knife only if really necessary. Allow to set and decorate with the chocolate rose leaves.

AMERICAN FROSTING

This is not a true American frosting. Its texture is rather meringue-like.

To cover the top of 1 × 20-cm/8-inch cake

175 g/6 oz caster sugar
2 tablespoons cold water
2 pinches cream of tartar
1 medium egg white

1. Stir the sugar into the water in a large heatproof bowl. Add all the remaining ingredients.
2. Suspend the bowl over a pan of simmering water and, using an electric hand whisk, beat until the frosting starts to thicken.
3. When the mixture stands up in a peak when you pull away, take the bowl off the heat and pour the frosting on the cake. Smooth the frosting over with a knife and, using a skewer, pull the icing into rough peaks in the manner of a Christmas scene.

SIMPLE BUTTER CREAM

This can be used as a coating or a filling. Margarine can be substituted for butter but of course the flavour is not so good. Try to find a butter which softens easily.

To fill and cover the top of 1 × 20-cm/8-inch cake

125 g/4 oz butter or margarine, softened but not oiled
225 g/8 oz icing sugar, sifted
A little milk
Flavouring (optional)

1. Put the butter or margarine into a mixing bowl and beat with a wooden spoon.
2. Add the icing sugar a little at a time and beat well. Add enough milk to give a soft consistency. Add flavouring, if using.

Providing it is tightly covered, will keep for up to 2 weeks in the fridge. Freezes well for up to 2 months.

VARIATIONS

CHOCOLATE

Beat 2 tablespoons of sifted cocoa powder into 2 tablespoons hot water. Allow to cool and beat into the butter cream before the milk. Then add milk to adjust the consistency.

VANILLA

Add 2–3 drops vanilla essence to the finished cream.

SHERRY OR BRANDY

Add 2 tablespoons sherry or brandy to the butter cream before the milk, then add milk to adjust the consistency to that of soft cream.

EXTRA SPECIAL BUTTER CREAM

This is a good deal more complicated to make than a simple butter cream but its mousse-like texture is beautifully light.

To fill and cover the top of 1 × 18-cm/7-inch sponge

65 g/2½ oz granulated sugar
4 tablespoons water
2 medium egg yolks
150 g/5 oz unsalted butter
Flavouring *(see above right)*

1. Over a low heat, dissolve the sugar and water in a small ground based or heavy pan.
2. Put the egg yolks in a heatproof glass bowl and whisk them with either a loop-headed wire whisk or an electric hand whisk until pale and creamy.
3. Bring the sugar and water to the boil and continue to boil without stirring until it reaches a temperature of 218°F/104°C on a sugar thermometer. It is handy to have a pastry brush in a bowl of water to brush away any crystals which form on the sides of the pan. This is to prevent more crystals forming.

   To test the syrup without a thermometer, take the pan off the heat when the liquid is reduced by half and is beginning to look sticky – this will take 1–2 minutes depending on how hard the boiling is. Dip the tip of a teaspoon into the syrup. Touch the syrup on the spoon with another spoon and pull away. A short sugar thread should appear. If it doesn't, return the pan to the heat for a further minute, then test again.
4. Pour the hot syrup slowly into the egg yolks, beating all the time or using a whisk, and continue beating until the mixture is thick and cool, almost like a mousse.
5. In another mixing bowl, cream the butter until it is smooth. Beat in the egg and sugar mixture, a little at a time, until it is all incorporated. Add the flavouring of your choice.

FLAVOURINGS

ORANGE

Beat in the finely grated rind of 1 orange.

LEMON

Beat in the finely grated rind of 1 lemon.

RUM

Beat in 1–2 tablespoons rum.

CHOCOLATE

Add 125 g/4 oz melted plain chocolate and beat well.

BUTTER CREAM MADE WITH MERINGUE

This is yet another way to make butter cream.

To fill and cover the top of 1 × 20-cm/8-inch cake

2 medium egg whites
125 g/4 oz icing sugar, sifted
225 g/8 oz unsalted butter, softened
Flavouring *(see below)*

1. Put the egg whites and icing sugar into a large heatproof glass bowl set over a pan of simmering water. Using an electric hand whisk, beat until the mixture is fluffy and meringue-like.
2. Take the bowl off the heat and continue whisking until the mixture is cool.
3. In another bowl, cream the butter until it is smooth, then add the meringue mixture a little at a time, beating well between each addition. Add the flavouring of your choice and use immediately.

FLAVOURINGS

CHOCOLATE

Add 125 g/4 oz melted chocolate and beat well.

RUM

Add 2 tablespoons rum and beat well.

COFFEE

Beat in 1 or 2 tablespoons extra strong coffee made with powder or granules.

MARZIPAN OR ALMOND PASTE

Marzipan and almond paste are almost the same. To make marzipan sweets it is usual to use all icing sugar to give a smooth texture. For almond paste the sugars are usually half caster sugar and half icing sugar. However, I don't think there is much difference and certainly I always use up leftover almond paste to make sweets or petits fours.

To cover the top and sides of 1 × 20-cm/8-inch round cake (see page 224)

325 g/12 oz ground almonds
175 g/6 oz caster sugar
175 g/6 oz icing sugar, sifted
2 teaspoons fresh lemon juice
3–4 drops almond essence
3–4 drops vanilla or ratafia essence
1 small egg, beaten

1. Put all the dry ingredients into a mixing bowl and mix well, checking that there are no lumps.
2. Add the lemon juice and essences and about half the beaten egg. Take great care that you do not get the paste too soft – the texture should be firm. If you do, add more ground almonds.
3. Knead very lightly.

Use at once or store in a polythene bag in the fridge for 7–10 days. The bag must be tightly closed to keep the marzipan in good condition.

SIEVED APRICOT GLAZE

Recipes often suggest sieved apricot jam for glazing a fresh fruit open tart or for helping to stick marzipan to a fruit cake.

450 g/1 lb apricot jam
3 tablespoons water
Squeeze of lemon juice

1. Put the jam, water and lemon juice into a heavy-based pan. Heat slowly, bring to the boil and allow to boil for 2–3 minutes, stirring continuously.
2. Strain the jam through a nylon sieve which will hold back the whole pieces of apricot. Return the strained jam to a jar with a screw-top lid and allow to go cold before putting the lid on.

Store the glaze in the fridge.

TOPPINGS

SIFTED ICING SUGAR AND CINNAMON TOPPING

This is a simple topping for a sponge but don't bother with it if you sneeze easily! There are two ways of applying it.

To cover the top of 1 × 20-cm/8-inch sponge

1 heaped tablespoon icing sugar
1 teaspoon ground cinnamon

1. The first method is to mix the two ingredients together and sprinkle on top of the sponge through a sieve. Put the sieve on a plate and put the icing sugar and cinnamon into it. Lift it carefully over the cake and knock the side of the sieve gently. The icing sugar and cinnamon will lightly coat the cake.
2. The other method is to dredge the sponge top with white icing sugar through a sieve, as directed above, and then use the cinnamon to make a pattern. Straight lines are easy or use a simple stencil. Lay the stencil gently on the icing sugar and carefully dredge the cinnamon over it so that no cinnamon creeps over the edge. Lift off the stencil gently leaving the cinnamon pattern behind.

COCONUT TOPPING

Buy creamed coconut in a hard block at a wholefood shop.

To cover the top of 1 × 20-cm/8-inch sponge sandwich

125 g/4 oz creamed coconut
100 ml/3 fl oz milk
3 tablespoons natural yoghurt
A little icing sugar, sifted
25 g/1 oz toasted coconut

1. Chop the creamed coconut into small pieces and melt it in the milk in a small pan over a low heat. Allow to cool.
2. Add the yoghurt and beat hard until the mixture looks like whipped cream.
3. Sweeten to taste with the icing sugar.
4. Swirl this over the top of a plain sandwich and sprinkle the toasted coconut in a thick border.

ICING TOPPING USING OIL

Enough for a thick topping for 1 × 18-cm/7-inch sponge

125 g/4 oz icing sugar, sifted
2 tablespoons sunflower or corn oil
Just under 1 tablespoon milk
5 drops vanilla essence

Beat all the ingredients together until very smooth.

Tightly covered, will keep for up to 1 week in the fridge. Will not freeze.

VARIATION

CHOCOLATE TOPPING

1 tablespoon cocoa powder
Just under 2 tablespoons hot milk
75 g/3 oz icing sugar, sifted
2 tablespoons sunflower oil

Mix the cocoa into a little hot milk until smooth. Stir in the icing sugar, oil and a little more of the milk to get a smooth consistency.

SIMPLE RASPBERRY AND COARSE COCONUT TOPPING

This is a delicious and easy topping. I buy my coconut loose from a wholefood shop.

To cover the top of 1 × 18-cm/7-inch sponge

1 heaped tablespoon home-made raspberry jam
25 g/1 oz coarse coconut (do not use packet coconut – it is nearly always too fine)

1. If the jam is stiff, warm it slightly either in the microwave for 3–4 seconds or stand the jar in a pan of hot water.
2. Spread a very thin layer of jam over the cold sponge.
3. Sprinkle the coconut evenly over the top.

CRUNCHY LEMON TOPPING

This is another very simple topping for a plain sponge. The topping must be applied swiftly before the sugar starts to melt.

To cover the top of 1 × 18-cm/7-inch sponge

75 g/3 oz granulated sugar
1 tablespoon fresh lemon juice

1. Stir the sugar into the lemon juice and immediately pour over the top of the sponge. Spread it carefully with a knife.
2. The lemon juice sinks into the sponge leaving a pleasant crunchy lemon topping.

CREAM CHEESE TOPPING

This is not really for putting on top of a cake but rather for serving a dollop with a cake. It is rather soft but the sweet sharp flavour is very pleasant.

175 g/6 oz cream cheese (full fat or low fat)
1½ tablespoons milk
Sifted icing sugar to sweeten

1. Blend the cream cheese with the milk until smooth.
2. Stir in a little sifted icing sugar to taste.

FILLINGS

CREAM

Double cream

Whip double cream with a loop-headed whisk, a balloon whisk, a rotary whisk, an electric hand whisk or an electric mixing machine with whisk attachment. It all depends on the quantity you are whipping. I would not think of using anything but a hand held wire whisk for a 150-g/5-oz carton of double cream. I also prefer double cream which is still liquid in the carton. Some of the big stores heat-treat their cream so that it sets in the carton – but I don't think this whips as well as the liquid type.

When whipping cream it is helpful to chill your bowl first in the fridge. Watch the consistency of the cream very carefully while you whip as it can suddenly turn to butter and it is very difficult to retrieve in this situation. The floppy stage is the one to aim for if you are filling a soft sponge. Cream needs to be firmer if, for example, you are filling choux buns, and firmer still if you are going to use the cream in a piping bag. I like to use a large piping bag – size 30 cm/12 inches – so that I can twist up the wide end to close it tightly and it gives me something to hang on to. A 1-cm/½-inch star nozzle is a good size for most sorts of piping work – whipped cream whirls, meringues and even creamed potato.

You can sweeten and flavour the cream to be whipped but do this very carefully; add too much and it will not whip well.

Rose water and violet water added in drops will give a delicate flavour to cream in a fatless sponge which could then be decorated with crystallized rose petals or crystallized violets.

Whipping cream

Because it is slightly lower in fat than double cream, whipping cream is excellent for filling a sponge or for topping a trifle. It has a good flavour but its volume tends to flop a bit after it has been whipped and it is therefore no good for piping work.

Single cream

Single cream has much less fat than double or whipping cream and is not suitable for whipping. Use it in baking only for pouring over puddings and desserts.

Frozen cream

Frozen cream is now readily available, and is extremely economical and sensible in the way it is packaged. The small pieces are easy to defrost and, of course, you can calculate exactly how much to use. However, the flavour is nowhere near as rich and full as fresh cream. Follow directions on the packaging when using frozen cream.

Canned cream

This, again, has a slightly different flavour to fresh cream – being very like that of boiled milk. However, it is pleasant to use and very economical.

Long-life cream

This is much more like normal cream, being liquid and available in cartons. It can be used whipped and as a pouring cream. The slight variation in flavour is not obtrusive.

FRESH CREAM AND LEMON FILLING

This filling is perfect for a pavlova, meringue baskets or a fatless sponge. It really should be made with home-made lemon curd to achieve the best result. You could liven up a shop-bought curd with ½ teaspoon fresh lemon juice beaten into the curd before you mix it with the whipped cream.

To cover the top of 1 × 23-cm/9-inch pavlova, or fill 10 meringue baskets or 1 × 20-cm/8-inch sponge

150 ml/¼ pint double cream
2 tablespoons home-made lemon curd

1. Whip the double cream until it is fairly firm.
2. Fold in the lemon curd. Keep the bowl covered in a cool place. Fill the meringues or cakes just before serving.

Eat on the day the cake is assembled.

CHOCOLATE CREAM FILLING

To cover and fill 1 × 20-cm/8-inch sponge, or sandwich 20 small meringues

125 g/4 oz plain chocolate, broken into pieces
60 ml/2 fl oz water
300 ml/½ pint double cream

1. Put the chocolate and water into a small heatproof bowl set over a pan of simmering water and stir until melted and smooth. Allow to cool.
2. Whip the cream with a loop-headed whisk or an electric whisk until it starts to thicken. Add the melted chocolate slowly and whisk again until the mixture is thick.

Use on the day it is made.

DECORATIONS

SUGARS

Caster sugar

Makes a pleasant dusting over the top of a traditional Victoria Sandwich.

Granulated sugar

Can be coloured for using on children's cakes. Just rub one or two drops of food colouring through the sugar.

Icing sugar

A light dusting is often very attractive on a tart or cake. A pretty effect is achieved with a paper doyley laid over the sponge and icing sugar dredged thickly over that. Lift the doyley carefully and you have an attractive pattern.

CHOCOLATE

Probably the most popular decoration of all.

Types of chocolate

Plain chocolate is easier to use than milk because it sets harder. Cooking chocolate is easier to work with but lacks good flavour. Rich plain chocolate sold in bars has an excellent flavour but takes longer to set than cooking chocolate.

Chocolate sometimes takes on a white/grey film – this can occur when it has been stored for a time. It is not easy to correct but the flavour is not affected. It also disappears on melting.

Chocolate curls

Hold a bar of chocolate over the cake or pudding to be decorated and draw the blade of a vegetable peeler along the thin edge of the chocolate. Do this over paper if you wish to store the curls, and lift into a tin.

Grated chocolate

Put the bar of chocolate in the freezer until very hard. Grate it on the largest holes of a metal grater directly onto the cake or onto greaseproof paper.

To melt chocolate

Put a small heatproof bowl over a pan of simmering water. Do not allow the hot water to touch the bottom of the bowl. Break the chocolate into pieces and put in the bowl. Stir very gently until the chocolate has melted.

Another way to melt chocolate is to put an empty heatproof bowl in the oven. When it is hot take it out and put the chocolate pieces into the bowl. Leave to melt and stir carefully.

Occasionally the chocolate coating on a cake may take on a whitish film; this is caused by uneven heat during the melting. The best solution is to cover it with a little grated chocolate.

Chocolate shapes

Spread melted chocolate on foil to an even thickness. To level the chocolate and get a really smooth finish, lift the corners of the foil and bang it down. Allow the chocolate to set, but not too hard, and quickly press metal cutters into it. Allow the shapes to set hard, then store in an airtight tin. Make flowers, hearts, half moons, circles, squares etc.

Chocolate leaves

Use mature rose leaves or bay leaves with well developed veins. Clean the leaves, then use an artist's brush to paint melted chocolate thickly on the back of the leaves. Put the leaves to dry on foil and, when the chocolate has set hard, start peeling off the leaves from the stem end. Small ivy leaves can also look very pretty. A snow effect can be achieved by a sprinkling of icing sugar over the chocolate leaves.

Chocolate caraque (scrolls)

Melt chocolate and, using a palette knife, spread the chocolate to the thickness of 3 mm/⅛ inch on a cool surface like marble or laminated wood. I like to oil the surface first with vegetable oil. When the chocolate has set, but not set really hard, take a long sharp, thin-bladed knife and, holding it at a slight angle, push the knife away from you across the chocolate in a continuous motion and thin chocolate scrolls will be formed. Store carefully in a tin. (Some people like to use a small clean wallpaper stripper for this job.)

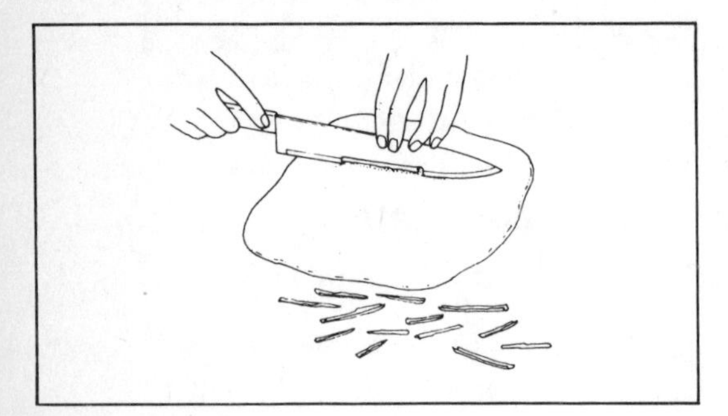

NUTS

Whole almonds

I like the long thin ones best. Skin almonds by pouring boiling water on them and leaving for a few minutes. You will find them much sweeter and softer than shop-bought blanched almonds which are often hard, dry and tasteless.

Flaked almonds

Buy carefully. Check that they are whole and not shattered. Good sprinkled on wet glacé icing. Toasted almonds are excellent over ice cream and other desserts. Toast a single layer on a baking tray under a hot grill. Remove as soon as they turn golden.

Nibbed almonds

I know you can buy these, but by skinning and chopping the almonds yourself you will have a much better nut – moist and not at all hard.

Desiccated coconut

Buy the very coarse loose kind as the packet variety is extremely fine. I get mine in a wholefood shop. Coconut is very good sprinkled over wet glacé icing. Toast it the same way as flaked almonds. Lay a thin layer on a baking tray and put under a hot grill. Watch carefully – it burns easily.

Coconut can easily be coloured for children's cakes. Just rub 1–2 drops of food colouring through the coconut.

Hazelnuts

Hazelnuts are rich in oil and add a distinctive taste to home baking. You can buy ground hazelnuts, but a far better flavour is achieved if you grind them yourself as you need them.

To prepare your own hazelnuts, roast them on a metal tray in a hot oven for about 7–10 minutes when the skins will go very dark and papery. Tip the nuts into a clean tea towel and rub them together through the cloth. You will find that most of the skins come away easily, but don't worry if some refuse to budge. Grind the nuts in a food processor, grinder or mouli grater.

Pistachio nuts

Often called green almonds. Skin in the same way as almonds. Usually used chopped to show off their green colour.

Walnuts

Buy carefully. I like very light-coloured walnuts – dark, black-streaked walnuts are often bitter. Walnuts go off more easily than other nuts so store them in the freezer. Whole or half walnuts placed round the edge of a cake often help to keep your fingers away from the icing. Chopped roughly they make a pleasant contrast in a light fruit cake. If you are using a food processor to chop them, do not over-process – you can easily end up with an oily mess.

SEEDS

Poppy seeds

This fine dark blue seed looks really good on bread. It is sprinkled on just before the bread goes in the oven. Buy in a wholefood shop.

Sesame seeds
Sunflower seeds

Pleasant additions to both sweet and savoury dishes. Lightly toasted, their flavour is even better. Toast in the same way as flaked almonds. Use on bread for different textures. Buy these seeds in a wholefood shop.

ORANGE AND LEMON RIND

Strands of orange and lemon rind are a popular decoration on puddings and cakes. To make these, cut the rind in very fine strips – finer than match-stick thickness. Put the strips in a pan, cover with water and boil for 2–3 minutes. Drain the strips and re-cover with fresh water, adding 1–2 tea-spoons of sugar. Boil again for 2–3 minutes and allow to go cold. Strain away the water, dry the rind and use within 2 days. All the boiling is to remove the very bitter flavour and soften the peel.

Recipes often call for the rind only of oranges and lemons and it is a simple matter to keep some rind in the freezer (*see page 16*).

To obtain orange and lemon rind, I cannot find any gadget which is better than my old metal grater. (I use a tooth brush for getting every last scrap of rind out of my grater. I hasten to add it is not used for anything else!) You can also use a 'zester'. This is a metal scraper with five tiny sharp-edged holes to scrape off the lemon and orange rind, but be extremely careful to scrape only the rind and none of the white pith underneath which is very bitter. The rind comes off in long strings which you will need to snip up very finely before the drying treatment.

Another way of preserving grated rind is to stir it into a little sugar in a jar and keep it tightly stoppered until you need it. Of course, this method is only suitable for baking sweet things.

CANDIED AND CRYSTALLIZED FRUIT

Angelica

This candied green stem of the angelica plant comes in very handy when simulating leaves. Use-ful in children's cake decorations.

Glacé cherries

Glacé cherries can be used in many decorative ways outside, as well as inside, cakes. If you are using them inside, cut the cherries in two pieces, wash away all the syrup and dry on kitchen paper. The slippery syrup is supposed to be the culprit if you end up with all your cherries at the bottom of your fruit cake.

Now available in four colours: red, yellow, green and a new one which is about the colour of a black grape. They are preserved without artificial colour.

Use coloured cherries carefully – it often looks better to decorate with just tiny bits of coloured cherry instead of whole ones.

CRYSTALLIZED FLOWERS AND LEAVES

You can buy crystallized violets and rose petals in some specialist shops and they are delightful for adding finishing touches to desserts and gâteaux. However, there are two simple ways of making them yourself. The first method gives a longer lasting result, but the second method is quicker and the flowers and leaves can be used within a very short time.

Flowers which are safe to use are: violets, prim-roses, mimosa, tiny rosebuds, rose petals and carnation petals. Herbs, of course, are all edible but the only one, as far as I know, which is popular is mint.

Buy the rose water and acacia or gum arabic powder from a chemist.

USING ROSE WATER, ACACIA OR GUM ARABIC POWDER AND CASTER SUGAR

4 tablespoons rose water
3 tablespoons acacia or gum arabic powder
Caster sugar for sprinkling

1. Put the rose water into a small heatproof bowl placed in a pan of simmering water and sprinkle on the acacia or gum arabic powder. Stir until the liquid is clear.
2. Using a small artist's brush, paint all parts of the flower, leaf or bud and, while it is still wet, sprinkle liberally with caster sugar until thoroughly coated. Shake off the excess and leave to dry on nonstick paper.
3. Next day, store the flowers, leaves or buds in an airtight tin for future use.

USING CASTER SUGAR AND EGG WHITE

1 medium egg white
Caster sugar for sprinkling

1. Using an artist's brush, paint the flower, leaf or bud back and front with egg white. While still wet, sprinkle liberally with caster sugar until thoroughly coated. Shake off the excess and leave to dry in the open air. They soon harden up.
2. Store in an airtight tin.

WHAT WENT WRONG?

This chapter contains some common reasons for less than perfect baking. The list is rather daunting and, in fact, there are umpteen other things I could have added. Every ingredient could be suspect.

For example, take flour – is it the correct flour for the job? Have you used self-raising when the recipe said plain with cream of tartar and bicarbonate of soda added? Was the flour at room temperature or did it come straight out of a freezing cupboard or from a hot shelf above the cooker? Has it absorbed the flavour of something else standing nearby because the top of the bag was not secure? If it is wholewheat flour, has it gone a long way past its 'use by' date and developed an 'off' flavour? (I am sure you will have noticed that wholewheat bread goes mouldy much more quickly than white.) Check the 'use by' dates whenever you buy flour, and if you keep flour in a bin or jar do use the flour in the bin first and resist the temptation to pour the freshly bought flour in on top of the last 1 cm/½ inch.

I could go on and on in this vein but, thank goodness, common sense usually comes to the rescue.

Do have all the ingredients and equipment needed for the recipe ready before you start, and give yourself time to weigh out everything carefully. Ensure all the ingredients are at room temperature (including eggs, which should not be stored in a fridge) unless otherwise specified in the recipe.

Try not to abandon a recipe which has disappointed you. The best cure is to try it again, and nine times out of ten you will find the way to a good result. I always think it is worthwhile also to make a written note beside the recipe to remind you next time you make it.

PASTRY

Most common problem of all

Unless using a fan oven, do check that the oven temperature is reached before you put your pie, flan or tart into the oven. Preheating will take about 15 minutes. Use the shelf above the middle of the oven for pastry baking in all but fan ovens. Only they have even heat at all levels.

Shortcrust, rich shortcrust, wholemeal and cheese pastry

Soft raw pastry under a flan
- Oven temperature too low.
- Oven not preheated.
- Baking tray not used under flan.
- Too much liquid in filling.

Flan or quiche sides collapsed when baking blind
- Oven temperature too low.
- Baking beans should be piled high up the sides of the flan to support the pastry.

Pastry over deep pie has sunk
- Oven temperature too cool.
- Not enough filling to support pastry until it is set.
- Pastry put over hot filling.
- No pie funnel to support pastry.

Shrunken pastry
- Oven temperature too cool.
- Pastry stretched during rolling and shaping.
- Rich shortcrust must be allowed to rest between making and using.

Cooked pastry soft and crumbly
- Too much fat used.
- Too little liquid.
- Do not use self-raising flour in rich shortcrust pastry.

Cooked pastry tough and hard
- Pastry over-handled.
- Too much water added.
- Too much extra flour incorporated during rolling and shaping.

Tacky dough
- Rich shortcrust pastry and cheese pastry must be chilled before rolling.
- Too much water added.
- Flour not weighed accurately.

Crumbly dough
- Not enough water added.
- Insufficient mixing.

Choux pastry

Sinking when removed from oven
- Not cooked long enough.

Soggy insides
- Not returned to oven after pricking to allow pastry to dry out.

Mixture flat
- Oven too cool.
- Wrong proportions.
- Too much liquid added.
- Not cooked long enough.

Mixture too soft to pipe
- Wrong proportions.
- Mixture is not cooked until it leaves the sides of the pan.
- Too much egg added at once.

Flaky pastry

Sticky dough
- Dough not chilled enough.
- Too much water added.
- Insufficient resting and chilling.
- Too heavy rolling.

Pastry not risen and flaky
- Dough not chilled enough.
- Not enough water added.
- Fat not cold enough.

Uneven rise
- Poor folding. Great care is needed to get a neat even shape.
- Uneven rolling.

Pastry tough
- Too much water added. The dough must be soft but not tacky.

Fat running out during baking
- Oven temperature too low.
- Fat so hard that it broke through during shaping and rolling.

CAKES AND SPONGES

Cracked or peaked top
- Oven too hot.
- Too much raising agent used.
- Too much mixture in the tin.
- Cake too near top of oven.

Top sunk in the middle
- Oven too cool.
- Too much raising agent used.
- Over-creaming of fat and sugar.
- Over-beating after egg added.
- Mixture too wet.
- Baking tin too small.
- Slamming oven door during baking.

Hard crust and over-browning of top
- Oven too hot.
- Too much sugar used.
- Cake too near top of oven.
- If rich fruit cake, cake was not protected with paper during the long cooking.

Cake sticks to bottom or sides of tin
- Poor quality tin used.
- Tin insufficiently greased and/or lined.

Over-browning of bottom
- Poor quality tin used.
- Tin insufficiently greased and/or lined.

Sides very crusty
- Tin probably over-greased.

Speckling on top
- Too much sugar used.
- Granulated instead of caster sugar used.
- Raising agent and flour poorly sifted.

Tunnelling in centre of cake or uneven texture
- Over-mixing or uneven mixing when adding flour or liquid.
- Mixture too dry causing air pockets.
- Raising agent and flour poorly sifted.

Fruit sunk to the bottom
- Oven too cool.
- Too much raising agent used.
- Mixture too wet.
- Fruit wet when added.
- Syrup left on glacé fruit (*see page 63*).
- Fruit too large and heavy for mixture.
- Oven opened too soon.

Coarse texture
- Oven too cool.
- Too much raising agent used.
- Fat not rubbed in or creamed properly.
- Inadequate mixing.

Rubbery texture
- Over-mixing.
- Too much egg and/or milk added.

Dry crumbly texture which stales quickly
- Too much raising agent used.
- Mixture too dry.
- Fat not creamed or rubbed in properly.
- Baked too slowly.

Close texture
- Oven too hot.
- Too little raising agent used.
- Too much fat, egg or flour used.
- Mixture too dry or too wet.
- Over-mixing.
- Inadequate creaming and/or beating.
- Under-baking.

Uneven rise
- Oven incorrectly preheated.
- Oven shelf or oven not level.
- Cake not in centre of oven shelf.

Small cakes spread
- Too much or too little raising agent used.
- Mixture too wet.
- Insufficient fat used.
- Too much mixture in paper cases.

BISCUITS

Soft
- Not baked long enough.
- Put into storage tin before cold.
- Left on plate too long (keep biscuits in airtight tin until needed).

Hard
- Mixture too stiff.
- Over-baked.

Sticking to baking tray
- Tray under-greased or dirty – use nonstick paper to line baking trays (*see page 20*).

MERINGUES

Soft meringues
- Egg whites not beaten long enough before sugar added. Ensure egg whites are stiff, and not just floppy, before adding sugar.
- Too much sugar added at once. Add only 1 tablespoon at a time and beat hard between each addition. You should end up with a very thick shiny meringue which cuts easily.
- Filled meringues left out too long on a plate. Always fill the meringues just before serving.

Weeping meringues
- Sugar not beaten in thoroughly enough. The beating is to ensure the crystals dissolve before baking, otherwise the undissolved sugar melts during baking and runs out. This often bakes into dark caramel streaks under the meringues.

SCONES

Close texture, heavy or tough
- Oven too cool.
- Too little raising agent used.
- Over-handling.
- Mixture too dry or too wet.

Too pale
- Oven too cool.
- Top not glazed with egg or milk.

Rough surface
- Inadequate mixing.
- Insufficient kneading.

Speckling
- Flour and raising agents poorly sifted.
- Incorrect proportions of bicarbonate of soda and cream of tartar used.
- Granulated instead of caster sugar used.

Scones spread out and have no shape
- Mixture too wet.
- Unevenly kneaded.
- Baking tray over-greased.

GIRDLE SCONES, PANCAKES AND WELSH CAKES

Sticking to girdle
- Girdle dirty or insufficiently greased.

Spreading
- Batter too thin – it should just pour from the spoon.

Pale and leathery
- Girdle too cool.

Over-browned and hard
- Girdle too hot.

YEAST COOKERY

Bread

Sour yeasty smell
- Too much yeast used.
- Over-proving.

Bread is crumbly and stales quickly
- Flour too soft.
- Rising too quickly in too hot a place.
- Under-rising.

'Flying top' – top crust breaks away from the loaf
- Oven too hot.
- Dough surface dried out during proving.
- Under-proving.

Flat top
- Flour too soft.
- Dough too set.
- Pour shaping of dough.

Dough collapses when put into oven
- Over-proving.

Coarse open texture
- Oven too cool.
- Too much liquid added.

Most of the problems which occur when baking bread apply to any baking using yeast. Correct mixing is important, and when using the batter method the mixture must be beaten really hard so that the yeast is well distributed.

Fruit and peel is often added to the yeast dough after the hard kneading has been done. This is to protect the fruit which would otherwise be broken and spoiled during the vigorous kneading.

MARZIPAN AND ICINGS

The most common fault when making marzipans and icings is to add too much liquid. You then have to add more icing sugar to correct the consistency and you often end up with double the quantity you intended to make. Always add the liquid no more than 1 teaspoon at a time and beat well between each addition.

Marzipan

Dry patches on marzipan

– Dried-out skin formed on uncovered marzipan was worked back into the ball. Always cover the bowl of marzipan with a damp cloth while you are not using it. Or put it into a plastic bag or cover with foil.

Icings

Icing is lumpy

– Icing sugar wasn't sifted properly and tiny balls of undissolved icing sugar spoil the smooth surface. They also clog up icing pipes very easily when doing decorative work.

Fondant or Glacé icing too thick or too thin

– Very carefully add either a little more water or icing sugar and beat well between each spoonful.

Icing dribbles down side of cake

– Leave it to harden and then scrape away excess.

Icings won't spread easily

– All icing is easier to work with if you apply more than you need. You can then work the icing back and forward with a palette knife until you get a smooth surface, and the excess icing can be skimmed off.

Icing when applied to top of cake is too stiff to spread smoothly

– Flash the cake under a hot grill and smooth the icing with a palette knife while it is still warm. This should be done with great care, and do ensure the grill is preheated before you put the cake under.

Royal icing discolours on cake

– Marzipan has not been allowed to dry out before applying the icing and oils in the marzipan are seeping through. Once the cake has been covered with marzipan it should be left to dry out for about 7 days. The surface of the marzipan forms a firm 'skin' and feels papery to the touch. Do not put the cake into a tin but just lightly cover it with tissue paper so that air can circulate.

Butter icing loses definition after piping

– Not enough icing sugar added.

Rich icings

Icings and fillings using cream can be spoiled if the cream has not been beaten sufficiently before being added to the icing. It is difficult to break up globules of cream in the icing after it has been mixed.

INDEX

A

B

C

D

E

F

G

H

I

J

K

L

M

N

O

P

Q

R

S

T

V

W

Y

Z

FOR YOUR
OWN NOTES

FOR YOUR OWN NOTES

FOR YOUR OWN NOTES

FOR YOUR OWN NOTES

FOR YOUR OWN NOTES

FOR YOUR OWN NOTES

FOR YOUR OWN NOTES

FOR YOUR OWN NOTES

FOR YOUR OWN NOTES

FOR YOUR OWN NOTES

FOR YOUR OWN NOTES

FOR YOUR OWN NOTES

FOR YOUR OWN NOTES